RICHARD RIEMERSCHMID'S EXTRAORDINARY LIVING THINGS

RICHARD RIEMERSCHMID'S EXTRAORDINARY LIVING THINGS

FREYJA HARTZELL

THE MIT PRESS
CAMBRIDGE, MASSACHUSETTS
LONDON, ENGLAND

Published with assistance from the Graham Foundation for Advanced Studies in the Fine Arts.

The MIT Press would like to thank the anonymous peer reviewers who provided comments on drafts of this book. The generous work of academic experts is essential for establishing the authority and quality of our publications. We acknowledge with gratitude the contributions of these otherwise uncredited readers.

This book was set in Arnhem Pro and Frank New by New Best-set Typesetters Ltd. Printed and bound in the United States of America.

Library of Congress Cataloging-in-Publication Data

Names: Hartzell, Freyja Thorbjørn, author.
Title: Richard Riemerschmid's extraordinary living things / Freyja Hartzell.
Description: Cambridge, Massachusetts : The MIT Press, [2022] | Includes bibliographical references and index.
Identifiers: LCCN 2021049761 | ISBN 9780262047425 (hardcover)
Subjects: LCSH: Riemerschmid, Richard, 1868-1957—Criticism and interpretation.
Classification: LCC NK1450.Z9 R5434 2022 | DDC 745.4—dc23/eng/20220423
LC record available at https://lccn.loc.gov/2021049761

10 9 8 7 6 5 4 3 2 1

For Sally and Jon

. . . with an eye made quiet by the power
Of harmony, and the deep power of joy,
We see into the life of things.
—William Wordsworth

CONTENTS

INTRODUCTION

EXTRAORDINARY LIVING THINGS

"It speaks, it talks in forms, it makes its personality visible."
—Hermann Obrist[1]

"Munich sparkled," wrote Thomas Mann in 1902 of the Bavarian city he called home.[2] And as Munich sparkled, Mann's desk chair trembled (figure 0.1). Perhaps it trembled vicariously with the writer's nerves; perhaps it trembled momentously on the brink of the modern century; or perhaps it trembled simply with joy—that irrational, animal joy of the organism coursing with life—the sheer joy of being alive. Or did it really tremble at all? Surely it seems unlikely that any chair should tremble, and especially that this small, unassuming, cherrywood desk chair would comport itself so shamelessly. So we look again. Yes, it still trembles. While its squared, splayed feet root it to the ground, and its generous seat and broadly curving backrest invite the writer's body, the limbs that connect them—the slender legs and supple arms—cannot keep still.

Mann's unruly desk chair was designed by his Munich compatriot, the artist, architect, and designer Richard Riemerschmid (1868–1957). It may come as something of a surprise, then, that when Riemerschmid's name appears within the canon of modern design, it is often accompanied by words such as *standardization*, *practicality*, or *Sachlichkeit*—that core tenet of German modernism, typically rendered as "objectivity" in English. In fact, surveys of design history tend to hail Riemerschmid as a pioneer of functionalism.[3] He is credited with being among the first of his Munich colleagues to reject the fanciful Jugendstil—the German

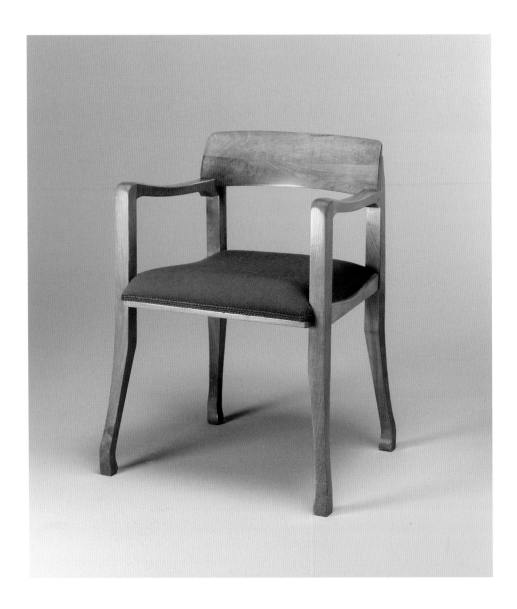

FIGURE 0.1

Richard Riemerschmid, *Desk Chair*, designed
1898 (this example purchased by Thomas
Mann 1902). © 2021 Artists Rights Society
(ARS), New York / VG Bild-Kunst, Bonn.

branch of Art Nouveau or the so-called "New Style" in design at the end of the nineteenth century—in the late 1890s; lauded for his invention of serially producible "machine furniture" in 1905; and recognized as a proponent of architect and cultural reformer Hermann Muthesius's 1914 program of *Typisierung*: the promotion of *types*, or reduced, standardized forms for utilitarian objects.[4] Riemerschmid has been understood as a transitional figure, conveniently bridging a stylistic "gap" between 1890s Art Nouveau and 1920s modernism. Unparalleled in their own time, Riemerschmid's things are repeatedly seen as "ahead" of that time. And so they are valued for their "anticipation" of the better-known industrial design of the Bauhaus school, celebrated in twentieth-century design scholarship for its dissemination of a functional, reductive design aesthetic in postwar Europe, Britain, and the United States through products that have since become synonymous with the words *modern design*.

So perhaps Thomas Mann's cherry chair trembled *toward* something; perhaps it shook in anticipation of its own future perfection—of a more definitively "modern" chair. Certainly, Bauhaus designer Marcel Breuer's B3 club chair, designed in 1925 and known by its affectionate nickname "Wassily" (for Wassily Kandinsky, Breuer's Bauhaus colleague at the time), has been seen as such a chair (figure 0.2). Design theorist Frederic J. Schwartz has written that Breuer's now iconic tubular steel and black canvas chair distilled "thousands of years of design into a few spare lines" and was, in this sense, the "final iteration of the image 'chair.'"[5] And the forms of these two "artist's" chairs—Mann's and Kandinsky's—do present both resemblance and evolution through their similarly sparse designs, their equally accommodating seats and embracing backrests, the upward springing of their legs, the lilting lines of their arms: Breuer's canvas flexible by nature, Riemerschmid's wood made so through design.

But the Wassily chair's "evolution" also held a threat for the trembling Munich desk chair, and for all chairs—for the very *presence* of the chair as a concrete thing. For, as Schwartz has noted, Breuer's tubular steel and fabric chair automatically reduced its material to a collection of abstract, floating lines and planes; even "the reflections on the chromed surfaces," Schwartz observes, "narrow the cylinders of steel into thin strokes of an imaginary pen."[6] Perhaps, then, Mann's Munich chair trembles not in anticipation after all, but in fear of its inevitable annihilation. "In the dialectic of dwelling," Schwartz writes, "the object was to dissolve in the service of living; the chair was to disappear in the liberation of sitting."[7] And so the most interesting image of this "final iteration of the image 'chair'" features not Wassily's

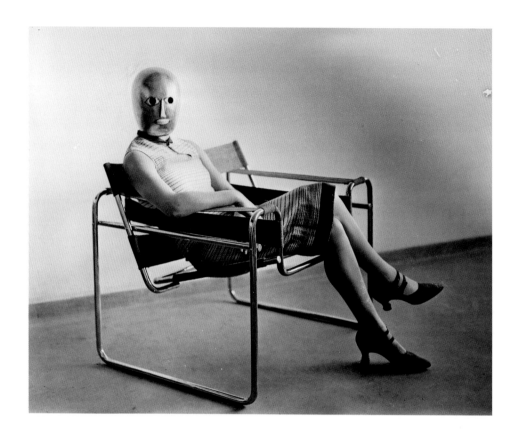

FIGURE 0.2

Erich Consemüller, *Untitled* (Lis Beyer or Ise
Gropius wearing mask by Oskar Schlemmer
in Breuer's "Wassily" chair), 1926. Bauhaus-
Archiv Berlin / © Stephan Consemüller.

abstract geometry but a mysterious, masked sitter. With the Wassily chair, then, the "dialectic of dwelling" had come to a standstill—or, in more comfortable terms, to a seat. In 1925, the human subject was framed by the subservient, inanimate object. But in 1902, Riemerschmid's obstreperous armchair was yet in motion—acting out. It contested the sitter's claim to subjecthood. Rather than dematerializing, it asserted its materiality, shaking and destabilizing the very relation of subject to object. While Breuer's chair may look more "modern" in the teleological terms of stylistic "evolution," it is Riemerschmid's chair that embodies the complexity of the conflicted modern self.

We can draw an even closer comparison between Breuer's 1928 B32 side chair (figure 0.3) and Riemerschmid's 1905 "machine chair" (figure 0.4). Both chairs are reduced in design, employ traditional caned seats, and were produced in multiples; Breuer's chair was mass-produced by the Thonet bentwood and tubular steel manufacturers, and Riemerschmid's was serially produced at the Dresden Workshops. An example of Riemerschmid's bare-bones machine chair in the collection of Berlin's Bauhaus Archive perpetuates the notion of Riemerschmid's supporting role in a modernism destined for the Bauhaus. The chair's remarkably spare form, its lack of ornament, and its straightforward construction from standardized, serially produced parts fabricated with the aid of machines seem to herald the advent of what has since been termed *Sachlichkeit*—sobriety, matter-of-factness, or objectivity—in modern design through the 1920s. But upon closer inspection, the machine chair transcends the sum of its rationalized parts. From the top of its stile to the tip of its foot runs a supple line of energy, a vital charge that courses through the chair's contour and is released in the "kick" of each small foot, articulating the chair's definitive stance. Fleshed out by the animated details of its design, the machine chair steps out of the Bauhaus lineage; its economy of form is not skeletal but muscular; to the B32's ghostly silhouette it offers a full body. Riemerschmid's *Sachlichkeit* cannot be reduced to sobriety or objectivity; rather, it is more intuitively and better understood as "thingliness": the vitality, character, or *personality* of specific material things.

Twenty-first-century scholars have set about retexturing the Bauhaus: their research has unraveled its theoretically uniform modernism into distinct threads of modernist practice—modernisms of gender, culture, and politics that, while they coexist historically, can never be rewoven into the smooth, seamless image of a "Bauhaus style."[8] While this critical, inclusive, and pluralist turn in Bauhaus scholarship has effectively negated the school's role as a historical or stylistic destination,

FIGURE 0.4

Richard Riemerschmid, *Machine Chair* (Maschinenmöbelprogramm II, Stuhl Nr. 79.5, manufactured by the Dresdner Werkstätten), 1904–06. Courtesy Die Neue Sammlung— The Design Museum. Photo: Die Neue Sammlung (A. Laurenzo). © 2021 Artists Rights Society (ARS), New York / VG Bild-Kunst, Bonn.

FIGURE 0.3

Marcel Breuer, *Cesca Side Chair (model B32)*, 1928. Chrome-plated tubular steel, wood, and cane. Manufactured by Gebrüder Thonet, Vienna, Austria. Purchase. Digital Image The Museum of Modern Art/Licensed by SCALA / Art Resource, NY.

accounts of Riemerschmid's work still show it moving in a Bauhaus direction. This book, however, looks closely at Riemerschmid's designed objects in their native historical habitat of pre–World War I Germany. Rather than anticipating landmarks or hallmarks of 1920s modernism, Riemerschmid's things, observed "at home" in their own time and place, recalibrate our vision of modernism itself by celebrating the irregular within rationalized structures, enlisting history as an agent of progress, and harnessing regional charm for their universal appeal. Regardless of their lineage, Riemerschmid's *extra-ordinary* everyday objects claim a seminal status in the development of a modern design that is just now coming to historical light. The aim of this book is to uncover a new yet historically grounded history of modernism—one that was there all along, but told now, and for the first time, by modernist things themselves.

These things are the protagonists of the chapters that follow. Although Riemerschmid's achievements as an architect, a community planner, an institutional leader, an educational reformer, and a teacher have all garnered scholarly praise, his work as a designer of everyday things has never been approached with the sustained intellectual focus or interpretive intuition that the designer himself devoted to his own practice.[9] Through close material analyses and cultural interpretations of his designs for the body and the home, I redefine Riemerschmid's historical legacy as far more pervasive than previous accounts have suggested, precisely (if counterintuitively) because it operated at a smaller scale. A number of years ago, architectural historian Winfried Nerdinger, curator of the 1982 Riemerschmid retrospective in Munich and editor of its catalog, told me that he believed Riemerschmid's *Kleinkunst* ("little arts" or designed objects) to have been works far less serious and of lower stakes than his architecture, adding that design was a place for Riemerschmid to experiment and "play."[10] At the time, Nerdinger's speculation seemed to relegate Riemerschmid's objects to a category of lesser significance than the rest of his production—both in Nerdinger's own view, and in his assumption about Riemerschmid's. But it is, ironically, this equation of design with *play* that supports the fundamental proposition of this book: that Riemerschmid was by nature a designer; he was a designer at heart. He was a capable, versatile creator who was nonetheless most inventive, playful, and free—most in his element—when designing things for everyday use.

Richard Riemerschmid's Extraordinary Living Things contends for his designs from 1896 through 1914, the formative years of his career, as the core of his creative practice. These things reveal their designer at his most imaginative, speculative, and hopeful—and, intersecting as they do with critical developments in modern social and political life, they have much to say that is new about what it meant to be "modern" during Germany's *Kaiserreich*: the Wilhelmine Empire. Riemerschmid's ardent, innovative, and prolific modernism radiates—sparkles, even—from his extraordinary things and glows in the cultural-aesthetic discourse first kindled around them during the period in which they were designed, made, and used.

Riemerschmid's things are products of the environment in which they were conceived: the material results of their designer's culture. His twentieth-century design practice was rooted in a network of nineteenth-century philosophical and scientific discourses: theories of evolution and biological interconnectedness spawned by Charles Darwin's revolutionary publication of *On the Origin of Species* in 1859, including microbiological studies like German artist and biologist Ernst Haeckel's *Radiolaria* (1862); new discoveries in neuroscience about the nature of aesthetic perception and its connection to bodily experience; philosophical and psychological questions about the nature of the soul and the vital essence of all things; as well as medical reforms that aimed to free women's bodies from the constrictions of fashionable dress. For Riemerschmid, to be a designer at the turn of the twentieth century was to explore the fundamental questions of being in the modern world—to investigate intimate relations among body, mind, and self through the creation of what I understand as *living things*.

But to be a designer at this same moment was also to be an artist, to have in one's power the ability to create a thoroughly modern art that was (or would be) for the first time available to all levels of society as part of the very texture and experience of everyday life. Riemerschmid's Germany was young; only in 1871 had it become a unified nation. It had come late and in haste to the European nationalist pursuits of industrialism, colonialism—and style. The creation of a new German style through the practice of design thus took on higher stakes than ever before, and designed objects—produced in multiples and thus available to many—began to replace unique and precious paintings and sculptures as the modern German art. This book proposes Riemerschmid's "modern German art" as both a contribution to and an index of modern German culture. His first drawings, paintings, and prints of the 1890s; his early interiors and household objects; his designs for women's dresses; his immensely popular wooden furniture; his serially produced ceramics; his complex and compelling pattern designs for textiles and wallpapers, which trace the full arc of his career from the 1890s to his death in 1957—these things are the memoirs of a complicated, conflicted, and often inscrutable Germany trying to determine how to be "modern" in a rapidly modernizing world.

Riemerschmid's things come alive not solely through their connections with nineteenth-century biology and psychology, but also more practically, in their key roles as sociopolitical instruments during the first decades of the twentieth century. Cultural reformers of his time understood Riemerschmid's household objects as active agents for social change—operating "undercover" in the home, but also impacting the wider world beyond its walls. While important recent scholarship on Germany's design discourse has offered valuable interpretations of German cultural aesthetics, many such texts position the material object as a concretization of the immaterial *word*. I suggest instead that Riemerschmid's things played a constitutive role in the thoughts about them. Because these objects participated in cultural reforms alongside politicians, philanthropists, and pedagogues, a close examination of their material qualities is essential to understanding the cultural vision they promoted. Astonishing responses to Riemerschmid's everyday objects from colleagues and critics grew into an intellectual discourse of design unprecedented in its significance for the development of cultural politics, yet to this day unrivaled in its imaginative implications for the lives of the things themselves.

The greatest contribution of this discourse to our understanding of modernism is its case—made through arresting material evidence—for a *Sachlichkeit* neither sober nor objective, but as essential and vital as the relation between body and soul. Riemerschmid explained this "body and soul" *Sachlichkeit* through the designer's relation of material to form. In his words, it is the designer "in whose hands the dead material comes to life, so that it too acquires a kind of soul, and then, as if of its own accord searches for its own most genuine form, reacts to stimuli, grows and becomes."[11] In Riemerschmid's hands, materials came to life: he was a designer of living things.

OBJECTIVITY, OLD AND NEW

The Anglo-German historian of architecture and design Nikolaus Pevsner wrote in 1936 that "the untranslatable word *sachlich*, meaning at the same time pertinent, matter-of-fact, and objective, became the catchword of the growing Modern Movement."[12] Despite its resistance to translation, *Sachlichkeit* was indeed a pivotal concept for modern culture in Germany as early as the 1890s. The term remains key to any comprehensive, astute interpretation of the history and theory of modern art, architecture, and design today. But neither its complex meanings nor its implications for the intersections of various branches of material and visual culture during the modern period has been fully understood. Historians have repeatedly extended Pevsner's emphasis on *Sachlichkeit*'s objectivity and matter-of-factness to advance even sterner interpretations, such as "sobriety" and even "austerity." And *Sachlichkeit*'s frequent reduction to the English word "functionalism" fails absolutely to capture the prismatic array of historical meanings that the term accrued over the course of its specialized use, beginning in the Wilhelmine Era (1871–1918) and continuing through the Weimar Republic (1918–1933) and into the Third Reich (1933–1945). *Sachlichkeit*'s paradoxically emotional, psychological, and even empathic import for the greater history of what Pevsner called the "Modern Movement" simply cannot be conveyed through such terms as "sobriety," "functionalism," and "objectivity." Now, in the interest of my own objectivity, I leave them behind.

Like his machine chair, however, Riemerschmid's things move beyond these verbal discrepancies to perform *Sachlichkeit* on a more intuitive level, embodying and illuminating the complexities and contradictions inherent in modernism. This material exhibition and performance of *Sachlichkeit* is what I understand as *thingliness*. But the idea that the nature and purpose of "things" might be distinct from the mundane function of mere "objects" is not new. Martin Heidegger drew attention to this thingly quality in a lecture titled "The Thing," delivered shortly after the Second World War had ended.[13] Heidegger opposes the ordinary object or *Gegenstand*—that which "stands before, over against, opposite us" as *subjects*—with the thing as "what stands forth."[14] "Standing forth," he continues, "has the sense of stemming from somewhere, whether this be a process of self-making or of being made by another . . . standing forth has the sense of the made thing's standing forth into the unconcealedness of what is already present."[15] The "essential nature" or "presencing" of an object, "so experienced and thought of in these terms, is what we call *thing*."[16]

At the turn of the current century, American scholar Bill Brown argued in his "thing theory" that what Heidegger identified as *things* express "what is excessive in objects to their mere utilization as objects—their force as a sensuous presence or a metaphysical presence."[17] While the conventional reading of *Sachlichkeit* as "objectivity" suggests the boiling down of an object to a clinical essence of form and function, thingliness contends, on the contrary, for the irreducible, living excess of the thing—its uncontainable self-expression. This thingly vitality resonates with a recent strain of materialist thinking that scholars Diana Coole and Samantha Frost have called a "new ontology."[18] They point to political theorist Jane Bennett's exploration of a "vital materialism" as one example of new materialist ontologies that resist distinctions between animate and inanimate matter.[19] But just as Bennett's new ontology taps into currents of vitalist thought flowing back through centuries, so Coole and Frost acknowledge the lately popular matter philosophies they discuss as "renewed" materialisms.[20]

While these theories support a thingly understanding of *Sachlichkeit*, thingliness insists on the primary role—the inherent vitality—not of theories, but of historical things themselves. Riemerschmid's designs argue that long before their theory, things exerted themselves in a way that destabilized and sometimes even reversed our conventional understanding of subject-object relations. Reading *Sachlichkeit* as thingliness, then, is no intellectual gimmick: it is the appropriate response to modernist things and their true yet frequently misinterpreted nature.

Sachlichkeit originated in common parlance, as one nearly untranslatable word among many in the German language. However, its connotations for the discourse of architecture and design developing in the 1890s and continuing roughly through 1918 are distinct from the more familiar meanings it adopted in discussions of painting, photography, and architecture during the 1920s. *Sachlichkeit* is best known for its part in Neue Sachlichkeit or "New Objectivity," the title that Mannheim Kunsthalle director Gustav Friedrich Hartlaub gave to new work by a group of painters exhibiting at his gallery in 1925. Created in reaction to the Expressionism that preceded them, Neue Sachlichkeit paintings by artists including Max Beckmann and Otto Dix represented for Hartlaub "a positively tangible reality" (figures 0.5 and 0.6).[21] Dix further solidified Hartlaub's claim in 1927 by arguing that the *object*—the painting's physical, material subject—was the central concern in his painting. "For me," Dix wrote, "the object is primary and determines the form. I have therefore always felt it vital to get as close as possible to the thing I see. 'What' matters more to me than 'How.' 'How' arises from 'what.'"[22]

FIGURE 0.5

Max Beckmann, *Self Portrait with Cigarette*, 1923. Oil on canvas, 23¾ × 15⅞". Gift of Dr. and Mrs. F. H. Hirschland (255.1956). Digital Image © The Museum of Modern Art/ Licensed by SCALA / Art Resource, NY. © 2021 Artists Rights Society (ARS), New York.

This potentially myopic focus on the object extended the designation of Neue Sachlichkeit to the work of contemporary photographers such as Albert Renger-Patzsch, whose close-cropped, crisp-focused, unmanipulated image of a rationally ordered troop of everyday flat irons appears to offer the viewer these things *themselves*—no more, no less (*Flatirons*, 1928; figure 0.7). Neue Sachlichkeit portrait photographer August Sander took a similar approach in his treatment of the human figure, capturing his subjects at their most identifiable, with a few key signifiers of their identity or occupation—the master bricklayer, poised between two piles of bricks, brick trowel in his left hand, finishing trowel in his right (*Master Bricklayer*, figure 0.8). Or Cologne design professor Richard Riemerschmid in 1930, his one brown and one blue eye peering at the camera through thick, round, bifocal spectacles, with his no-nonsense linen work coat—a sketchbook poking out from its slack breast pocket—pulled roughly over his dark tweed suit (figure 0.9). But just as Riemerschmid's weary eyes, thinning disheveled hair, drooping shoulders, creased and rumpled clothes, and worn worrying hands communicate a poignancy that overflows the objectivity of his deadpan pose, so the luminous, larger-than-life quality of Renger-Patzsch's flatirons—the *what*, in Dix's terms—extends beyond the object's materiality. Beckmann had already articulated this liminal capacity of Neue Sachlichkeit in 1920, when he described his paintings as "transcendental objectivity."[23] Neue Sachlichkeit art could convey an almost eerie hyperrealism, a magical sense of an object's full-bodied, three-dimensional presence within the viewer's visual world. These postexpressionist works appeared to historian, photographer, and critic Franz Roh to "crystallize" raw matter into resonant objects, prompting him to give the movement its alternate name, Magical Realism.[24]

At the same time that *Sachlichkeit* defined such magical images, however, it also indicated objects and buildings that were anything but. During the 1920s, progressive architects and designers—including those working at the Bauhaus—developed

FIGURE 0.6

Otto Dix, *Portrait of the Journalist Sylvia von Harden*, 1926. Oil and tempera on wood, 121 × 89 cm. AM3899P. Photo: Audrey Laurans. Musée National d'Art Moderne, Centre Georges Pompidou, Paris, France. © CNAC/MNAM, Dist. RMN-Grand Palais / Art Resource, NY. © 2021 Artists Rights Society (ARS), New York / VG Bild-Kunst, Bonn.

FIGURE 0.7

Albert Renger-Patzsch, *Flatirons for Shoe Manufacture*, 1928. Gelatin silver print. Sheet: 22.9 × 16.8 cm (9 × 6⅝ in.). The J. Paul Getty Museum, Los Angeles © Albert Renger-Patzsch Archiv / Ann u. Jürgen Wilde, Zülpich / Artists Rights Society (ARS), New York, 2021.

FIGURE 0.8

August Sander, *Master Mason (Building a Chimney)*, 1932. Gelatin silver print. Image: 28.9 × 17.9 cm (11⅜ × 7¹⁄₁₆ in.). Mount (beige original): 43.8 × 33.9 cm (17¼ × 13⅜ in.). The J. Paul Getty Museum, Los Angeles. © J. Paul Getty Trust. © Die Photographische Sammlung / SK Stiftung Kultur—August Sander Archiv, Cologne / ARS, NY 2021.

the concept of *Sachlichkeit* into that principle of objectivity that came to be equated with functionalism. Like Dix, architects and designers of the Neues Bauen—the New Building, or Neue Sachlichkeit architecture—believed that the *how* of construction should arise from the *what* of the project's immediate circumstances—or, in more familiar terms, that form should follow function.[25] One of the most publicized examples of *Sachlichkeit* in Neues Bauen architecture, interiors, and furniture, was the 1927 exhibition Die Wohnung (The Dwelling), mounted by the German Werkbund—the organization founded in 1907 by artists, architects, designers, educators, museum professionals, and merchant retailers to modernize German culture through the redesign of utilitarian objects and the built environment. The Dwelling showcased new types of apartments, single-family houses, and their interiors as part of the Weissenhof Siedlung, a housing settlement designed by a group of international modernist architects and built in Stuttgart (figure 0.10).[26]

FIGURE 0.9

August Sander, *The Architect [Richard Riemerschmid]*, 1930. © 2021 Die Photographische Sammlung/SK Stiftung Kultur—August Sander Archiv, Cologne; ARS, NY 2021.

FIGURE 0.10

Weissenhof Housing Settlement (part of the German Werkbund's "The Dwelling" Exhibition), 1927. Weissenhof, Stuttgart, Germany. © Bildarchiv Foto Marburg / Art Resource, NY.

As architectural historian Rosemarie Haag Bletter has shown, Berlin architect and critic Adolf Behne developed a nuanced theory of *Sachlichkeit* in his influential writings of the 1920s. In *Der moderne Zweckbau* (The Modern Functional Building) of 1926, Behne uses the words *Zweck* (purpose) and *Funktion* (function) as synonyms for *Sachlichkeit* in its architectural application. However, just a year later in his *Neues Wohnen—Neues Bauen* (New Dwelling—New Building) of 1927, Behne refutes the assumption that *Sachlichkeit* implies dry, sober, or strictly mathematical architecture. *Sachlichkeit*, he explains, simply means that the architectural solution develops in response to the *Sache*—the matter at hand: "Each *Sache* is a nodal point, a crossing point of relations between human being and human being. . . . To work *sachlich* means therefore to work socially in each discipline. To build *sachlich* means to build socially."[27]

But before *Sachlichkeit* was conjured into Magical Realism, and before it choreographed the "social" life of architecture, it had a simpler life of its own. Neither Hartlaub nor Behne had invented the term; it was already waiting for them when the 1920s arrived. *Sachlichkeit*, like its root word, *Sache*, did not originate as a theoretical term but as an everyday German word. The primary synonyms for *Sache* that appear in Duden's *Stilwörterbuch* (dictionary of style) are *Ding* (thing) and *Gegenstand* (object), linking the concept of *Sachlichkeit* both to the hard, factual world of the object and to the more ephemeral, even spiritual world of the thing.[28] A more versatile translation of *Sache*, however, is "matter," a word that implies both the concrete, physical stuff that crystallizes into objects and also a more abstract problem or issue, as in the "matter at hand" or "the heart of the matter." Heidegger's excavation of the old German words *thing* and *dinc*—ancestors of the modern-day *Ding*—supports this dualistic apprehension of *Sachlichkeit* as "matter": "The Old High German word *thing* means a gathering, and specifically a gathering to deliberate on a matter under discussion, a contested matter. In consequence, the Old German words *thing* and *dinc* become the names for an affair or matter of pertinence."[29]

Modern architects seized on the term *Sachlichkeit* in the mid-1890s precisely because of its common, unsophisticated heritage. An architecture that considered above all the matter at hand—an architecture that got to the heart of the matter, a matter-of-fact architecture—could be comprehended intuitively by most Germans. In this late nineteenth-century context, *Sachlichkeit* was a variant of architectural *realism*. Architectural historian Harry Francis Mallgrave has shown that Austrian architect Otto Wagner, whose Vienna Postal Savings Bank was hailed as a model of rationalism in 1906, situated realism (as opposed to the perceived artifice of historical styles popular in the nineteenth century) at the center of his creative project already in 1894: "Our living conditions and methods of construction must be fully and completely expressed if architecture is not to be reduced to a caricature. The realism of our time must pervade the developing work of art. . . . It will breathe a new and pulsating life into forms."[30]

A year later in his *Moderne Architektur* (Modern Architecture) of 1895, Wagner stressed "need, purpose, construction" as the "primitive germs" of artistic creation. That same year, Berlin Applied Arts Museum director Julius Lessing joined Wagner's campaign, averring, "our work has to be based on the soil of the practical life of our time; it has to create those forms that correspond to our needs, our technology, and our materials."[31] As Mallgrave has argued, the architectural realism of the first half of the 1890s paid "scrupulous attention to the attributes of convenience, comfort, health, and cleanliness," while at the same time attempting to reassure potential critics that a down-to-earth approach to architecture could still be an artistic one.[32]

However, *sachlich* design was down-to-earth in a way that was not just sensible, but familiar and homey as well.[33] In addition to being straightforward and matter-of-fact, *Sachlichkeit* was styleless: it was unencumbered by any specific historical or stylistic tradition and thus recommended itself in the 1890s to progressive architects who longed to break free of the foreign and historical styles that had dominated German architecture and design throughout the nineteenth century. *Sachlichkeit* arose neither from the distant past nor from a foreign land, but from the national vernacular; it was the visual language of the German *Volk*. Some histories of German design would suggest that *Sachlichkeit* was itself yet another style—the style of the German Werkbund, whose proponents advanced it as an antidote to fashionable turn-of-the-century Jugendstil.[34] And the Werkbund was indeed responsible for promulgating, during the 1910s, the dry, sober, mathematical caricature of *Sachlichkeit* that Behne contested in the 1920s. But Behne's social vision of *Sachlichkeit* tapped its vernacular essence, replacing clinical functionalism with the expansive, animating principle that I call *thingliness*, making room not only for "relations between human being and human being," but also for those between humans and their things.

In human terms, *Sachlichkeit* is the "soul" of the thing. But the notion that inanimate objects might possess a soul was by no means a late nineteenth-century invention. Its Western tradition dates back to the fourth century BCE with Aristotle's "De Anima (On the Soul)," in which the philosopher explored what he called the "essential whatness" of all things: human, animal, plant, and object. Aristotle defined the soul as "the definitive formula of a thing's essence."[35] For Aristotle, the "soul" of the eye was its capacity for sight; remove or disable this capacity, and the eye became an eye in name only. Sight was the eye's animating and defining principle; without it, the eye was no longer itself. "As the pupil *plus* the power of sight constitutes the eye, so the soul *plus* the body constitutes the animal [animated being]."[36] Remarkably, though, Aristotle extended his analogy into the realm of things that were literally lacking *anima*: *in*animate objects. If an axe, for instance, were a "natural body," the essential whatness of the thing called *axe* would then be its potential, purpose, or function—its capacity to chop: "if this disappeared from it, it would have ceased to be an axe."[37] Aristotle acknowledges, however, that axes do not and cannot have souls: "As it is, it is just an axe; it wants the character which is required to make its whatness or formulable essence a soul; for that, it would have to be a *natural* body . . . having *in itself* the power of setting itself in movement and arresting itself."[38] In other words, an inanimate object can have no soul because it is just as its name defines it: it cannot move of its own free will, and thus it can express no character; or, to be more precise, even if it *did* have a character, it would have no way of letting us know.

Aristotle's reservations notwithstanding, however, we persist in endowing inanimate objects with souls on a daily basis: the small child bestows on a beloved toy the capacity to return her love; the grieving widower invests a photograph, or even a familiar possession of his wife's, with the ability to perpetuate a relationship that death has severed. One of the nineteenth century's most penetrating thinkers, the author and de facto sociologist George Eliot (penname of Mary Ann Evans), interprets the power of attachment and loss to animate material objects in her 1861 novel, *Silas Marner: The Weaver of Raveloe*. Eliot traces the life of a weaver who in his youth is framed as a criminal by his closest friend, cast out from his church, jilted by his betrothed, and shunned by his provincial community, from which he ultimately flees to Raveloe, a faraway village that seems as unfamiliar to him as a foreign country. Struggling with his profound sense of betrayal and loss, Silas turns inward, shutting himself off, so that his neighbors come to regard him as a suspicious hermit. "Yet even in this stage of withering," Eliot writes,

a little incident happened, which showed that the sap of affection was not all gone. It was one of his daily tasks to fetch his water from a well a couple of fields off, and for this purpose, ever since he came to Raveloe, he had had a brown earthenware pot, which he held as his most precious utensil among the very few conveniences he had granted himself. It had been his companion for twelve years, always standing on the same spot, always lending its handle to him in the early morning, so that its form had an expression for him of willing help-fulness, and the impress of its handle on his palm gave a satisfaction mingled with that of having the fresh clear water. One day as he was returning from the well, he stumbled against the step of the stile, and his brown pot, falling with force against the stones that overarched the ditch below him, was broken in three pieces. Silas picked up the pieces and carried them home with grief in his heart. The brown pot could never be of use to him any more, but he stuck the bits together and propped the ruin in its old place for a memorial.[39]

In Aristotle's terms, it was the brown pot's "essential whatness" that had grad-ually endeared this thing to Silas. In its capacity to help him, it had proved more useful, more straightforward, and far more reliable than previous friends had been. Even in "death"—even when, according to Aristotle's "essential whatness" logic, it was no longer a pot at all—it retained a claim upon the weaver's heart. Rather than simply disposing of the useless earthenware shards that had once constituted his useful brown pot, Silas arranges them so that they still resemble his trusty com-panion. Although the pot is, in Aristotelian essence, dead, the weaver's memorial gives it a kind of afterlife. But if the pot could no longer serve and companion him, what true attraction could its ruin have retained for Silas? During the twelve years of their relationship, the pot had acquired symbolic meaning for him: every day it stood waiting for him, the touch of its handle was a promise in his hand, so that, by and by, "its form had an expression for him of willing helpfulness." Even when the pot's thingliness had passed, Silas's powerful associations with its form continued. It is *form*, then, that endows inanimate objects with character and seems—by the magic of association—to grant them souls.

As "wax and the shape given to it by the stamp are one," wrote Aristotle, so the soul was in a sense material: its expression could only be perceived materially, through the language of the body.[40] Just as Aristotle's conceptions of soul and body could not be separated, so the nineteenth century's philosophically based, though scientifically influenced, forerunner to modern psychology—known in German as *Seelenlehre* (the doctrine of the soul)—was bound up with the body and its forms. The clinical pioneer in this regard was the French founder of neurology, Jean-Martin Charcot. His studies, beginning in the 1880s, of neurasthenia and hysteria (nineteenth-century nervous disorders) revealed striking correspondences between the dramatic facial expressions and bodily gestures of his patients and their var-ious types of mental disarray.[41] As early as the 1860s and 1870s, however, German studies, including those by psychophysicist Gustav Theodor Fechner and aesthetic philosopher Robert Vischer, pursued connections between the feelings of the soul and forms of the body.[42] By the end of the century there were even those, like the philosopher Friedrich Nietzsche, who interpreted Aristotle's analogy not as a depiction of the unity of matter and spirit, but as an utter negation of any spiritual concept of soul: the body's form and its animating substance were both material; matter, not spirit, was the stuff of life.[43] Zoologist, philosopher, and artist Ernst Haeckel, a follower of Darwin and of naturalist Alexander von Humboldt, replaced the traditional Christian notion of a spiritual soul inhabiting a physical body with his theory of *monism*—the belief that all organisms were united through their cellular life force and through their ever-changing material *forms*.[44]

This fascination with the origins, nature, and specific location of animate life developed in a century during which human life was perceived as much more mysterious and precarious than it is today. Eliot's narrative, for example, addresses precious but fleeting human attachments within a rural community effectively cut off from nineteenth-century advances in medical science and still reliant for its understanding of the world on religious mysticism and superstition. Just as mysterious individuals might possess strange powers for good or ill, so material things might also exert talismanic or apotropaic influences. And it was during Eliot's century, with its blending of science and spiritualism, that Riemerschmid came of age. By 1900, critics began to report on Riemerschmid's uncanny ability to identify the soul of the material for which he designed, and to allow the essential whatness of that material to determine the form of the object it constituted.[45] Riemerschmid's sensitive *Materialgerechtigkeit*, or "justice to materials," was inherent in his practice of the animating principle of *Sachlichkeit*. Part of the object's thingliness for Riemerschmid, like Aristotle's wax in its mold, was the nature of its substance. While Aristotle's axe could have been made out of any number of combinations of materials that enabled its "axeness"—its capacity for chopping—the essence of each of Riemerschmid's things depended on the definitive character of its chosen material.

And yet the object's purpose took an equal part in the thingliness of Riemerschmid's things. Their functional capacity was demonstrated in their *Zweckmäßigkeit*, or "fitness for purpose." Riemerschmid's approach to *Zweckmäßigkeit* was remarkable, however, in its extension beyond the functional parameters of purpose, into the expressive realm of personality. Aristotle makes no requirement that the design of his axe express its capacity to chop (its so-called "soul"), nor does he draw any parallels between the physical form of the eye and the activity of sight. Like the symbolic, emotional associations Silas Marner formed with his brown pot, one might indeed, as the result of experience, associate the form of an axe with the act of chopping, or an image of an eye with vision. And although the pot's rounded belly suggests its ability to hold water, just as the axe's tapered form and sharp edge suggests its capacity to chop, there is only latency—no *action*—in these forms. The brown pot makes no outward gesture to signal the living fluid it holds; the axe at rest makes no motion towards chopping; and the physical form of the eye could never embody the complex dynamics inherent in the act of seeing. There is no mimetic relationship between the forms of any of these objects and their active purposes—their animated souls.

In contrast to these nonmimetic examples of purposiveness, Riemerschmid's *zweckmäßig* chairs were felt to "squat" in anticipation of their sitters; his tables to "stretch themselves out to receive dishes"; and his wardrobes to adopt a "comfortable, broad stance" that gave those who stored things in them a "reassuring sense of security and stability."[46] These were not associations formed over time through particular experience and individual use, but the immediate impressions of many period observers. It was as if, in his unique articulation of *Materialgerechtigkeit* and *Zweckmäßigkeit*, Riemerschmid challenged Aristotle's conclusion about the inherent lack of anima in the inanimate object. While *Materialgerechtigkeit*'s justice to materials provided the object with a soul's character, *Zweckmäßigkeit*'s fitness for purpose seemed to endow it with its own capacity to express itself, through gestures of form suggestive of impulsion, action—movement. Riemerschmid's *Sachlichkeit*—the animating principle that, rather than imposing the will of the artist, exposed the soul of the thing—defined him as a new kind of designer, whose things themselves advanced a compelling vision for the modern age.

ARTIST X AND THE NEW STYLE

"The only remarkable one is Riemerschmid," wrote the young designer August Endell in an 1897 letter describing his artist cohort in Munich to his cousin (cultural historian Kurt Breysig) in Berlin.[47] Richard Anton Adolf Riemerschmid came into the world on June 20, 1868, in one of the houses that made up the so-called "Riemerschmid-Block," the property located on Munich's fashionable Maximilianstraße, the inner courtyard of which would later become the site of the Münchner Schauspielhaus, the avant-garde theater renovated by Riemerschmid in 1901. Richard was born into one of Munich's wealthiest and most influential *Bildungsbürger*, or "cultured middle-class" families. The Riemerschmids moved in musical and artistic circles, kept abreast of cultural trends and events, and encouraged all of their children (Richard was the sixth of nine) to pursue their own interests. The curly auburn-haired Richard, with his striking mismatched blue and brown eyes, grew up in a liberal, loving household during the Gründerzeit, or "founders' time," the heady and formative episode in German history characterized first by euphoric speculation and then by economic depression and social anxiety—but by nationalism throughout—that followed Germany's 1871 unification as a result of victory in the Franco-Prussian War. The Riemerschmid family business—the Royal Bavarian Private Wine, Spirit, Liqueur, and Vinegar Factory—was one of many to benefit from the Gründerzeit's immediate postwar economic boom: by 1878, Riemerschmid's father Eduard and uncles Adolf and Heinrich owned two branches, in Munich and Vienna, and in 1883 Eduard became sole director of the Munich branch.[48]

Richard Riemerschmid came of age in a time and place characterized not simply by political, social, and economic upheaval, but simultaneously defined by a multitude of cultural reforms—especially by new directions in the arts. This was the period when composer Richard Wagner developed his theory of the *Gesamtkunstwerk*, or "total artwork," drawing together music, poetry, and theatre in his epic, path-breaking opera cycles, whose influence moved far beyond music to impact literature, the visual arts, philosophy, and politics.[49] And since the 1850s, British social reformers, including the "father" of the Arts and Crafts Movement, William Morris, had been rethinking the design of everyday objects to make them more useful, beautiful, and available to greater numbers of people.[50] Riemerschmid subscribed to the British Arts and Crafts journal *The Studio* from its founding in 1893, by which time radical artists in Belgium and France, too, were identifying the everyday art of design as the area where the greatest and swiftest aesthetic changes and social impact could be made. Their New Style or Art Nouveau rejected old, historical forms of ornament, taking inspiration instead from the natural shapes, patterns, and colors of plants and animals that were also the focus of developments in contemporary science.[51] Toward the close of the century, Austrian artists like designer Josef Hoffmann and painter Gustav Klimt would abandon the traditional structure and training of the art academy to embrace this youthful fervor for growth and change in what would be called, in 1898, the Vienna Secession. But first it was Munich's turn. In 1892, a group of young, progressive Bavarian artists broke from Munich's prestigious art academy to embark on a fresh, unconventional approach to art, at the forefront of which was design. Riemerschmid, who had enrolled in the academy in 1888 but dropped out in 1891 to pursue his own course as a painter, joined the Secession in 1893. It was this group of radical young artists that pioneered Munich's new take on art and design: the "youth style," or Jugendstil.

August Endell, originally from Berlin, joined Riemerschmid's cause a few years later, in 1896. Endell had come to Munich in the mid-1890s to study mathematics; however, after dropping that all-too-rational pursuit, he took up philosophy, and then psychology. Endell became a devoté of Munich's notorious *Seelenlehre* and began to experiment with design as a kind of public testing ground for new psychological theories. In the slightly older and better-established Riemerschmid—who, unlike Endell, could claim both an artistic upbringing and actual training in art—Endell recognized that "remarkable" impulse toward the *Beseelung* ("ensouling" or animation) of design to which he, the neophyte designer, aspired. Endell's mentor was Professor Theodor Lipps, the aesthetic philosopher and psychologist who, during the 1890s, attracted international attention (including that of Sigmund Freud) for his theories of empathy and the unconscious. Under Lipps, Endell developed a dissertation on the "construction of feelings," which makes his singling out of Riemerschmid even more significant—and tantalizing.[52]

Endell's deepest devotion, however, was to the Swiss sculptor and designer Hermann Obrist, whose Munich exhibition of botanically inspired embroideries in April 1896 was hailed as a breakthrough not just in decorative art, but in the arts generally (figure 0.11). Obrist's exhibition has since been understood as one of the inaugural events of Jugendstil. In another letter home to Berlin, the enraptured Endell writes: "This is the new style that everybody seeks and whose possibilities many doubt. Here the great riddle is solved, like child's play, of course. This is totally new, independent, mature, great art. What a plethora of forms, what splendor of color! It is the dawn of a new era."[53]

Like Endell, Obrist had received no formal artistic instruction but had instead developed his interest in decorative design through the study of botany. Natural science—especially biological discovery—had become a catalyst not simply for developments in art and design toward the end of the nineteenth century, but for the transformation of German cultural life more broadly. Extending well into the twentieth century, this pan-German fascination with the visible and invisible worlds of nature in popular and rarefied circles, entwining the fields of biology, psychology, philosophy, ecology, and occultism, was part of a unique, discursive network that has since been termed *German holism*.[54] Hybrid careers that paired the empirical study of nature with the imaginative practices of art and design generated some

of the most intriguing innovations in both science and style toward the close of the nineteenth century. Without his artistic training and virtuosity as a draftsman and watercolorist, for instance, German biologist Ernst Haeckel would not have been able to record his microscopic discoveries in their minute and lifelike detail; moreover, Haeckel's controversial evolutionary theories would never have been popularized had it not been for the vibrant and compelling illustrations of never-before-seen creatures that made up the bulk of his published portfolios, such as his widely disseminated *Art Forms in Nature* of 1899. The benefits from this relationship were not accrued by science alone, however: some of the most forward-looking

FIGURE 0.11

Hermann Obrist, *Cyclamen* (wallhanging with silk embroidery), 1895. Münchner Stadtmuseum, Sammlung Mode/Textilien/ Kostümbibliothek.

designs of the nineteenth century were created by German-trained British botanist Christopher Dresser, who, during the 1850s, began to apply his botanical training to the development of a practical design theory rooted in plant morphology.

Biological processes of growth, development, and evolution, demonstrating organic, responsive relations between outer form and inner life, suggested parallels between the animate being's soul and the "purpose" of the designed object, so that even inanimate objects might be considered ontologically as "living things." In Obrist's embroideries and, later, in Riemerschmid's designs, Endell identified an ensouled quality that, according to architectural historian Tilmann Buddensieg, manifested itself as "an emotional expression that had, until then, been reserved for the fine arts."[55] In other words, to approach the design of everyday objects not as a workman approaches his trade but rather as a creator approaches his creature was to breathe life into the "dead material." Though Obrist's embroidery designs sprang from vegetal life, plant forms served him only as the vehicle to a loftier destination. What he and his protégé Endell ultimately sought to harness for design was the wordless energy and affective power of abstract form.

In a series of articles published between 1897 and 1898 in the Munich journal *Dekorative Kunst* (Decorative Art), Endell traces a path from Obrist's nature-based abstractions to an outright rejection of objective forms in an entirely new *Formenkunst* (form-art)—an art made purely of forms: "An art with forms which signify nothing, represent nothing and remind us of nothing, which arouse our souls as deeply and as strongly as music. . . . This is the power of form upon the mind, a direct, immediate influence without any intermediary stage, by no means an anthropomorphic effect, but one of direct empathy."[56] Endell's first large-scale experiment in these abstract yet affecting forms received mixed reviews. The avant-garde studio he designed in 1897 for photographers Anita Augspurg and Sophia Goudstikker—radical feminists, open lesbians, and Germany's first women business owners[57]—stood out from its neighbors on Munich's An-der-Tann-Straße by virtue of the brightly painted, churning, whipping, seething relief sculpture applied to its facade (figure 0.12). Although Riemerschmid would never embark on the kind of purely ornamental excess of Endell's *Formenkunst*, a chair that squatted, a table that stretched out its surface, or a wardrobe that secured its contents with a sturdy broad-shouldered stance would doubtless have affected the designer of the Elvira studio in a "remarkable" way.

The distinction between Endell's and Riemerschmid's designs—and the reactions they evoked—lay in the Aristotelian essential whatness determining each

man's forms. Endell remarked that Riemerschmid's constructions could too easily be reduced to "sheer naked lines," much like the designs of Belgian artist Henry van de Velde, whose theories of line proved highly influential for German designers during the 1890s and early 1900s.[58] Endell's critique arose from his own practice in which ornament—not structural lines—was primary. "Ornament," he wrote in 1897, "is luxury and needs space for itself."[59] The embellished surface was like an image projected on a screen: the screen (the construction to which the ornament adhered) was merely a vehicle for the ornament's impact on the soul, a way of exposing people to pure *form-art* on a daily basis, and so affecting their experience. Like Studio Elvira, Endell's furniture and interiors were psychological experiments.

FIGURE 0.12

August Endell, *Atelier Elvira*, 1897. Münchner Stadtmuseum, Sammlung Fotografie.

While Riemerschmid's designs too manifest what art historian Maria Makela has termed the "emphatic" forms of Munich Jugendstil, their impact is less a product of their users' psyches; their affective power derives instead from their own inherent drive to self-expression, located not on an ornamental surface but within their very bones—at the level of *form*.[60] While the abstract ornamental forms of an Endell chair might have the power to "arouse our souls," the purposeful structures of Riemerschmid's chairs bare their souls to us.

In a 1901 article titled "The Future of Our Architecture," Obrist drew a line between modern objects whose thoughtlessly applied ornament obscured their essential purpose and those whose expressive, decorative qualities served actively to heighten and enliven their purpose—whose ornament *and* purpose came from the same place: "das Wesen der Sache," or the essential being of the thing.[61] To illustrate his theory, Obrist compared three imaginary chairs: an old German Gothic councilor's chair, an English lady's boudoir chair, and a chair designed by "Artist X." The first two chairs, Obrist argued, were products of certain styles—one historical, the other foreign. Neither bore any relation to the lifestyles or concerns of modern Germans in 1901. But Artist X's chair seemed to spring from a more profound and personal source, which it demonstrated through design:

Its entire appearance is thoroughly unique. Everything about its construction gives us the impression of energetic life. The powerfully bowed legs carry the generous seat energetically, the back legs pass into the backrest, supporting it energetically, and this age-old problem [of constructing a chair] is solved in a striking new way. The backrest embraces the back fully and broadly, supporting the whole body; its pronouncedly rippling form emphasizes its function . . . Artist X understands and loves this powerful kind of coziness, energetic life pulses inside him, he loves to emphasize, accentuate, and accent. You see, this chair, as the outpouring of his own imagination, expresses his entire self; it could never have been made like this by anyone else. It speaks, it talks in forms, it makes its personality visible.[62]

Obrist's description of this ideal chair underscores his appeal for a designer like Endell, who believed in the power of form to speak directly to the observer or user. But the corporeal, anthropomorphic language of the chair's forms flouts Endell's requirement of "pure" forms that "signify nothing, represent nothing and remind us of nothing." Obrist's imagined chair, with its intimate relationship among purpose, structure, and expression, was meant to represent not his 1890s protégé, but that protégé's only "remarkable" Munich colleague. Artist X was

Richard Riemerschmid. Although Artist X's chair is ostensibly drawn from Obrist's imagination, its energetically bowed legs, "rippling form," and overall fluid articulation of structure in which one component passes seamlessly into the next constitute the hallmarks of a Riemerschmid chair, undoubtedly known to Obrist, from 1898—that same energetic design that would serve as Thomas Mann's desk chair in 1902 (figure 0.1).

Obrist's chief concern in his 1901 article was Germany's failure to arrive at a style for the new century: "We still have no new style," he lamented.[63] "Does the Empire style express the soul of our German people, or does van de Velde-ornament express the soul of our German Volk? Absolutely not, and yet they are both fashionable. Even small-time carpenters . . . rush to imitate their forms."[64] For Obrist, the foreignness of the French Empire style and the Belgian "van de Velde-ornament" disqualified them both from representing the modern German soul. The Empire style committed a second sin by being unmodern, but the use of "van de Velde-ornament," while ultramodern, was something even worse: it was *inauthentic*, the commercial imitation and corruption of that artist's original designs into a fashion; it was *kitsch*. According to Obrist, the solution was to abandon the concept of style altogether: tired motifs should be exchanged for spontaneous inspiration; historicism should be replaced by more familiar and natural forms. Modern German design should be characterized by unselfconsciousness and integrity.[65]

But the achievement of this unstudied, spontaneous, authentic design would not be the accomplishment of professionally trained designers; on the contrary, Obrist believed that those unschooled in the design trade were best suited to bring about its twentieth-century renewal. Artist X, for instance, "created his chair without looking back at other chairs from previous stylistic periods, he didn't bother at all with chairs that already existed, he just designed it the only way he could. That happy man! He had never languished in a [design] school, he had never learned anything; instead, his personality lived as freely as that of a poet, to whom a song occurs spontaneously—his own song, not a song in the style of the seventeenth century!"[66] The modern designer Obrist envisions is not a trained professional, but a sensitive individual with an artistic temperament—someone who feels deeply and is driven to express. This artist-designer was a relatively new phenomenon in Europe, and especially in Munich, at the time of Obrist's article. In fact, many of the day's most prominent designers were untrained in the practice: Obrist himself had come from botany, van de Velde had been an Impressionist painter, and Riemerschmid was a landscape painter—a "colorist"—by training. With childlike humility, Obrist believed, artists like Riemerschmid had applied themselves to the new task of design in the 1890s, realizing, with the dawn of the twentieth century, a contemporary, creative, and personal style. There was no single "style of the future," Obrist proclaimed; there must be instead as many styles as there were artistic personalities. "Style," then, could no longer be understood as the visual homogenizer of a historical period but had become, in the modern age, the infinitely varying expression of the modern individual.[67] This was in 1901—and is again today—a new vision of modernism: one in which *Sachlichkeit* materializes inward character through outward form.

Obrist traced the path of the modern artist-designer from fine art to object design to architecture. Indeed, by 1901, Riemerschmid, the landscape painter, had designed and built his own home in suburban Munich and had just completed the interiors of Munich's first modern theater—the Münchner Schauspielhaus.[68] For the first time in centuries, Obrist rejoiced, Germany was finally in a position to show something of its own architecture to the world. But this "architecture of the future" would not be accompanied by the fanfare and bombast of previous national styles. (And it is worth pausing here to note that the heavy-handed fascist aesthetics of the 1930s were, as we shall see, no realization of Obrist's "future" German architecture.) Instead, like *Sachlichkeit*, it would be straightforward, down-to-earth, and representative of the matter at hand: "Let us exploit the economic boom of the new century and show ourselves worthy of today's social progress, inasmuch as we build our homes authentically, genuinely, and appropriately to our own age, upon that in which we ourselves take pleasure. Let us leave behind to our progeny a monument not to that which we imitated, but to what and how we ourselves, at the beginning of the twentieth century, actually were."[69] Rather than embellishing the surface of the national character, *Sachlichkeit* penetrated to the multiple, unvarnished essences of "what and how we ourselves, at the beginning of the twentieth century, actually were." Like Riemerschmid—who served in Obrist's eyes as their exemplar—Germany's modern artist-designers, each in his or her own way, got to the heart of modernity's many matters.

THINGS AND THOUGHTS

The German designed object was the catalyst for some of the most lively, creative, interdisciplinary, and impactful criticism and debate of the twentieth century. During the Wilhelmine period (1890–1918)—which is the focus, though not the limit, of this book—an intellectual discourse, unparalleled in its cultural insight and political significance, grew up around everyday things. This discourse, revivified through the words of its most compelling voices, is central not only to my interpretation of Riemerschmid's "living things," but to understanding the character of modern life at the turn of the twentieth century. This was a time when design became a pivotal force in the redefinition of German culture for the modern age, a time when designers were understood not simply as makers but as *thinkers* who influenced the intellectual culture of their day. Just as designed objects became visual and material "terms" in Wilhelmine cultural debates, the language of the design reformers and critics who wrote about them has become for us a type of artifact: both concrete evidence of and a direct connection with a historically unique way of thinking about the relationship among objects, people, and cultural institutions.

The terms of Riemerschmid's Wilhelmine design discourse—the terms of this book's debate—are both conceptually and socially distinct. Words like *Sachlichkeit*, *Gemütlichkeit*, and *Kultur*, for instance, while they can be expounded upon and explored in English, lose some of their essential whatness in direct, single-word translations. They are the product of a historical marriage of things and thoughts: German ideas about German objects conceived them. Born through native speech, they have since acquired their own discursive life; they have developed what might be called a *material culture* of words. Their special aural texture and cadence, too, act as material links to the conversations that put them in play: to read and speak them is to catch the reverberations of long-passed debates, to breathe the breath of those who uttered them. As much as possible in this book, I let German things and thoughts speak for themselves. I want readers to hear the remarkable interchanges among manufacturers, academics, government officials, cultural critics, artists, architects, and designers that these interdependent objects and ideas generated.[70] Inasmuch as the following chapters explore, analyze, and offer Riemerschmid's things to the reader, they also unfold and illuminate the dynamic debates about how these things defined what it was—and is—to be modern.

Chapter 1, "Ties of the Flesh," grounds Riemerschmid's design practice, and especially its unique expression of *Sachlichkeit*, in relation to his dynamic conception of the human body as he explores it through his early work as a Symbolist painter in the 1890s. During this explosive period in the development of modern art, when Symbolist artists pushed form and color to the brink of abstraction, Riemerschmid depicts embattled, eroticized bodies engaged in athletic acts that blur the boundaries between affection and violence. In this chapter, I invoke philosophical and medical discourses peculiar to the late nineteenth century to interpret Riemerschmid's straining, struggling bodies and their import for his approach to the three-dimensional, utilitarian objects he would begin to design as early as 1895, while yet identifying as a painter. I propose the popular nineteenth-century theory of physiognomy, in which a person's emotions, character, or even soul could be "read" in their facial expressions or body language, as key to understanding Riemerschmid's relational conception of *Sachlichkeit*, in which the designed object's outward, material form reveals its inner function, purpose, and essence.

At the dawn of the twentieth century, cultural reformers recognized utilitarian design as both the newest adaptation and most radical iteration of Art: a new, useful, democratic art designed to infuse a potent aesthetic current into the flow of everyday life. The book's second chapter, "At Home with the Uncanny," connects Riemerschmid's turn-of-the-century conversion from painting to design with the broader social and psychological consequences of this modernist shift from exclusive image to accessible object. This drive toward universalism links design to modernism's grander aspirations, which have conventionally been understood as transcending the particular, the regional, the rural, and the traditional in order to attain the openness and versatility of urban cosmopolitanism. The modernist dream of universality has often been taken to imply a complete "cultural amnesia"—a suppression of the past in an attempt to achieve a clinically clean slate. I propose, however, that this suppressed—or, in the terms of Riemerschmid's contemporary, Sigmund Freud, *repressed*—past is not only part of but essential to modern consciousness. Paying close attention to relations among the specialized discourse of *Sachlichkeit*, the cultural resonance of the vernacular, and the psychology of the *Unheimliche* (uncanny), "At Home with the Uncanny" reveals how, in the comfortable and familiar space of the domestic interior, Riemerschmid's animated designs perform modernism's unconscious as they mobilize material traditions and reiterate regional fantasies within the boundaries of simplified, modernized forms.

Chapter 3, "Close as Skin," draws together *Sachlichkeit* as the "vital essence" of material things with Riemerschmid's artistic focus on the forms and movements of the human body by examining his integration of a particular body—his wife's—into his schemes for aesthetically unified interiors. As part of the 1901 debut of the Münchner Schauspielhaus, a theater for avant-garde drama whose interiors Riemerschmid had reconceptualized as a total artwork or *Gesamtkunstwerk*, the artist also designed a "reform dress"—a type of medically and aesthetically progressive gown that reformers promoted in reaction to the physically restrictive women's garments fashionable at the time—for his wife to wear at the theater's opening gala. Ida Riemerschmid's simple theater dress becomes the centerpiece of a more expansive discussion of relations among bodies, forms, and spaces in Riemerschmid's designs for garments and interiors between 1900 and 1903. This chapter advances the book's central argument for *Sachlichkeit* as the visible, tangible relation of body to soul by bringing nineteenth-century architect Gottfried Semper's theory of symbolic *Bekleidung* (dressing) to bear on Riemerschmid's clothing of the female body and his cladding of interior space.

Inherent in an embrace of the new is a rejection of the old—or so the story of modernism has largely been told. Structured around the 1906 Third German Applied Arts Exhibition in Dresden, a watershed event during which modern design gained more visibility and popularity with the middle class than ever before, chapter 4, "A Forest in the Living Room," tells a different tale. While it was at Dresden in 1906 that Riemerschmid unveiled his newly conceived "machine furniture"—simple wooden furnishings that were serially produced using standardized, component parts and that could be quickly assembled and disassembled to facilitate cost-effective production, convenient shipping, and, importantly, more sales—Riemerschmid's exhibition displays also reveal a reverence for the past. Portraits of German cultural heroes like Albrecht Dürer and Richard Wagner hang on the walls of his avant-garde interiors, and simplified wooden furniture, fabricated using machine tools, alludes to forms familiar from the Renaissance. Even more than these images and forms, however, it is these displays' chief element—wood—in its ubiquity and materiality, that occupies the past and the future at once. Through the medium of wood, I propose that *Sachlichkeit*'s inextricable relation of surface and substance conveys not only material essence but also immaterial *time*. This chapter traces the rapprochement between German Renaissance art of the early sixteenth century and Riemerschmid's modernist design of the early twentieth century via the cultural currency of wood, present in his Dresden displays in such quantity that one critic described his experience as encountering "a forest in the living room."

Chapter 5, "Filling Empty Hands," problematizes the relationship between utilitarian function and political agenda in the modernist object by considering Riemerschmid's things in the service of a larger, nationalist cause. Riemerschmid's designs for blue-and-gray salt-glazed stoneware ceramics—commonplace items like beer mugs and kitchen canisters—were especially attractive to the German

Werkbund, which selected and deployed Riemerschmid's tankards, egg cups, and butter dishes in its campaign to reform Germany from the domestic interior outward.[71] Building on the previous chapter's interpretation of *Sachlichkeit* at the 1906 Dresden exhibition as revealing both timeless essence and collective memory, I argue for *Sachlichkeit*, in a context of increasingly heightening nationalism from 1907 to 1914, as the communicator of material "instructions" on how to be German in the modern age. At a time when an imperialist Germany struggled to maintain control of its colonies in Africa and Asia, Riemerschmid's cheerful beer mugs became model servants, placing reassuringly German values into the "empty hands" of the young nation's cultured middle class, or *Bildungsbürgertum*.

Chapter 6, "Cells and Souls," gathers the book's interpretive strands and material studies in an exploration of Riemerschmid's vast body of patterns for textiles and wallpapers, many of which play on the cellular structures of plants. Riemerschmid's patterns are the only aspect of his creative practice that persists over the full arc of his career and the span of his long life; together, they provide a map to his larger project as a designer. I contend that Riemerschmid's relationship to his pattern designs mirrors the *Sachlichkeit* at work within his designed objects, which express their inner thingly nature in their outer, utilitarian forms. Riemerschmid's mesmerizing patterns are a visual index of his thoughts and feelings about his relevance and purpose within an increasingly threatening modern world. "Cells and Souls" revisits key discussions of biology, empathy, perception, aesthetics, spirituality, and materiality in the book's previous chapters, interweaving them with pivotal events, both historical and personal, in Riemerschmid's later career. This culminating chapter moves beyond the Wilhelmine era to consider the impact of the two world wars, and of National Socialism in particular, on Riemerschmid's life and work. His patterns transgress the boundaries of art and design, wordlessly invoking and engaging in modernist debates around self-referentiality, medium specificity, and abstraction. Just as *Sachlichkeit* lays bare the secret soul on the sensible surface, Riemerschmid's patterns reveal the complexity of his life's work as the complexity of modernism.

But was Riemerschmid's modernism truly modernism? Or was it simply a repackaging of old-timey clichés for a *Volk* reluctant to embrace the realities of their own time? Or was he, perhaps, as Nietzsche felt about the Germans in general, "of the day before yesterday and the day after tomorrow," yet unable to come to terms with the requirements of "today"?[72] I believe not. Riemerschmid's designed objects offered average Germans a modernism that reflected themselves. It patterned itself on what German people, at the beginning of the twentieth century, "actually were," as Obrist put it. Riemerschmid's was a modernism both comfortable and comforting, nestling into "today" with what Obrist called a "powerful kind of coziness." Riemerschmid's things expressed the yearning aroused by and nurtured within industrialized, urbanized, globalized modernism for something—like Silas Marner's brown pot—dear and familiar in an ever-stranger land. Riemerschmid's efficiently designed and produced, mass-market products carried within them—in gestures, textures, and ornaments—the collective cultural memory. His things promised the survival of German heritage precisely because they succeeded in housing it safely within standardized, modernized forms designed to withstand the winds of fashion. In Riemershmid's designs, *Sachlichkeit* got to the heart of the matter: they painted no sleek image of what twentieth-century Germans *wished* to be; rather, they revealed the conflicted and contradictory nature of who and how they actually were.

No mere object could have accomplished this hybridization of past, present, and future; no mere object could be a bearer of cultural memory. Riemerschmid's *Sachlichkeit* resulted in something more than simple objects: it expressed expressive *things*. In Bill Brown's "object/thing" dialectic, as he calls it, "the story of objects asserting themselves as things is the story of a changed relation to the human subject and thus the story of how the thing really names less an object than a particular subject-object relation. . . . You could imagine things . . . as what is excessive in objects to their mere utilization as objects—their force as a sensuous presence or as a metaphysical presence, the magic by which objects become values, fetishes, idols, and totems."[73] It is the *thingliness*—the active emotional, psychological, social, personal, and even magical appeal—of Riemerschmid's designed objects that is our *Sache*, our matter at hand. The uniquely designed form that allows us to recognize the thing not just as a tool, but as an individual being, will be my focus in the chapters to come. Riemerschmid's forms give his things souls because it is form that actualizes their thingliness for all to see. His business, in fact, was to actualize— and activate. In contrast to the heady debates that hummed around him and his designs, Riemerschmid favored the concrete over the abstract, saying very little of his work (and even less of himself), and instead allowing his things to speak for him and, more importantly, for themselves. In 1908, he urged the German Werkbund to exchange its words for deeds, arguing that "even with the most beautiful and best words we will never achieve much."[74] I have sought out the "most beautiful and best words" to reveal the nature of Riemerschmid's *Sachlichkeit* and its significance for modernism. But words ultimately fail *Sachlichkeit*, and living things must and will speak for themselves. Like Riemerschmid, *Sachlichkeit* demands a shift from words to deeds and from thoughts to things.

Now to the matter at hand.

1

TIES OF THE FLESH

Body am I through and through, and nothing besides; and soul is merely a word for something about the body.
—Friedrich Nietzsche[1]

Richard Riemerschmid's 1905 "machine chair" is a *thing* (figure 0.4). Despite its celebrated functional efficiency, it is determined to exert its "force as a sensuous presence or as a metaphysical presence"—to invoke "the magic," as Bill Brown puts it, "excessive in objects to their mere utilization as objects" that transforms a utilitarian object into a living thing.[2] At the same time, however, the machine chair's formal restraint scorns the very notion of excess. How then, does this piece of serially produced, everyday furniture accomplish its metamorphosis from object to thing? The principle of *Sachlichkeit*—getting to the heart of the matter and externalizing the machine chair's vital essence—reveals its animating "magic," or thingliness, as inherent in (never excessive to) the chair's functional form. Riemerschmid articulates the chair's personality through its unique anatomy: his design gives voice to its "body language." Though its posture is controlled, the chair's body is fully engaged: its back arches, its legs flex, and its feet kick. And yet for all its mounting energy, the machine chair still hesitates: while its back feet kick forward with the impulse to bound ahead, its front feet turn in toward each other, pausing in pigeon-toed diffidence.

How should we interpret the machine chair's body language? This chapter proposes the human body—its forms and structures, materiality and movements, as well as its relations with other bodies and its surrounding environment—as the source of the expressive, communicative qualities of Riemerschmid's designs. To establish the rich complexity of the body's influence on his entire aesthetic project, I will look closely at the very first phase of Riemerschmid's career: as a figurative painter in 1890s Munich. While Riemerschmid's early two-dimensional art—his paintings, drawings, and the prints he published in popular magazines—is generally seen as merely a precursor to his later work as an architect and designer, I argue that it is only through an understanding of Riemerschmid's approach to the body within the frames of his paintings that we can appreciate the true vitality of his "living things."

This chapter considers ways of representing, reading, and experiencing the body that grew out of nineteenth-century visual practices and aesthetic discourses. It foregrounds new theories of perception, emotion, and affect as critical not only to an understanding of Riemerschmid's paintings and prints but to his work—and his time—as a whole. Independent yet ever-intersecting tendrils of nineteenth-century thought stemming from the newly developing sciences of neurology and psychology, from philosophy and popular notions on spirituality, and from social reform movements and the aesthetic avant-garde together generated and interpreted late nineteenth-century works of art that employed the energized body as modernity's living symbol.

BODY LANGUAGE: MUSCLES IN MOTION

Riemerschmid's designs have been noted for their accommodation of the human body, but the role of the body as a leitmotif throughout his career has yet to be acknowledged.[3] Far beyond a kind of ergonomics or *Körpergerechtigkeit* (body-suitedness), Riemerschmid's furniture mirrors the active, youthful body in its forms and construction. His design process was a mimetic one: through observation and *imitation* of the body as an object in nature, Riemerschmid created a second object. The animated forms and gestures of his machine chair could thus be understood as anthropomorphic—mimicking the human body. But a purely anthropomorphic perception of the chair assumes a kind of subject-object one-way street: we imagine the chair responding to our bodies, imitating our *selves*. In his 1933 essay "On the Mimetic Faculty," Walter Benjamin writes that "children's play is permeated by mimetic behavior, and its realm is by no means limited to what one person can imitate in another. The child plays at being not only a shopkeeper or teacher, but also a windmill and a train."[4] It is possible, then, to see the machine chair in a position of command: as the emitter of a physiological impulse to which we, the sitters, unconsciously—yet imperatively—respond. Could the chair's animated design, instead of communicating its humanity, be inviting us to imagine our own thingliness? Rather than pretending to be human, the chair's real magic is designing a human who plays at being a chair.

The word *anthropomorphic*, Bruno Latour has suggested, can mean more than "human in shape"; together, the roots *anthropos* and *morphos* may also mean "that which gives shape to humans" or that which "shapes human action."[5] Again, George Eliot's solitary, miserly weaver, Silas Marner, provides a poignant example of this reverse mimesis, or formative, object-driven anthropomorphism: "His affections made desolate, he had clung with all the force of his nature to his work and his money; and like all objects to which a man devotes himself, they had fashioned in him a correspondence with themselves. His loom, as he wrought in it without ceasing, had in its turn wrought on him, and confirmed more and more the monotonous craving for its monotonous response. His gold, as he hung over it and saw it grow, gathered his power of loving together into a hard isolation like his own."[6] If objects—like Silas's wooden loom or his hoarded gold sovereigns—that lack any direct visual or structural similarity to their human counterparts can still elicit a "correspondence with themselves" through contact and association, then this correspondence can only be amplified by formal mimesis—that is, when an object resembles the subject in its form as well as its affect. So Riemerschmid's doubly mimetic—or doubly anthropomorphic—objects, before they ever came into contact with their prospective users, anticipated a "correspondence with themselves" through their design.

Shifting our attention from Riemerschmid's creation of the chair to its subsequent actuality within the constructed environment, we witness a second relationship both more profoundly mimetic than the first and more actively, affectively anthropomorphic. As a thing in the world, the machine chair becomes suddenly social. Its intention is to make our body feel with (or against) it: not simply the physical sensation of cool, smooth, varnished wood against warm skin, but—even before these touch—the complex, electric emotion of eagerness tinged with hesitation, desire cautioned by restraint. This simple, everyday chair exudes a bottled-up life force capable not simply of simulating but of rivaling its sitter's vitality. Its accommodating form elicits in the sitter the urge to mimic its gestures. Though frozen in space and rooted to its spot, the chair instigates an impulse for the occupant to follow—with her body, she traces its curves. The machine chair's mimesis, then, suggested by its body-based design, is expanded and extended through its affect: in enticing its occupant, it initiates a corporeal rapport between the two—an intricate intercourse of mirrored sensation and emotion.

The figures depicted in Riemerschmid's paintings and other works of graphic art produced during the latter half of the 1890s offer the human body as an organic model for bringing inorganic things to life. But the painted figures model a fluidity of subject and object, wherein bodies blur the two categories by slipping back and forth between them. Riemerschmid's flat representations of space and the figures inhabiting it may be understood metaphorically as a kind of choreographic notation or "blocking" for the domestic interior as a stage set where people and things, within their particular drama, take on roles in relation to one another. Starting then with Riemerschmid's painted bodies in their illusionistic space, we entertain that elastic, imaginative, childlike mimesis that Benjamin explores, in which humans not only play at being one another but also bring inanimate things into the circle of their game.

The boisterous bodies in Riemerschmid's representational art provide blueprints for the lively exchanges that would soon take place in his designed interiors. Whether on their own or engaged with one another, Riemerschmid's bodies and objects strove to express: their forms were designed to communicate their inner being. The idea that physical form or anatomy was knit together with spirit, mind, or soul in such a way as to objectify or corporealize personality had been the subject of study and debate in the fields of physiology and aesthetic philosophy long before Riemerschmid came to explore it. Over the course of the seventeenth, eighteenth, and nineteenth centuries, the mechanics of affect were studied in two ways: first as *physiognomy*, or how one's inner character was believed essentially to be pressed outward through the features of the face; and second as *pathognomy*, or how, inversely, changes in facial musculature manifested the surrounding environment's external "pressures."[7] Linked to this mechanical question of how facial or bodily form could generate affect was the dilemma of how form was perceived—how visual phenomena affected the perceiver, or what happened (and where) during the process of perception.

Riemerschmid came of age during a fundamental shift in the understanding of perception and its relation to the acquisition of knowledge. Perceptual experiences that had been considered in the eighteenth century as primarily ideal, metaphysical, and cognitive occurrences—things transpiring in the mind—began to be seen as external phenomena: real, physical events and experiences that could be measured through empirical data. The nineteenth century's focus on natural science and its radical developments, such as the publication, translation, and popular dissemination of Darwin's theories of evolution and sexual selection, as well as the specifically German emphasis on the capacity of biological science to draw together various fields of study and experience—or *biocentrism*—all contributed to a late nineteenth-century culture riveted on the body.[8] Turning toward the body meant turning away not simply from the metaphysical or the purely mental, but also from the intellectual and the rational.

During the latter half of the nineteenth century, the body—its muscles, specifically—became the direct focus of theories about aesthetics—and, even more practically, of design strategies for architecture and utilitarian objects. According to architectural historian Zeynep Çelik Alexander, studies of perception began to take a kineasthetic turn as early as midcentury. Alexander describes what she has termed *kinaesthetic knowing* as "nondiscursive and nonconceptual knowledge assumed to be gathered from the body's experiential exchanges in the world."[9] During the 1860s, renowned German physicist and physiologist Hermann von Helmholtz began to draw on earlier studies in muscle sense—a sixth sense perceptible in the body though not directly connected with any one of the five senses—to develop a theory of kinaesthesia especially useful to students and practitioners of aesthetics. Helmholtz understood the knowledge acquired through *Kennen*—"muscle sense," or physical familiarity—as equally valuable to that achieved through *Wissen*, or cognitive awareness. He describes the contrast between mental *Wissen* and muscle-made *Kennen* in a lecture from 1868 (the year of Riemerschmid's birth):

When we say that we "know" [*kennen*] a man, a road, a fruit, a perfume, we mean that we have seen, or tasted, or smelt, these objects. We keep the sensible impression fast in our memory, and we shall recognise it again when it is repeated, but we cannot describe the impression in words, even to ourselves. And yet it is certain that this kind of knowledge (*Kennen*) may attain the highest possible degree of precision and certainly, and is so far not inferior to any knowledge (*Wissen*) which can be expressed in words; but it is not directly communicable, unless the object in question can be brought actually forward, or the impression it produces can be otherwise represented—as by drawing the portrait of a man instead of producing the man himself.[10]

During the century's final decades, then, nonverbal, visceral experience began to be seen as a viable, and in some cases preferred, means of acquiring knowledge; and all sorts of aesthetic events—from watching the crashing of ocean waves on a beach to viewing a painted seascape in a museum gallery—were increasingly believed to be apprehended not solely by the eyes or the mind, but *felt* in the whole body, through the fibers of the muscles and on the surface of the skin.

While Helmholtz's "body language" could not be expressed verbally, the preexisting tradition of physiognomy, or reading the features of the face in order to deduce specific traits of character, relied on the belief that muscular expression could be translated into words. Developed in the seventeenth century, physiognomy was well established in aesthetic discourse by Helmholtz's (and Riemerschmid's) day and had become closely connected with architectural theory. The tradition of physiognomic thinking concerned with affect as an outward projection of inward dispositions was defined by two primary figures: seventeenth-century French court painter, décorator, and aesthetic theorist Charles le Brun, whose physiognomic studies of twenty-two categories of emotion, or "passions," were consulted widely during the eighteenth century; and almost a century later, Swiss philosopher and theologian Johann Caspar Lavater, who explored physiognomic permutations as manifestations of character traits in individuals (as opposed to Le Brun's more generalized types). Far from transcending words, these *types* and traits had to be classified through their verbal equivalents in terms of *character*.[11]

Already in the eighteenth century, physiognomy's proposition of an interior structure that projected itself outward, producing a "character" legible on the body and face, had found its way into architectural theory. Antoine-Chrysosthôme Quatremère de Quincy (1755–1849), of the French Académie des Beaux-Arts, traced the word *character* to the technology of imprinting, such that character in architecture meant "the art of impressing each building with a state so appropriate to its nature or its use that one can read in its salient traits what it is and what it cannot be."[12] This apprehension of architectural character as an imprinting of appropriateness onto the building's "skin" recalls Aristotle's discussion of the relation of soul and body as "wax and the shape given to it by the stamp." In Claude-Nicholas Ledoux's Ideal City of Chaux (an ambitious unrealized project that the architect began in 1789 and intended to build around the Royal Saltworks at Arc-et-Senans), the hoopmakers' houses were shaped like barrels, the river inspector's house straddled the river, and a brothel was housed inside a phallic structure.[13] This "speaking architecture" (*architecture parlante*) of mimetic relations resulting from the physiognomic correspondence of a building's inside and its outside—its soul and its body—laid the groundwork for Riemerschmid's *Sachlichkeit*. What began with eighteenth-century physiognomic fantasy had become, by the late nineteenth century, an architectural realism in which an object's affect was at the same time the expression of its essence and the impression of its environment.

The notion that a thing's affect—what it is like or how it comes across to the perceiver—was the result not just of something internal pushing itself outward but equally of opposing, external forces pressing in on it was the nineteenth century's critical addition to eighteenth-century physiognomy. This new theory of pathognomy presented philosophers, scientists, and aesthetic communities with two revelations about the nature of motion and emotion—and the intimacy of their relation. First, pathognomy proposed that emotion, though a physiological event, did not originate in the body but was instead a bodily *response* to outside stimulus. In the 1884 essay "What Is an Emotion?," psychologist William James argued that not only was emotion triggered externally, but the individual's perception of that emotion was, essentially, an awareness of muscular changes in the body—or *motion*.[14] Two decades prior to James's argument for emotion as muscles in motion, French neurologist Guillaume-Benjamin-Amand Duchenne de Boulogne had documented his electrophysiological studies in pathognomy in his *Mechanism of Human Physiognomy, or The Electrophysiological Analysis of the Expression of the Passions* of 1862, which contained photographs of his subjects' faces as they experienced a spectrum of electrically induced "emotions" (figure 1.1).[15] Pathognomy, then, as the study of changes in the facial muscles during the experience of emotion, was at its core the study of movement. This "discovery" of emotion as corporeal motion was revolutionary—and yet it did not dispel faith in an interior *animus*. For Duchenne, facial expressions were the "gymnastics of the soul."

AU NATURALE: BODIES IN NATURE

Riemerschmid's *In Arcadia*, an oil painting of 1897, presents an open field of wildflowers sprawling out toward the viewer from a stand of trees (figure 1.2). This meadow is punctuated on the far right, at the composition's very edge, by two figures so small as to be missed at first glance. A naked figure (possibly a child) wearing a floral garland appears to be running forward, open-mouthed and laughing, while a naked woman (perhaps the child's mother) follows several yards behind.

FIGURE 1.1

Guillaume-Benjamin Duchenne and Adrien Alban Tournachon, *Électro-Physiologie Photographique*, Planche 7, negative 1852–1856; print 1876. Albumen silver print. Image: 13.3 × 10.7 cm (5¼ × 4³/₁₆ in.). Mount: 27.5 × 18.2 cm (10¹³/₁₆ × 7³/₁₆ in.). The J. Paul Getty Museum, Los Angeles.

FIGURE 1.2

Richard Riemerschmid, *In Arcadia*, 1897.
Oil on canvas. Städtische Galerie im
Lenbachhaus, Munich. © 2021 Artists Rights
Society (ARS), New York / VG Bild-Kunst, Bonn.

Although these tiny figures seem at first incidental to the vast, natural landscape that dwarfs them, as soon as we spot them, they command our attention, and the painting changes: it is no longer just a landscape, but a story—a mystery. Who are these figures? Why are they naked? Where have they come from? And where are they going? While the figures are far too small for their bodies to be "read" in a physiognomic sense, their animated presence affects the nature of the picture: its impact on *us*, the viewers, now depends on *them*; their active bodies connect the painting's imagined space and our own kinaesthetic experience.

Two color lithographs—covers for *Jugend* (Youth: The Munich Illustrated Weekly Magazine of Art and Life)—depict similarly vibrant landscapes into which naked human figures have wandered. On the cover of a June issue from 1896, a lithe young girl holding a flowering branch has just entered a picture of softly budding spring (figure 1.3). The wind sweeps her hair toward a central cluster of white birches, drawing her graceful body toward its counterpart in nature, her tall, white, androgynous form mimicking the slender birch trunks. A year later, on another cover, a second naked girl is more deeply embedded in her landscape. Recumbent in the sun-warmed grass, she contemplates the rustic bouquet she must just have picked (figure 1.4). Long afternoon shadows cast on the gently rolling turf echo her relaxed posture, conveying again the sense of imitative play between body and landscape.

In Arcadia and the two *Jugend* covers convey the longing for a reunion of humans with nature, a blending of the two—a concept exalted by progressive artistic and social trends of Riemerschmid's day. But Riemerschmid's treatment of this prelapsarian theme is unusual: it suggests the peculiar nature of humankind's imprint upon the natural world. While this human presence corrupts the purity of uninhabited nature, it also enlivens the composition, warming the cool perfection of paradise. Riemerschmid's bodies break the silence: they commune and communicate with nature, creating a conduit between it and us.

Between 1888 and late 1891, Riemerschmid studied painting at the Munich Academy of Fine Art, then one of the most prestigious art schools in Europe. The academic painting tradition, dominant in Europe since the seventeenth century, prioritized verisimilitude and emphasized the close study of the human figure. However, a number of progressive artists had challenged its strictures and standards throughout the nineteenth century, and it was during the final decades of the century that the academy's residual value as an institution was called into question and its influence on contemporary art-making began sharply to decline. At the

1896 · 27. JUNI   · JUGEND ·   I. JAHRGANG · NR. 26

Münchner illustrierte Wochenschrift für Kunst und Leben. — G. Hirth's Verlag in München & Leipzig.
ALLE RECHTE VORBEHALTEN.

FIGURE 1.3

Richard Riemerschmid, Cover for *Jugend* 1,
no. 26 (27 June 1896).

FIGURE 1.4

Richard Riemerschmid, Cover for *Jugend* 2,
no. 25 (19 June 1897).

academy, Riemerschmid trained under two painters whose influence pervades his graphic work of the 1890s. The first was drawing instructor Gabriel von Hackl, the son of a doctor, who emphasized accuracy in anatomical rendering. The second was the relatively progressive Ludwig von Löfftz, who took up the position of the academy's director in 1891. Löfftz was interested in the manipulation of color and form in the depiction of nature, and Riemerschmid notes in his diaries from 1891 that Löfftz recommended landscape painting to him as an artistic path. In November 1891, however, feeling that the academy no longer served his needs as a developing artist, Riemerschmid left off his studies there to establish his own Munich studio.[16] While his earliest surviving plein air paintings executed in Munich's environs cling closely to naturalism, by the end of the century his preoccupation with the body in nature expresses itself in bolder, more abstract colors and interpretive, imaginative forms.

The notion of the body's muscular motion as the soul's "gymnastics" was not exclusive to studies in pathognomy. Inventor of psychophysics and pioneer of experimental psychology Gustav Theodor Fechner (1801–1887) understood all things—human beings, animals, plants, and even inanimate objects—as possessing souls, and described the body as the "medium of the soul's processes."[17] Fechner's vision of the human body as the externalizer of activities that were inherently invisible, unquantifiable, inexplicable, and irrational resonated with concurrent trends in philosophy and science. This newly theorized body—starkly objective and mysteriously subjective at the same time—also played a central role in the late nineteenth-century social movement of Lebensreform (Life Reform), which developed in reaction to specifically German conditions of modernization. Following its relatively late unification in 1871, the new German nation experienced an immediate economic boom accompanied by wild financial speculation. This Gründerzeit—so named for the speculators, or *Gründer*—was a time of rapid industrialization, urbanization, and general social upheaval.[18] It was also short-lived, however, imploding in 1873 with a market crash and aftermath of recession and general financial instability, lasting until 1896. The Gründerzeit thus cultivated in its wake a climate of anxiety in the newly unified Germany. Marked increases in crime and venereal disease (resulting from unprecedented population growth and the further expansion of already large cities), as well as new nervous disorders understood as symptomatic of these modern metropolitan ills, became topics of popular concern.[19] The *Großstadt* or "Great City" exerted mesmeric attraction, creating a rift between Germany's rural, regional past and its urban, national future. The poet Rainer Maria Rilke wrote shortly after the turn of the century that city dwellers had "lost their connection to the earth" and seemed to "float directionless through the air," echoing Karl Marx's dictum that in modern urban life "all that is solid melts into air, all that is holy is profaned."[20]

Beginning in the 1880s, the Life Reformers attempted to ward off this darkly encroaching modernity with naturopathy, vegetarianism, new forms of exercise and dance, sun worshiping, and therapeutic nudity; they defined and celebrated their endeavors with the image of the "natural" (naked) body set within romanticized nature as a talisman against the gritty realities of city life. The pervasive longing for and striving toward a "return to nature" became a theme of the Lebensreform movement—and naked bodies in paradisiacal landscapes became one of its visual tropes.[21] Art historian Annette Wagner has proposed the idealized natural landscape in the paintings of Riemerschmid and several of his German contemporaries working around the turn of the twentieth century as the "theater of the soul," where human figures (predominantly women), through their bodily gestures and facial expressions, determined the atmosphere.[22] Riemerschmid's covers for *Jugend* are by no means the only examples of this motif in the Munich journal. Drawings by Hugo Höppener, a contemporary of Riemerschmid's known to the public simply as "Fidus," pepper *Jugend*'s pages (figure 1.5). Fidus's wiry, energetic, and very young nudes, engaged in humorous high jinks in nature's playground or absorbed in sentimental scenes of adolescent love, conflate realist and romantic sentiments, emblematizing the Life Reformer's utopian vision.

Fidus's active, athletic bodies were examples of a new kind of nudity in late nineteenth-century art. They represented what art historian Klaus Wolbert has described as a "new, naked, artistic image of mankind," in contrast to the established academic tradition of languid, voluptuous nudes, generally presented in confined and refined contexts to avoid shocking or provoking the viewer.[23] Art historian Hilke Peckmann has discussed Fidus's figures as prime examples of Fechner's influential idea that the purpose of the body was to realize the inward sensitivity of the soul in direct, corporeal expression.[24] Fidus's explicitly physiognomical studies in his 1899 *Theoretische Physiognomik* (Theoretical Physiognomics) harness his belief in the direct, communicative power of facial expression and body language for his troubling though by no means unique promotion of white supremacy and anti-Semitism.[25]

Moving beyond Fidus's notion of a soul that was legible via the body, Friedrich Nietzsche (also featured in *Jugend*) flatly denied the existence of a soul except as a thoroughly corporeal phenomenon originating in and *of* the body. In *Thus Spoke Zarathustra* (1883), he writes: "'Body am I and soul'—thus talks the child. And why should one not talk like children? But the awakened one, the one who knows, says:

FIGURE 1.5

Fidus, *Wasser Rosen* (Water Lilies),
Jugend 1 (1896).

Body am I through and through, and nothing besides; and soul is merely a word for something about the body."[26] For Nietzsche there could be in reality no "relationship" between body and soul, because the body was in itself the "great reason," generating, animating, and enfolding all capacities called *spirit* or *soul*. In Nietzsche's conception, interior emotion and exterior expression were one flesh.[27]

Riemerschmid's bodies express the Life Reformers' longing to recover, in Rilke's words, their lost connection to the earth. But while Fidus's caricatured nudes seem to hurl themselves at this project in sport and play, Riemerschmid's are more tentative—rendered less fussily, yet articulated with greater nuance. They stand timidly on the edges of things and yet, when invited into the picture, plant themselves shamelessly in the landscape. Riemerschmid's naked bodies describe an originary state of innocence, as if just discovering their material connection with the rest of the wide, organic world. His careful choreography of human body and natural landscape alludes at the same time to the Life Reformers' sociospiritual quest for a return to natural innocence and articulates a distinctly modern understanding of the body as a material vessel for its expression. Many of his works from the latter half of the 1890s reveal a neo-Christian vision of the uninhabited, untouched "garden" as both a lament of that which modernity had lost and a hint at what might yet be regained.

Riemerschmid explored this combination of longing and hope in a series of artworks picturing the Biblical Garden of Eden, which he worked on between 1896 and 1900. This was a period of particular sweetness, ardor, and promise in Riemerschmid's personal life, too. In the early spring of 1895, he married the celebrated Munich actress Ida Hofmann (1873–1962), whom Thomas Mann recalled years later as "the loveliest thing that the stage had ever offered my eyes (and ears—in short, my entire aesthetic sense)" (figure 1.6).[28] Riemerschmid's bride clearly inspired him: not only did he begin designing his earliest furniture for the couple's apartment in the Riemerschmid-Block (the family property in the center of Munich) directly after their marriage, but their first son, Helmut, was born in 1896, and their daughter Ilse

FIGURE 1.6

Actress Ida Hofmann, age 17. Munich, 1890.
Germanisches Nationalmuseum, Deutsches
Kunstarchiv und Historisches Archiv,
Nuremberg.

followed close on the heels of her brother in 1897. We can imagine the tiny, exhilarated bodies in Riemerschmid's 1897 *Arcadia* as those he knew—and loved—best. Indeed, these years seem to have been a true Arcadia for the young lovers, who also shared a passion for art and music (figure 1.7). Peering through the window of Riemerschmid's diary on September 18, 1897, we find him playing the piano with his wife—perhaps as a respite from that year's all-absorbing project: the house he was designing for his growing family in Pasing bei München, then a newly developing colony of villas on the outskirts of Munich. Just a few days earlier, on September 15, he had written: "We entered our plot of land . . . to tread on our *own* ground for the very first time. Laughing and happy despite the dreary, rainy weather, we clambered around the site . . . filled with hope in anticipation of cozy, delightful times to come."[29] Completed in 1898, the Riemerschmid House was not only the artist's first architectural experiment but also a lasting achievement (figure 1.8).

Eden—and the possibility of recreating it on his very "*own*" ground"—preoccupied Riemerschmid during these first, blooming years of his marriage and career. A rough oil-study for an 1896 painting titled, *And the Lord God planted a Garden in Eden* (the fully realized work was purchased by the Royal Picture Gallery in Dresden and likely destroyed in the city's February 1945 bombing) depicts a glowing garden flanked by a wooden frame carved in the form of two naked bodies—Adam and Eve (figure 1.9). The landscape is sketched in pure, unmixed oil colors directly from the tube and applied with a palette knife to create a vibrant impasto, with a ring of thickly caked yellow haloing the central, fruit-laden Tree of Life. While the framing figures seem poised to enter the scene, they hesitate; and the round, ripe tree remains unmarred. Riemerschmid imagines the moment before the Biblical "fall" of humanity, before human contact with hallowed nature would propel man, woman—and nature itself—toward degeneration. But his bodies remain—for the moment of the painting, at least—solitary: merging neither with one another, nor with the landscape that stretches out before them.

FIGURE 1.7

Richard and Ida Riemerschmid, Munich, 1900. Germanisches Nationalmuseum, Deutsches Kunstarchiv und Historisches Archiv, Nuremberg.

Cartoons for the finished frame underscore the artist's investment in anatomy, gesture, and mien (figure 1.10). The subtle language of these bodies calls to mind the confronted figures of Ida and Richard, like bookends, holding between them the yet unopened chapters of those bountiful, innocent years. We imagine husband and wife "entering" their own land, each setting foot for the first time, together, upon their newly turned earth. The pivotal tension of Riemerschmid's bodies, their muscular contraction upon the fulcrum of motion, visualized the exhilaration of this young man, young lover, young father—young creator. But even more than all of this, it represented the zeal and optimism of the Life Reformer poised on the cusp of the new. Without words, Riemerschmid's prelapsarian bodies articulate, in the context of late nineteenth-century Lebensreform, the rejuvenation implied in the term *Jugendstil*: the warm, solid, *living* recompense for all that modernity had "melted into air."

ANATOMICAL AMBIVALENCE: THE EMPATHIC, EMBATTLED BODY

Hesitation and expectancy take on new forms—and meanings—in Riemerschmid's most sinister Eden. *Eve and the Snake* (also from 1896) depicts a tranquil, golden landscape marked by a surprisingly tall and slender apple tree that tempts us with its abundance of ripe, rosy fruit (figure 1.11). Tracing the trunk's slim line to the

FIGURE 1.8

Richard Riemerschmid, *Riemerschmid House* (Pasing bei München), 1898. Photograph, 1907. Architekturmuseum der TUM. © 2021 ARS, New York / VG Bild-Kunst, Bonn.

FIGURE 1.9

Richard Riemerschmid, *And the Lord God Planted a Garden in Eden* (study), 1896. Oil on board in original frame, hand-carved by the artist. Städtische Galerie im Lenbachhaus und Kunstbau München. © 2021 Artists Rights Society (ARS), New York / VG Bild-Kunst, Bonn.

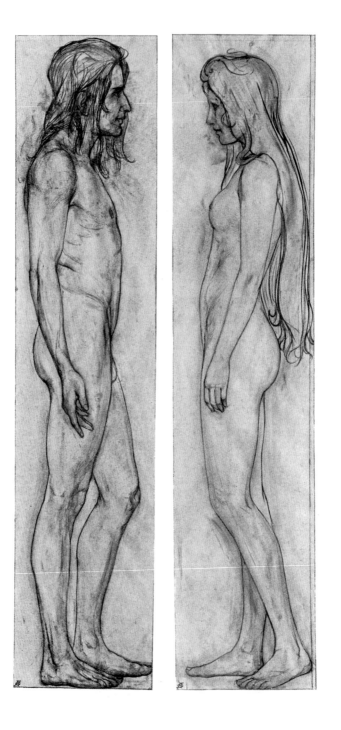

FIGURE 1.10

Richard Riemerschmid, *Cartoons for Wooden Frame*, *Dekorative Kunst* 4, no. 9 (June 1901): 330–331.

FIGURE 1.11

Richard Riemerschmid, *Eve and the Snake*, 1896. Oil on canvas. Museum Tempelhof-Schöneberg, Berlin. Photo: Malte Nies (cequi). © 2021 ARS, New York / VG Bild-Kunst, Bonn.

ground, we discover the tail of a large snake coiled around the tree's base. Patterns playing and echoing between the tree's bark and the snake's skin suggest an intimacy between them, as if the snake, chameleon-like, could mimic the tree's tones and textures, or hinting, perhaps that the two had been formed from the same material. The snake's body at its thickest matches the trunk's narrow circumference, enabling a visual understanding of plant and animal as a single line. Following the snake's contortions through the gold-green grass, we arrive finally at the figure of a young woman whose golden skin seems brushed with the blush of the apples. This naked, kneeling Eve is at once exposed and protected: her folded limbs and curved back conceal from view the details of her anatomy, while her greenish-gold hair flows over her body and into the grass beneath. Her downturned gaze is gentle but curious as she regards the snake raising its sleek oval head to address her, its delicate, forked tongue just visible.

Eve and the Snake offers a different, more intimate moment "before." It seems mild, fluid, placid—swaddled and sedated by the heavy, golden tones of body, turf, and sky. And yet just as the muscles of Riemerschmid's framing bodies seemed coiled in anticipation, so the crouching Eve and the insinuating serpent, locked in their hypnotic exchange, together embody a tension which action must follow. The result of this inevitable attraction had been rendered three years earlier by Munich artist Franz von Stuck in a wildly popular painting, titled simply *Die Sünde*— or *Sin* (figure 1.12). While Eve and the snake are the focus of Stuck's composition, too, it is more explicit: where Riemerschmid presents possibilities, Stuck supplies us with their cautionary—and tantalizing—conclusions. Here, the dark-haired, voluptuous Eve is already in league with the monstrous snake, its massive muscular mechanism wound about her torso like a vise and draped across her shoulders like a cabaret dancer's risqué boa. In contrast to Riemerschmid's characters engaged in their private, contemplative interchange, Stuck's Eve and snake confront the viewer—the one seductively and the other in open-mouthed malice. Stuck's erect and naked female torso, framed teasingly by the venomous pair's conspiracy of scales and hair, scorns the crouched modesty of Riemerschmid's girl.

Although Stuck's and Riemerschmid's paintings approach the same story from strikingly different angles, their choice of the theme itself—its mixing of eroticism and theology, materiality and mysticism—aligns both artists with the Symbolist movement in late nineteenth-century art. Riemerschmid's reverence for what he depicts as the holiness of nature links him not only to the social goals of Lebensreform but also to the idealism-cum-materialism of Symbolism. Riemerschmid's

FIGURE 1.12

Franz von Stuck, *Die Sünde* (*Sin*), 1893. Oil
on canvas, 94.5 × 59.5 cm. Inv. 7925. bpk
Bildagentur / Neue Pinakothek, Bayerische
Staatsgemaeldesammlungen, Munich,
Germany / Art Resource, NY.

interpretations of the familiar religious theme rely heavily on the manipulation of the real, physical elements of painting—a rethinking of compositional "choreography"; the exaggeration of color; and the stylization of form—to present the viewer with a psychological complexity that defies transliteration. His Eden paintings propose that the internal, spiritual idea can be read in the material presence of color and form, or on the surface of the body. Riemerschmid's physiognomic painting, in which, as Nietzsche believed, the idea of the soul became simply "something about the body," claimed a place within the larger Symbolist project.

Inherent in Symbolism from its inception as a literary movement in the 1880s was the belief in a bond between matter and spirit; embedded in this belief was the inevitable compulsion to tease out the strands of that binding. In 1886, when asked to formulate the fundamental principles of Symbolism for the literary supplement of the French newspaper *Le Figaro*, Jean Moréas, a Greek-born poet living in Paris, wrote that Symbolism "endeavors to clothe the Idea in a form perceptible to the senses."[30] In her study of four Symbolist painters, art historian Allison Morehead addresses what she terms a "dialectic between form and content," explaining that Symbolists' "most pressing problem became the search for appropriate forms in which to 'clothe' or 'envelop' that capital-I Idea, forms that would then ideally become completely inextricable from content."[31] While the chosen form was the artist's individual decision, then, the resulting relationship between the metaphysical and the empirical—or the Ideal and the Real—was physiognomic: form externalized content just as musculature spoke the soul.

Only days after Moréas's manifesto appeared in *Le Figaro*, another Symbolist poet, Gustave Kahn, wrote in *L'Evénément* that "the essential aim of our art is to objectify the subjective (the externalization of the Idea) instead of subjectifying the objective (nature seen through a temperament)."[32] Kahn refers, like Moréas, to what Morehead terms "the capital-I Idea," Symbolism's link to the metaphysics of Idealism, a philosophy that ascribes reality and priority to the immaterial phenomena of the mind, thus promoting the belief that subjective ideas and emotions, not objective depictions of the world, were art's proper subject matter. As the product of avant-garde French, Belgian, and German writers and artists who began in the mid-1880s to break away from established, government-sponsored institutions such as the academy and its tradition of naturalism, Symbolism was, from its very inception, considered modern. But, as Kahn's statement infers, Symbolists' response to the conditions and experience of modern life was very different from that of their contemporaries, the Naturalists. Epitomized by the writer Émile Zola and his meticulously detailed, gritty, and emotionally wrenching descriptions of modern French life, Naturalism could be understood in Kahn's terms as "subjectifying the objective"—harsh, worldly reality rendered familiar and personal. The task of the Symbolist, on the contrary, was, as art historian Michelle Facos has described it, "to discern and convey invisible realities."[33] Symbolist painting was a visual channel connecting the psyches of artist and viewer through the material facts of form.

The central paradox of Symbolism was, as historian Debora Silverman has put it, to "express the inexpressible," and yet to do this through forms that would "convey and evoke emotional states" in the average middle-class viewer.[34] For Morehead, this was a twofold formal problem: "to create form that could be read as corresponding to an individual's . . . interior emotive world, and to render that form objectively understandable, even truthful, without using what were understood to be caricatured or traditional, academic, naturalist modes of art making."[35] In 1892, the search for concrete forms through which to express immaterial ideas took a radical turn in Munich. The Munich Academy's conservative embrace of traditional history painting, and its support from the Bavarian government, constrained Munich's younger, more progressive painters—most notably, those who identified as Impressionists and Symbolists.[36] In the spring of 1892, a group of ninety-six artists broke away from the official, academy-affiliated Munich Artists' Association to found what soon became Europe's first secession movement. The Munich Secession's debut exhibition, which took place not in Munich but in Berlin in the summer of 1893, included a significant number of Symbolist paintings—Stuck's gold-framed *Die Sünde* glowing shamelessly among them like an erotic antimonument.[37] Riemerschmid first exhibited work with the Secession in 1894, and his *Garden of Eden* later acquired by the Dresden Gemäldegalerie was first displayed in the Secession's 1896 exhibition.[38]

In the year of the Secession, Munich poet Stefan George, protégé of the noted French Symbolist Stéphane Mallarmé, promoted Symbolism in Munich's intellectual circles via his poetry journal, *Blätter für die Kunst* (Pages for Art), which called for "spiritual art on the basis of a new manner of feeling and doing."[39] As art historian Peg Weiss has shown, George also manifested interests in contemporary developments in fine and applied arts. The George-Kreis—the poet's Munich circle—rejected the notion of Symbolism as a dreamy escapism, taking up Symbolist art instead as an "active power, which would regenerate and lead the world."[40] An awakening from Symbolist dreams to potentially revolutionary realities depended on form.

To this end, artists developed a repertoire of images that probed areas of special fascination for a late nineteenth-century audience; artwork addressing such characteristically Symbolist themes abounded in Munich during the 1890s. Images exploring sensualism and seduction, like Stuck's *Sin*, as well as those depicting ambiguous or disquieting relationships between mind and body, proliferated in Germany's artistic capital. Weekly issues of *Jugend* were flooded with prints and drawings exploiting provocative topics ranging from the notorious archetype of the femme fatale to the terrain of the unconscious mind to the mystical and occult. All of these images focused the viewer's attention directly on the sexualized, hypnotized, or spellbound body, employing it as a fleshly vehicle for externalizing the mysteries of the mind.

This fascination with a "physiology of the mind," or, conversely, a physical theory of the soul (like Fechner's or Nietzsche's) overflows from the mythological paintings of Arnold Böcklin, one of the greatest influences on Munich's young Symbolists. Böcklin enlisted popular scientific color theories in his development of a particular type of realism, creating startling yet believable spatial effects through the deft opposition of warm and cool tones. Rather than mythologizing the mundane, his pioneering "proto-Symbolism" strove to convince the viewer of the real, corporeal presence of things that were entirely a product of historical and cultural—or personal—imagination. The Swiss painter lived and worked in Munich in the 1850s and 1870s, sowing seeds for the themes and approaches of Munich's younger generation of modern painters—among them, Secession members Stuck and Riemerschmid. Although Böcklin was trained as a landscape painter, it was the distinctive appearance and attitudes of the bodies within his landscapes that quickly came to distinguish his work. Böcklin's mythological subjects appeared to reunite humans with nature, aligning him to some degree with the goals of Lebensreform; but his startlingly fleshy realism, often humorous or grotesque, lent him a special allure for German Symbolists keen to objectify the subjective. Symbolism scholar Rodolphe Rapetti has argued that "Böcklin literally gave body to mythology . . . bringing it to life, thereby revealing himself . . . as a man of his times, attuned to reality."[41]

Böcklin's large painting of 1883, *Im Spiel der Wellen* (*In the Play of the Waves*), depicts an entirely fantastical, mythological scene in detailed, animated naturalism (figure 1.13). Fleshy merfolk cavort in the swell of a wave that occupies the greater part of the composition, pitching sickeningly away from the picture's lower frame and arching powerfully upward, as if to break momentarily over the viewer. The

FIGURE 1.13

Arnold Böcklin, *In the Play of the Waves*, 1883. Oil on canvas, 180 × 238 cm (70.9 × 93.7 in). Inv. 7754. bpk Bildagentur / Neue Pinakothek, Bayerische Staatsgemaeldesammlungen, Munich, Germany / Art Resource, NY.

swimmers' voluptuous yet agile bodies occupy real space, displacing their own volumes within the glassy water of the dangerously mounting swells. The undeniable, massive presence of these mythical beings, heightened and complicated by each figure's bodily gestures and facial expression, mesmerizes the viewer. The play of bodies within the play of the waves resonates with our individual, bodily knowledge of flesh, wind, and water—that wordless yet flawless precision that Helmholtz called *Kennen*. And yet the literal meaning of this scene is veiled, inaccessible. The emotional tumult, whatever its cause or key, expressed between the two central figures, is mirrored and amplified in the churning waves. Or perhaps the waves do not mimic their occupants at all; rather, it is the swimmers whose complex, unfathomable emotions are triggered by the impulse and impact of the exhilarating, terrifying water.

Viewing *In the Play of the Waves* in the 1880s, as now, involved more than just looking; this active painting demands the viewer's active, bodily participation. It was not simply a pathognomic "reading" of muscular changes—on the face or across the body—within a work of art itself, but, more importantly, muscular events taking place in and being noticed by the body *during* that reading that characterized this kind of embodied perception. Çelik Alexander argues that this new understanding of embodied experience became the focus of aesthetic science and philosophy in the final decades of the nineteenth century. She writes that "artworks were imagined to impact the physiology of the human body in an immediate and forceful manner by means of effects (*Wirkungen*). The recipient was presumed to react by producing unconscious, automatic, and reflex-like reactions to the formal qualities of the work."[42]

The idea that an aesthetic effect (*aesthetitsche Wirkung*) could not only alter the musculature of the body but also be read on the body's surfaces implies a kind of kinaesthetic circuit. This phenomenon, central to Çelik Alexander's exploration of a *New Aesthetics* developing toward the close of the nineteenth century, has also played a key role in architectural historian Harry Francis Mallgrave's discussion of the neurological simulation that we experience in relation to our surroundings, including not just the natural environment, but architecture and designed objects as well.[43] Working with twenty-first-century neurological studies rooted in the thinking of nineteenth-century figures like Helmholtz and James, Mallgrave addresses emotions as *gut feelings*: "somatic, visceral, electrical, and chemical events" that arise in a process of mimicry even more natural, more involuntary than Benjamin's mimetic children's games. Exchanging aesthetic *Wirkung* for the more recent neurological understanding of *embodied simulation*, Mallgrave brings to bear on the phenomena of the built environment new research showing that, by means of the systemic firing of specialized neurons, we "mentally simulate or embody most of what we apprehend through the senses, whether we are aware of it or not."[44] Through these mimetic "mirror neurons," Mallgrave explains, "we animate the inanimate physical environment with which we come into contact."[45]

Empathy and animation are key components in perception understood as neurological simulation, and both can be traced to aesthetic philosopher Robert Vischer's 1873 theory of *Einfühlung*—literally "in-feeling" or "feeling into" (approximated in English as "empathy" in 1904)—which he proposed in his doctoral dissertation, *On the Optical Feeling of Form: A Contribution to Aesthetics*, published in 1873.[46] The son of a Hegelian aesthetician, Vischer was grounded in Idealist aesthetics, but was also interested in more current physiological studies of perception—including Helmholtz's. As part of his intricate conceptualization of *Einfühlung*, Vischer theorized a mode of viewing things in which the viewer's ego was projected *inside* the object. Art historian Juliet Koss has characterized the late nineteenth-century concept of *Einfühlung* as an "embodied response to an image, object, or spatial environment . . . a form of spectatorship that was simultaneously haptic and optic."[47] Architectural historians Mallgrave and Eleftherios Ikonomou have explained that while in English *empathy* suggests a strong emotional response to an object, for Vischer *Einfühlung* indicated a state in which the whole personality merged with the object: "In essence, we fill out the appearance with the content of our soul."[48] Considered as an act of aesthetic simulation, *Einfühlung* animated both subject and object at the same time, destabilizing each by blurring the conventional sense of a boundary between them. In the case of Riemerschmid's 1905 machine chair, for instance, while the chair is responding to, mimicking, our body, our soul is experiencing the body of the chair. In *Einfühlung*, in fact, the soul—human or thingly—is no longer a separate entity but only, after all, "something about the body," be it flesh or wood.

The experience of *Einfühlung* was at once optic and haptic because Vischer's understanding of viewing—*Schauen* (scanning)—was directly linked to touch: "Scanning is a much more active process than seeing . . . I run my hand, as it were, over the planes, convexities and concavities of the object, the paths of light."[49] *Wolkengespenster* (*Cloud Ghosts*) of 1897, Riemerschmid's next major painting (and theme) after his *Garden of Eden* period, provided the embodied, empathic viewer with myriad "paths of light": brilliant needles of moonlight painted in delicate tempera, for the eye's fingers to trace as they emanate from a large full moon and extend outward from the painting's center and actually *into* its frame, radiating over the surface of Riemerschmid's carved and silvered wood (figure 1.14). Our scanning accelerates as an acrobatic cloud-man chases an agile cloud-woman across the piercing moon. Here *Einfühlung* is not limited to our "feeling in," with embodied eyes, to these ethereal bodies; we can also perceive a second empathic relation between the painted human subjects and objects of nature: the actual blurring of figure and ground as mist becomes flesh and these vaporous "natural" bodies are, in turn, penetrated by moonbeams. But the most important instance of empathic exchange takes place between the painting's two individual subjects themselves. True to the nature of the clouds from which they emerge, these nebulous bodies are permeable: they flow into and *feel* into each other in a manner unknown to flesh and bone. While *Einfühlung* animates the cosmos—giving athletic bodies and active wills to that which is literally vapid—it also projects the subject's will directly into the object's form.

Riemerschmid's animism maps erotic drive onto an inherently empathic activity: in *Wolkengespenster*, the child's game of identifying familiar forms in a cloudy sky becomes an intensely adult pursuit. As Böcklin had done before him, Riemerschmid brings to corporeal life that which should exist only within the confines of the imagination. Earlier studies for the *Cloud Ghosts* reveal Riemerschmid's interest in Germanic mythology—specifically, the Witches' Sabbath on Walpurgis Night, a theme beloved in Symbolist literature for its favoring of feeling over reason. As an erotic witch-hunt, *Cloud Ghosts* responds directly to Böcklin by transposing his dangerous "play" in the waves to equally treacherous games among the stars. In Riemerschmid's hunt, bodily gestures and facial expressions are indeed, as Duchenne had understood them, the soul's gymnastics: a wide-eyed, open-mouthed expression of agitation just visible on the cloud-woman's face as she looks back over her shoulder at her pursuant recalls the inexplicable look of dread on the face of Böcklin's mermaid. In both paintings, the active and interactive bodies speak a muscular language comprehensible to the senses, yet indecipherable to the mind: we "feel into" them, know them precisely with our own bodies, and yet what they mean we cannot think.

The extended limbs, taut musculature, and dynamically engaged bodies of Riemerschmid's *Cloud Ghosts* exude an almost assaultive energy. While its tone may be difficult to define, its pitch is certain: here we find bodies fully employed, straining, stretched to capacity—doing to their utmost what bodies are designed

to do. An undated charcoal sketch from the late 1890s intensifies this full, bodily engagement (figure 1.15). A young man and woman, both naked, embrace within a hurriedly drawn, natural landscape. The man kneels in a wide, open-legged posture, his face elevated to meet that of his lover and his arms encircling her shoulders. She, crouching, though still on her feet, bends her body toward him and meets his face with hers; while she grasps his head in her hands, it is unclear whether her gesture and posture—a lunge with left leg forward, right leg behind, knee bent and foot flexed—indicate a moment of passionate reunion, or one of immanent separation: has she just run into his arms or will she tear herself away? The tangle of arms and the interjecting volumes and vectors of buttocks, thighs, knees, and calves suggest as much a violent struggle as they do a lovers' embrace. The quick, breathy strokes of the charcoal that signify the surrounding landscape amplify the exhilaration, tension, and, ultimately, confusion that an empathic "scanning" of the sketch delivers.

In its scratchy hapticity, its resistance to formal resolution, and also in the solid corporeality of its figures, Riemerschmid's sketch may be compared to another rendering of the same theme by the Norwegian Symbolist Edward Munch (figure 1.16). Munch's black-and-white etching *The Kiss* (1895) represents a motif to which the artist returned in a variety of media during the decade's latter half. But the formal commonalities of the two figure studies only accentuate their visceral disparities: while Munch's *Kiss* is set within an urban interior, Riemerschmid's embrace is wild and windblown. And while Munch's figures seem almost to melt into one another, their soft bodies puzzle-like—one supplying moment by moment the convexity to the other's concavity—and their faces merging into a single form, Riemerschmid's angular, amorous combatants, though entangled, remain fundamentally separate, as if at any moment their explosive energy will propel them apart.

Riemerschmid's Symbolist paintings of the 1890s model anatomical ambivalence. Whether this manifests itself in the hesitation of figures on the threshold, feet about to step, or whether it takes on the contortions of erotic conflict, Riemerschmid's bodies, in repeatedly reenacting the opposing forces of excitement and restraint, impulsion and repulsion, generate an electric tension—a vital energy—that we not only see, but physiologically mimic and *feel*. These embattled bodies, whether made of ghostly mist or firm flesh, force us to dispense with preconceptions about relations between "subject" and "object," compelling us to

FIGURE 1.15

Richard Riemerschmid, *Untitled Charcoal Sketch*, 1890s. Städtische Galerie im Lenbachhaus und Kunstbau München. © 2021 Artists Rights Society (ARS), New York / VG Bild-Kunst, Bonn.

project ourselves instead into a tangle of matted limbs, or the ever-shifting shapes of clouds. Within the world of Riemerschmid's anatomical analogies, the soul is, as Nietzche perceived it, "something about the body": the body that realizes both the ungodly fear and the unearthly hope of being human; the body that strives, that wrestles in love. In their full physical engagement and complete emotional complexity, Riemerschmid's body images provide the vital essence—that magic, bittersweet elixir—that will animate his utilitarian designs.

FIGURE 1.16

Edvard Munch, *The Kiss* (*Kyss*), 1895. Etching and drypoint. Plate: 13 ½ × 11" (34.3 × 28 cm); sheet (irreg.): 21¹⁵/₁₆ × 17³/₈" (55.8 × 44.1 cm). Publisher: The artist, Berlin. Printer: probably L. Angerer, Berlin, or Carl Sabo, Berlin. Edition: more than 50 impressions. The William B. Jaffe and Evelyn A. J. Hall Collection. Digital Image © The Museum of Modern Art/Licensed by SCALA / Art Resource, NY. © 2021 Artists Rights Society (ARS), New York.

2

AT HOME WITH THE UNCANNY

One can read now and then in old accounts of journeys that someone sat down in an ancient forest on a tree trunk and that, to the horror of the traveler, this trunk suddenly *began to move* and showed itself to be a giant snake. . . . The mass that at first seemed completely lifeless suddenly reveals an inherent energy because of its *movement*.
—Ernst Jentsch[1]

In 1886, Swiss art historian Heinrich Wölfflin explored connections between the human body and the animation of architectural form in his doctoral dissertation, "Prolegomena to a Psychology of Architecture."[2] Wölfflin dismissed Robert Vischer's prior theory of *Einfühlung*: the subject's empathic projection into the object's form. But this was not because Wöfflin found the notion of animating inanimate objects absurd—far from it. Wölfflin simply believed that we animate aesthetic objects because "we ourselves possess a body," that we read *forms* (objects whose visual forms are laden with meaning) as animated because we perceive and understand them through the organization of our own bodies. Particular forms please us, he argued, because they reflect the "basic conditions of organic life."[3]

Riemerschmid spent the critical first years of his career as a visual artist in the 1890s exploring the significance of the body as a visual, symbolic communicator: an arrangement of forms that spoke wordlessly through musculature, posture, gesture, and expression, not only with other forms in the same composition, but with their surrounding environment, and, ultimately, with the sentient, sensitive viewer. But by the time Riemerschmid was completing his most important paintings, *Garden of*

Eden (1896; figure 1.9) and *Cloud Ghosts* (1897; figure 1.14), he was also beginning to expand his scope from the embodied vision required by these flat, figurative works to true, material embodiment. The roles that had up until this point been assumed by the figures in his two-dimensional compositions were about to be played out in three dimensions by designed objects within the fully realized space of the home.

This chapter argues for the significance of Riemerschmid's transition from flat painting to full-bodied design at a time when modern, utilitarian design came increasingly to be seen as not only the newest adaptation of art, but also its most radical iteration. Designed objects became a useful, democratic, and *activist* art whose mission it was to infuse a strong aesthetic current into the flow of everyone's everyday life. Modern design's drive toward universalism linked it to the grander aspirations of modernism itself. Modernism's commitment to expressing the essence of its own time has generally equated it with a transcendence of the particular, the regional, the rural, and the traditional. The modernist dream of universality has often been taken to imply collective amnesia—a suppression of the past and the destruction of its souvenirs, the loss of its memories. I suggest, however, that this suppressed—or *repressed*—past is integral to modernism, just as memories are by definition a phenomenon of present experience, and just as the unconscious, in psychoanalytic terms, is not merely part of but actually constitutive of consciousness. Riemerschmid's living things perform modernism's unconscious as they mobilize material traditions and reiterate regional fantasies within deliberately modern forms.

DESIGNS ON THE BODY

Riemerschmid was one among many socially concerned, progressive artists in the 1890s who believed that if their two-dimensional images could make a physiological impact on the viewer, then their three-dimensional objects—objects that could be sat in, picked up, worn against the skin, or put to the lips—might accomplish much more. Zeynep Çelik Alexander has argued for the heightened power of architecture and design at this moment, and especially in Munich's circles of design reform, where Riemerschmid's career took shape: "Designed objects seemed to acquire magical properties, striking their recipient, as it were, with aesthetic effects. This was how 'design' would function in the twentieth century: it would be taken for granted that designed objects—whether teacups, chairs, or buildings—had the immanent ability to affect the body and alter its own behavior patterns. The assumed immediacy between form and affect, a relationship forged at the end of the nineteenth century, would thereby be transformed into an assumed immediacy between design and behavior in twentieth-century modernism."[4] The constellation of mimetic relationships designed into Riemerschmid's things—their mirroring of organic, bodily forms, in conjunction with the mental and physical mimicry they compel in their users—maps out the questions of affect and perception fundamental not simply to a new understanding of aesthetics at the turn of the twentieth century but, more specifically, to the simultaneously optic and haptic body language that endows design with agency. Riemerschmid's sketchbooks from the 1890s show a playful imagination bent on making the fantastic part of ordinary life (figure 2.1). The experience of embodied viewing that Riemerschmid offered through his paintings, in which an optical event triggers in the viewer a simultaneous haptic one, became something *more*—both more intense and more important—in his three-dimensional things, designed to be seen, touched, and *used*.

Arnold Böcklin, the early Symbolist painter whose work had proven so influential for Riemerschmid and other members of the Munich Secession of 1892, harbored concerns about the disjuncture between the lofty pursuit of art and the grim circumstances of modern life in the late nineteenth century: "Life as it is lived today is a hindrance to creativity. . . . Look at our habitat—it barely suffices for survival. We are piled one upon the other in houses that don't belong to us, presented with a landscape cluttered with buildings, dark and airless. . . . From what can we draw inspiration? How can we light up our gaze, make it more joyful?"[5] Böcklin breathed life into imaginary creatures like mermaids and nymphs as symbols of his longing for a more colorful, more lively approach to modern living. Riemerschmid and his colleagues, however, responded to this longing by exchanging the visionary for the practical—two dimensions for three.

Democratizing beauty by applying it to everyday things was the impulse at the core of the nineteenth-century British Arts and Crafts movement and in the heart of William Morris, its founder and father. Morris's "romantic" socialism was adopted and adapted in the early 1890s by Belgian artist Henry van de Velde, who proclaimed in 1895 that use was the only way to unite art with life.[6] Art, according to van de Velde, was the animator of life; one could not do without it. But use was the connective tissue, the very sinew that brought artistic ideals to corporeal presence; it was what made them come alive. Like Riemerschmid, van de Velde also trained as a naturalist painter, studying at the Antwerp Academy and later moving to Paris

FIGURE 2.1

Richard Riemerschmid, *Sketch for a
Pouring Vessel*, late 1890s. Riemerschmid
sketchbooks, Städtische Galerie im
Lenbachhaus und Kunstbau München.
Nachlaß-Nr. 3958. © 2021 Artists Rights
Society (ARS), New York / VG Bild-Kunst, Bonn.

where he became fascinated with the pointillist works of Georges Seurat and Paul Signac. In 1888, he joined the Brussels secessionist group Les XX ("The Twenty"), which displayed not only avant-garde paintings but also modern applied arts at its exhibitions—as the Munich Secession exhibitions would soon do. Van de Velde soon began experimenting with designs for graphic art and objects, developing a theory of "energized line," which, along with his bold deployment of color, distinguished his earliest works as a designer: colorfully embroidered wall-hangings, such as *The Angels' Vigil* of 1893, in which bright patches of embroidered appliqué construct the figures of four Flemish peasant "angels" keeping watch over a sleeping Christ child (figure 2.2).[7]

FIGURE 2.2

Henry van de Velde, *The Angels' Vigil*, 1893. Embroidered appliqué (wool and silk). Museum für Gestaltung Zürich, Decorative Arts Collection, ZHdK. © 2021 Artists Right Society (ARS), New York / c/o Pictoright Amsterdam.

Riemerschmid, too, cultivated a strong, complementary palette in his paintings and prints. But though these saturated color contrasts would become hallmarks of his domestic interiors, his true "conversion" to the new occupation of designer was more corporeal than chromatic. In contrast to van de Velde's colorfully clothed figures, the bodies in Riemerschmid's images are naked, emphasizing not the formal possibilities of dress, but the forms and gestures of the body itself. Where van de Velde's embroidered appliqué unifies its subjects optically with abstracted shapes and lines, Riemerschmid's impulse, even as a painter, was toward the haptic: making image flesh as he carved his Adam and Eve out in solid, tactile wood beside their painted paradise.

Articulating the expressive body in his Symbolist paintings pushed Riemerschmid toward the real body, whose construction, needs, and considerations would dictate his approach to design: *Sachlichkeit*. Though one occupied itself with the Ideal and the other with the Real, both Symbolism and *Sachlichkeit* relied upon the intimate correspondence between inside and outside, soul and body, to accomplish their goal of expression through form. The "free" and often eroticized body was the focus of much attention in Munich, and especially in Schwabing, the city's bohemian quarter, home to Stefan George's circle of Symbolist poets. Despite George's ostensible espousal of the virtues of celibacy, the George-Kreis was nevertheless embroiled in Schwabing's body-centered, countercultural hedonism, also sharing members with the self-consciously modern Munich Psychological Society, founded in 1888 to investigate occult phenomena and the relation of body and mind.[8]

One of the society's most important members was empathy theorist Theodor Lipps, whose influence had been felt in Munich since he began teaching in 1894 at the Ludwig-Maximilian University. Lipps developed Vischer's theory of *Einfühlung* ("feeling into" or empathy) in a more overtly aesthetic direction, adapting it to support a psychology of perception founded on the belief in embodied responses to art and architecture. For Lipps, aesthetic empathy amounted to an objectified enjoyment of the *self*—a pleasure in self externalized only to be reinternalized—hinging on one's mimetic faculty, or the capacity for inner "imitation" of external phenomena. Stacy Hand has discussed Lipps's theory of perception as analogous to a spectator's identification with the body of a performer on stage: our experience of form arises from our imaginative imitation of the object's gesture or posture and our assessment of the physical pleasure or displeasure it appears to convey.[9] *Einfühlung* could be experienced in a number of ways, however, including the muscular mimicry of perceived forms and lines, the reading of another person's body language as an expression of their inner thoughts, or a somatic or visceral experience of objects or buildings: "In architecture everywhere we see unified masses advancing and receding," Lipps writes. "Mass is thereby transformed into a living rhythm of tension and relaxation."[10]

In 1895, the Munich-born architect Richard Streiter gave up his Berlin practice and returned to his native city to study under Lipps.[11] And in 1896, Streiter published an article in Berlin's literary and art journal, *Pan*, which routinely featured the poetry of French Symbolists, including Paul Verlaine and Stéphane Mallarmé, along with reproductions of Symbolist art by painters such as Stuck and Böcklin, as well as articles on design theory by internationally known figures like van de Velde. Ostensibly out of place within *Pan*'s context of Symbolist imagination and immateriality, then, was Streiter's advocacy a new kind of "realism" in architecture, based on existing living conditions, specific locality, locally available materials and technology, and utilitarian purpose. Streiter named this new realism *Sachlichkeit*.

This was the first time that the common term *Sachlichkeit* had been applied in a specialized, aesthetic sense. In selecting it, Streiter assigned *Sachlichkeit* new and pointed meanings for modern architecture and design reform—meanings that would both persist and permutate through the 1930s. In *Pan*'s "Notes from Munich" section, Streiter argued—using the vernacular-inspired buildings and interiors of the more established Munich architect Gabriel von Seidl as examples (figure 2.3)—that in Munich a promising tendency toward unpretentiousness in architecture and applied arts had begun; this new realism was defined by "the most perfect fulfillment of the requirements of fitness for purpose [*Zweckmäßigkeit*], comfort, health—in a word: *Sachlichkeit*."[12]

Also writing frequently for *Pan* was Alfred Lichtwark, the director of the Hamburger Kunsthalle (Hamburg Art Museum), who understood aesthetic experience as a form of bodily enjoyment rather than intellectual judgment.[13] Like Streiter, Lichtwark was a proponent of realistic architecture. In the October 1897 inaugural issue of Munich's design journal, *Dekorative Kunst*, Lichtwark considered the topic from the inside—the domestic interior—in an article titled "Der Praktische Zweck" (Practical Purpose). Lichtwark argued, from a housewife's perspective, for the elimination of excessive draperies and elaborate decoration in the domestic interior and recommended instead simply constructed, comfortable furniture, which—being easy both to use and to clean—would make for a more practical, hygienic, and thus modern home.[14]

FIGURE 2.3

Gabriel von Seidl, *Renovation Drawing
for Steinach Castle, Baden-Württemberg*
(originally erected in 1549), gable view, 19
May 1906. Project dates: 1902 to 1908.
Architekturmuseum der TUM.

To be *sachlich*, Streiter and Lichtwark believed, the forms of modern buildings and objects must result from the material circumstances of real, everyday life. But "that is not all," Streiter writes. *Sachlichkeit* is much more than a dry, objective relation of material cause and formal effect: "Just as the realism of poetry considers it one of its central tasks to delineate the character in relation to his milieu, so the parallel program in architecture sees as the most desirable goal of artistic truth the development of the character of a built work not solely out of a determination of needs [*Zweckbestimmung*] but also from the milieu, from the qualities of available materials, and from the environmentally and historically conditioned feeling of the place [*Stimmung der Örtlichkeit*]."[15]

It is here that the influence of Lipps's empathy theory on the otherwise pragmatic thinking of his student appears. Perception, for both, is a straightforward, embodied event determined by nervous and muscular responses—by material circumstances—but it is at the same time "objectified self-enjoyment": the subject "feeling into" his surroundings, so that the first is no longer a subject but an expressive "character," and the second are no longer empirically observed surroundings but a romantic "milieu." Streiter's *Sachlichkeit*—the development of the work's character from the qualities of its materials and the feeling of its place—lays the foundation for all modern *Sachlichkeits* to come. The word *functionalism* simply cannot contain it.

The "character of a built work," while it arises from the material and tangible, is, in itself, immaterial and *intangible*. Like the body in Riemerschmid's Symbolist paintings, the real, in the *sachlich* object, functions as a medium to invoke something more than itself. For Streiter, the *sachlich* form of Munich's local architecture was distinctly expressive: it communicated immediately and intuitively Munich's particular lifestyle or character—the feeling of that particular place.[16] Lichtwark, too, stressed the expressive nature of *Sachlichkeit* in his focus on the vernacular element in German regional architecture, in which strong colors and specific aesthetic qualities of materials conveyed, for him, a feeling of "Germanness."[17] Both Streiter and Lichtwark recognized *sachlich* form, despite its foundation on the real and actual, as inherently symbolic: an approach to the outer, visible surface of the object that communicated, without words, not only what but *how* that object really was.

At the same time that Streiter and Lichtwark were theorizing *Sachlichkeit*, van de Velde, too, was attempting to rationalize the relation between inner purpose and outer appearance. In an article on the design and construction of modern furniture published in *Pan* in 1897, van de Velde called for modern designers to define the utilitarian purpose of every object they designed, and to ensure its suitability to mass-production. In a statement of *Sachlichkeit* remarkable in the Morris devotee and creator of the ornamental *Angels' Vigil*, van de Velde continues: "We can succeed in completely renewing the appearances of things by carrying out the simple intention to be strictly logical, by following the principle of rejecting without exception all forms and ornamentation that a modern (machine-operated) factory could not easily manufacture and reproduce, by revealing the essential organism of every piece of furniture and object and by constantly bearing in mind that they must be easy to use . . . in other words unconditionally and resolutely following the functional logic of an article and being unreservedly honest about the materials employed."[18] "Revealing the essential organism" of an object in visible, tangible terms was *Sachlichkeit*'s central ambition. In practice, however, van de Velde tended to subsume both functional requirements and social goals within the primary cause of beauty: his designs were never narrowly functional but expansively, idiosyncratically expressive and, as such never achieved the social impact their designer had envisioned for them during the mid-1890s. Nevertheless, his promotion of the union of domestic life with abstract art did produce immediate and transformative effects in the German art world of the 1890s.

At the 1897 Dresden International Art Exhibition, van de Velde installed a domestic *Gesamtkunstwerk*: an aesthetically orchestrated *Ruheraum* (lounge) with stoneware tiles and upholstery fabric by French designer Alexandre Bigot (figure 2.4). Carefully placed decorative objects functioned as artistic accents.[19] To van de Velde, the contents of the well-designed room were its "living organs," and the Dresden exhibition provided him with the opportunity to model his vision of a domestic interior as a beautiful, useful, living thing.[20] In addition to van de Velde's *Ruheraum*, the Hamburg-born Parisian art dealer and entrepreneur Siegfried Bing displayed four rooms at Dresden that van de Velde had designed in 1895 for Bing's Paris gallery and shop, L'Art Nouveau. Van de Velde's interiors created a sensation in Dresden, bringing him overnight renown followed closely by numerous German commissions.[21]

This was Germany's first taste of van de Velde's organic approach to design, but more importantly, it also represented a revolution in the exhibition of modern *Kunstgewerbe* (applied arts products) in Germany. While La Libre Esthétique ("the Free Aesthetic," successor to Les XX) had displayed complete interiors in its Brussels exhibitions of 1894 and 1895, and while Bing's L'Art Nouveau had already promoted the concept through van de Velde's display rooms in Paris, van de Velde's *Ruheraum*,

FIGURE 2.4

Henry van de Velde, *Lounge at the Dresden International Art Exhibition*, 1897. © 2021 Artists Rights Society (ARS), New York / c/o Pictoright Amsterdam.

designed specifically for the 1897 Dresden exhibition, set a precedent for the display of modern applied arts in Germany. These would henceforth be shown most frequently in complete domestic environments: this meant that German exhibition goers were now active, bodily participants in modern design.[22]

Riemerschmid's tempera painting *Cloud Ghosts* was first exhibited in the autumn of that same year (figure 2.5). But rather than taking a conventional place in a picture gallery as Riemerschmid's *Garden of Eden* had done in 1896, the *Cloud Ghosts* played a special role in a collaboratively contrived interior—a *Gesamtkunstwerk* orchestrated not by a single artistic "conductor" but by several pairs of hands—at the Seventh International Art Exhibition in Munich's Glaspalast (glass palace), the city's mammoth iron-and-glass exhibition hall modeled on London's 1851 Crystal Palace. The cloud ghosts graced a portiere designed by August Endell, next to a chair by sculptor Bernhard Pankok, in a room arranged by architect Theodor Fischer. Placed against a large landscape mural in blues and greens (which Riemerschmid also painted expressly for the space), the smaller painting in its carved wooden frame acted as a coat of arms for the room, as well as the larger project of its creators.

Early in 1897, Riemerschmid and a group of Munich's young, progressive artists issued a call for entries to their planned display of avant-garde applied arts at the Glaspalast exhibition. This new section would be quite limited, however; its very existence was the result of a hard-won battle between the established designers of the Bavarian Applied Arts Society, who organized the Glaspalast's applied arts displays, and Munich's new generation of design reformers, many of whom had only recently come to design from painting or, like Riemerschmid, were practicing fine and applied art simultaneously. The Applied Arts Society's adherence to historicism and advocacy of traditional craft practices put it at odds with reformers like Riemerschmid and his colleagues, who only after trying negotiations were granted two *Zimmerchen*, or "little rooms," for what were accordingly (and pejoratively) designated *Kleinkunst*, or "little arts."[23]

Riemerschmid had designed his very first pieces of furniture in a relatively rough, heavy, neo-Gothic aesthetic in 1895, after his marriage to Ida Hofmann, to outfit the couple's apartment in the Riemerschmid-Block on Hildegardstrasse. Gradually, he began designing household objects and pieces of furniture that manifested the same preoccupation with "unspoiled" nature evident in his contemporaneous paintings. At the Glaspalast in 1897, Riemerschmid exhibited a large buffet, sparingly designed and sparsely ornamented with iron hardware originating in functional, medievalizing hinges, but growing into plant tendrils that stretched

CHAPTER 2

FIGURE 2.5

Theodor Fischer, Richard Riemerschmid,
Bernhard Pankok, and August Endell,
*Kleinkunst Room at the Seventh International
Art Exhibition*, Glaspalast, Munich, 1897.
Kunst und Handwerk 47 (1997/1998): 43.

toward the center of the buffet's lower cupboard like vines reaching toward the light (figure 2.6). The natural grain of the yew boards beneath, with their knots, irregularities, and imperfections, was plainly visible, not merely creating a contrast to the sinuous, stylized plant forms but acting as a second, staccato strain of ornament—metal and wood generating in their conjunction a visual syncopation.

The "art" in Riemerschmid's applied art was not simply a result of his design work; vital too were the properties and qualities of the materials used to execute it, as well as the intelligence and skill with which they were executed. Some of the more decorative aspects of Riemerschmid's things (the idiosyncrasies of woodgrain, for instance) might seem entirely haphazard: the "simple" byproducts of natural processes. But it was the craftsman—in this case, Munich cabinet maker Wenzel Till, with whom Riemerschmid worked frequently around 1900—who drew out that material's particular charms, through his hands-on interpretation of the design. For the artists of the 1897 *Kleinkunst* rooms (some of them working in the capacity of designers for the first time), sensitive, interpretive fabrication was the factor on which their entire venture depended. For unless the fabricator was receptive to the design of the modern artist and technically capable of carrying it out in the appropriate materials, the artist's vision remained merely that. The call for entries to the *Kleinkunst* displays, issued in February 1897 by a committee of six artists including Riemerschmid, stated that submissions would be judged not just on "originality of invention," but equally on "the perfect artistic and technical execution" of "such artistic objects as fulfill the requirements of our modern life."[24]

Much to the conservative Applied Arts Society's dismay, the begrudged *Kleinkunst* rooms stole the show from the Glaspalast's more established fine art sections, garnering celebratory reactions from both public and press.[25] Their success proclaimed the birth of a utilitarian beauty in Munich, a style that gave body and purpose to the flat graphics in the pages of *Jugend*. This, then, was Jugendstil: a new, youthful style for a fresh, modern way of living. One of the exhibition's practical results was the establishment by the *Kleinkunst* committee members of the Vereinigte Werkstätten für Kunst im Handwerk (United Workshops for Art in Handcraft), which registered its allegiance to social and cultural reform by taking its name straight from William Morris's 1890 utopian novel *News from Nowhere*, which depicted handcraftsmanship as key to the high quality of life achieved by Britons after an imagined socialist revolution.[26]

Founded in the spring of 1898, the Vereinigte Werkstätten did indeed aspire to specific ideals in the design and fabrication of new applied arts products, but not

FIGURE 2.6

Richard Riemerschmid, *Buffet* (yew with iron
hardware), 1897. Executed by Wenzel Till,
Munich. Landesmuseum Württemberg, P.
Frankenstein / H. Zwietasch. © 2021 Artists
Rights Society (ARS), New York / VG Bild-
Kunst, Bonn.

necessarily Morris's. The Workshops' founders aimed to disseminate high-quality modern products by fostering collaborations between modern artists and several carefully selected firms of technically progressive and artistically inclined craftspeople. Without the corporate support of the Vereinigte Werkstätten (which also took the responsibility of marketing and selling the modern products), these artisans could not have taken the financial risk of producing applied arts in modern styles.[27]

Relationships between Munich's new designers and progressive craft firms had been developing organically since the mid-1890s, but the Vereinigte Werkstätten cemented a corporate relationship between modern designers and craftspeople, underscoring the significance that its artists placed on the execution of their designs. In contrast to Morris's emphasis on the conditions of labor and the redemptive value of engagement in the craft process, the Vereinigte Werkstätten targeted the product itself—how it looked, felt, and functioned—as the most important aspect of design reform. Mechanized production methods were readily adopted if appropriate to a particular aspect of fabrication. But though the Vereinigte Werkstätten embraced machines as tools that could ease fabrication, speed production, and so reduce costs, thereby allowing the modern applied arts to be more broadly affordable, sensuous materiality and expressive form were equally prized.[28]

Regardless of how they were actually made, however, the Werkstätten's furniture and housewares *looked* handmade; they conveyed a sense of artistic originality and authenticity—the touch of the artist's hand—that recommended them to those discerning members of the cultured middle class, or *Bildungbürgertum*, seeking to enhance their domestic lives with applied art. Just as the framing figures of Riemerschmid's *Garden of Eden* triptych represented a transition from purely optic to solidly haptic, so in the minds of the Vereinigte Werkstätten's designers and in the hands of their artisans did the images of late nineteenth-century German art become flesh and step out into real, everyday life.

BODY BUILDING

Like the buffet he exhibited at the Glaspalast in 1897, many of Riemerschmid's earliest household objects produced with the Vereinigten Werkstätten seemed drawn from the natural world envisioned in his landscapes. Candlesticks in brass, bronze, and copper clambered up from leaf-like bases, their stems swelling in places as if a green bud might burst forth from the inorganic material, or shooting off at a peculiar angle as if straining toward an unseen source of light (figure 2.7). The taut, active forms of Riemerschmid's candlesticks suggest not simply growth but motion. A set of silver cutlery fabricated with the Werkstätten in 1899 embodies this vegetable-animal hybridity, the handles of the knives in particular confounding distinction between gently curling vines and stretched sinews, or smoothed, yet knobbly bones (figure 2.8). The combination, though cognitively baffling, was optically—and haptically—enticing: the utensils' twining tendrils crept into the hand, while their animality rested them there, rounding into the palm and pressing against the fingers like a pet inviting a caress.

One of Riemerschmid's first furniture designs produced after the founding of the Werkstätten in April 1898 was his oak "musician's chair," part of a suite of music-room furniture, including a piano, that he showed at the 1899 Deutsche Kunst-Ausstellung Dresden (German Art Exhibition in Dresden; figures 2.9 and 2.10). The musician's chair, perhaps Riemerschmid's best-known design, is remarkable for its sparse construction that appears, from some angles, almost to dematerialize or dissolve the chair's very form, as if it were being reduced to its simplest, barest essence right before our eyes. The chair's salient feature—its long, bowed diagonal strut that seems to sway as it connects the backrest to the gently flared front feet—reinforces this sense of attenuation approaching dissolution.

Despite its delicate appearance, however, the musician's chair's design was eminently practical. It suited the musician's needs by being not only light and portable, but also sturdy: the curved diagonal strut served to brace the chair at the same time that it allowed for the free movement of the musician's active arms. Paul Schultze-Naumburg, a colleague of Riemerschmid's at the Werkstätten, praised the furniture in Riemerschmid's Dresden music room, calling it "*sachlich* and comfortable right down to every edge and corner," and noting in particular the musician's chair's thoughtful accommodation of the body, "so that the pieces conform to and cuddle the relaxed body, and through them the problem of fitness for purpose [*Zweckmäßigkeit*] is solved in exemplary style." But Schultze-Naumburg also recognized in the musician's chair something beyond fitness for function, concluding that Riemerschmid "achieves this solution through original constructive ideas, which in his hands become lines of decoration."[29]

In 1900, the musician's chair made a second appearance in Riemerschmid's *Room of an Art Lover*, installed in Paris at the Exposition Universelle, a triumphal event for Europe's New Style—Art Nouveau in France, Jugendstil in Germany—and for Riemerschmid, who received a grand prize for his display (figure 2.11). This "art

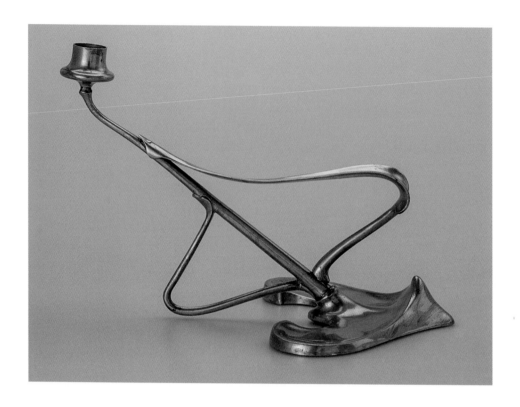

FIGURE 2.7

Richard Riemerschmid, *Candlestick*, 1898.
Brass. Vereinigte Werkstätten, Munich,
model no. 1459. Münchner Stadtmuseum,
Sammlung Angewandte Kunst. © 2021
Artists Rights Society (ARS), New York / VG
Bild-Kunst, Bonn.

FIGURE 2.8

Richard Riemerschmid, *Cutlery*, 1899/1900.
Silver. Designed for the Vereinigte
Werkstätten, Munich and manufactured
by Bruckmann & Söhne. Münchner
Stadtmuseum, Sammlung Angewandte Kunst.
© 2021 Artists Rights Society (ARS),
New York / VG Bild-Kunst, Bonn.

FIGURE 2.9

Richard Riemerschmid, *Chair*, 1898–99
(Vereinigte Werkstätten für Kunst im
Handwerk). Oak and replacement leather;
31⅜ × 18⅛ × 22½ inches; Saint Louis
Art Museum, Richard Brumbaugh Trust
in memory of Richard Irving Brumbaugh
and in honor of Grace Lischer Brumbaugh
248:1992. © 2021 Artists Rights Society
(ARS), New York / VG Bild-Kunst, Bonn.

FIGURE 2.10

Richard Riemerschmid, *Music Room*,
Deutsche Kunstausstellung Dresden, 1899.
Vereinigte Werkstätten, Munich. *Dekorative
Kunst* 4 (1899): 99.

FIGURE 2.11

Richard Riemerschmid, *Room of an Art Lover*,
Exposition Universelle, Paris, 1900. *Deutsche
Kunst und Dekoration* 7 (Oct. 1900): 26.

lover's room" was a quintessential *Gesamtkunstwerk*, a space where the cultured aesthete might transcend the mundane. Riemerschmid designed a sinuous, interlacing frieze that not only graced the room's entrance but also enclosed the entire space within its tendrils, framing a living picture in which the prospective art lover was the subject. The inventive handcrafted frames of Riemerschmid's *Garden of Eden* and *Cloud Ghosts* paintings had hinted at his investment in the frame as a structural device with spatial implications, but it was not until Paris 1900 that he expanded the frame to truly encompass his vision for dwelling.

While surviving black-and-white photographs emphasize the frieze's frame-like three-dimensionality, Riemerschmid's colored pencil drawings attest to the equal significance of its blue-green color scheme (figure 2.12). In conjunction with his original designs for the blue frieze, color lithographs of his designs for the room's chartreuse wallpaper and vermilion carpet, published in the journal *Dekorative Kunst*, help to reconstruct the room's vivid contrasts and suggest how astonishingly vibrant it must have seemed to visitors in 1900 (figure 2.13). The lively complementary colors deployed in the *Room of an Art Lover* evoked the lush, Symbolist palettes of Riemerschmid's landscapes, while also offsetting the subtler tones of his oak furniture.

Within the new framework of the art lover's room, the musician's chair recalls the compositions of Riemerschmid's earlier graphic art. Positioned just inside the frieze-framed doorway, the simple wooden chair sits in opposition to the room's saturated hues and to the frieze's intricate tangle. As the solitary girl on his 1896 *Jugend* cover seems to hesitate on the verge of communion with the slender birch trees (figure 1.3), so the plain little chair appears slightly out of place within the room's grandiose, ornamental frame. In contrast to the clambering abstraction of the framing frieze, the practical chair produces an effect like that of the bodies that intrude upon Riemerschmid's imagined Edens: its slender, lilting limbs trace the lines of the *Jugend* girl's body.

Against the complex frieze, the simple, purposeful chair acts as a surrogate for the body, its struts suggesting sinews, and its backrest and limbs evoking the forms of bones. The chair's combination of expressive design and sensitive execution— its deliberate, splayed stance, with front feet thickening toward the bottom, as if rooting themselves to their spot, coupled with its softened contours and lithe silhouette—conveys the youthful affect of Riemerschmid's figures. The subtly rounded edges and gently caressing curves that Schulze-Naumburg saw as cradling the human body simultaneously described the chair's own "body" as supple and

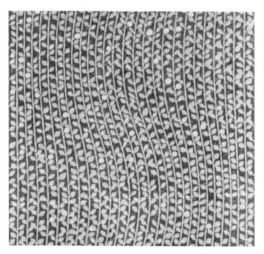

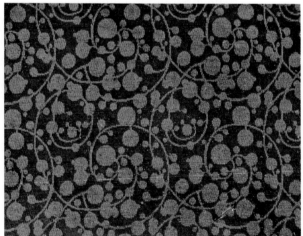

FIGURE 2.12

Richard Riemerschmid, *Design Drawing for Room of an Art Lover* (colored pencil and pen), 1900. Architekturmuseum der TUM. © 2021 Artists Rights Society (ARS), New York / VG Bild-Kunst, Bonn.

FIGURE 2.13

Richard Riemerschmid, *Wallpaper* (left) and *Carpet* (right) for *Room of an Art Lover* (color lithographs), *Dekorative Kunst* 4, no. 9 (June 1901): 352 and 353.

yielding. In Lipps's terms, we naturally follow the chair's structural lines to discover our own pleasure in them: a pleasure derived from "feeling into" and neurologically mirroring the chair's formal expression of its urge to "cuddle," and from our imagining of what being cuddled by this chair might feel like.

In 1902, architect, design reform advocate, and civil servant Hermann Muthesius theorized the attraction of the curved line for Jugendstil designers in terms resonant with theories of *Einfühlung*. Muthesius theorized that "expressiveness" could help to "clarify certain static images"—in other words, to assign meaning to aesthetic experience; but this was only possible "with the vigorous assistance of human 'empathy'": "The chair becomes something straddle-legged and crouching, the table leg an elastic line like the weight-bearing human foot. The constructive parts clasp one another; a metal attachment claws into the wood and extends itself like an arm; a brass handle indicates through its lines the motion with which it should be used. Or one may try to increase the utility of furniture through the rigorous adaptation of form to the physical movements of the human being."[30] What Muthesius describes here is not simply the application of empathy aesthetics to utilitarian forms, however; it is the perception of pathognomic forms designed to elicit embodied responses: bodily forms intended to communicate with and be understood directly through the body—a *Sachlichkeit* in which corporeal form explained anatomical function.

The musician's chair's *Körpergerechtigkeit*—its appropriateness to the body—may be attributed to its intended purpose. But its "straddled-legged and crouching" *Körperlichkeit*—its corporeality of form—cannot be rationalized by the demands of function alone. Architectural historian Dolf Sternberger has suggested that Riemerschmid's furniture exhibits an "anatomical construction principle" with limbs that remind one of muscles and bones, or joints that protrude slightly to suggest elbows and knees.[31] This pervasive impulse to animate inanimate utilitarian objects through associations with the human body, though not antagonistic to functional concerns, has yet no logical foundation in the requirements of function. The plain fact that an object is equipped for use by the human body does not dictate the more complex proposition that it should also suggest or ressemble bodily forms. The vision of these two conditions existing together as an integrated whole—a *body* at once functioning and expressing—was Riemerschmid's own. The musician's chair stood, within the art lover's framework of symbolic aesthetics, not simply as a reference to the human body but as an embodiment of the *self* in its conflation of inherent need and excessive desire. And this recognition of the self as simultaneously rational and irrational, inextricably physical and spiritual, characterizes the full-ness and inclusiveness of Riemerschmid's *Sachlichkeit*.

In his short essay, "On the Mimetic Faculty," Walter Benjamin introduces the concept of "imitative behavior" in the formation of language—or onomatopoeia.[32] The "body language" of Riemerschmid's things could be described as a kind of visual, material onomatopoeia: their thingliness, *Sachlichkeit*, appeared to depend on an imitative relationship in which the object's core meaning (what it was, what it did, and *how* it did it) was expressed through the imitative behavior of its outer "rind": its appearance. While this linguistic analogy conveys a one-to-one corre-spondence between surface and substance, the example of fruit and rind—and indeed, the truly organic, integrated model of the body—demonstrate more pre-cisely and intuitively the natural inextricability that thingliness implies. We can imagine a theoretical relationship between inward purpose and outward expression playing itself out during Riemerschmid's design process, and deconstructing the construction of such a relationship might help us, in part at least, to understand its workings, its mechanism—in practice. But we can no more speak of such mim-icry in Riemerschmid's realized designs—his actual *things*—than we can speak of a human being as a relationship between muscle and mind, or skin and flesh. The German adjective *hautnah*—"as close as skin"—approaches this intimacy of surface and substance. In both cases—humanity and thingliness—the fullness of being escapes and exceeds merely clinical relations of function and form.

Ideas about the body, function, animation, and empathy overlap and inter-sect in Riemerschmid's utilitarian designs; each object articulates their relations afresh in a manner unique to its particular purpose and character. Whereas Wölf-flin believed that humans animated objects as part of a natural, bodily response, we might conversely correlate the potency of an object's Wirkung—its capacity to affect us, to "work upon" us—to the degree that it mirrors our own basic condi-tions of organic life: in other words, the more the inanimate mimics the animate, the more naturally we relate to it as a living thing. But although the *Wirkung* of Riemerschmid's things relies on their capacity to arouse in us their apperception as organic beings, it does not propose them as fellow humans, *Doppelgänger* of the prospective user. The formal sparseness and restraint of his designs instead enlists the user's imagination to uncover, gradually and naturally, as in a process of acquaintance and endearment, the thing's true nature. In this sense, although they provoke a mimetic response in their users, Riemerschmid's objects themselves are not mimetic: they do not take on other bodies—of humans or animals; they are not directly biomorphic or anthropomorphic, but are intensely, insistently, *themselves*.

August Endell, the philosopher turned designer who in 1897 singled out Riemerschmid's designs as "remarkable," was also a contributor to the *Kleinkunst* displays at the Glaspalast exhibition that same year. Endell, a student of Lipps, shared with his design colleagues a profound interest in the evocative possibilities of form in applied art. Though Endell and Lipps differed over the latter's insistence on a mimetic correspondence between observer and form, Endell shared Lipps's preoccupation with the empathic pull of line, relying on visual effects engineered at the level of surface to generate an embodied optical experience, or arousal, in the viewer.[33] Endell's design for a side chair, executed in 1902, underscores his preoccupation with flat, abstract form through an unusual arrangement of solids and voids, whose formal relationships are further dramatized by Endell's choice to stain the chair black—emphasizing its striking contours while suppressing the details of its construction and effacing the texture of its materials (figure 2.14). The chair becomes an abstract silhouette. Endell's conception of the chair's primary purpose as a vehicle for optical *Wirkung* dovetails with Munich philosopher, psychologist, and graphologist Ludwig Klages's belief that images were the "souls of things": that it was the embodied optical experience—neither cognition, nor the practical, utilitarian employment of objects—that was actually the most real and hence made the deepest impression on both mind and body.[34]

Compared with the flat surfaces and clean contours that form the optical image or "soul" of Endell's chair, Thomas Mann's 1902 desk chair (initially designed by Riemerschmid in 1898 and executed by the Vereinigte Werkstätten) is far simpler in its construction, yet far subtler in the nuanced articulation of its few components (figure 0.1). On either side, the chair's front and back legs form vertical sections of one continuous strand, which grows up like a vine from a thickened, root-like front foot, then levels off and dips slightly to form the chair's horizontal arm, and ultimately makes its way downward again, replanting itself with the second root-foot of its back leg. If, following Lipps's trajectory of *Einfühlung*, we "feel into" the chair's lines, we experience fluidity, as though the chair has been brought into being not by dry, dusty carpentry, but by the swift, sure motion of an ink-soaked brush, or by stretching moist clay into long, supple strands.

Where Endell's ghostly dematerialization or conspicuous *absence* of body might work upon us to feel our own bodily presence all the more intensely, Riemerschmid's chair, though slender, *takes up space*—space that we might otherwise

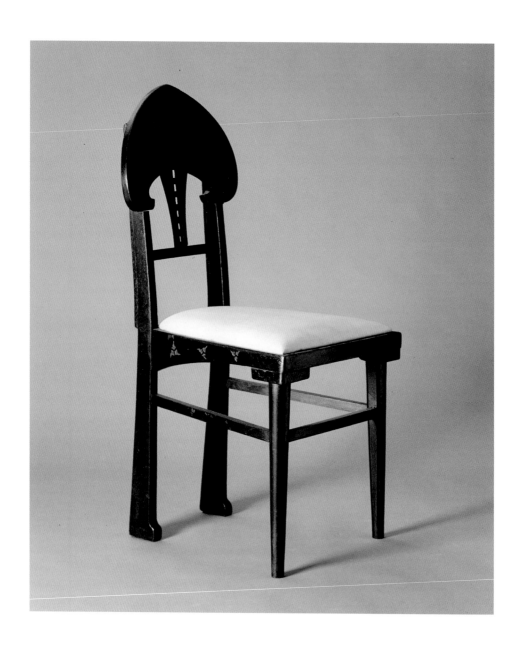

FIGURE 2.14

August Endell, *Side Chair*, 1902. Münchner
Stadtmuseum, Sammlung Angewandte Kunst.

occupy. Ironically, it is the very slightness of its frame that makes its volume undeniable: it is only by virtue of its lithe musculature that we perceive its motion. Like Endell's biomorphic abstraction, Riemerschmid's chair, too, generates an image—though a different one. The soul of Riemerschmid's armchair is a *moving picture*: unlike Endell's chair, whose black, static graphic is stamped on our vision, Riemerschmid's chair tends to slip away from our optical memory; we have to keep looking, revisiting it, touching it—with our eyes as well as our bodies—to know how it really is. If the soul of the thing is its image, then the soul of Riemerschmid's chair is *alive*.

But alive in what sense? Its moving, growing forms, its root-like feet and clambering legs and arms, and its silky, varnished surfaces stir up associations with familiar images of plant life—tender leaves just unfurling, newly emerging shoots, and stems glittering with dew. Biologists like Haeckel and psychophysicists like Fechner believed in the souls of plants; might these not look something like Riemerschmid's armchair?[35] But the three-dimensional precision with which the chair was designed and fabricated transforms its loosely plant-based forms into something less identifiable, though more compelling. The slight inward turning of the front feet (in contrast to the forward-facing back feet) were not conceived and carved in flat contour but sculpted in full volume, like roots, hooves, or fleshy limbs, each flaring and expanding at the base, as if bearing weight. While the delicate tremor of the chair's attenuated legs and its shyly confronted feet echo the demeanor of Riemerschmid's *Jugend* girls, its lilting limbs are ultimately not stems, vines, or legs; instead, they animate an entirely new being: a chair that quivers with expectancy.

Van de Velde, by contrast, whose theory of line formed the basis for many of his designs, employed line to stylize rather than animate.[36] While a dining chair of van de Velde's from 1898 also possesses visibly curving legs, their lines serve only to extend the forms of the backrest, not to suggest movement (figure 2.15). Compared with the expressively articulated feet on Riemerschmid's chair, the feet of van de Velde's chair remain undifferentiated from the contour of the leg. Riemerschmid's lovingly sculpted, hoof-like, root-like, but ultimately *chair*-like feet—arrested, for a heartbeat, on restless tiptoe—set the chair's legs gently akimbo, lending them a sense of immanent, dynamic expansion, as if Mann's writing chair, in anticipation (or perhaps in imitation) of its occupant, yearns to stretch its legs.

Moving beyond illustration, representation, image, and line, Riemerschmid's designs gave things their own individual, naturally evolved, three-dimensional bodies. It was as if, in van de Velde's words, Riemerschmid had revealed their "essential organism." This was their unique thingliness: their inner character expressed

FIGURE 2.15

Henry van de Velde, *Dining Chair for Mme. De Craene-Van Mons, Brussels*, ca. 1898. Design Museum Gent. Photo: Studio Claerhout. © 2021 Artists Rights Society (ARS), New York / c/o Pictoright Amsterdam.

through material means. A human body, after all, was made of quite different materials than a chair. While pencil, oil paint, and tempera had inflected the various aspects of Riemerschmid's practice as a graphic artist, as a designer, the consideration and selection of appropriate materials for each design concept defined the character of the resulting object. Comparing the vigorous, muscular rendering of his design drawings with their realized counterparts, it becomes clear that Riemerschmid designed with the specific, sensuous properties of his intended materials in mind. The cross-hatching and gestural marks of his pencil drawings are materialized in his furniture as patterns created by the grained surfaces of thoughtfully arranged wood veneers (figure 2.16), while the bold chiaroscuro that describes the

FIGURE 2.16

Richard Riemerschmid, *Table Top* (detail showing wood grain patterns), 1900. Kunstgewerbemuseum, Berlin. © 2021 Artists Rights Society (ARS), New York / VG Bild-Kunst, Bonn.

bulbous, spiny body of a water jug becomes the prickly skin of salt-glazed stoneware (figure 2.17). Materials also transported the theme of ambivalence and imperfection from Riemerschmid's graphic art into his designed objects. Despite his rational attention to the requirements of function and the radical restraint of his construction, he intentionally avoided any sense of strict, mathematical or industrial precision that might rob his objects of their organic lifelikeness. Even when his furniture and ceramics could be produced with the aid of mechanized processes, Riemerschmid was careful to incorporate the presence of "the hand," whether through the character of a particular material and its reference to handcraft traditions or through the deft insertion of small irregularities—which, like the mildly unruly figures that invade his pristine landscapes, enliven their sober surfaces.

The mother-of-pearl inlays in an otherwise somber wooden wardrobe of 1902 reenact the dynamic of figure and ground well established in Riemerschmid's art (figure 2.18). While an initial glance affords gratifying bursts of decoration within the broad expanse of unornamented wood, a closer look reveals that these lustrous, milky lozenges, sprinkled in a casual symmetry to either side of the wardrobe doors and along its crowning frame, are irregular in shape. This unconformity becomes more obvious in the "window" of mother-of-pearl laid into each of the wardrobe's doors. While together the four pearly panes form what appears as a grid, each one is actually slightly off-kilter—cut just a bit differently from its neighbor. It is this delight in the uncontainable, the imperfect and forgivable—the *human*—stemming from the delicately clumsy, yet exuberant organicism of his paintings, that defines Riemerschmid's *Sachlichkeit*. But it is the mother-of-pearl "eyes" peering out from the face of the Riemerschmid's wardrobe that animate it—projecting its presence into our space, with curious consequences.

AT HOME WITH THE *UNHEIMLICH*

Through their animated physiognomies, objects like Riemerschmid's 1902 wardrobe united the *Einfühlung* and *Sachlichkeit* already connected in 1890s discourse in an organically integrated whole—a *body* that occupied space and lived alongside other, human bodies in the modern home. Writing in 1908 of new developments in German design since the turn of the century, the Austrian critic and architectural theorist Joseph August Lux illuminates the mother-of-pearl accents on Riemerschmid's wardrobe: "Squeezing together in pairs towards the centers of broad

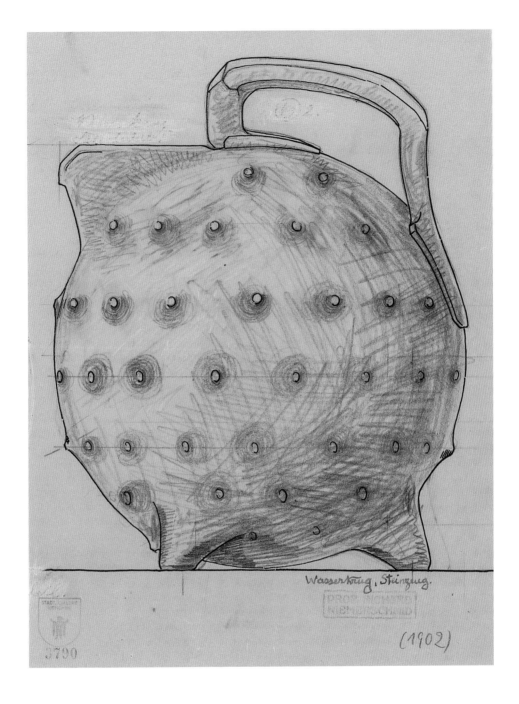

FIGURE 2.17

Richard Riemerschmid, *Design for Stoneware Water Jug*, 1902. Architekturmuseum der TUM. © 2021 Artists Rights Society (ARS), New York / VG Bild-Kunst, Bonn.

FIGURE 2.18

Richard Riemerschmid, *Wardrobe for the Thieme House*, 1902–03. Münchner Stadtmuseum, Sammlung Angewandte Kunst. © 2021 Artist Rights Society (ARS), New York / VG Bild-Kunst, Bonn.

wooden surfaces," these little morsels of inlaid ornament express, for Lux, "an unmistakable sense of inner, spiritual life."[37]

But even before Lux's retrospective, other period writings celebrated Riemerschmid's imaginative capacity to reveal this inner life as a result of his *Sachlichkeit*. Hermann Muthesius, just returned from his post as technical attaché in England, where he had gathered information for the German government about recent English dwelling reforms, identified Riemerschmid in 1904 as one of Germany's most important modern designers. According to Muthesius, Riemerschmid had reawakened the German dwelling, revealing a new, lively domestic interior where "the chairs squat in a bow-legged stance that invites you to sit down, the tables stretch out their surfaces to receive your dishes," and the wardrobes assume "a comfortably broad stance that gives their bodies an altogether secure and reassuring stability."[38] In both Lux's and Muthesius's readings of Riemerschmid's wardrobe, *Einfühlung* enables *Sachlichkeit*: staring into the wardrobe's opalescent "eyes," Lux perceives its true nature. And the wardrobe presents its strong, stocky body to Muthesius as proof of its inner strength and reliability. Wardrobe and user converse with each other, each alternating in the position of subject and object naturally, as in a conversation.

Nuremberg art historian Paul Johannes Rée corroborates Muthesius's affectionate testimony of hospitable chairs, generous tables, and trusty wardrobes. "Everything courses with life," Rée writes in 1906.[39] He describes objects full of "character" with "faces that testify to their inner cheerfulness and freedom." These faces, Rée proceeds, regard us with "the friendly, quiet smiles that we look for in our fellow men and in every aspect of our environment."[40] Rée's empathy with Riemerschmid's things, as if they were his "fellow men," both informs and proves—in an ever-repeating cycle—his perception of Riemerschmid's *Sachlichkeit* as comprising two components: the object's inner being (*Wesen*) and its outer expression, or form. More than once, Rée notes that Riemerschmid's first priority in designing is "die Sache" (the matter at hand): "The *Sache* is everything to him, the form is totally secondary."[41] But Rée recognizes this *Sache* as inseparable from expressive form: Riemerschmid's art is "full of the warm expression of life"; the forms of his objects demonstrate not just their practical purpose, but their "particular feeling or disposition" as well.[42] Just as emotion arranges the muscles of the face into a physical expression, so there is no form without *Sache*; but conversely, as facial expression is the physical revelation of inner being, there can be no *Sache* without form. Riemerschmid's *Sachlichkeit* was, in Rée's eyes, a physiognomy of function and form.

For Muthesius, Riemerschmid's art was a *sachliche Kunst*, or *Sachkunst*—a rational art.[43] The forms of his objects were dictated by their utilitarian purpose, not by historical or foreign styles; they rejected superficial applied ornament, and they honored the working properties and aesthetic qualities of individual materials. All of these attributes made them identifiably and self-consciously modern. But there was another aspect of *Sachlichkeit*, implied in the writings of Lux, Muthesius, and Rée and inherent in the development of the discourse by such figures as Streiter and Lichtwark, that seemed unselfconscious and *un*modern. This was the vernacular. Streiter had invoked the vernacular's regional authenticity in his discussion of local materials and traditions through his emphasis on the *milieu*: the idea that the specific geographical or physical setting and sociocultural context should dictate the functions and forms of built objects. And Lichtwark, in "Palace Window and Swinging Door," had proposed Germany's various regional architectures, developed prior to unification, as points of departure for a modern, middle-class, national architecture. Muthesius linked Riemerschmid's *Sachlichkeit* with an idealized vernacular, claiming that his work had a decidedly German character. Just like "the old German art," Riemerschmid's was "naively loyal, a little bit bumbling, strictly *sachlich*, but always mitigated by feeling." In short, it was *Gemütlich* (cozy, homely, *canny*).[44]

While Muthesius invokes images of domestic tradition to connect Riemerschmid's modern designs with a shared past, exactly to which "old German art" he refers remains obscure. But this inexactitude was precisely the appeal of the vernacular ideal for turn-of-the-century cultural reformers, like Lichtwark and Muthesius. The notion of an old-fashioned, unspoiled, rural culture—firmly grounded in the past yet still accessible in the present—offered modern reformers a critical approach to their own experience of modernity; it seemed to provide an antidote to the metropolitan ills of urbanism and industrialism, which had initially incited the Life Reformers. While reassuringly rooted in an agrarian past, the vernacular was also perpetual and ahistorical and so could be integrated with an antihistoricist modernism. From a safe intellectual distance, vernacular forms seemed "natural," unassuming, and naive. In concrete, architectural terms, vernacular forms were those that had survived a stylistic natural selection through time to become ostensibly timeless. And it was this timelessness, reformers felt, that made vernacular forms appropriate for a German modern design that rejected historical styles but still required cultural legitimacy if it were to pervade and influence German domestic culture. For the newly unified nation, the construct of a modern German vernacular promised a perpetuation and unification of regional cultures, as well as a symbolic return to an idealized agrarianism tainted by neither foreign nor modern adulterations.[45]

For most of the twentieth century, historians positioned the characteristics and values typically associated with the vernacular—regional specificity, material authenticity, cultural tradition, nostalgia or sentimentality, social and/or political conservatism—in opposition to a modernism that was universal, cosmopolitan, rational, functional, and progressive. More recently, however, scholars have proposed a *vernacular modernism*, within which the vernacular "lived on as a strong subcurrent of modern praxis."[46] Instead of positioning the vernacular in modernity's wake, historians Bernd Hüppauf and Maiken Umbach have described it as "one of the generative principles of the modern condition."[47] They replace the vernacular's stereotypical timelessness with the more specific historically and culturally determined concepts of *cultural memory* and childhood. As such, modernism retains its defining contemporaneity, but also accommodates the persistence of its own memory: nostalgia's longing is embraced as an inherent and necessary part of the new. Hüppauf and Umbach argue that as long as modernity is "exclusively equated" with the universal, the rational, and the contemporary, "an important constituent of the modern psyche is repressed."[48] Framing the vernacular, then, not as modernism's other, but as its Freudian unconscious, reveals it as a deep though forceful current—an undertow—in the relentless torrent of modernity.

The vernacular's power as an engine of modern life derived not simply from its associations with memory and childhood, but more profoundly from their primary locus and primal attachment: the home. Hüppauf and Umbach explain that the vernacular's Latin root, *verna*, indicated a connection to the domestic sphere. To *vernacularize* was to make someone "feel at home."[49] They identify the German term *Heimat*, home or homeland, as an analogue to the vernacular: "*Heimisch* or *einheimisch* refers to a space defined in terms of a mental and emotional place of belonging, and by implication, exclusion of others. . . . In combination with knowledge or information, *heimlich* means secret, known only inside a closed circle and concealed to others. *Heimisch* in the sense of being at home, being familiar with, or dwelling at a place is the opposite of being alien, *fremd*."[50] In this context, then, the vernacular supplied the *heimisch* to modernity's foreign or alien *fremd*. For Hüppauf and Umbach, it is no coincidence that "the desire for *Heimat* emerges within the parameters of modernism."[51]

The vernacular held special relevance for design reform as it implied not only nostalgia for a preindustrial Heimat, or homeland, but also the material texture of domesticity, of the home, or *Heim*, itself. Umbach writes that the spirit of the vernacular "emanated from things pertaining to the home."[52] Rée imbues Riemerschmid's domestic interiors with vernacular nostalgia through the use of the idiomatic German verb *anheimeln*: to seem homelike or familiar, to convey a sense of intimacy. *Anheimeln* is an exclusively transitive verb: it requires a direct object upon which to act. An interior capable of *anheimeln*, was, like Riemerschmid's animated objects, an active agent—it *did* something *to* its occupant—so that its effect was really its affect: "the room *makes me* feel at home." As in the process or experience of *Einfühlung*, the subject-object relation is upset, inverted: the human subject becomes the object of the room's action, when the room, rather than its inhabitant, is the homemaker. Rée writes that the "poetic element" in Riemerschmid's interiors is the same quality that is eternally "alive in our [German] folksongs." And, "like an old folksong," Rée believes, Riemerschmid's intimate, domestic poetry—a quality that Lux later named *Hauspoesie*—"makes us feel at home [*heimelt es uns an*]."[53]

As in the popular folksong, Rée continues, "we feel [in Riemerschmid's interiors] that the old has renewed itself and is now forever young."[54] The metaphor of the folksong foregrounds a particularly compelling aspect of the vernacular, one that recommended it as a palliative for modernity's urban *Heimweh*, or homesickness: the possibility of sensory contact with a "lost" and longed for regional past, or cultural home.[55] Like hearing a folksong, touching a vernacular object delivered an immediate, physiological experience of that which might otherwise seem remote from modern cosmopolitan life. And yet for all its implications of authenticity, directness, and simplicity, the memory that the vernacular promised was a false one—not drawn from actual personal or historical experience but constructed in the present by modern culture. Though the timeless vernacular tune evoked the life of the rural peasant, it was not sung for that peasant but for the German *Bürgertum* (middle class). "Riemerschmid has achieved broadly significant middle-class [*bürgerliche*] art," Muthesius proclaimed. "This is the people's art [*Volkskunst*]."[56]

The visual and tactile qualities of materials understood as "vernacular" played an important role in evoking the cultural heritage of objects.[57] For Rée, the rough, gritty surface of the salt-glazed stoneware tankard possessed a masculine character stemming directly from its cultural heritage—a "manly honesty [*männlicher Biederkeit*]" and "beer-coziness [*Biergemütlichkeit*]" that stood in opposition to the refined femininity of a porcelain tea service.[58] For Muthesius, Riemerschmid's stoneware

beer service of 1903 (figure 2.19) derived its nature not simply from the texture of its material, but through the design of its forms: "The little baby tankards offer themselves in an orderly fashion to the loving embrace of the empty hand, while the large pitcher seems, in his [*seiner*] already half-tipping motion, to be just waiting for the moment when he will be next called upon to perform his accommodating service with drink."[59] Muthesius's personification of the beer service's bulbous tankards and pitcher, each perched jauntily on three stubby feet, resonates with his prior description of Riemerschmid's "old German art" as "naively loyal" and "a little bit bumbling," connecting the vernacular ideal not simply with the corporealization of form, but with busy forms—forms in *motion*. Here, the established image of vernacular objects as practical and useful beings is realized in animated forms that express what Rée calls "purpose [*Zweck*] in its broadest sense, not to be simply equated with practical utility."[60] For Muthesius, Riemerschmid's beer vessels had hardy, agrarian, *working* bodies—bodies designed to render utilitarian service. Their materials, however, spoke wordlessly of ease and joviality to those who used them.

Muthesius's description of the beer vessels as bustling bodies—active forms that seemed only momentarily suspended, midgesture, in the performance of their task—connects them to the fanciful illustrations in period journals (figure 2.20). The forward-leaning posture of Little Red Riding Hood entering, at lower right, a *Jugend* illustration from 1896 by Munich artist Adolf Hofer, for instance, bears an

FIGURE 2.19

Richard Riemerschmid, *Beer Service*, 1903.
Dekorative Kunst 7, no. 7 (April 1904): 273.

Rothkäppchen

Adolf Hofer (München).

FIGURE 2.20

Adolf Hofer, "Little Red Riding Hood," *Jugend*
1, no. 48 (1896).

uncanny resemblance to the "half-tipping" motion of Riemerschmid's stoneware pitcher. The girl's raised right arm, bent at the elbow, her hand to her mouth as she calls out for her grandmother (we see the wolf at the upper left; she does not), seems to prefigure the angle and gesture of the pitcher's handle. Hofer's fairy-tale image presented a romanticized vernacular: seemingly authentic, un(self)conscious, and childlike, but—like the electric moment before girl meets wolf—prickling with latency. Early in the nineteenth century, Johann Wolfgang von Goethe and other German Romantic writers had mined the peasant folktale—the *Volksmärchen*— for a cultured middle class in their artistic, psychologically charged *Kunstmärchen*, or literary fairy tales; Hofer's "Rothkäppchen" provides the end-of-century visual equivalent for *Jugend* readers. Like Hofer, Riemerschmid also appropriated familiar, vernacular imagery as the *Volksmärchen* from which to fashion his modern *Kunstmärchen*; but where Hofer's characters enlivened the pages of *Jugend*, Riemerschmid's actors animated real domestic life.

Muthesius's account of the beer service implies a magical narrative in which inanimate objects come to life; but Rée actually likens Riemerschmid's forms to "the figures of our fairy tales who are fully alive to us, even though we have never seen them in reality." In Riemerschmid's interiors, he continues, "there is nothing dead, rather, everything is alive."[61] Riemerschmid's *Sachlichkeit* dictated that an object express its inner purpose in tangible form, and the embodied perception inherent in Lipps's theory of *Einfühlung* gives us a sense of how "feeling into" this form might simultaneously animate or enliven it. But why such a form should recall the figures of fairy tales is a question that reaches beyond Lipps's aesthetic theories, beyond Streiter's and Lichtwark's fact-based conceptions of *Sachlichkeit*, and into the realm of fiction. In a sense, Riemerschmid's tankards and pitcher preempt *Einfühlung*: we need not feel into them and fill them out with our souls because they project *their* souls into us.

Inanimate forms that suggest movement are destabilizing—or even disruptive—by nature. In his 1906 article "On the Psychology of the Uncanny," German psychologist Ernst Jentsch defines the sense of the *uncanny* as a basic lack of orientation brought on by "psychical uncertainties," the most powerful of which is "doubt as to whether an apparently living being is animate, and conversely, doubt as to whether a lifeless object may in fact be animate—and more precisely, when this doubt makes itself felt obscurely in one's consciousness."[62] Jentsch notes that doubt about an object's animacy is innately human and corresponds, as Wölfflin also believed, to the possession of a living, human body. Jentsch writes of "the natural tendency of man to infer, in a kind of naïve analogy with his own animatedness, that things in the natural world are also animate . . . or animate in the same way."[63]

In his 1933 essay on the activity of mimesis, Walter Benjamin demonstrates the possibility of a mimetic transaction between the animate and the inanimate through the example of play: a child's mimicking of an inanimate object—a windmill or a train.[64] In Benjamin's relation, the dead object is given (in the child's fantasy) a vicarious life. But decades earlier, Jentsch interprets the child's animation of the inanimate not as the subject's assumption of the object's identity—or the projection of animate self into inanimate other—but rather as a simple assumption of all things being *like*: "animate in the same way." Jentsch observes that "small children speak in all seriousness to a chair, to their spoon, to an old rag . . . hitting out full of anger at lifeless things in order to punish them."[65] Swiss-German philosopher and psychiatrist Karl Jaspers, in his 1909 disquisition on the concept of *Heimweh* (homesickness), located the development of this complex emotional response, too, in childhood: the child is a kind of "spiritual plant," whose "roots penetrate his youthful world" and whose "tendrils twine themselves around it . . . growing up with and becoming one and the same with it . . . animating everything, even lifeless things, with his imaginings."[66]

The child's imaginative, dreamlike world, in which objects are invested with and enlivened by untempered emotion and irrational fantasy, informs the adult construction of the fairy-tale realm. But here the child's purer, more optimistic, naïve belief in the likeness of things may degenerate (in the hands of the grown-up storyteller) into the dubious territory of the uncanny. To illustrate, Jentsch invokes a generic fairy-tale narrative in which a traveler on a long journey sits down to rest on a tree trunk in an ancient forest. "To the horror of the traveler," Jentsch rehearses, "this trunk suddenly *began to move* and showed itself to be a giant snake . . . The mass that at first seemed completely lifeless suddenly reveals an inherent energy because of its *movement*."[67]

The unconscious naïveté of childhood play, the animation of the inanimate inherent in the act of mimesis, and the genre of the fairy tale as a kind of domesticated sublime in which things "come alive," much to the horror of the story's characters, are all manifestations of the vernacular as modernism's unconscious. Inherent in modernity's newness—its foreignness—was the nostalgia for tradition, the longing for the familiar: that "space of belonging," dwelling, or home implied in the Latin root, *verna*. Jentsch defined *unheimlich*—uncanny, or literally unhomely—in its most basic sense as "not quite 'at home' or 'at ease.'" "It is an old experience," he proposes, "that the traditional, the usual and the hereditary is dear and familiar to most people, and that they incorporate the new and the unusual with mistrust, unease, and even hostility (misoneism). This can be explained to a great extent by the difficulty of establishing quickly and completely the conceptual connections that the object strives to make with the previous ideational sphere of the individual—in other words, the intellectual mastery of the new thing."[68] The confusion—or "lack of orientation"—brought on by the appearance of a new "object" within the individual's "previous ideational sphere" defined for Jentsch the peculiar sensation of the uncanny, the unhomely. This liminal, transitional feeling of knowing and recalling a state or place called *home* and at the same time being distinctly, physiologically aware of not *being* "at home" is one way to understand a vernacular modernism. This arousal and anxiety was the electric energy of modern life at the turn of the twentieth century, the moment when Jentsch was writing and when Riemerschmid was designing. But the ambivalence of excitement and unrest inherent in the uncertainty of modernity could never have been produced by the self-consciously new or the amnesiac modern alone. Operating as a counterforce to what architectural historian Anthony Vidler has termed modernism's "urge to escape history," it was the pull of the vernacular—the memory of *Heim* necessary for the recognition of the unfamiliar and *new*—that generated both the uncertain *unheimlich* and the disorienting dynamic of modernism.[69]

Vidler's reading of Jentsch's *unheimlich*—an uncanny provoked by a "lack of orientation"—as "a sense of something new, foreign, and hostile invading an old, familiar, customary world" supports a modern-vernacular dialectic.[70] Sigmund Freud—also, like Jentsch, Riemerschmid's direct contemporary—began work on his own essay on the uncanny ("Das Unheimliche") in 1913.[71] While Freud's essay builds on Jentsch's earlier definition of the uncanny as the sense of doubt arising from "intellectual uncertainty," it delves deeper into the etymological relation of *unheimlich* and *heimlich* to argue for a dialectical swing from homely to unhomely, not unlike the volatile yet necessary connection of modernism and all that it appears to forget, reject, or suppress. While in Jentsch's construction we might position modernity as that which, in the context of the familiar or "homely," triggers intellectual uncertainty, in Freud's analysis, these roles are reversed. Although, as Vidler writes, Freud's uncanny is "situated firmly in the domestic and homely,"[72] Freud's *heimlich* is better correlated with the up-to-date, regular, functional, comprehensible world of modernity, and his *unheimlich* with the old-fashioned, idiosyncratic, fairy-tale world of the vernacular. For Jentsch, it is the shock of the new that provokes uncanny disorientation, whereas for Freud this same dislocation or discomfort is conjured up by the unbidden reappearing of the old. This emphasis on reappearing or "returning" suggests the unrest that might result from trying to accommodate in a single thought, place, or *object* both the modern and its memory. Within the scientifically rational, modernist sphere, the vernacular reappears as a ghost—the restless and relentless "return" of all that modernism has repressed.

For Freud, as for Jentsch, the sensation of the uncanny was bound up with the destabilizing mimetic play of animate and inanimate—specifically, with the familiar, vernacular genre of the fairy tale. Rather than the milder disconcertion that arises from an unresolved doubt, however, Freud's uncanny is an eerie sense of dread or terror that can occur as a result of transgression, "when the boundary between fantasy and reality is blurred, when we are faced with the reality of something that we have until now considered imaginary, when a symbol takes on the full function and significance of what it symbolizes."[73] While Freund acknowledges, as Jentsch did, this blurring of the real and the imaginary as the stuff of fairy tales, he also distinguishes the fictional from the real, physiological experience of the uncanny in life: "Many things that would be bound to seem uncanny if they happened in real life," including the "animation of the inanimate," can seem quite plausible in fiction, the free province of the imagination.[74] It is only in real life, if the "symbol takes on the full function and significance of what it symbolizes"—if familiar things that we know to be lifeless show signs of coming to life—that we experience the shock of the uncanny.

Which sphere, then, the real or the fairy tale, do Riemerschmid's beer mugs inhabit? Their weighty, solid bodies and gritty, salt-glazed skins place them squarely within the realm of real, everyday life. But the expectations that their animated forms elicit from us as they offer themselves to our empty hands or tip forward to quench our thirst complicate their position, relocating them within the landscape of our imagination. Their appropriation of the *Volksmärchen*, the authentic, vernacular fairy tale, suspends Riemerschmid's objects between the fictional (where their animated qualities are normalized by the imaginary narrative) and the factual, where their aspirations to animation might produce uncanny effects.

Riemerschmid's reassuring yet self-assured wooden wardrobe of 1902, whose broad stance convinced its owner that it would safeguard his treasured possessions, and whose mother-of-pearl "eyes" regarded all comers accordingly with vigilant suspicion, occupied a position in a series of complete interiors that Riemerschmid installed between 1898 and 1906 in Munich's Georgenstrasse at the urban villa of his friend Carl Thieme, the director of a Munich insurance company. Bold, complementary color schemes, the showcasing of natural materials, and references to handcraft all invoked vernacular ideals. But Riemerschmid's designs for the Thiemes' home were precisely harmonized, refined, and orchestrated for its wealthy, modern, middle-class occupants. At the modern Haus Thieme, the vernacular made a luxe return.

In the salon, where the Thiemes received their guests, the watchful wardrobe, stationed on the west wall (figure 2.21), stared across at a row of red-velvet side chairs assembled against the east wall, signaling allegiance to the wardrobe with scatterings of mother-of-pearl inlays and crowned with an irregular appliqué of gold fabric (figure 2.22). Viewed from the front, each chair offers these ornaments, set within the planes of its backrest and seat-frame, in benign, decorative flatness (figure 2.23). Yet the backs and profiles of three chairs drawn up to a table piled with books reveal the curious, agitated motion of their spindly legs, as well as the perked alertness of their pearl-studded ears (see figure 2.22). A gaggle of these eager, attentive chairs congregating in the Thiemes' salon might impose a bit too eagerly upon an unsuspecting visitor, each chair poised on its spidery legs as if ready to spring. The inanimate objects that occupied this Munich interior seem to have had designs on its animate inhabitants—on its *real* bodies. In the Thiemes' respectable, well-appointed, middle-class salon, distinctions between fact and fiction, animate and inanimate, subject and object, temporarily relaxed to create a permissive, hybrid space where emphatic things—often enchanting but sometimes threatening—could express their inherent, affective thingliness.

Like Riemerschmid's cozy domestic interiors, in which objects might delight and disconcert by turns, Freud's etymologically based exploration of *das Unheimliche*—the uncanny—is itself characterized by ambivalence. Vidler points out that Freud's understanding of *unheimlich* (literally, "unhomely") is dependent on its intimate yet ambivalent relationship with its antonym, *heimlich*, which can mean both "homely" and "secret."[75] Freud's consultation of nineteenth-century German dictionaries (the same ones available Riemerschmid)—especially the 1877 *Wörterbuch* compiled by the fairy-tale-collecting folklorist Brothers Grimm—prompted him to present the concept of the *unheimlich* as impossible without its antonym, *heimlich*: the homely or domestic—that which shelters, offers security and refuge from fear. The Grimms' definition of *heimlich* in particular, however, demonstrates its rapid slippage into its ostensible opposite, in Vidler's terms "from home, to private, to privy . . . to secret and thereby magic."[76] Freud's *heimlich* was

FIGURE 2.21

Richard Riemerschmid, *Salon of the
Thieme House* (west wall), Munich, 1903.
Architekturmuseum der TUM. © 2021 Artists
Rights Society (ARS), New York / VG Bild-
Kunst, Bonn.

FIGURE 2.22

Richard Riemerschmid, *Salon of the Thieme House* (east wall) *with Side Chairs*, Munich, 1903. Architekturmuseum der TUM. © 2021 Artists Rights Society (ARS), New York / VG Bild-Kunst, Bonn.

FIGURE 2.23

Richard Riemerschmid, *Side Chair for the Thieme House*, Munich, 1903. Quittenbaum. © 2021 Artists Rights Society (ARS), New York / VG Bild-Kunst, Bonn.

at once domestic and *private*: the *Heim* (home) was a refuge from the public world, and also a place where things could be kept secret, or hidden, from the public eye. The *unheimlich*, then, connoted a moment in which the familiar or homely became somehow defamiliarized, or when something that should have been kept secret— *repressed*—makes its way into the open.[77] Latent in the *heimlich*, the homely, lies the anxiety of exposure, while inherent in the *unheimlich* is the longing for home.

The "return" of a "repressed" past generated a certain kind of energy—an animating spark. One way to understand this is in the Grimms' terms of the fairy tale. Vidler ties the *heimlich-unheimlich* paradox to the nineteenth-century bourgeois interior, where, he argues, the awesome thrill of the sublime becomes "a domesticated version of absolute terror, to be experienced in the comfort of the home and relegated to the minor genre of the *Märchen* or fairy tale."[78] The nineteenth-century *Kunstmärchen* (literary fairy tale) provokes, for Vidler, the "quintessential bourgeois kind of fear . . . carefully bounded by the limits of real material security and the pleasure principle afforded by a terror that was, artistically at least, kept well under control . . . a sensation best experienced in the privacy of the interior." It was within the very privacy and seeming security of these fictional domestic interiors, Vidler remarks, that the familiar could "turn on its owners, suddenly become defamiliarized, derealized, as in a dream."[79]

The animating sparks that flew in Riemerschmid's interiors for the Munich House Thieme emanated not simply from form, but from forms *within* forms—or from how decorative motifs were situated, insulated, and regulated by the structures of the objects they ornamented. While forms like those of the Thiemes' magnolia-wood wardrobe initially appeared simple and rational in accordance with newly emerging modernist principles of design reform in Germany, upon closer examination, those same regular "framing" forms might be destabilized, unsettled, and *animated* by intrusions of the irregular, unruly past. Muthesius wrote that Riemerschmid's inlaid ornaments were always conservative in size, never dominating the wooden surfaces they embellished, and yet they always had something to *say*— "here, a funny story," while over there, they reported on "earnest, sturdy work."[80] In addition to the two grids of gently skewed mother-of-pearl chips that served as the wardrobe's eyes, little mother-of-pearl fragments, gradually decreasing in size as they ascended, bubbled up along either side of the wardrobe's frame, their irreverent luster emphasizing the gravity of the wardrobe's sober, bottom-heavy form. Paul Rée admired Riemerschmid's talent for repeating an ornamental motif while assiduously avoiding the deadening effect of "mathematical regularity." As Rée saw it, the "little coincidences" popping up throughout Riemerschmid's designs played an important role in creating a sense of movement within his otherwise sturdy, stable objects.[81] Ornament in the Thieme salon was unpredictable, moving like fairy dust from one object to another and from one material to the next, suggesting the lively imperfections one might expect to find in the craftsmanship of the vernacular artisan.

Where urban modernity might be equated with the homely in Freud's configuration of the uncanny, and the irregular, fanciful past of the regional vernacular might be likened to the mischievous magic of the unhomely, Riemerschmid's ornament is the vernacular's return. At the turn of the twentieth century, when modern design was beginning to strip away applied ornament to uncover a smooth, minimal, unornamented surface, the unexpected eruption of gleeful glints from solid, dutiful and dependable objects like the Thiemes' wardrobe embodies the fundamental ambivalence of the *heimlich-unheimlich* interchange. Just as the homely by its very nature both perpetuated and domesticated the unhomely, so modernism both recalled and reframed the unruly vernacular—its obstreperous unconscious.

Riemerschmid never truly abandoned the Symbolist bodies that had interrupted the serenity of his early paintings; instead, he brought these bodies home. The erotic occult of the *Cloud Ghosts* had to be reframed, domesticated for design reform; Riemerschmid accomplished this by infusing their primal energy into household objects that both accommodate the body and possess active bodies of their own. Riemerschmid brought back the vernacular and redeemed the unhomely for the modern home, rendering it once again *heimlich* in the original, dual sense: both homely and secret. Working at the intersectiom of *Einfühlung* and *Sachlichkeit*, he enfolded the object's soul within its functional form, giving it a secret life.

The vernacular's figuration as a kind of cultural childhood, as well as its conflation with the magical *Märchen*, binds it to the uncanny through the act of animation: the bringing to life of inanimate objects common to the child's mimetic play and to the fairy tale's eerie tingle. But the ambivalence of inanimate objects that seem perpetually poised on the brink of animation arises not from a childish impulse to "bring things to life," but from the unearthing of a deeply buried memory: the child*like* imagining of what things, in secret, *might be*. Both the resuscitation of the past and the returning of the repressed bring up ostensibly opposed emotions: in tandem with the desire to "bring back," to reanimate, arises the fear of the ungovernable other—the threat of its "acting out" in ways that we can neither predict nor control. Looking at Riemerschmid's beer vessels, chairs, and wardrobe, we do not truly believe they will begin to move (and neither did his contemporaries). And yet these objects remind us of a childhood thrill: the sensation that, just before we turned our heads, *things might have been moving.*

For Freud (and for Jentsch before him), this ambivalence or *doubt* about the status of things—living or dead—was troubling, unnerving, sometimes even terrifying. But theater historian John Bell has more recently argued that while at the dawn of the twentieth century, "their concept of the uncanny defines the power of objects as a problem," a century on, we might instead turn the uncanny to our advantage, making *use* of it as "a window into the nature of the material world and its agency."[82] Playing with inanimate objects—whether as fanciful child, imaginative designer, or curious consumer—generates a type or *condition* of thing that Bell calls the *performing object*. In this act of play, the categories of animate and inanimate are destabilized—but rather than attempting to cordon off this unstable terrain with the concept of the uncanny, Bell suggests that we take these transient, unsettled moments to "consider the possibility of the agency of things."[83] Like the vernacular, which reawakens modernism's dormant memory, the uncanny is, according to Bell, "a force that tugs back on the civilizing and rationalizing thrust of modern thinking."[84] With Bell, I reclaim the uncanny here as a force for good.

———

In 1901, Henry van de Velde wrote to Richard Riemerschmid, requesting photographs of his work for an upcoming article that van de Velde was about to publish in the Darmstadt journal *Deutsche Kunst und Dekoration*. To Riemerschmid he wrote, "I would rightfully like to give you the first place" in this overview of design reform in Germany.[85] Van de Velde, a leader in modern design reform whose conversion to applied art, and especially his celebrated *Gesamtkunstwerk* interiors at Dresden in 1897, had served as a catalyst in the development of Munich Jugendstil hails Riemerschmid as the exemplar of Germany's achievements in its modern *Kunstgewerbebewegung*, or Art-Industry Movement. Riemerschmid had indeed responded to van de Velde's call to "reveal the essential organisms" of objects. But where van de Velde's theory of line contained and fixed his objects within prescribed and perfected formal boundaries, Riemerschmid's deep affection for the human body and empathic insight into the idiosyncrasies of bodily experience opened his designs, from their origins in rationality, to the possibilities—and uncertainties—of irrationality and imagination. Where van de Velde envisioned the room as a "skeleton" waiting to be clinically populated with aesthetically stylized "organs," Riemerschmid saw a fertile interior landscape, corrupted—but at the same time enlivened—by living things.[86] While van de Velde was stylizing the structures of things, Riemerschmid was interpreting their personalities, which, like the personalities of loved ones, may be punctuated with quirks and imperfections that lend them character and endear them to the lover.

Riemerschmid's attachment to the forms of the body as a figural painter, his perception of the body's functional/expressive duality, his adaptation of the regional vernacular for a middle-class modernity, and his sensitivity to materials and production processes all contributed to his empathic *Sachlichkeit*. But it is his embrace of ambivalence, his sanctioning of irrationality within the rational structures of utility, that truly animates his designs, transforming them into "performing objects": destabilizing *things* that change, from one moment to the next, in response to those who live with and use them. It is their unpredictability that endows Riemerschmid's objects with the basic human capacity of agency, making them seem to us as though they might possess, in addition to their own bodies, *heimlich* thoughts and lives of their own.

Jentsch and Freud understood the uncanny as an elusive kind of *experience*—something that, out of nowhere and beyond our control, just *happens* to us. But if, as Bell has it, the uncanny can be a "window into the nature of the material world and its agency," perhaps we can understand it more productively now as a way of *seeing*. Perhaps the uncanny is a type of *double vision*—the term that puppetry scholar Steve Tillis has used to identify the cognitive balancing act that occurs when an audience encounters a manipulated puppet simultaneously as "perceived object" and "imagined life."[87] This is an overlooked kind of looking, a rare penetration: as when a single photograph captures both the trees reflected on the surface of a woodland pool and the aquatic life inhabiting its depths.

The uncanny, then, is a double-vision lens: through it we can, all at once, apprehend the inanimate object and perceive the living thing. Bill Brown has suggested that "as they circulate through our lives, we look *through* objects (to see what they disclose about history, society, nature, or culture—above all what they disclose about *us*), but we only catch a glimpse of things."[88] The symbolic *Sachlichkeit* of Riemerschmid's objects hinted at "a world beyond," or perhaps more accurately *beneath*, the surface of "appearances." His admission, through the animated forms and exuberant decoration of his objects, that within modernism's rational, orderly framework irrationality and disorder might at any moment return and make mischief, was his way of welcoming home those forces conventionally considered unhomely to progressive, no-nonsense modern life. These animating forces, long regarded as antagonistic to modernism, are only beginning to be understood as its constituents—its generators. The more we accept the ambivalence of modernity—the more we relax into double vision—the more uncanny glimpses of modern things we will catch.

3

CLOSE AS SKIN

I wrap myself within its contours as in a garment.
—Robert Vischer[1]

On the evening of April 20, 1901, Munich's new theater, with interiors by the local painter and designer Richard Riemerschmid, opened to the public. The radically intimate scale and startling décor of the Münchner Schauspielhaus immediately earned it the title of Germany's "first modern theater," and its progression of interiors, intricately coordinated from street door to stage, has more recently been called the "jewel of Jugendstil" (figure 3.1).[2] Riemerschmid's friends and colleagues showered his first major architectural commission with praise. Munich architect Carl Hocheder averred in a letter to Riemerschmid that the young painter had achieved something not only new but also unique with the design of this public interior: "As a painter you certainly have an advantage over professional architects: you are much less prejudiced and freer in your relationship to things, to the design of interiors. Through your design process, you experience much more than the architect, for whom so much is determined by his professional training, and this pedantic approach never speaks so penetratingly and in such a vivid and haunting way to the viewer as that which is experienced, that which is lived through."[3]

The painter and designer Hans Berlepsch-Valendas, in attendance on opening night, wrote to Riemerschmid the very next day of his personal impression: "Everything that I saw yesterday in the brilliance of illumination and decoration. . . . A space like that, filled with lights and with dressed-up ladies, many of whose

decolletés should, perhaps, have been adjusted in the interest of good taste, always strikes one [*wirkt*] as a complete thing, as a picture, as a decorative apparition."[4] Universally admired as part of this "complete picture" were the guests of honor: Riemerschmid and his wife, the celebrated actress Ida Riemerschmid (figure 3.2), who wore a strawberry-colored evening gown designed for the occasion by her husband (figure 3.3).

These two firsthand accounts of the Schauspielhaus interiors are neither objective reviews nor critical analyses: they are subjective accounts of personal experience. Hocheder's remarks emphasize the striking, penetrating qualities of

FIGURE 3.1

Richard Riemerschmid, *Münchner Schauspielhaus* (auditorium), completed 1901. Photograph courtesy of Atelier Achatz Architekten & Andreas Huber Fotografie. © 2021 Artists Rights Society (ARS), New York / VG Bild-Kunst, Bonn.

Riemerschmid's artistically conceived interiors, and Berlepsch-Valendas confides how the Schauspielhaus affects him—its "impression" (*Eindruck*) and "effect" (*Wirkung*) *on* him. These descriptions of the theater's interiors—not the performance—in specific, experiential terms, point to an empathic, bodily understanding not simply of form but, more expansively, of *space*.

By the final decade of the nineteenth century, bodily experience had become the focus of inquiry for the developing study of psychophysical aesthetics. In his 1886 "Prolegomena to a Psychology of Architecture," Heinrich Wölfflin had set forth his theory that all aesthetic questions were negotiated through the human body, whose forms and functions served as the common denominator in all human evaluation of both the natural and built environment.[5] Theodor Lipps had foregrounded the spatial experience of the body in his *Aesthetics of Space and Geometric-Optical Illusions* of 1893 and was, around 1900, developing and reformulating Robert Vischer's 1873 theory of empathy (*Einfühlung*) in relation to art and architecture.[6] Vischer's conceptualization of *Einfühlung* described the act of viewing as a psychophysical

FIGURE 3.2

Actress Ida Riemerschmid, age 22. Munich, 1895. Germanisches Nationalmuseum, Deutsches Kunstarchiv und Historisches Archiv, Nuremberg.

process during which the subject "felt into" the object, or projected his or her ego—or soul—within its formal bounds, thus filling up or filling out its material vessel with spiritual or psychological content.[7] In addition to its application to a variety of types of public spectatorship toward the end of the nineteenth century, *Einfühlung* also implied a fundamental, physical intimacy that was, in German terms, *hautnah*—"as close as skin."[8] *Einfühlung* allowed external phenomena encountered in everyday experience to become personalized as analogies for one's own bodily structure. In the experience of viewing a specific object, Vischer believed, "I wrap myself within its contours as in a garment."[9]

This chapter turns to Riemerschmid's experimentation with the design of real garments; the connection between his clothing of bodies and his cladding of interiors; and the possibility of empathic relations among bodies, forms, and two spaces—one public, one private—that he designed just after the turn of the twentieth century. Parallels between building and clothing in architectural theory date back at least to the mid-nineteenth-century writings of German architect Gottfried Semper, and the notion of a dialogue between dwelling reforms and the reform of clothing during the Wilhelmine period is well established.[10] Art historian August Schmarsow writes in his 1893 "Essence of Architectural Creation" of a sense of space which we "erect around ourselves and consider more necessary than the form of our own body," made up of "residues of sensory experience to which the muscular sensations of the body, the sensitivity of our skin, and the structure of our body all contribute."[11] Schmarsow's construct offers the spatial or architectural equivalent to Vischer's earlier, sartorial picturing of *Einfühlung*: in both cases, the embodied self is *wrapped up in* and so becomes *one with* its surroundings. Riemerschmid's specific enactment of this relationship through his designs, both for reformed dresses and reformed interiors, reveals the intimate, yet dynamic nature of the exchange—or *absorption*—that was possible between the body and its clothing,

FIGURE 3.3

Richard Riemerschmid, *Dress Designed for Ida Riemerschmid for Münchner Schauspielhaus Debut, 1901.* Fabricated at Salon Rosipal, Munich. Münchner Stadtmuseum, Sammlung Mode/Textilien/Kostümbibliothek. © 2021 Artists Rights Society (ARS), New York / VG Bild-Kunst, Bonn.

between the clothed body and the design of its environment, and, finally, between inhabiting subjects and their "animated" objects. Riemerschmid's reformed, modern dresses and interiors that, through the language of their forms, pleaded to be invested with bodies propose a resensualized, close-as-skin account of both dress and interior architecture at the beginning of the twentieth century.

THE DOMESTIC INTERIOR AND MODERN *BEKLEIDUNG*

In his seminal *Style-Architecture and Building Art* of 1902, Hermann Muthesius wrote that the lightness and cleanliness desirable in the modern household should follow "the same tendency as our clothing, that enveloping dwelling that is closest to us."[12] In an April 1904 article entitled "Culture and Art," Muthesius inverted this same idea: "The dwelling is surely just that more expansive dress that enfolds us."[13] The easy fluidity in Muthesius's image of the familiar, enfolding dwelling that contracts into a comfortable garment and, conversely, in the garment that expands generously to become a dwelling, suggests a permissive sense of flux in which modern dwellings and dresses alike invited their occupants to live and breathe. Muthesius's vision of garment-like domestic space implied the intimate, bodily contact of fabric on skin.

Exactly contemporaneous to "Culture and Art," Muthesius published a comprehensive, retrospective article on Riemerschmid. In "The Art of Richard Riemerschmid," he touted the artist's modern interiors as livable and comfortable, concluding that "in his rooms Riemerschmid has arrived at something comparable to that which we are now seeing in our contemporary outfits, in which we also no longer want to parade around with art."[14] Muthesius's use of the term *art* is deliberately cynical. He elaborates on his contempt for artificial "artiness" in the modern interior in "Culture and Art": "Everybody who wants to redecorate these days has to hire an 'artist.' So [interior decoration] becomes an 'art for art's sake' like painting. Just as one would acquire a painting or a sculpture, one acquires finished rooms. These interior designs are not the familiar, experienced arrangements of our personal surroundings, which they should be, but foreign invaders, to whom the occupant must conform, when the interiors should really conform themselves to him."[15] Although much German design reform was, notwithstanding Muthesius's critique, instigated and accomplished by professional artists, and though Riemerschmid had himself been trained as a painter, Muthesius credited him with placing the wishes of the homeowner above his own and so absolved him from the idiosyncrasies of self-absorbed "art for art's sake."

Four years earlier in 1900, the Viennese architect and polemicist Adolf Loos had lambasted the artist-designed interior with his notorious satire, "About a Poor Little Rich Man." This short essay told the story of a wealthy man who employs a famous architect to design the interiors of his luxurious home. While the rich man is initially overjoyed at the beauty of his private *Gesamtkunstwerk*, in which even the tiniest detail exudes "Art," he quickly finds that his museum-dwelling aestheticizes, and thus restricts, his day-to-day activities to the point that normal domestic life becomes impossible. His every action, from the placement of his personal objects to which clothes he wears, is prescribed by uncompromising Art. Art—quite literally—absorbs him. The story's punchline arrives when the rich man, desperate for some comfort in his museum-life hell, slides his feet into the embroidered slippers that the architect has designed expressly for him. The architect, on entering the house, immediately challenges him on his choice of footwear: "What are those slippers you have on?!" The rich man innocently replies, "But Herr Architekt, don't you remember? You designed these slippers yourself!" "Certainly," the architect thunders back, "but for the *bedroom*! With those two *impossible* specks of color, you've ruptured the entire mood of the room!"[16]

While Loos's tone is playful, his closing comment on the meaning of "completeness" for the poor little rich man living in the *Gesamtkunstwerk* interior is chilling: "He was shut out of all future life and longing, all striving and struggle. The time had come, he felt, to learn how to go around with his own corpse. Yes, he's finished. He is complete."[17] It was this rigid, overdetermined vision of the artistic interior, the *Gesamtkunstwerk* dwelling that absorbed and terminally "completed" its occupant, against which Muthesius railed. Loos's parody of the *Gesamtkunstwerk* interior resonates with Juliet Koss's discussion of *Einfühlung* as a kind of absorption, or an interchange between viewer and object in which the viewer animates the inanimate object with the contents of his soul, but finds his own identity destabilized—shaken—as a result.[18] The poor little rich man's designer slippers are an ostensibly trivial metaphor for the more unsettling effects of *Einfühlung*. Were he to slip into his slippers in the bedroom for which they were designed, the rich man would literally animate the architect's interior scheme, but at a price: he would lose something of himself; his agency, his identity, would be masked by design. By wearing the slippers out of context, however, the poor little rich man breaks the spell of the empathic interior, dispelling the mesmeric hold of dwelling upon dweller.

But was it possible to *settle into* an empathic interior rather than being *unsettled by* it? Could feeling into one's material surroundings produce a sensation not of estrangement, but of coming home? For Muthesius, modern dress was a relationship: while clothing *impressed* itself upon its wearer, the wearer simultaneously pushed back, making an individual, corporeal impression on (or *in*) the garment. This seemed the right metaphor for the organic, intimate, and constantly changing bodily experience of the domestic interior.

For reformers like Muthesius and Riemerschmid, everyday lived experience was the primary vehicle for social and cultural change. The concept of the *Gesamtkunstwerk* seemed to have originated far from such mundane concerns, however, with Richard Wagner's dramatic, elaborately staged nineteenth-century operas, in which music, poetry, and movement were understood to unite in a "synthesis of the arts," or complete artwork. But in the middle-class, domestic *Gesamtkunstwerk*, the comfortably wealthy, cultured citizen could wear his slippers when and where he liked. Instead of a seamless, fully completed work of art, the *Gesamtkunstwerk* that Muthesius described and Riemerschmid orchestrated remained open, perpetually unfinished, incomplete by design: an artwork that coaxed the occupant to engage with it, feel into it—actively *put it on*.

Color played a primary and pivotal role in dressing both bodies and interiors. Indeed, color was essential for Riemerschmid: his pared-down, sparsely ornamented designs relied on bold, vibrant color for much of their expressive effect. *Bekleidung*, Gottfried Semper's architectural theory of "dressing," which he began to develop in the late 1840s, hinged on his hypothesis that Greek architecture had originally been painted in rich, polychrome designs. Mallgrave has argued that Semper's vision of art can be encapsulated in the "Dionysian frenzy" of Greek drama, which Semper understood to be expressed symbolically in the classical Greek temple's brightly painted facade. This festive, theatrical, multimedia conception of the function of art was one that Semper shared with Wagner during the 1840s, when both men were in the process of developing their notions of the synthetic *Gesamtkunstwerk*.[19]

Semper's *Bekleidung* principle does not originate with color as such, however, but with textiles as its material bearers. Mallgrave is careful to emphasize the literal connection between Semper's *Bekleidung* and the clothing or dressing of the body in contrast to the more frequently employed and more strictly architectural "cladding": "The root word of the concept is the German verb *kleiden*, which means 'to clothe, to dress,' and this sartorial association is critically important to Semper's use of the term, which he introduces as a textile concept."[20] In brief, Semper believed that aboriginal societies had defined their dwelling spaces through the hanging of mats and, later, more complex woven textiles, first used alone but soon applied as coverings for more durable, structural walls. These textile hangings underwent a transformation when Mesopotamian societies transposed them into nontextile dressings or claddings for walls, such as mosaic and alabaster. Semper felt that in Greek architecture the *Bekleidung* attained its "artistic culmination" as a thin veil of paint covering entire architectural facades. At this point, he argued, form became entirely dematerialized: the sole purpose of the colored paint was to evoke or symbolize the functions and associations that prior, material dressings had previously performed.[21]

Semper envisioned color as "the subtlest, most bodiless coating. It was the most perfect means to do away with reality, for while it dressed the material, it was itself immaterial."[22] But as Mallgrave and Eleftherios Ikonomou point out, while Semper's bright *Bekleidung* dematerialized corporeal form, it simultaneously filled this physical void with spiritual significance—by animating form with symbolic (or human) content.[23] Color could operate empathically, investing objects with sentient souls. At the turn of the twentieth century, color became the key term in Riemerschmid's articulation of the complex act of dressing both bodies and spaces. It was, in a sense, the most versatile and plastic of all materials: it could be applied and manipulated at the artist's whim. But, as Semper understood, color was also a dangerous dematerializer: it had the seemingly supernatural power to collapse, absorb, and consume the corporeal. Whether Riemerschmid was envisioning the literal clothing of his wife's body within a dress of his own design, calculating the effect of her clothed body within the painted interiors of his Schauspielhaus, or carefully orchestrating the symphony of tones in carpets, upholstery, and wall paintings that were to harmonize a domestic interior, he was exploring the liminal space between material presence and dematerializing effects—between flesh and spirit—through color.

REFORMKLEIDUNG AND THE STYLE/FASHION PROBLEM

In 1896, just as Riemerschmid's willowy young nude was entering the spring landscape on his first *Jugend* cover (figure 1.3), the health, structure, and clothing of real female bodies had become a topic of both medical and aesthetic debate. In September of that year, the concept of *Reformkleidung*, clothing that was literally re-formed to provide alternatives to conventional or fashionable forms of dress, was brought to the attention of the German public with the founding in Berlin of Germany's first official dress reform organization, the Association for the Improvement of Women's Clothing (Der Allgemeine Verein für Verbesserung der Frauenkleidung).[24] From the mid-1890s through the First World War, at the same time that the *Körperkultur* (body culture) of the *Lebensreformer* was emphasizing the cultivation of a healthy body in connection with the development of a healthy mind and spirit, this German middle-class women's movement—inspired by earlier dress-reform movements in the United States (beginning in the 1850s) and Britain (from the 1880s)—called specifically for rationalization in German women's clothing.[25] Through numerous lectures and exhibitions, German dress reform received enough publicity between 1896 and 1918 to become a favorite target of satire and caricature. Though Germany embarked rather later on the project of dress reform in comparison to America and Britain, it was German women who embraced the reform dress most whole-heartedly: one result of this was the opening of an entire *Reformkleid* (reform dress) department at Berlin's gargantuan department store, Wertheim, in 1903.[26]

The motto of the Association for the Improvement of Women's Clothing, "Healthy—Beautiful—Practical," points to the wide range of issues at stake in Germany's dress reform debates. For its earliest proponents in Germany, as well as in other nations, the reform of women's clothing was primarily a medical and hygienic concern, represented most notoriously by the corset debate. Medical professionals, along with members of the women's movement, attacked the corset—the hidden yet defining feature of women's dress that facilitated the fashionable hourglass silhouette—arguing, with the aid of photographs and medical drawings, that corsets deformed the female body, fostered and even caused a number of illnesses and disorders, and interfered with pregnancy and childbirth.[27] Male and female dress reformers alike considered the restriction of body movement in dresses that bound the arms and/or waist, or weighed the body down with excessive amounts of heavy drapery, impractical for the demands placed on modern women. Long skirts with trains that trailed in the street were deemed unhygienic as they brought dirt and bacteria (newly discovered) into contact with a woman's body, as well as ushering these unwelcome guests into her home.[28]

The central criterion of the association's motto, beauty, was the most complex and subjective of the three. Among the organization's practical goals of "simplifying undergarments, freeing the hips, maintaining the natural forms of the body," and "shortening the street dress," the directive that the outer portion of the garment should be "freely constructed" but "according to fashion" highlighted the enduring significance of aesthetics—and the enduring association of fashion and beauty—in women's clothing.[29] The very mention of "fashion" in the association's program points to the problem of fashion as a hotly contested topic in late nineteenth-century discourses of social and cultural reform. As historian Patricia Ober has noted, the *Reformkleid*, in presenting an alternative to more conventional clothing for women, constituted an explicit critique of fashionable dress and an implicit challenge—at least in part—to the idea of fashion itself.[30]

While the rapidly changing styles of women's dresses epitomized the concept of fashion, cultural reformers of the Wilhelmine period, as design theorist Frederic J. Schwartz has discussed, understood fashion not simply as a question of clothing styles but as a "general social phenomenon of modernity," characterized by the "chaotic behavior of consumer commodities on the mass market."[31] Anxieties about the effects of fashion on modern society and culture had been articulated as early as 1879, when Robert Vischer's father, Friedrich Theodor Vischer, published his *Mode und Zynismus* (Fashion and Cynicism). In 1895, just a year before the Association for the Improvement of Women's Clothing was founded, sociologist Georg Simmel published the first version of his essay "The Theory of Fashion in the Public Realm," in which he argued that the intricately constructed system of fashion in female dress allowed women to signal their allegiance to a certain social group while simultaneously differentiating themselves from it as individuals. Although the German dress reform discourse eagerly assimilated Simmel's theories, much of the nuance of his argument was sacrificed to the primary idea that women were "slaves to fashion" who must be liberated.[32]

The simpler theory of fashion slavery was useful, however, in the development of a turn-of-the-century ideological opposition between the concepts of *fashion* and *style*. Those—both female and male—who were slaves to fashion were also slaves to capitalism. Economist Werner Sombart used women's fashion as the primary example of the capitalist alienation of consumer from producer, writing in 1902: "Fashion is the favorite child of capitalism: it has emerged out of the innermost essence of capitalism and reveals its nature like few other phenomena of the social life of our age." For Sombart, perhaps most characteristic and also most threatening in this regard was "the frantic speed of changes in Fashion."[33] To counter the adverse effects of tumultuous, transitory fashion, German cultural reformers theorized and promoted the idea of an epochal style: an accurate and *permanent* aesthetic expression of their modern age. Sociologist and dress reform advocate

Heinrich Pudor summarized this period understanding of the dynamic between fashion and style in a brief statement: "Fashion [*Mode*] is the transient, style [*Stil*] is the enduring."[34]

Schwartz has shown that in their binary relation, *fashion* and *style* mirrored the discursive pair, specific to German cultural theory, of *Zivilisation* and *Kultur*, inexactly translated in English as "civilization" and "culture." While the English concept of *culture* can also be understood as inherent in the English concept of *civilization*, the historically accrued meanings of *Zivilisation* and *Kultur* are diametrically opposed in German scholarly usage. Style, like *Kultur*, connoted that which was innate, enduring, and noble in the German self-identity (embodied by the cultured middle class, or *Bildungsbürgertum*); but *Zivilisation* signified the external imposition of transitory novelties and foreign frivolities—the tyranny of fashion.[35] The project of determining a style for the age, which began in the late 1890s with the Art-Industry Movement (*Kunstgewerbebewegung*) and which the German Werkbund pursued systematically after its founding in 1907, was thus not simply a scheme to escape the arbitrary pressures of the market; it was more fundamentally a rejection of the foreign (predominantly French) fashions that had "enslaved" Germans throughout the nineteenth century and a desire to reinstate, through modern forms, that which was indigenously, inherently German.

The question for design reformers—and for dress reformers in particular—became, then, how one might design products that would appeal to the consumer without resorting to the seduction of fashion. Straightforward *Sachlichkeit*, however, promised a solution to this dilemma: its rootedness in time and place offered an enduring style based on a familiar, timeless German vernacular that transcended transitory novelty and foreign frivolity; and in the special case of women's dress, *Sachlichkeit* refocused design on the most fundamental matter at hand—the female body. For Riemerschmid, the concrete, corporeal relationship between the structure and materials of clothing and the structure and forms of the body itself expressed a new facet of thingliness, in which two material things—the dress and the body—together articulated a definitive, expressive relationship.

THE ARTISTIC ELEVATION OF WOMEN'S DRESS

In the winter of 1900, Friedrich Deneken, founder and director of the Kaiser Wilhelm Museum in Krefeld, met with Riemerschmid at the Paris Exposition Universelle and invited him to participate in an exhibition of modern, artist-designed women's dresses slated to open at Krefeld in August of the same year.[36] Deneken had conceived the project jointly with Hamburg painter Alfred Mohrbutter and with the Belgian Henry van de Velde, whose designs had become increasingly popular in Germany since the exhibition of his *Gesamtkunstwerk* salon at Dresden in 1897.[37] For van de Velde, who had been designing dresses for his wife since 1895 as part of his total vision for the couple's domestic life together in their private house outside of Brussels, the Krefeld exhibition presented a public opportunity to elevate the practical German *Reformkleid*—which the general public in 1900 saw either as an inelegant, formless sack or as a strictly therapeutic garment—to an object of beauty.

Munich designer Bruno Paul ridiculed this stereotypical *Reformkleid* by juxtaposing a thin, androgynous woman in an austere reform dress with a buxom woman, squeezed and deformed by the tight, high collar and narrow wasp waist of a flounced and frilled "fashionable" dress, in his "Quarrel of the Fashions" caricature for the satirical journal *Simplicissimus* (figure 3.4). In this ironic rendition of the *Reformkleidung* debate, dress pits the sex appeal of fashion against the very capacity for sexual reproduction. At Krefeld, van de Velde hoped to bypass this binary cliché altogether by proposing sophisticated alternatives to both the clinical reform dress, which he found "puritanical, rather dry, plain, and off-putting," and the alluring Paris toilette.[38] In van de Velde's conception, the *artistic* reform dress, neither medical accessory nor fashion commodity, was an artwork to be integrated—via a woman's body—into the grander project of the domestic *Gesamtkunstwerk*.[39]

For Deneken, the Krefeld exhibition carried direct implications not only for domestic *Kultur* but also for Krefeld's local (and Germany's national) economy. Before founding the Kaiser Wilhelm Museum in 1897, Deneken had served as assistant to Justus Brinckmann, the forward-thinking director of the Hamburg Museum of Art and Trade (Hamburg Museum für Kunst und Gewerbe). Brinckmann collected groundbreaking applied arts objects for the Hamburg museum, whose teaching collections he opened to local craftspeople and designers for study and to promote awareness of new ideas in design. Deneken founded his Krefeld museum on similar principles, conceiving it as a vehicle for the dissemination of artistic reforms within his own community, throughout Germany, and, he hoped, beyond. But he also had a special project in mind for Krefeld—one designed to link art with industry. Krefeld was Germany's textile capital: silk weaving had been its primary industry since the seventeenth century. By 1900, however, the native industry was suffering at the hands of Paris fashion. Deneken targeted what he called the city's major "taste

Streit der Moden

(Zeichnung von Bruno Paul)

„Das Reformkleid ist vor allem hygienisch und erhält den Körper tüchtig für die Mutterpflichten." — „So lange Sie den Fetzen anhaben, werden Sie nie in diese Verlegenheit kommen."

industry" with "taste education" programs—in particular, with strategies for the "artistic influencing" of the Krefeld silk industry.[40]

Deneken concerned himself not merely with the design of artistic reform dresses, but equally with the manufacture of modern silks from patterns designed by German artists, and with the fabrication of garments by progressive workshops and dress salons in Krefeld.[41] The Krefeld exhibition of 1900 was one of the earliest German attempts at collaboration between modern German artists and a preestablished German industry.[42] Deneken planned his straightforwardly titled Special Exhibition of Modern Ladies' Dresses Executed from Artists' Designs in conjunction with the annual meeting of the Union of German Tailors and Dressmakers and its Great Comprehensive Exhibition of Clothing Types, slated to take place in Krefeld in August 1900. Deneken's special exhibition would be the first show of artistically designed reform dresses in Germany, and the museum director would take every opportunity to make its impact as profound and wide-reaching as possible, from its display in a public, community-oriented space to the publication of its stylish, richly illustrated catalog. By exhibiting the artist-designed dresses beside the other clothing displays at Krefeld's city hall, amid the greater context of the scheduled *Schneidertag* (tailors and dressmakers' convention), Deneken sought both to link the new "art dresses" with the more established branches of the German industry in the public eye, and also to set the innovative, artistic dresses apart from more standard production. This dual strategy was designed to reassure more traditional, conservative clients while at the same time piquing the curiosity of well-to-do, sophisticated, trendsetting ladies. Deneken strove to demonstrate that Krefeld's indigenous industry could, entirely independent of Paris fashion, produce dress designs elegant and modern enough to tempt German women back from Paris to Krefeld. In a 1904 essay, "Artistic Dress and Personalized Dress," Deneken argued for the national significance of defining a specifically German style of modern dress:

FIGURE 3.4

"The Reform Dress is hygienic, and conditions the body for the demands of motherhood." "As long as you're wearing those rags, you'll never find yourself in that predicament!" Bruno Paul, "Streit der Moden" ("Quarrel of the Fashions"), *Simplicissimus* 9, no. 36 (1904): 351.

"Is not the French influence on women's dress in our country a humiliating sign of intellectual poverty? While we strive to eradicate Gallicisms from the German language and to reinforce a feeling of national pride in all areas, the very idea of imitating Parisian women makes our wives feel superior. They get themselves up in all that shoddy French stuff, in trimmings and spangles: in other words, in innumerable items that are as tasteless as they are anti-German! Moreover, the impact of Parisian fashions is an anachronism. It is short-sighted and completely contradicts our own cultural evolution."[43] For Deneken, the urgency of dress reform as a national issue derived from its origin and daily impact as a personal, domestic, aesthetic, and economic issue. While German women were increasingly instructed in the serious impact that their choice of clothing could have on the appearance and health of their own bodies, German men were encouraged to see the *Reformkleid* as having a direct impact on *them*—an impact as personal and intimate as marriage itself.

The theme of intimacy recurred in each aspect of Deneken's approach to the Krefeld project, from his relationship with the designers to the process of fabrication to the fact that each exhibition dress was designed for a specific client, who worked closely with the designer and dressmakers. The antidote to the alienating effect of Paris fashion on German women, Deneken believed, could be found at home. In addition to van de Velde, Mohrbutter, and Riemerschmid, Deneken invited a group of promising young German artists—Margarethe von Brauchitsch (a colleague of Riemerschmid's at Munich's Vereinigte Werkstätten and head of the Women's Atelier for Ornamental Design there), Curt Hermann, F. A. Krüger, Bernard Pankok, Hugo van de Woude, and Krefeld textile designer Paul Schulze. These designers were, as he put it, "trying to integrate art and life" and were "already involved with women's dress." "As well as designing furniture for their own homes," Deneken wrote, "they wanted to create garments for their young wives."[44] (Apparently Deneken had forgotten about von Brauchitsch for the moment.)

As the photographs published in the Krefeld catalog attest, both van de Velde and Mohrbutter designed numerous dresses for their respective wives. While Frau Mohrbutter models her husband's dresses in the exhibition catalog, Frau van de Velde was not only visible but also vocal in publicizing the exhibition, writing both the introductory essay for the catalog and an illustrated review of the show for *Dekorative Kunst* in October 1900.[45] Together, Henry and Maria Sèthe van de Velde embraced and advanced Deneken's vision of a dress reform developed organically from, and in harmony with, the modern domestic interior. Deneken's selection of

German applied artists, with Henry van de Velde as their spokesperson, expressed the former's recognition that although health concerns had initially launched the dress reform movement in Germany, it was the aesthetic impact of the dress that would not only link it to other branches of applied arts reform but also *sell it* to German women. If the new dresses failed to attract the attention of modern German women, Deneken knew, both the dress reform movement and the revitalization of his Krefeld industry would fail with them.

In his address at the opening of the Krefeld exhibition on August 4, 1900, entitled "The Artistic Elevation of Women's Garb" ("Die künstlerische Hebung der Frauentracht"), van de Velde named women's dress the final project of applied arts reforms, prophesying that dresses would soon appear in art exhibitions, just as works of design had begun to do.[46] He argued that "as with the cupboard or the lamp . . . one also has to design dress according to general tectonic principles." Each object—the cupboard, the lamp, and now the dress—was integrated into the larger aesthetic whole of the *Gesamtkunstwerk* interior through its design. Elegantly choreographed photographs, published in the Krefeld catalog, modeled van de Velde's ideal of formal harmony between women in artistically designed dresses and their artistically designed surroundings.

Van de Velde's critique of French fashions, which he believed seduced women with the artifice of their hidden, structuring undergarments and the ostensibly seamless—and therefore "dishonest"—appearance of the gown itself, lay at the heart of his tectonically principled approach to dress construction.[47] Advancing an agenda of revealed construction, van de Velde identified the seam as the dress's primary structural element and principle in his 1902 retrospective article on "The New Art-Principle in Modern Women's Clothing." His new art principle, governing both dress and utilitarian objects, comprised in reality two core principles—both in copious evidence at the Krefeld exhibition of 1900, which would characterize the development of the artistic reform dress in Germany.

The first principle, van de Velde wrote, "consists of conceiving an object in relation to its intended function. It requires that we abandon anything that conceals this aim and that we bring out whatever can help make it visible."[48] Though a dress's purpose and construction varied according to the precise function required, the primary purpose of all clothing was to protect the body while allowing for movement; the dress's seam (as a structural marker) enabled both of these necessities. "What I expect from visible seams," van de Velde stated at Krefeld in 1900, "is honesty in bringing out how a dress was made."[49] Van de Velde aestheticizes the structure of his uncorseted velvet evening gown by emphasizing its seams through the strategic placement of decorative appliqués at the collar, shoulder, back, cuffs, and hem (figure 3.5). A closer inspection of van de Velde's evening gown reveals that the abstract, linear motifs of his ornamental appliqués are not simply "honest" indicators of the construction process; their abstracted forms refer systematically, rationally—but also symbolically—to the structure of the body *beneath* the dress: to the collarbone, spine, shoulder blades, and wrists. In the case of this dress, abstraction's inner necessity acquires a second, symbolic meaning as its structural ornament mimics the structure of the body itself.

In his Krefeld address on the artistic elevation of women's dress, van de Velde warned that "lacking a visible skeleton allows a cloud of laces, puffs, flounces, and pleats to overrun all the forms of the body, and reshape it into an amorphous flesh-mass, which gives no sense of limbs or joints, and within which the beauty of the human figure is entirely lost."[50] After the Krefeld exhibition, "The Artistic Elevation of Women's Garb" was published as a pamphlet in 1901, contemporaneously with the influential *Culture of the Female Body as Foundation for Women's Clothing* by socially conservative design reformer Paul Schultze-Naumburg (not to be confused with the previously mentioned Krefeld textile designer, Paul Schulze).[51] Like van de Velde, Schultze-Naumburg promoted an aesthetic approach to dress reform based on the forms of the body and its structure. Unlike van de Velde, however, Schultze-Naumburg marshaled popular medical and scientific "evidence" (much of it in the form of provocative photographs of naked women) to make a physiognomic argument for the cultural significance of what he envisioned as the "healthy" female body. This body was one that had escaped the deforming influence of the corset and thus, according to Schultze-Naumburg's comparative images, resembled the perpetually undefiled "antique" figure familiar from classical Greek sculpture. The reactionary politics of his argument notwithstanding, the formal, practical application of his *Reformkleid* theory emphasized the aesthetic virtues of the idealized body to a far greater extent than the design of the *Reformkleid* itself. In keeping with his antique muses, Schultze-Naumburg's own designs for reform dresses present the

FIGURE 3.5

Henry van de Velde, Velvet evening gown,
*Album moderner nach Künstlerentwürfen
Damenkleider*, Krefeld 1900.

dress predominantly as drapery for the classical silhouette (figure 3.6). Without this all-important body, Schultze-Naumburg's dress is nothing but a heap of fabric—lifeless, formless.

Van de Velde's velvet evening gown, on the other hand, while it derives its seamed construction from the jointed structure of the body and its ornamental motifs from the body's forms, remains distinct from this body, which serves not simply as its armature but as the point of departure for its formal stylization. The dress maps its stylized, organic ornaments onto the living body to perform a Semperian *Bekleidung*: the dress's abstracted decorative forms become symbolic representations of the very body on which they superimpose themselves—and which, in so doing, they cannot help but dematerialize. As signs for the structures they cover, van de Velde's ornaments collapse the dress as signifier into its referent body. At the same time that its velvet fabric touches and amplifies the softness of the skin beneath, van de Velde's dress consumes the actual, living body, presenting instead its aestheticized index for public admiration. Even vacated by the body, van de Velde's dress lives on as corporeal simulacrum.

In contrast to Schultze-Naumburg's glorified draperies, van de Velde's *Doppelgänger* dress recommended itself to the basic, commercial aspect of Deneken's taste-making project: selling artistic reform dresses to style-conscious German women. In his 1902 article on the dress's new "art principle," van de Velde criticized German dress reformers for misunderstanding "feminine psychology" and suggested that instead of abandoning fashion altogether, "they should have opposed a different fashion to the dominant tendency, presenting it as the latest innovation—a 'German' style, for example, rather than a French one."[52] While van de Velde's statement abandons somewhat the firm foundation of *Kultur* suggested by Schultze-Naumburg's classical claddings in order to flirt with fashion, Schultze-Naumburg's myopic and misogynistic beholding of an ideal female body overlooks the intimate, individual relation between the dress and its prospective wearer. While both approaches are presumptuous and paternalistic, van de Velde attempts at least the integration of inside and outside—mind and body. His dresses, even before they were worn, expressed their essential nature, their *thingliness*—their

FIGURE 3.6

Figures 109 and 110 in Schultze-Naumburg,
Kultur des weiblichen Körpers, 1901.

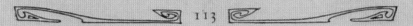

weder anatomisch noch ästhetisch begründet ist und nur durch
Irrtümer und perversen Geschmack einer Zeit entstanden ist, die
hinter uns liegen muss. —

Wenn ich hier (Abb. 109—111) einige Bilder nach einem be-
kleideten, ganz normalen Frauenkörper, der nie ein Korset getragen
hat, anführe, so geschieht dies nicht in der Absicht, fertige Mode-
vorbilder zu geben. Ich möchte es nochmals aufs ausdrücklichste
betonen: es sollen in keiner Weise direkte Vorbilder für Kleider-

Abb. 109

Abb. 110

8

visible correspondence to the articulated body of the potential wearer. Through its revealed structure and precisely calculated ornament, his evening dress announced to the consumer the specific subject-object dynamic of body and garment: "Here are my cuffs (your wrists); here is my collar (your neck); here are my back seams (your shoulder blades)." With the assurance of *Sachlichkeit*, the dress proclaimed: "This is what I am! Try me on!" With its structure on its surface and without the distraction of flounces and frills, van de Velde's anthropomorphic dress appealed directly to the imagination of the client, through the thingliness of *Sachlichkeit*.

The dress's accentuated structure could only signify (not bring about) animation; but with the body's aid, its materials could achieve motion. Van de Velde asserted that "each material has its own intrinsic beauty through which it expresses its existence. Each material aspires to life, and it is the artist's task to awaken its dormant life."[53] Within the rational structure of his "logically" cut evening gown, van de Velde delighted in the free play of velvet drapery, insisting that "the real beauty of the cloth lies in the play of its folds, in how it falls. This is what one should start from when creating a design. It is necessary to make the folds stand out, bring the cloth alive."[54] Just as the seam was the symbol of revealed structure, so the fold became liberated fabric's synecdoche.

Even the abstract, linear motifs of van de Velde's decorative appliqués took their cues not just from the organic forms of the body they covered but from the material properties of the dress fabric to which they were applied. Van de Velde arrests and repeats the unpredictable, body-propelled motion of velvet folds in the pattern of regularized swirls that ornaments the hem of his evening gown. But just as the dress's mimetic structure threatened to dissolve the body's presence within it, so its symbolic ornament competed for visual attention with the very thing it symbolized: the perpetually folding and unfolding fabric. Van de Velde's deliberate appliqués loomed above the soft, retiring folds of his evening gown, their luminous *Bekleidung* determining the dress's optical effect and relegating the corporeal—both the materiality of the dress and the physicality of the body—to the shadows.

LOVERS' SNAPSHOTS

Deneken wrote to Riemerschmid directly after their meeting at the 1900 Paris World's Fair, informing him that their mutual friend, van de Velde, had assured him of Riemerschmid's "sound taste" and expected great things from the Munich artist in this new field of dress design.[55] But Riemerschmid's few existing designs for reform dresses, all from about 1900, adopt neither van de Velde's stylized anthropomorphism nor Schultze-Naumburg's "style-less" classicism. Instead, Riemerschmid's designs propose an identifiably German solution to the problem of style while revealing his uniquely corporeal vision for the reform of women's dress.

Before Paris 1900, Riemerschmid had been a Munich painter whose designs were drawing increasing attention among select German circles. But after winning the exposition's grand prix for his art lover's room, he was quickly recognized as one of Germany's most innovative designers—one who represented the promise of design reform as an avenue to an internationally visible, modern German culture. In the *Room of an Art Lover*, Deneken beheld the lean lines of the emphatic musician's chair framed within its tangle of Jugendstil tendrils (figure 2.11). But dressed in its bold, saturated greens, blues, and reds, Riemerschmid's room simultaneously signaled an old-German *Gemütlichkeit*, or coziness, evoked by this traditional alpine color scheme (figures 2.12 and 2.13).[56] As the frieze's late nineteenth-century complexity played up the wooden chair's radically sparse yet sturdily serviceable design, so Paris presented Riemerschmid as a confident, self-consciously modern artist whose innovations were still grounded in the cultural soil of his homeland. For Deneken, the intimate character of Riemerschmid's designs promised a corrective to the alienation of a fashion industry driven by French novelties. But the homespun texture of Riemerschmid's approach to women's clothing proved a challenge for Deneken as he attempted to straddle the gulf between *Heimat* (homeland) and *Mode* (fashion), which the nineteenth-century fashion system had so firmly established in the minds of its increasingly sophisticated consumers.

In her introduction to the catalog for the *sachlich*-titled Exhibition of Modern Ladies' Dresses Executed from Artists' Designs, Maria van de Velde explains that these dresses are "not produced as display pieces; they are without exception functional dresses designed by artists for and in agreement with specific ladies. Artists and dressmakers worked hand in hand in their fabrication."[57] This central criterion, in conjunction with logistical realities, determined the exhibition's content. Deneken initially expected that Riemerschmid would play a significant role in the exhibition, hoping too that the Bavarian designer would direct the fabrication of his dress designs on site in Krefeld. "From all I've heard and learned from my own experience," he wrote to Riemerschmid in April, "it amounts to nothing when the artist simply draws the dress and the dressmaker is expected to just execute the drawing. Herr van de Velde keeps coming back to the idea that the design really emerges, so to speak, from actually working with the fabrics on the figure of the client."[58]

But direct contact with Krefeld clients proved problematic for the Munich-based Riemerschmid. And to compound this logistical hurdle, the Krefeld ladies did not immediately take to his proposed designs. Deneken wrote in June that "the ladies can't quite get comfortable with your unusual type of garb [*Trachtform*]. They find it too reminiscent of rural folk costumes."[59] While Deneken pleaded with Riemerschmid to come to Krefeld in person to discuss his designs and get the fabrication underway, frequently holding up van de Velde's and Mohrbutter's collaborative work with clients and dressmakers as examples of the correct approach, Riemerschmid never did. And the lavender wool street dress created for his one Krefeld client, a schoolteacher named Kathi Lotz, was made up entirely without his practical input.

Maria van de Velde writes in her catalog essay that "the execution of a piece of clothing that aspires to artistic quality requires as much time and energy as the execution of a good piece of furniture, fine jewelry, or a house."[60] Her assessment draws on firsthand experience as her husband's model, "dressform"—and wife. The artist's wife was the ideal candidate for Deneken's collaborative idea of reform dressmaking: it was more practical for her to work closely with her husband than it would have been for a regular paying client, and the design of her dress—like her furniture, jewelry, and even her house—could arise organically from and harmonize with its surroundings. Finally, while integrated within the *Gesamtkunstwerk* of the domestic interior, this dress, designed by a husband for his wife, should suit her in every detail: it would be the truly personal, individual dress, or *Eigenkleid*—a concept that Anna Muthesius, dress reformer and wife of Hermann Muthesius, would soon develop in her book on the topic.[61] Deneken encouraged Riemerschmid to have a dress made for his wife, "so that you can oversee the process completely," and had special yellow silk sent from Krefeld to Munich's preeminent Reform-Kleid Salon of Hirschberg & Co., where Riemerschmid worked with progressive dressmakers to create what Deneken termed an "adorable" yellow-and-white-striped costume for his Ida.[62] This noncommission—originating in the context of the German home, conceived by a German artist, and executed with Krefeld materials in a progressive Munich workshop—wove into a tangible fabric the various strands of Deneken's ambition for the *Reformkleid* as the embodiment of regional and national *style*.

At the center of Deneken's exhibition program was the production and broad dissemination of a catalog—in German and French editions—with design drawings in color lithograph, as well as black-and-white photographs of the dresses. This catalog would be the critical tool in asserting "a strong artistic influence on women's fashions in order to promote the discerning abstinence from the arbitrariness and bad taste of Paris fashion."[63] But Deneken's correspondence with Riemerschmid concerning the production of the all-important catalog shows Riemerschmid to have been out of step with Deneken's publicity goals. While van de Velde churned out carefully orchestrated, professional photographs showing his wife and furniture arranged in artistic ensembles for the exhibition catalog, Deneken prodded Riemerschmid for good images of Ida wearing the yellow dress, entreating him to have his wife pose for a professional photograph "in one of your interiors, or at least next to one of your chairs" and sending him some of van de Velde's sophisticated photographs as samples.[64]

Why Riemerschmid failed to meet Deneken's requirements and take his rightful place alongside van de Velde—as the director wished—is ultimately unclear. However, the tone of Deneken's final two letters on the subject, as he informs Riemerschmid that neither his color design drawings nor his black-and-white photographs of Ida's yellow dress will appear in the catalog, is telling: "Don't be angry with me, because I can't have your drawing made into a lithograph. It would look lost in the album, like a curiosity. If you were strongly represented like van de Velde, this wouldn't be an issue."[65] And then, just days before the opening, Deneken writes, "Your yellow costume could *unfortunately* not appear in the catalogue. Nothing could really be done with these little lovers' photos."[66] Despite Deneken's specific and increasingly insistent reminders, it appears that in lieu of the large 18 × 24 cm professional photograph Deneken had requested, Riemerschmid had sent a pocket-sized snapshot of Ida wearing the yellow dress—taken not from the front, but from the back.[67]

One explanation of Riemerschmid's amateurish approach to what Deneken impressed upon him as a thoroughly professional project is haste: perhaps Riemerschmid's other commissions—not least among which would have been his interiors for the Munich Schauspielhaus—took precedence over Deneken's project. However, there may be another, more intimate interpretation: perhaps Riemerschmid shared idiosyncratic, irreproducible renderings of his wife's dress and slightly coy, homemade pictures of Ida herself because though dress reform had the potential to become a national campaign, it was first, for him, a personal one.

While neither of Riemerschmid's two dresses appeared in the Krefeld catalog, both were included in the exhibition. According to Deneken, however, the lavender wool walking costume executed in Krefeld for Frau Lotz was not a success. "It looks as if it were only half-finished, too bald. This is of course because you [Riemerschmid] were not involved in the fabrication."[68] But the *Kölnische Zeitung* reviewed the "violet-gray" dress's "peculiar cut," defined by its long, tapered, pointed piece of cloth, or *Schnebbe*, extending from waist to knee, and its broad lapel fastened with a single button over the breast, in a more positive light, calling it "a revolution, a departure from tradition" (figure 3.7).[69]

Deneken's praise of the "exemplary" cut and color of Ida Riemerschmid's yellow dress must have come as a welcome relief to her husband.[70] The *Kölnische Zeitung* compares the dress—with its skirt of yellow-and-white striped silk and iridescent silk bodice in the form of a loose camisole held in place by two shoulder straps—to Dutch and south Bavarian folk costumes (*Volkstrachten*).[71] For Deneken, this old-German element in Riemerschmid's modern dresses was especially endearing.[72] Van de Velde explored the concept of *Tracht* in his "künstlerische Hebung der Frauentracht" speech at the opening of the Krefeld exhibition. *Tracht* (regional garb, or costume) stood in opposition to the more popular French-derived term for fashion: *Mode*. *Tracht* aligned itself with the German concept of style as opposed to fashion as it referred to indigenous, traditional, rural dress supposedly free from fashion's transience. For van de Velde, the term *Frauentracht* conveyed an artistic yet enduring women's dress, endowed with enough inherent style to make it impervious to the allure of novelty.[73] But implicit in the idea of vernacular *Tracht* was the longing to return to a preindustrial age. In her catalog introduction, Maria van de Velde laments the alienation between dress and wearer that had resulted from the decline of vernacular dress, placing "the destiny of the dress" in the "cunning and dangerous hands of the dressmaker."[74] She numbers Riemerschmid, along with her husband and Margarete von Brauchitsch, as one of the few truly innovative participants in the Krefeld exhibition. But she is quick to qualify her praise of Riemerschmid by noting that unlike her husband, who deals with "real life," Riemerschmid is more interested in the "artistic effect" of historical or vernacular costumes.[75]

FIGURE 3.7

Richard Riemerschmid, *Design for a Street Dress*, 1900. Städtische Galerie im Lenbachhaus und Kunstbau München. © 2021 Artists Rights Society (ARS), New York / VG Bild-Kunst, Bonn.

I.

4255

Their engagement with historical dress allowed Riemerschmid's designs to appear peculiar, innovative, even revolutionary in one instance, and deeply traditional, vernacular, and even anti-modern in the next. The form-fitting bodice of Riemerschmid's lavender street dress, the vertical plunge of the *Schnebbe*, and the loose folds of sleeves and skirt echo the late fifteenth-century women's costumes seen in south-German drawings and prints, including Albrecht Dürer's *Nuremburg Lady in Dancing Dress* of 1500 (figure 3.8). The Renaissance reverence for costly fabrics, manifested in the plentiful pleats, darts, and folds that at once articulated and ornamented their costumes, resonated with those modern dress reformers who, like van de Velde, looked to the inherent properties of materials to bring the dress to life.

Van de Velde's stylized *Frauentracht* recalls the abstraction of vernacular costume in his decorative appliqué of 1893, *The Angels' Vigil* (figure 2.2). But Riemerschmid's dress designs incorporated structure, function, and decoration into one organic whole—*one body*. Where van de Velde enunciated his dress construction with embroidered appliqués, Riemerschmid fused function and decoration through sculptural cuts and functional details, like the unusual arrangement of buttons fastening the two swirling, off-center flaps of a jacket with a striking, central perforation in his design for a street dress (figure 3.9). The solids, voids, and overlaps of his dress designs prefigure the framing and inlays of his later wooden furniture: Riemerschmid's graphic rendering of the central reveal in his street dress, for example, evokes the texture of the figured wood he would use for the bosses on an otherwise unornamented cabinet door in 1906 (figure 4.13). And the explicit buttons, clasps, and cinches of his modern old-German dresses (figure 3.10) paralleled the stark medievalizing hardware—be it shiny brass hinges, pocked pewter drawer pulls, or sparkling silver nails—that acted as the principal ornaments on his cupboards, bookcases, and sideboards. In both dresses and dressers, construction, for Riemerschmid, was not so much revealed as *revealing*: decoration was not the marker of construction, as it was for van de Velde, but was instead construction's inevitable disclosure—its revelation.

FIGURE 3.8

Albrecht Dürer, *Nuremberg Lady in Dancing Dress*, Pen and watercolor, 1500. The Albertina Museum, Vienna.

FIGURE 3.9

Richard Riemerschmid, *Street Dress*, 1900.
Städtische Galerie im Lenbachhaus und
Kunstbau München. © 2021 Artists Rights
Society (ARS), New York / VG Bild-Kunst, Bonn.

FIGURE 3.10

Richard Riemerschmid, *Society Dress*, 1900.
Städtische Galerie im Lenbachhaus und
Kunstbau München. © 2021 Artists Rights
Society (ARS), New York / VG Bild-Kunst, Bonn.

Riemerschmid's revealed construction, though formally efficient and anatomically precise, never strove to duplicate human anatomy through form or ornament. The purpose of the dress—a second skin for the female body—complicated the expression of its *Sachlichkeit*. The dress must suppress its own thingly being in order to promote the wearer's bodily presence. Rather than challenging the body, Riemerschmid's dress must attend to it. The dress's necessary suppression of its thingly self represented a modified *Sachlichkeit*: this was not the emphatic agency of sprightly musician's chairs and bustling beer mugs, but a more yielding dependency—an attachment.

Riemerschmid's dresses acknowledged the body's contours through the form-fitting bodice and natural waist, the accentuation of neck and wrists by unusual collars, tapering sleeves, and attenuated cuffs, and the modest drapery of their unstructured A-line skirts. However, even in his design for a loose tea gown (figure 3.11), rather than apply a strip of horizontal ornament above the chest and across the shoulders as van de Velde had in a tea gown for his wife (figure 3.12), Riemerschmid angles the collar, peaks the shoulders, and arches the yoke over each breast to articulate the upper body. Between the two horizontal bands of decorative collar and hem, Maria van de Velde's body would have been lost in a sea of velvet. Riemerschmid's dress, by contrast, bifurcates the body with a single seam running visibly from the V of the narrow collar to the foot. Though unfitted and unornamented, Riemerschmid's vertical design is alive: yielding and responding to the dynamic curves of the faintly sketched body beneath.

Riemerschmid's only surviving *Reformkleid*, his wife's theater dress (figure 3.3), gently marks the neck, waist, and wrists, adopting neither the skintight bodice of a conventionally fashionable corseted gown nor the rigorous, ornamentally accentuated structure of van de Velde's velvet evening dress. Instead, Riemerschmid's rustic frock of strawberry-pink wool voile projects a homespun approachability in defiance of established formal conventions for theater attire. Its defining features are its playfully exaggerated sleeves and fluid, adjustable collar. Changing its arrangement with each movement and gesture of the body, the creamy satin collar was the dress's animating feature—the turbine of its thingliness. While van de Velde allocated the play of the fold to the unornamented segments of fabric within his framework of ornamented seams, Riemerschmid bypassed ornament altogether, freeing the whole dress to respond to, engage with, and emphasize the kinetic engagements of the body itself.

FIGURE 3.11

Richard Riemerschmid, *Tea Gown*, 1900.
Städtische Galerie im Lenbachhaus und
Kunstbau München. © 2021 Artists Rights
Society (ARS), New York / VG Bild-Kunst, Bonn.

As a *Reformkleid*, Ida Riemerschmid's theater dress collaborated with her body in more than aesthetics: her husband had conceived its construction in the terms he typically applied to the design of a utilitarian object, which must be practical, *sachlich*, and comfortable for its user. The dress's two-piece construction, with a front-fastening bodice and a skirt that attached to it by two sets of buttons at front and back, precluded conventionally restrictive binding at the waist and also made dressing and undressing relatively simple acts, to be completed by the wearer herself without the assistance of servants. A narrow, internal linen band to hold the loose-fitting bodice in place and a thin, white satin slip under the skirt were the dress's only "hidden" structural elements—and these, compared with the typical structuring aids of corset, crinoline, and bustle, did not constrain the body's movement. For the fabric, Riemerschmid chose wool voile, a diaphanous material woven from fine, tightly twisted wool fibers, which created a sense of depth through its slight translucency and subtle sheen. Both satin and wool voile are soft to the touch, pleasant to wear, and appropriate for an early spring occasion. The wool fabric exchanged the formal crispness of silk for a touched and touchable look. The fall of Ida's tissue-thin gown was gentle and fluid, and unlike rustling silk, it would have been silent—a natural extension of her body, like hair or skin.[76] Instead of performing a symbolic commentary on her body, Ida's theater dress enacted a symbiotic relationship with it. Closer than *Bekleidung*, Ida's dress whispered its *Sachlichkeit* like a caress.

Ida's theater gown was fabricated at the well-known *Reformkleid* salon of C. M. Rosipal in Munich. Strawberry voile, creamy satin, and red embroidery silk were the only materials used for both construction and decoration. The dress relied primarily on color for its effect—the lustrous pink of the voile, deepened by the red embroidery thread on the shirred bodice and exposed darts on the skirt and cuffs, and offset by the pearly sash and collar. Red silk thread—stitched at Salon Rosipal with exaggerated, self-conscious naivete—fulfilled functional and ornamental purposes simultaneously: an unconventional outer seam ran prominently down the

FIGURE 3.12

Henry van de Velde, *Tea Gown*, c. 1896 (reproduction 1983, Deutsches Textilmuseum Krefeld, No. 16483). © 2021 Artists Rights Society (ARS), New York / c/o Pictoright Amsterdam.

sleeve, and even the darts that drew billowing sleeve into slender cuff performed decorative duty.

This intentional lack of refinement on the part of professional urban dressmakers was a conscious opposition to the seamless elegance of Paris fashion. In fact, Ida's dress seems to parody the roughness of vernacular dressmaking, with its unusually conspicuous stitches that almost beg to be unraveled. Rather than articulating the structure of his dress through applied ornament in a symbolic secondary step, Riemerschmid deconstructs the construction process by rendering it both visible and tangible in decorative exaggeration. The theater dress's deliberately "unfinished" quality feeds its thingly being: not just the folds of its fabric, but also each imprecise stitch seems to be awakening, coming to life. This was not van de Velde's artistic elevation, where ornament paid symbolic tribute to the dress's seamed construction and the folds of fabric that enlivened it. Unaided by ornament, Riemerschmid's theater dress celebrated the spontaneity of "raw" materials caught up in the tumult of making. Instead of attempting to rival fashion, Riemerschmid offered a German *style* free of stylization.

When compared with the lapidary finish of van de Velde's velvet evening gown, Riemerschmid's strawberry voile theater dress seems indeterminate, unresolved. Van de Velde's definitive dress is monumentalized by the Krefeld catalog photograph, where the ornamental stamp that seals the logic of the dress's construction extends its claim to the abstracted forms of the display stand where the model's hand rests—and, further, to the undulating graphic designs in the framed prints on the wall above her (figure 3.5). The Krefeld catalog contains not a single photograph—artistic or domestic—of Riemerschmid's dresses, however. The history of his *Gesamtkunstwerk* is not the seamless image of Loosian lore but a patchwork of historical fragments—objects, interiors, people, and events. Riemerschmid's inability—or refusal—to "complete the picture" has largely obscured his contribution to the history of dress reform. But it is this very resistance to cohesion and closure that defines Riemerschmid's *Sachlichkeit* and, in turn, animates his designs. In contrast to the poor little rich man's ultradesigned experience, defined and delimited by the décor that surrounded him, Riemerschmid's dresses never completed or "finished" their wearers. The true ornament of Riemerschmid's unadorned dress was its wearer's presence—life itself. Where the formal relationships and optical effects of van de Velde's evening gown were predetermined by its designer, Riemerschmid's theater dress left these undefined: its kinetic forms had to be activated in collaboration with its wearer but could never be entirely arrested, or *completed*, by her. The dress, as its facture suggested, was incomplete by design: it demanded not only a body to occupy it, but a *space* for them both to inhabit.

A COMPLETE THING

At Krefeld, the artistic reform dress had completed the *Gesamtkunstwerk* of everyday life. Ida Riemerschmid wore hers on an auspicious evening in first spring at the beginning of the modern century, marking (for her husband) both the fruition of the past and a budding future. With the debut of the Münchner Schauspielhaus on April 20, 1901, Riemerschmid's career as a painter was over, but his life as one of Germany's most influential architect-designers was just beginning. Seven years later, after her husband's cofounding of the Deutscher Werkbund in late 1907, Ida Riemerschmid sewed a replica of her theater dress, using the original strawberry-colored fabric, to clothe a Nymphenburg porcelain doll for the Bavarian Art-Industry Society's 1908 bazaar—suggesting not just the significance of the original dress but of the event it commemorated (figure 3.13).

What was hailed in 1901 as Riemerschmid's first architectural commission had more in common with the design of his wife's dress—sheathing a preexisting structure in form and color—than it did with an accepted definition of architecture as the actual creation of structure. Around 1900, a popular Munich theater troupe that had been performing risqué French farces as well as more serious contemporary plays to wild acclaim on the stage of a former vaudeville hall since 1898 was in need of a new home. Its Viennese director, Georg Stollberg, approached Riemerschmid's brothers, Karl and Arthur, who owned the block of adjoining buildings situated on the fashionable Maximilianstraße known as the Riemerschmid-Houses, about building a new theater within their large inner courtyard. The Riemerschmid brothers agreed to rent their 6,800-square-meter courtyard to the Schauspielhaus on a long-term lease and took full charge of the commission. At their suggestion, Richard took on the complete design of the new theater's interiors, but as he was still known mainly for his paintings and furniture designs, the established Munich architectural firm of Heilmann & Littmann was hired to design and construct the building itself.[77]

The architects worked closely with Riemerschmid to achieve an intimate enclosure. Intimacy, in fact, was the primary goal and dominant effect of the Schauspielhaus: a brochure celebrating its debut promoted the Schauspielhaus as the "ideal

FIGURE 3.13

Ida Riemerschmid, *Dress for Nymphenburg Porcelain Doll*, 1908. Münchner Stadtmuseum, Sammlung Stadtkultur. © 2021 Artist Rights Society (ARS), New York / VG Bild-Kunst, Bonn.

of an intimate theater—Germany's first intimate theater altogether."[78] Constructed entirely within the interior courtyard, the Schauspielhaus possessed no formal exterior at all—theatergoers had actually to pass *through* the Riemerschmid-Houses in order to reach their destination. In lieu of a facade, Riemerschmid designed a placard holder for Schauspielhaus playbills (figure 3.14) and two sets of broad red doors, opening from Maximilianstraße into two separate, enclosed passageways leading directly through the Riemerschmid-Houses to two corresponding sets of red doors opening into the theater's vestibule (figure 3.15), which contained a box office ensconced in a leafy painted vine in the same full red of the wooden doors. Riemerschmid's touches were also palpable in the architectural details of the secluded inner courtyard, with its folkloric, farmhouse window frames and organically curling brass door handles that seemed both to reach for and yield to the hand's grasp. But as the theater's truly public face, Riemerschmid's placard holder and doors on Maximilianstraße must have created a singular impression. The placard holder, with its vegetal motifs and deliberately rustic, hand-hammered metalwork, placed between the squat, arching wooden doors, with their boards painted a cheerful red and their brass handles curling like leaves, suggested a fairy-tale scene: a mysterious door in a hollow tree leading down into an enchanted, underground kingdom. Schauspielhaus patrons opened these magic doors and descended their hidden passages, tunneling their way from the bustling city street to somewhere rich and strange.

In his study of modernist theater in Munich, Peter Jelavich has suggested that in addition to its remove from the street's commercial activity, the Schauspielhaus's interior space and design "made the theatergoer aware of his separation from the larger world and his organic amalgamation into a select cultural community . . . it gave the impression of a secluded haven . . . a womb—hidden, vitalizing."[79] This cocoon-like sensation originated in the auditorium—the Schauspielhaus's structural and conceptual core. According to the celebratory brochure, the auditorium was designed specifically to meet the functional requirements of "modern drama," characterized by naturalistic gestures and nuanced dialogue, in contrast to the histrionics of grand oratory.[80] The audience required sufficient proximity to the stage and its actors to appreciate the subtleties of the modern plays. In recognition of this, architect Max Littmann opted for an amphitheater construction with only 727 seats in total, including the orchestra, balcony, two boxes, and rear loggia, to achieve the "the closest accommodation of the spectators and the most intimate spatial design."[81]

FIGURE 3.14

Richard Riemerschmid, *Placard Holder*,
Münchner Schauspielhaus, 1901, in *Kunst
und Handwerk* 51, no. 10 (1901): 284.

FIGURE 3.15

Richard Riemerschmid, *Vestibule Doors*,
Münchner Schauspielhaus, 1901, in *Kunst
und Handwerk* 51, no. 10 (1901): 285.

Riemerschmid's Munich Schauspielhaus has been compared with August En-dell's contemporaneous Wolzogen Theater or "Buntes Theater," designed for the cultural critic and founder of German cabaret, Ernst von Wolzogen. Endell's was another modern theater, opening in Berlin a little more than six months after the Munich Schauspielhaus, on November 28, 1901. The "Colorful Theater," so nick-named for its abstract, pointillistic wallpaintings, was also constructed within an interior court and was likewise intended to house intimate modern drama.[82] But Endell's cavernous auditorium—with seating arranged in straight rows across a wide, ungraded floor, and a starkly flat, graphically decorated proscenium wall op-posing a balcony equally flush with the rear wall—created at once an imposing and an *exposing* architectural effect (figure 3.16).[83] Endell used color and form *against* architecture: dematerializing constructed space in order to suspend his audience in a shared, hypnotic experience, employing architecture not as womb, but as *screen*. Stacy Hand has noted that while the theater's architecture was rather ordinary, its decoration was avant-garde. She argues for Endell's kinaestethic conception of the space through his use of dynamic patterns intended to be activated by bodily mo-tion, patterns that called for the "infusion" of the visitors' "vital energy."[84] In a sense, just as van de Velde's velvet evening gown, through its mimicking of the body's structure, effaced that body's actual presence within the dress, so the decoration of Endell's theater supplanted the very presence of the theater itself.

Riemerschmid's Munich auditorium, by contrast, deployed haptic architec-tural strategies to generate physical closeness and psychological empathy among the audience members. An encircling, forward-jutting balcony brooded over the snug, gently graduated seating in the orchestra below, effectively shortening the distance from rear wall to proscenium wall and projecting the spectators seated in the balcony toward the stage. This arrangement enhanced each spectator's capac-ity to identify bodily with the actors—to empathize with them—and so facilitated imaginative participation in the drama. As the theater's debut brochure noted, no matter where one sat, there was never any separation between audience and actors to inhibit the "intimate co-experiencing" of the action.[85] Designer Hermann Obrist expressed his hope that, in response to the configuration of Riemerschmid's theater, more new dramas relaxing boundaries between audience and performance would be written from then on.[86] The physical proximity of one seat to the next heightened the experience of *Einfühlung*, which promoted a sense of camaraderie among the audience members so that the play became a truly collective experience.[87]

FIGURE 3.16

August Endell, *"Buntes Theater" Berlin*
(auditorium), 1901. Akademie der
Künste, Berlin.

Just as concern for his wife's bodily comfort played a major role in Riemerschmid's design for her theater dress, so his interiors for the Schauspielhaus fostered the physical ease of its patrons. The auditorium's human scale—dramatized by the sheltering balcony with its organically curved underbelly, rippling with ribs for optimal acoustics, slung low over the orchestra—was intensified by the voluptuous embrace of its fleshy forms (figure 3.17). The Schauspielhaus brochure affirmed that "absolutely everything has been done with the security and comfort of the audience in mind."[88] Riemerschmid's design for simple yet comfortable auditorium seating was manufactured by the German branch of Thonet Brothers, the Austrian firm known since the mid-nineteenth century for its innovative, inexpensive, industrially produced bentwood furniture.[89] Rows of ergonomically designed flip-up seats echoed the simplicity and practicality of the *Reformkleid*—and the sealed wood surfaces were more hygienic than the plush upholstery of conventional theater seats.

Despite the theater's small size and cozy arrangement, multiple carefully placed exits allowed spectators to file out efficiently from the performance into the two corridors flanking the auditorium, where ample cloakrooms awaited them. Both the orchestra and balcony foyers, with their electric lighting calculated not only for decorative effect but for congenial socializing, were pronounced exceedingly *gemütlich*. Low-pressure steam heating units maintained a comfortable temperature in both winter and summer. Riemerschmid housed these modern contraptions in originally designed cladding: little copper plates chained delicately together formed a metallic curtain that swayed gently as steam was expelled, and the polished copper surface of each small plate reflected flashes of light from the electric bulbs (figure 3.18).[90] With each flicker of warm light, Riemerschmid's *Heizkörperverkleidung* (heating-unit dressing) enacted Semperian *Bekleidung*: its kinetic copper cladding

FIGURE 3.17

The Schauspielhaus's sheltering balcony, featuring acoustical ribbing on its underside, projects over the orchestra seating. Photograph courtesy of Atelier Achatz Architekten & Andreas Huber Fotografie. © 2021 Artist Rights Society (ARS), New York / VG Bild-Kunst, Bonn.

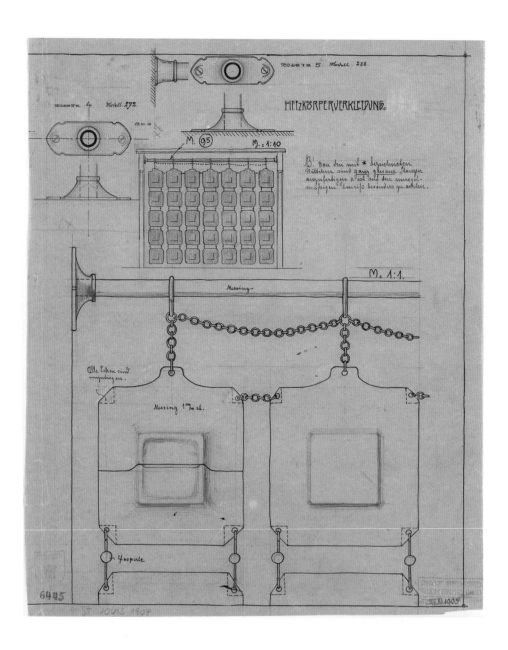

FIGURE 3.18

Richard Riemerschmid,
Heizkörperverkleidung (brass plates), 1905.
Architekturmuseum der TUM. © 2021 Artists
Rights Society (ARS), New York / VG Bild-
Kunst, Bonn.

symbolized the heater's practical function and, in the process, rendered visible its otherwise invisible vapors.

A review in Munich's *Dekorative Kunst* praised Riemerschmid for his material honesty, remarking that "none of his materials lies by acting like another, or pretends to qualities it does not actually possess."[91] Here was a primal *Sachlichkeit*, present in the materials themselves: "inspired by their essence [*Wesen*], Riemerschmid listened to what they each had to say, and in exchange for their confidence, gave them life."[92] Riemerschmid used costly metals sparingly as glittering accents scattered about the theater—the heaters' copper plates, the bronze-paneled doors opening into the orchestra, and the brass-clad columns that ornamented the balcony and its adjoining foyer. But his favored materials were much humbler. Texture and color—plaster and paint—defined the spatial progression of his interiors, from cool, airy periphery to warm, enveloping sanctum. Color acted simultaneously as embodied material and disembodying optical phenomenon: Riemerschmid's painted stucco *Bekleidung* both corporealized and dematerialized.[93]

In "Notes on Color," an article published shortly before the Schauspielhaus debut, critic Karl Scheffler argued that when artists designed interiors, Symbolist painters, who thought in "translated colors," found themselves most at ease.[94] Riemerschmid swathed the Schauspielhaus's sculptural ceiling treatments in expanses of bold, pure color, beginning with the cool, blue-green harmonies of the orchestra foyer and its adjoining cloakrooms. The smoky lavender-gray foyer featured a ceiling decorated with successive, receding stucco rings painted in incrementally darkening shades of blue (figure 3.19). The greenish patina of the two bronze-paneled doors introduced the green cloakrooms, which flanked the auditorium on right and left. In the cloakrooms, dark blue wainscoting met light green walls, and slender columns of the same blue articulated structural arches. Small violet-blue rings laid into the green walls repeated the foyer's large, striking ceiling treatments in miniature. Bright red leaf motifs clustered around circles of electric lights in the ceilings, recalling the red vines in the vestibule and foretelling the auditorium's chromatic explosion. Ascending either of the stairways leading up to the balcony, one was embraced in golden yellows and warm grays, while brass-clad columns "shimmering yet not ostentatious, unique but not bizarre" smoldered softly at restrained intervals.[95] Here the ceiling, as below, was treated in sculptural relief: pearly gray, bone-like limbs, each holding a single electric light bulb, extended from the tops of the gray walls to reach partway across the yellow coffered ceiling (figure 3.20).

Juliet Koss has described the experience of entering the Schauspielhaus as "walking into the aestheticized interior of a body."[96] In the auditorium, the patron arrived at the theater's beating heart. Here Riemerschmid unleashed his bright, hot red in its full electric intensity, freeing it to vibrate against an equally energized chartreuse green. Red has a festive history and had in 1901 long been considered appropriate for the theater. Wilhelm von Bezold, a Bavarian physicist who had worked in Munich during the 1870s and associated with prominent modern artists, including the renowned colorist Arnold Böcklin, reasoned in his *Theory of Color in*

FIGURE 3.19

Richard Riemerschmid, *Orchestra Foyer with Stucco Ceiling Decoration*, Münchner Schauspielhaus, 1901. Photograph courtesy of Atelier Achatz Architekten & Andreas Huber Fotografie. © 2021 Artists Rights Society (ARS), New York / VG Bild-Kunst, Bonn.

FIGURE 3.20

Richard Riemerschmid, *Balcony Foyer*, Münchner Schauspielhaus, 1901. Photograph courtesy of Atelier Achatz Architekten & Andreas Huber Fotografie. © 2021 Artists Rights Society (ARS), New York / VG Bild-Kunst, Bonn.

Its Relation to Art and Art-Industry that because red was the rarest color in nature, it held "the first rank as a decorative color."[97] Also to red's credit was its star performance under artificial light.

Sprouting vines spanned the bright green ceiling and crept in bold relief down the walls and toward the spectators. These fleshy yet plant-like forms vie for attention with the auditorium's robust, complementary palette. In one moment, the auditorium's sensual stucco forms encroach on the occupant with their smothering corporeality; in the next moment, the aggressive pulsation of color dissolves the auditorium's solid flesh as it transforms embodied occupant into bodiless spectator, transporting her out of the body and into pure opticality. As the interior absorbed the occupant, so the occupant gave her body to the interior, becoming more and more bodiless. This empathic transfer between subject and object evoked the uncanny sensation of an otherworldly encounter: the enchantment hinted by Maximilianstraße's curious red doors was actualized on entering the Schauspielhaus's auditorium, where the patron penetrated at last into a marvelous cave, hidden beneath the surface of rationalized urban life. Stalactite-shaped light bulbs, hanging from organically shaped voids in the coffered ceiling, corporealized light itself. This living material set form on fire.

Surrounding the stage, a giant wreath of clambering shoots recalled Riemerschmid's outsized frame for his Paris *Room of an Art Lover* of the previous year (figure 3.21). Indeed, the auditorium's homey scale—the dimensions of its seating area in exact proportion to those of the stage—aligned the Schauspielhaus interiors more closely with those of a dwelling than a public space. Sprawling out from the proscenium-frame in three dimensions was Riemerschmid's full-scale, fully functional realization of the artistic vision he had developed over the preceding decade. The theater's red-and-green palette was familiar not only from Paris 1900, but also from Riemerschmid's 1890s graphics, and the auditorium's fleshy protrusions and creeping stems, along with the bony coffers of the yellow foyer, called to mind both figures and furnishings from Riemerschmid's past. These complements of form and color implied, in the spirit of his Edenic paintings, a totality of living things: human flesh enmeshed with plant life in what Berlepsch-Valendas had experienced "as a complete thing, as a picture, as a decorative apparition"—a *Gesamtkunstwerk*.

The Schauspielhaus brochure closed with a benediction on the new theater, identifying the structure itself as a frame for human drama: "May . . . this beautiful frame . . . enclose now and always the most beautiful picture known to the world: the constantly changing, ever self-renewing and rejuvenating reflection of human

FIGURE 3.21

Richard Riemerschmid, *Schauspielhaus
Stage with Curtain and Thonet Seating*
(photograph hand-colored by designer),
1901. Architekturmuseum der TUM. © 2021
Artists Rights Society (ARS), New York / VG
Bild-Kunst, Bonn.

life."[98] As the image of the body had been embedded in Riemerschmid's landscapes, and as the musician's chair had animated his art lover's interior, so his wife's dress (figure 3.3) enfolded her within his living picture. While Riemerschmid eschewed anthropomorphic mimicry in his dress designs, thus precluding any overtly symbolic relationship between his wife's body and her dress, there were nevertheless conspicuous formal correspondences between Ida's theater dress and its surroundings. Dress and auditorium performed each other's analogue, their shared expanses of warm red each wrapped in a horizontal band—a balcony, a sash—and crowned with a collar (and a painted frieze), dipping gently into a red field below. Boundless, bottomless color performed the conjunction of *Reformkleid* and *Bekleidung*.

Riemerschmid's Schauspielhaus was not Wagner's *Gesamtkunstwerk* of poetry, motion, and music. And it was far from the type of theater that Wagner envisioned for his synthesis of the "sister arts": a theater that created the illusion of a mystical connection between audience and performers through what Koss has termed the "purity of the optical arrangement," in which each spectator claimed a direct, unmediated optical connection with the activity on stage, and so could identify with—feel into—the performance, becoming emotionally, psychologically, and even physically absorbed within it.[99] While Riemerschmid's auditorium fostered an intimacy both among audience members and between spectators and performers, his was not the intimacy of mystical absorption in high drama, but a humbler, familial relation. Riemerschmid's stage was not the all-consuming optical focus of his theater; instead, it was the expansion and completion of his *Room for an Art Lover*. Though these interiors threatened at times to devour or disintegrate their occupants, their ultimate aim was not to consume, but gently to enfold, like a lover wrapping his beloved in warm, red cloth.

THE *GESAMTKUNSTWERK*'S GHOST

Two intersecting rings of small electric light bulbs, sheathed in glass petals and set into a large painted medallion interlaced with leafy vines, formed the theatrical ceiling decoration of the dining room at the Munich villa of Carl Thieme and his family (figure 3.22). The ceiling's electric efflorescence reenacted the marvelous illumination of the Schauspielhaus auditorium for a private audience. Simultaneous to its accommodation of everyday activities, the dining room offered an alternative

FIGURE 3.22

Richard Riemerschmid, *Speisezimmer in the Thieme House*, Munich, 1903. Architekturmuseum der TUM. © 2021 Artists Rights Society (ARS), New York / VG Bild-Kunst, Bonn.

experience—the possibility of floating up, above the surface of mundane reality, into a field of stars. While the Schauspielhaus's theatrical pretext had sanctioned Riemerschmid's expressionistic forms and dramatic use of color, the Thieme house's middle-class, domestic context called for a more restrained, evenhanded tempering of formal expressionism with everyday, functional ease. As Hermann Muthesius put it in 1904, rather than "parading around with art," the Thiemes' rooms seemed as livable and flexible as "our contemporary outfits." The materials and colors Riemerschmid employed in his 1903 redesign of the Thiemes' salon and dining room employed symbolic *Bekleidung* in a remarkably down-to-earth, utilitarian fashion.

Born in 1844, Carl Thieme had come to Munich after Germany's 1871 unification to take charge of the local branch of the Thuringia Insurance Company. Prospering throughout the economic boom (and even during the subsequent downturn), the so-called "Gründerzeit" that followed unification, Thieme and his family were by the late 1890s in a very comfortable financial position. In the space of seven years, the Thiemes commissioned Riemerschmid to redesign seven rooms in their urban villa on Munich's Georgenstraße. A suite of rooms on the ground floor—a salon with a small adjoining reception room and a multipurpose living-dining room—were the richest in materials, colors, and decorative schemes.[100] The salon, a room intended for the festive yet comfortable entertainment of guests, constituted a complete decorative program (figures 2.21, 2.22, and 3.23). A *Wandverkleidung*, or wall dressing, of intarsia panels wrapped around the entire salon and framed an arched mirror and doorways on the west wall; above this, bare white wall extended up to meet a stenciled cornice frieze. Each wooden panel's construction of vertical stems, leaves, and buds was articulated by the careful placement of subtly contrasting light- and dark-stained magnolia during the intarsia process.

The unifying decorative motif of small, irregular trapezoids—appearing in mother-of-pearl on the magnolia wardrobe (figure 2.18) and in gold appliqué on the red velvet–upholstered side chairs (figure 2.23)—repeated itself in velvet club chairs and sofas, a stenciled cornice frieze, and even in the linked brass plates of a steam heater similar in design to those at the Schauspielhaus (figure 2.21, left, and figure 3.23, right). Directly adjacent to the wardrobe on the salon's west wall, a large mirror, framed like a doorway, reflected the side chairs and octagonal table arranged against the east wall (figure 2.22). The appliqués of clustered golden leaves stitched into the side chairs' red-velvet backs transposed the imperfect trapezoids from hard-edged mineral to yielding vegetation. Chandeliers, placed at the

FIGURE 3.23

Richard Riemerschmid, *Salon (south wall) in the Thieme House with Heizkörperverkleidung (right) and view into small reception room.* Architekturmuseum der TUM. © 2021 Artists Rights Society (ARS), New York / VG Bild-Kunst, Bonn.

indentations created by the four lobes of a large oval ceiling decoration of flowering garlands, hung down from brass plates like trapezoidal leaves. And the rounded brass squares of the steam heater—whose gleaming metal surfaces seemed almost an ossification of the side chairs' pliable golden appliqués—swayed gently in the warm steam, reflecting and dispersing the chandeliers' electric shower.

Art critic Joseph August Lux celebrated Riemerschmid's "twinkling, ever-changing, continually animated metal surfaces," which created unpredictable "artistic effects" of light.[101] Through the luster and sparkle of these reflective surfaces (even the velvet upholstery produced a softly reflective effect), Riemerschmid revealed the innately decorative nature of his materials. But reflection—treacherous and fugitive—simultaneously betrayed the individualities of the materials it enlivened: at the same time that it played innocently upon the material surface, it accomplished the more aggressive, destabilizing act of dematerialization. Within Riemerschmid's Thieme interiors, color was always escaping, constantly eluding the materials themselves—as if in outright defiance of its solid, corporeal vehicles—into uncontainable, intangible, disembodied light. And in the end, in the handful of black-and-white photographs of Haus Thieme, it is light itself, penetrating the windows, that leaves the most vivid impression.

Two large windows in the north wall of the Thiemes' salon create, within the borders of the period photographs, a haunting, almost otherworldly effect—not through any kind of material presence, but through the very lack of it. In fact, the window closest to the west wall is almost imperceptible in the photographs; the only hints of its presence are a section of hanging curtain just visible at the far right of the image, and the reflection of the window's light in the brass plates of the heating unit stationed against the south wall (figure 2.21). Placing the heater, with its reflective cladding, on the south wall of a room with a northern exposure was almost certainly a practical decision on Riemerschmid's part. But beyond its pragmatic amplification of natural light, the heater, positioned as it was, staged the paradoxical sequencing of Semperian *Bekleidung*. The material "dressing" of its metal costume (literally, its "heating body clothing" or *Heizkörperverkleidung*), with the motion and reflection symbolic of its utilitarian purpose, was undone in the very act of its function: the swaying brass plates seemed to evaporate, along with the steam that animated them, into pure heat and light.

In contrast to its invisible partner, the second large window, adjacent to the spidery side chairs in the photograph of the east wall, threatens to overpower the rest of the image with the brilliant burst of light that both penetrates it and pours from it (figure 2.22). The window's glass has become, under the photograph's spell, more aura than object, its spectral luminosity replacing material absence with unearthly presence. Like a memory—or a ghost—this most immaterial of dressings fills physical void with spiritual life.

Semper's *Bekleidung* functioned in Bezold's color theory as the principle that distinguished between the applied arts of interior decoration and the fine art of painting. Whereas in illusionistic painting one endeavored to disguise the presence of the picture plane, Bezold argued, "in the decorative arts the plane as such must be allowed to assert itself."[102] The red-clad backs of Riemerschmid's eagerly advancing, overly hospitable velvet side chairs activate—and personify—the "assertive" planes that characterize Bezold's conception of color in the applied art object. In a manner entirely opposed to the artistic reification that terrorized Loos's poor little rich man, Riemerschmid's garments, objects, and interiors entreated the engagement of their wearers, users, and occupants. His objects enticed their subjects not through passive display, but through active *play*. Riemerschmid relaxed the requirement for the "rich man" to conform to the sophistication of a museum-like habitat and so saved him from being absorbed by his surroundings—and losing his identity. Instead, Riemerschmid extended an invitation to return to a state of innocence, where useful objects appealed to the users who needed them not merely because they were pleasant to behold, but also as the result of designs that demonstrated their desire for employment.

According to Riemerschmid's furniture and interiors, the primary purpose of design was to delight the user. But engineered by *Sachlichkeit*, Riemerschmid's furniture and household objects began to appeal, from 1903 onward, not only to the cultured members of the *Bildungsbürgertum*, the educated middle class, who owned them, but also to cultural reformers as a delightful means of inculcating a new German style in a modern merchant class. Riemerschmid's deliberately imperfected motifs and intentional evidence of making promised liberation from the tyrannical overrefinements of foreign fashion, offering in their place a permissive, "unstylized" German *style*, playfully rich and yet rich enough in *Spielraum* to outlive the current season.[103]

Ultimately, it was Riemerschmid's *Einfühlung*—that empathy that not only feels with but feels *into*—that fascinated and compelled the user, engaging him (and also her) in an intimate relationship. Or perhaps it was a charming parlor game, in which the subject must "feel into" the object and fill out its appearance with the soul's subjective contents. Like a young woman stepping gracefully into a theater dress before a grand debut, these exchanges were both completely natural and entirely transformative: they seemed to take place effortlessly, and yet, as if by magic, the results of these subject-object fusions—whether enacted between the body and its clothing, the clothed form and the cladding of its surroundings, or the delightful object and the delighted subject—were unique, perpetually new, and pulsing with life. Within the animated contours of Riemerschmid's empathic *Gesamtkunstwerk*, as livable and lively as a modern dress, one might truly wrap oneself "as in a garment."

A FOREST IN THE LIVING ROOM

Full fathom five thy father lies;
Of his bones are coral made;
Those are pearls that were his eyes;
Nothing of him that doth fade,
But doth suffer a sea change
Into something rich and strange.
—William Shakespeare[1]

"OF HIS BONES ARE CORAL MADE": GERMAN CULTURE RE-FORMED

In 1906, modern design became the new German art. This was the year of the Third German Applied Arts Exhibition, which took place between May and October in the historic cultural center of Dresden. This third exhibition was, for Germany, a first. Brand-new designs for furniture and household objects, celebrating the extensive use of machine technology, took center stage. Handcrafted products and historicist interiors, which had occupied positions of honor at previous exhibitions, were brushed aside to make room for modern *Kunstgewerbe*: industrially produced applied arts objects. This audacious move by Dresden's exhibition committee brought simmering disputes over the relationship between the hand and the machine in the fabrication of everyday things to a boiling point, leading directly to the founding in 1907 of the German Werkbund. An organization of artists, architects, educators, industrialists, and retailers—in short, everyone and anyone who had a stake in the modernization of Germany's cultural and commercial life—the Werkbund systematically targeted the design of utilitarian objects as the key to reforming Germany and its people for the twentieth century. Considering its reform agenda, we might assume that the Werkbund was fundamentally modern. This chapter proposes, however, that deeply embedded in the Werkbund's modernism was a profound reverence for a collective German past. Richard Riemerschmid's furniture displayed at Dresden in 1906 materialized this counterintuitive approach to modernism through the timeless, living substance of wood.

The Dresden exhibition was a first for Riemerschmid, too: it was here that his new "machine furniture," efficiently constructed from serially produced, standardized components and fabricated using newly available machine tools, was first displayed before the German public (figure 4.1). His machine chair promised not simply to democratize artistic furniture, but simultaneously to open a new chapter in the history of German art (figure 0.4). The vivacious machine chair epitomized the physiognomic practice of *Sachlichkeit* that Riemerschmid had been developing since the mid-1890s. The simple chair modeled a fluid relation of surface and substance: the round, polished heads of its pegs signaled its construction, while its natural patterning demonstrated the seamlessness of material and decoration—of wood grain and wood. Its sparse, straightforward structure of slatted backrest supported by supple flexed legs, terminating in the upturned toes of staunchly planted feet, merged practical purpose with expressive disposition. Riemerschmid's machine chair compressed decoration into form and collapsed form into function—reducing the concept of *chair* to its primal elements: material and purpose.

The economically designed, functional, unornamented machine chair has served historians ever since as one of modern design's points of departure. Missing from history, however, is what looks like an entirely antithetical approach to furnishing the domestic interior, which Riemerschmid presented alongside his machine furniture, at the very same exhibition in 1906. This was a gentleman's study—literally a "man's room," or *Herrenzimmer*—designed specifically for his long-standing client Carl Thieme but displayed at Dresden before it was permanently installed at the family's Munich villa directly after the exhibition closed (figures 4.2 and 4.14). Riemerschmid's *Herrenzimmer* seems to champion everything that the modern Dresden exhibition was attempting to reject: the emphasis on traditional woodwork appears to glorify handcraft, and its stylistic leanings toward nineteenth-century historicism are unmistakable. Its dark wood paneling and coffered ceiling suggest a nineteenth-century Renaissance-style dining room, and its

chairs would have felt at home in a rustic German family living room, or *Wohnstube* (figure 4.3). Like the stamp on an official decree, a portrait of Richard Wagner—celebrated nineteenth-century composer and originator of the *Gesamtkunstwerk* or "total artwork" paradigm—hangs to the left of a large wooden cupboard, certifying the room's historical reference. But a second picture, to Wagner's right, digs more deeply into the young nation's root system and penetrates more pointedly into the collective German psyche: hanging against the wooden wall is a lithographic reproduction of Albrecht Dürer's *Self-Portrait* from the year 1500 (figure 4.4).

What was this four-hundred-year-old, meticulously crafted image of a Renaissance artist doing at a landmark exhibition of modern industrial design in 1906?

FIGURE 4.1

Richard Riemerschmid, *Machine Furniture: Living Room from Collection I* (spruce with brass fittings), Dresden, 1906, in the exhibition catalog *Das Deutsche Kunstgewerbe 1906*, 162.

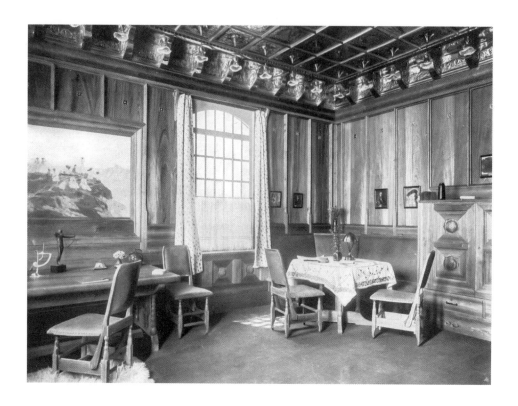

FIGURE 4.2

Richard Riemerschmid, *Herrenzimmer
installed at Third German Applied Arts
Exhibition,* Dresden, summer 1906, in *Das
Deutsche Kunstgewerbe 1906,* 159.

And why had the inventor of machine furniture created an interior where such an image would feel at home in the first place? History has avoided these puzzles by exalting the machine chair within the modernist canon while discounting Riemerschmid's more complex and perplexing design schemes. Was Riemerschmid's anachronistic Renaissance room a lapse—or a failure—of his modernism? Was he too conservative or too nostalgic to be truly progressive? Or did he simply bend his design principles to the whims of each new client? Is there, in short, a way to reconcile the avant-garde appearance and agenda of Riemerschmid's machine chair with furnishings and figures calculated to revive the spirit of a faded era? The 1906 sales catalog of the Dresden Workshops, where the machine chair is listed for purchase, gives us the beginnings of an answer—though in the form of a riddle:

FIGURE 4.3

Gabriel von Seidl, *Deutsche Wohnstube*,
German Art and Applied Art Exhibition,
Munich, 1876.

Riemerschmid's furniture, it tells us, animated by the "spirit of the machine," would "rebuild the world of Albrecht Dürer, from the inside out."[2]

This chapter unravels the riddle. It digs beneath these appealing yet elusive words to uncover how Riemerschmid's furniture designs—and his approach to their material, wood—tap into German cultural memory. Rather than approaching Riemerschmid's Dresden displays piecemeal—considering some successes and others failures—I take them as the intentional, unified product of a sophisticated, successful designer who saw how Renaissance culture might not simply inform but actually *enable* an emphatically modernist project. Riemerschmid saw the 1906 exhibition not just as an opportunity for more affordable, democratic, industrial design to overtake its handcrafted predecessor in the hearts and hands of consumers, but as the critical moment when Art itself could become truly democratic: when universally affordable modern German design would be hailed as the New German Art. And it was the material of wood—modest and useful, yet naturally ornamented; as ancient as Nature, yet renewed in each age—that bound the Renaissance concept of *Kunst* (art) to the modern invention of *Alltagskunst*: the art of everyday life.[3]

OLD-GERMAN ART AND MODERN ART-INDUSTRY

Hermann Muthesius wrote in 1901 that "only when art has once again become a common necessity, will we enter the new Age of Art [*Kunstzeit*]."[4] This was the core belief of the *Kunstgewerbebewegung* or Art-Industry Movement, the design reform movement begun in the 1890s as a branch of the broader *Lebensreform*. By 1906, the Art-Industry Movement was represented by the 17,000-member Verband des deutschen Kunstgewerbes (German Art-Industry Association), led by Muthesius. It would be succeeded in 1907 by the German Werkbund.[5] According to the Art-Industry Movement's proponents, twentieth-century art must be made accessible

FIGURE 4.4

Albrecht Dürer, *Self-Portrait in Fur Cloak*, 1500. Oil on wood panel, 48.9 × 67.1 cm. Inv. No. 537. bpk Bildagentur/Alte Pinakothek, Bayerische Staatsgemaeldesammlungen, Munich, Germany / Art Resource, NY.

to German society as a whole. But rather than attempting to bring "high art" down to the *Volk* through museum programs and reproducible media, these reformers decided to reinvent the concept of art altogether. If useful objects were also aesthetic ones, they argued, then art could truly penetrate the German household and integrate itself into everyday life, ennobling German culture as a whole. By 1906, modern art meant utilitarian art in *Kunstgewerbe* discourse. Visitors to the Dresden exhibition read in the exhibition catalog that "the modern man . . . wants to feel his art as the living breath that breathes through his house and all of its housewares: art as room-art [*Raumkunst*]."[6]

To "breathe" through the house, modern industrial art had to combine beauty and utility naturally—organically. This meant rejecting the popular nineteenth-century practice of applying decoration (as a secondary step) to useful objects, and embracing instead the object's *purpose* as the source of its aesthetic expression. How well the object served its particular purpose or *Zweck* was determined by its *Zweckmäßigkeit*. In a literal sense, *Zweckmäßigkeit* was a measure of the way a tool performed its specific function; but in a more intuitive sense, *Zweckmäßigkeit* was an index of *thingliness*: To what extent did the object's outer form capture its unique, essential nature, its reason for being? Inseparable from *Zweckmäßigkeit* was *Materialgerechtigkeit*, "material justice," or the manner in which an object's form responded to or honored the precise materials from which it was made. Despite their distinct definitions, however, *Zweckmäßigkeit* and *Materialgerechtigkeit* were bound together by *Sachlichkeit*. Material and purpose were as essential to a thing's thingliness as cardinal traits are to a human personality: change them, and the thing was no longer itself.

This new focus on purpose and material as the primary ways to determine an object's form was part of modern art-industry's opposition to the nineteenth-century's catalog of historical styles—including Neorococo, Neoclasscisim, Neo-Renaissance, and, surprisingly, the more recent Art Nouveau or Jugendstil. Despite the fact that Jugendstil—Youth Style—had itself been devised as the antidote to a preoccupation with styles of the past, twentieth-century *Kunstgewerbe* reformers nonetheless classed it among the very styles it had sought to replace. This was because the mass production of Jugendstil's most characteristic formal elements—like the whiplash curve—had rapidly commercialized it, relegating it (in the eyes of German reformers, at least) to an ornamental style just as superficial as any of its predecessors. In his 1902 *Stilarchitektur und Baukunst* (*Style-Architecture and Building-Art*), Muthesius makes short work of Jugendstil's rise and demise: "For a moment the world opened itself to welcome a liberation; the style-machine of the last twenty years had been driven to the absurd and the clockwork of stylistic imitation stood still. But this was only true for a moment. Immediately this opportunity closed upon itself as the whiplash curve and the little flower ornament emerged and worked with redoubled energy. Again there was a style, and now one that was indubitably the very latest . . . The factories today stamp out Jugendstil ornament just as they previously stamped out Rococo ornament."[7]

By 1906, although the energy of the curved line was still latent in Riemerschmid's machine chair, the taut whiplash had visibly relaxed. The more fanciful *Sachlichkeit* of the late 1890s had been brought down to earth in a mature twentieth-century version, which, according to Muthesius, simply "tacks down the inner essence of the problem, and seeks to express everything outwardly."[8] But whether critics like Muthesius approved of it or not, Jugendstil had come to be seen as "art furniture." And the new, more forthright *Sachlichkeit* appeared to be anything but. The aesthetic by-products of *Sachlichkeit*'s straightforward problem-solving—revealed structures and natural materials—were hardly the elements that the general German public would have looked for in artistic furniture, much less in art itself. While Jugendstil was synonymous with the idea of art, the machine chair seemed to scoff at it. How, then, could machine furniture usher in a new age of German art, when its naked surfaces and shameless flaunting of mechanization openly rejected everything that average Germans could have recognized as art?

Muthesius's new German art was to emphasize the innate properties of natural materials and the significance of these materials for practical, everyday life. This approach undoubtedly shared ground with British Arts and Crafts principles, promoted during the latter half of the nineteenth century by such reformers as William Morris; but for Muthesius it was rooted far earlier, in a uniquely Germanic understanding of *Kunst* (art), founded on an idealized vision of the medieval craft guild, or *Bauhütte*. Muthesius explained the *Bauhütte* as a "timeless local guild tradition" in which "one remained simple and natural" and "limited oneself to the necessary and familiar."[9] The "necessary" and "familiar" Germanic art Muthesius had in mind was not placed on a pedestal nor hung on a gallery wall: it was both accessible and essential to all Germans because it was the true "art of the people."[10]

Muthesius hails Riemerschmid's interiors and furniture in 1904 in precisely these terms: they are "simple and German," he writes, and therefore "worthy of the name" *Volkskunst* (folk art, or the people's art).[11] In 1908, the Austrian critic Joseph August Lux illustrated Muthesius's theory, writing that Riemerschmid's art was like the "German folksong, echoing through the German forest . . . on those long winter spinning-wheel evenings."[12] It was the material of spinning wheels and forests—*wood*—that epitomized the self-conscious roughness, earthiness, and familiarity inherent in Muthesius's and Lux's conceptions of German art. The floor-to-ceiling woodiness of Riemerschmid's 1906 *Herrenzimmer*, in conjunction with the Germanic heroes of art that graced its wood-paneled walls, marks this room as something more significant and complex than the old-timey foil to Riemerschmid's progressive machine furniture suites. This *Gesamtkunstwerk* interior, presided over by Dürer and Wagner, becomes the historical, cultural, and even material context in which the full meaning of the machine chair may unfold. In its sophisticated deployment of symbolic materials and forms, as well as its calculated references to "ancient" and "modern" fathers of German art, Riemerschmid's *Herrenzimmer* unites the old-German art tradition with Germany's modern art-industry, welcoming exhibition visitors in 1906 to what Muthesius called "the new Age of Art."

Muthesius's New Age of Art was founded on what he called a German "feeling." This feeling spurned the aesthetic standards of antiquity, the majestic "outward sweep of the classical line," and longed instead for something far more homey: "emotional warmth, inventiveness, and a sense of workmanship, construction, and proficiency in the applied arts." Muthesius argued that this German art-feeling was a "yearning for spiritualization, that desire for an intimacy suited to the circumstances of the individual task."[13] If this constellation of ideas feels familiar, it is because Muthesius's relation of the spiritual and the material, his connection of intimacy with outer "circumstances," and, finally, the specificity of the "individual task," coexist and *define* one central concept: *Sachlichkeit*. In fact, Muthesius's characterization in 1902 of the German art feeling is strikingly similar to Richard Streiter's 1896 definition of *Sachlichkeit* as "the character of a built work not solely out of a determination of needs but also from the milieu, from the qualities of available materials, and from the environmentally and historically conditioned feeling of the place."[14]

But in 1902, Muthesius takes a monumental step: rather than allowing *Sachlichkeit* to remain simply one approach to architecture and design, limited to individual cases and regional vernaculars, he proclaims it to be the historically, culturally, and *nationally* German approach not only to the applied arts, but to Art itself. Or, to state it as a logical proposition: the German mode of artmaking was *Sachlichkeit*; *Sachlichkeit* necessarily generated art with a practical, utilitarian purpose; and so, logically, true German Art was applied art—not just *Kunst*, but *Kunstgewerbe*. *Sachlichkeit*, the collective, pan-German "feeling for art," had manifested itself originally in Gothic architecture and applied arts, then in the art of the nineteenth-century Romantics, and was perceptible once again in the first years of the twentieth century. One of its most iconic incarnations—alive and well in the public imagination at the time of Muthesius's text—was in the paintings and prints executed around 1500 by the Nuremberg goldsmith's son, Albrecht Dürer.

VAGUENESS AND LOVE IN THE FOUNDERS' TIME

Since the beginning of the nineteenth century, when Albrecht Dürer's half-timbered house in Nuremberg was first opened to the public, the age in which he lived (around the turn of the sixteenth century) had suggested itself as the right epoch for culture-conscious Germans to replicate in their domestic interiors. During the two decades between the Great Exhibition at London's Crystal Palace in 1851 and the founding of the new Germany, a fascination with all things *altdeutsch*, or "old German," began to occupy the Germanic imagination. Design historian Stefan Muthesius has shown how the designation *altdeutsch* was linked to the late medieval German Gothic, which his great uncle, Hermann Muthesius, designated in 1902 as the inaugural epoch of German art.[15] During the 1850s and 1860s, Germans welcomed the revival of unpretentious, middle-class *altdeutsche* décor and decorative objects. These things opposed the fashionable elegance of their French competitors by celebrating that which seemed inherent, enduring, and uncontrived in German culture.

In 1868, Riemerschmid was born into this atmosphere of fierce nationalism and intense international competition, which came to a head in the Franco-Prussian War of 1870–1871. Germany's unification in 1871 as a result of pan-German collaboration and victory in the war was marked at the outset by wild speculation. This was the Gründerzeit, or "age of the founders," named for the *Gründer*—the speculators who founded the many new companies that sprouted up on the heels of unification. Underpinning the initial sense of euphoric optimism regarding German endeavor was the very real availability of capital facilitated by the French indemnity payment of five million francs, as well as the German annexation of Alsace and Lorraine, French territories known for their thriving industries. Economic expansion led to a building boom and an increased demand for everyday objects of all kinds, especially luxury goods to adorn the lavish new dwellings of the nouveau riche *Gründer*. But the Gründerzeit heyday would not last long: in 1873, the market crashed and the

Gründerkrise (*Gründer* crisis) ensued—a bitter aftermath of recession and general financial instability lasting until 1896.[16]

But unification had fueled the preexisting desire for a national style, and financial instability stimulated it even further. As the French recovered from war and began to reclaim their position on the luxury market, the British continued to pose a threat to a German applied arts industry now weakened by financial downturn. For many Germans, unification had signified not simply the triumph of German military power, but the ascendency of German cultural values at the expense of their French counterparts. In the sobering aftermath of the freewheeling Gründerzeit, those with a stake in the fate of German culture began to scan the past more deeply than ever for a way to reestablish German identity in a modern, industrial world.

Germany celebrated 1871 not just as the year of unification, but also as the four hundredth anniversary of Dürer's birth. Fascination with the artist's age—the German Renaissance—intensified after unification, but was also quickly corrupted into something much more flexible and livable than a slavish devotion to a historical style. The sixteenth century seemed to present a number of parallels with the 1870s Gründerzeit: Dürer's time glowed in cultural retrospect as a golden age of art, culture, and *comfort*—not just for aristocratic arts patrons, but in the simpler homes of merchants as well. Although Germans acknowledged the beauty and elegance of Italian Renaissance art and decor, they believed the German Renaissance to have been more intimate—*gemütlich*, or cozy. This view of a German Renaissance, characterized, in the words of nineteenth-century architectural historian Wilhelm Lübke, at once by "original ability, even native genius, individual freedom," and "a familiar warmth and liveliness," elasticized the "deutsche Renaissance" in the 1870s, expanding it to encompass already favored old-German medieval and vernacular attributes.[17] Before long, instead of referring merely to the *deutsche Renaissance*, decorators employed the hybridized term *altdeutsche Renaissance* to describe a composite yet still thoroughly German style of decor. To Stefan Muthesius, this shift away from stylistic purity and historical accuracy toward a cozy, old-German pastiche indicated "a greater vagueness, but also a much deeper love."[18]

Riemerschmid's native Bavarian city of Munich folded vagueness and love into a confection of past and present, simplicity and sophistication, amounting to a local style. As Germany's gateway to the Alps, Munich was a tourist destination for Germans and foreigners alike. It offered visitors the cosmopolitan culture of the opera, coffee house, and grand encyclopedic museum, as well as the iconic alpine vernacular culture of *Lederhosen*, *Dirndl*, and *Bierkeller*. The Bavarian alpine peasant house was the first vernacular building type to undergo ethnographic study in Germany, and the materials, colors, and textures that made up its interior exerted a decided influence on Munich's artists, architects, and designers.[19] Munich's local designers wove the two strands of "Munich-ness"—its sophisticated cosmopolitanism and its naive vernacular—into a fresh, yet cozily familiar upholstery for the domestic interior. On July 15, 1876, at the German Art and Art-Industry Exhibition, the Bavarian Applied Arts Association unveiled the new "Munich Style" of interior decor at Munich's Crystal Palace. Munich architect Gabriel von Seidl's room at the 1876 exhibition would become the touchstone of the new Munich movement (figure 4.3).

AN OLD-GERMAN *STUBE* FOR MODERN LIVING

Seidl's room—officially titled the *Deutsche Wohnstube* (*German Living Room*), but casually called the *Seidlzimmer* (Seidl room)—was a *Stube*, a type of room that had become popular in southern Germany, including the alpine region, around 1300 and remained a standard component of the southern middle-class house through the sixteenth century. Seidl's *Wohnstube* featured light-brown, untreated pine paneling, white-washed walls, a carved wood ceiling, and emphasized particular material characteristics: coarse wood grain, the lead-glazed ceramic tiles of a large heating stove, and a bottle-glass window that bathed the room in milky light.

The word *Stube*, cognate with the English "stove," referred to a heated parlor whose central feature was a large ceramic-tiled stove. In contrast to the other rooms in the late-medieval and early Renaissance southern German house, the *Stube* could be heated to a comfortable warmth in winter (20°C or 68°F). In place of an open hearth, the tile stove not only provided much more efficient radiant heat but also guaranteed a clean, smoke-free atmosphere, thereby making the *Stube* the most desirable space for family activities, including working, reading, playing games, and eating. Although the *Stube*'s primary function was to create winter-proof warmth, it was also richly punctuated by windows that yielded unusually generous amounts of daylight. The pleasantly warm and surprisingly bright *Stube* quickly became both the most comfortable and the most prestigious room in the late medieval house: a space where the family gathered, but also where they entertained guests.[20]

Enabling this warmth and comfort was the *Stube*'s distinctive construction. In order to conserve the heat generated by the tile stove and counter the effects of the abundant windows, the room was built as an outsized wooden cabinet set within the existing structure of the half-timbered house. Its floor, walls, and ceiling were all made of solid timber. To enhance its powers of insulation, the *Stube* was positioned in a back corner of the house and always entered through a vestibule, a hallway, or another room—never directly from the street. The *Stube*'s costly floor-to-ceiling wood construction and state-of-the-art amenities demonstrated the owner's wealth and status. And yet the atmosphere of the south German *Stube* was the opposite of stiff elegance: its wooden ceilings were low, its wooden walls were unadorned, and its wooden floors bare. Its large tile stove was minimally ornamented. Aside from built-in wooden benches, wooden tables, and chairs, the *Stube* was sparsely furnished. The *Stube* was, in a word, *schlicht*—plain, homey, and homespun. Its construction and materials reflected an individual, and by extension a family, who, far from aloof and ceremonious, were warm-hearted, content, at ease, and magnanimous.

The second-floor study, or *Schreibstube* (writing room), in Albrecht Dürer's Nuremberg house became a particular attraction for visitors in the 1870s and 1880s. A late nineteenth-century photograph of the study displays *altdeutsche Renaissance* comfort: a *Stube* with its characteristic wooden floor, walls, and ceiling, its bottle-glass windows, its built-in wooden benches, and its few furnishings, also of wood, as well as a bow-legged Luther chair and a heavy, scantily carved writing table (figure 4.5). The pewter hand-washing basin mounted on the left wall with its accompanying pewter kettle hanging above, along with the candle chandelier constructed from antlers and carved wood that dangled from the ceiling, testify to the practical, yet refined nature of the study—a place where the artist could wash his hands of the outside world and engage in interior pursuits. Dürer depicts this quiet, contemplative inner life in his copperplate etching of *Saint Jerome in His Study* (figure 4.6). In meticulous anachronism, the fifth-century saint occupies a *Stube* very like Dürer's own: as Jerome stoops over a wooden writing stand placed on a wooden table with inverted U-shaped legs, he works not merely by the "inner light" radiating out from the nimbus around his head, but by the milky rays streaming in from two bottle-glass windows. Like Dürer's *Stube*, Jerome's study is thoroughly woody: the grained texture of floor, walls, and ceiling have all been carefully etched into the copperplate. Even the built-in wooden benches recall those in Dürer's *Stube*. Jerome's tile stove is probably just out of our view, to the saint's left.

The tile stove was a prominent feature of the 1876 *Seidlzimmer*. And its simple board floor, natural wood paneling, hand-washing kettle and basin, and recessed,

arched bottle-glass window are all present both in Dürer's etching and in his own *Stube*. The *Seidlzimmer*, with its high ceilings and more elaborate furnishings, was, however, a better reflection of nineteenth-century taste than a facsimile of sixteenth-century domesticity; still, its bones—the bare pine floor and the untreated wood panels, along with the whitewashed plaster above them—identified it as a simple, informal family room meant for everyday living. Jerome's study is a cozy coincidence of order and disorder: while each implement hangs neatly in its proper place on the wall behind his desk, little signs of the benign material disarray that results from mental industry abound. Even the sun renders the regular patterns of the bottle-glass windows unruly by reproducing them in gay distortion on the window

FIGURE 4.5

Albrecht Dürer's study, Nuremberg.
Photograph ca. 1896–98. Schlesinger
Library, Harvard Radcliffe Institute.

FIGURE 4.6

Albrecht Dürer, *St. Jerome in his Study*,
1514. Copper engraving. Germanisches
Nationalmuseum, Nuremberg. On loan from
the city of Nuremberg's art collections.
Photo: M. Runge.

arches. And the Luther chair in Dürer's own room, pulled out at a slight angle from his desk, suggests that the artist has only moments before gotten up from his work and will shortly return to it.

Unusually for an exhibition room in 1876, the *Seidlzimmer* echoed the impression, given by both Dürer's actual and fictional *Stuben*, of a room in use: a towel hung ready next to the hand-washing basin; the chairs on either side of the little table, fitted cozily into the bay window nook, were angled invitingly toward the visitor; and the dining table in front of the tile stove was laid for a casual family meal. This was in truth a *Wohn- und Eßstube*, or living and eating room, identical in concept to the machine furniture room Riemerschmid would exhibit in 1906 at Dresden (figure 4.1). The artfully staged *Seidlzimmer* set the tone for the *altdeutsche Renaissance* room, which, despite its historicizing name, should be not simply livable in terms of contemporary needs and comforts, but *lively*—animated by character and personality. This sensation of liveliness was one of the most significant aspects of the *altdeutsche Renaissance* concept.[21] Underscoring the *Seidlzimmer*'s ironic mixture of everyday ease and self-conscious theatricality, observers remarked that the *Wohnstube* seemed to have been "staged for a painter of genre paintings."[22] Here was a room where "our forefathers enjoyed their lives in youthful freshness,"[23] a room whose tile-stove acted as a true "comrade, warm with life."[24]

THE MUNICH DIALECTIC

The notion of a living past enlivening the present pervaded Munich's applied arts discourse, which hinged on two descriptive terms: the first was *derb*, meaning rough, coarse, or earthy; and the second was *gemütvoll*—full of feeling and imagination, or, literally, soulful. The paired terms evoked a specifically Bavarian approach to interior decoration, associated with Munich in particular.[25] Bavarians celebrated *Derbheit*—a casual roughness of character—as a regional virtue. *Gemütvoll*, on the other hand, stemmed from the noun *Gemüt*, referring to the spiritual capacities of the mind or soul. The adjective *derb* might connote the rough-and-ready construction of a chair or the coarse grain of its wood surface. By contrast, an object of transcendent cultural import, such as a painting by Albrecht Dürer, was *gemütvoll*. Within the new Munich interior, the *derb* and the *gemütvoll* performed a dialectic. If *Derbheit* advanced a thesis of vernacular materiality, *Gemüt* might be understood as its antithesis. Against the austere *Derbheit* of Seidl's white-washed walls and pine panels, accents of strong, saturated color provided imaginative, inspiriting *Gemüt*. Munich publisher Georg Hirth described how the Seidlzimmer's dashes of color were at the same time embedded in the Germanic past and imperative to the future of German domestic culture: "How the simple man, living in frugal circumstances in our cold Germany can arrive at a cozy, modestly beautiful, heart-warming domesticity, if we don't seek to reconnect with the classic examples from our 'good old days'—this I can't understand. Yes, I believe these models—I'll just mention the sap-green tile stove against the golden-brown wooden wall, and the deep blue stoneware jug on the red-embroidered tablecloth—would have to be invented all over again out of a sense of sheer, natural necessity, if they didn't already exist."[26] Hirth located these models of timeless German domesticity in the new old-German Renaissance interiors designed by the group of Munich artists and architects whose leading light was Gabriel von Seidl.

During the late 1870s, Hirth became a major proponent of Munich's *altdeutsche* Renaissance movement and the spokesperson for its designers; in 1880 he published *Das Deutsche Zimmer der Renaissance: Anregungen zu Häuslicher Kunstpflege* (*The German Room of the Renaissance: Hints on the Domestic Cultivation of Art*). This immensely popular manual on interior decoration, revised and reissued numerous times between 1880 and 1900, was filled with illustrations of both historical and contemporary interiors, including a print of the *Seidlzimmer*. In the Munich *Wohnstube*, Hirth found the spirit of Albrecht Dürer resurrected, and he assured his readers that this great man who had played such a significant part in the rebirth of art in the German lands during the sixteenth century now wanted to "live again in and through us."[27] It was this vision of a German past reanimated right before the viewer's eyes that informed Hirth's discussion of the Munich style. For Hirth, *altdeutsche* Renaissance was something more than one of many styles; it was an expression of character. Hirth believed that an old-German Renaissance room could emit the same sort of expressive richness that one associated with a warm personality.[28] Warmth was, in Hirth's estimation, the salient trait of the German character; he asserted that during the Renaissance period, while "southerners" (Italians) had devised "cool," academic theories on interior decoration, "northerners" (Germans) had warmed these theories up by putting them into domestic practice on northern soil—where warmth was a necessity.[29]

In the context of German domestic life, warmth had developed over the centuries as a condition at once physical and psychological. The tile stove, radiating smokeless heat and enabling physical comfort in the half-timbered south-German house, had defined the purpose and function—the *Zweckmäßigkeit*—of the sixteenth-century *Stube*. But by the advent of Seidl's nineteenth-century old-German Renaissance *Wohnstube* and Hirth's publication of *The German Room of the Renaissance*, the stove had become more than an old-fashioned amenity: it was now an agent of coziness—a "comrade, warm with life." Warmth was inherent in the German term *Gemütlichkeit*, most often translated as "coziness." But through its etymological relation to *Gemüt*, *Gemütlichkeit* implied something far beyond mere physical comfort. Though generally evoked through contact with material things, *Gemütlichkeit* itself was a sense of well-being, originating in the mind or soul and coloring one's physiological experience. A comfortably appointed room could foster a sense of *Gemütlichkeit*, but it was the symbolic associations of particular forms, materials, and colors—a room's aesthetic effect and emotional affect—that made it "gemütlich." Hirth writes that if one asked a German homeowner why he had arranged his room in a certain way, he would be far less likely to say "because the German Renaissance dictates that it be just so" than to say "because it delights me this way, because it goes together, and because it's beautiful, pleasant, cozy [*Gemütlich*], and cheerful."[30] For Hirth, Munich's domestic design was not simply a process of applying Renaissance style to nineteenth-century interiors. Rather, it channeled the creative spirit or soul—the *Gemüt*—of the old-German Renaissance that Hirth and his contemporaries understood as the key to reincarnating its affective genius and kindling the "heartwarming" glow of *Gemütlichkeit*.

Hirth viewed the Renaissance as a period when the objects of daily life had been held in high esteem, when even the smallest things were alive with artistic spirit.[31] But, he countered, this *Gemüt* of everyday things was rooted firmly in *Derbheit*. Renaissance materials seemed to possess a heightened "realness," emphasized in workmanship that foregrounded their defining qualities.[32] Above all, Hirth prized natural materials in their natural state, and the material that conducted the pulse of Nature most directly into the bourgeois parlor was wood. The spirit of the wood, in its unrefined and unpredictable wildness, was manifested in the visual and tactile irregularities of its natural surface. And the German people, Hirth proposed, at home in the forest, loved natural wood for its personality and character, for its peculiarities and deformities—"grain, annual rings, knots," and all.[33]

But the forest offered the German interior more than texture: wood brought color into the *Wohnstube*; it was in fact *the* color of the *altdeutsche* Renaissance room, providing the platform for Hirth's *Prinzip des Braunen* (principle of brown), in which wood, now understood as *color*, dappled the German interior with all the varied tones of mellow autumn light: "warm, juicy colors . . . browns, brown-reds, brown-greens, and brown-yellows . . . shot through with warm rays."[34] Like the *Stube* it lined and furnished, wood was warm, both chromatically and in the traditional, comfortable, and familiar associations it evoked. Wood was, for Hirth, both the principal color and primary material of the German interior. But for all its warmth, wood was still *derb*: its burls and figures were works of Nature rather than Art. To set the Munich dialectic of *Derbheit* and *Gemüt* in motion, then, Hirth studded his *Prinzip des Braunen* with gem-like accents. These touches of brilliant color were exemplified in the otherwise woody *Seidlzimmer*: Hirth's descriptions of its "sap-green tile-stove," its "deep blue stoneware jug," and its "red-embroidered tablecloth" brought his monochrome print to polychrome life. This sparing, selective use of bold, saturated color—those "glorious, raw tones that Nature lent to the Renaissance color-world"—he felt, was a distinctly northern practice, dating back to the rich *cloisons* that glowed from the surface of Jan van Eyck's early fifteenth-century panel paintings. The Renaissance had possessed "the right feeling for light and color," and it was Hirth's project to reawaken this feeling in nineteenth-century designers and dwellers.[35]

Although Hirth borrowed richly and openly from color theories of the first half of the nineteenth century—including Goethe's 1810 psychophysical *Farbenlehre* (*Color Doctrine*), Michel-Eugène Chevreul's 1839 theory of simultaneous color contrasts, and Hermann von Helmholtz's work in the 1850s on the distinction between light and pigment in color-mixing—toward the century's conclusion, color choice in the domestic interior was becoming a matter of feeling.[36] But the ongoing investigation, over the course of the nineteenth century, into the affective, physiological power of color and its operation had laid the groundwork for the preoccupation with color in the design literature of Hirth's day. After the invention of the first chemical dyes in 1856, intensely bright synthetic colors in previously unknown shades began to appear in women's fashions and domestic interiors. By the 1870s, the new technology of color lithography allowed homemakers to envision their domestic surroundings pulsating with vibrant carpets, rich upholstery, and brilliant wallpapers as they thumbed through the latest taste manuals and pattern books. Though Hirth's principle of brown precluded him from advocating a rainbow scheme for the German interior, his vision of a revivified Renaissance was anything but antiquarian: each material in the new old-German room was alive with its own robust, indigenous color.

In 1905, Hermann Muthesius announced the advent of an "unheard-of" phenomenon: "The applied arts [*Kunstgewerbe*] have achieved, in the public consciousness, a place next to the previously privileged monopoly-art, painting."[37] Riemerschmid, whom only the year before Muthesius had identified as the inaugurator of a new German art, had brought his training in that "monopolizing" art of painting to bear in his decoration of modern interiors. Or perhaps what he had done was far more intuitive: he had simply expanded the boundaries of his painting practice to embrace graphic art, furniture, household objects, and interiors. Around 1900, Riemerschmid had begun adapting the bold, complementary palettes of Munich's nineteenth-century neo-Renaissance, deploying their luminous shades in striking new ways. He had extended Seidl's lively accents to clothe the walls and floor of his *Room of an Art Lover*, the modern interior displayed at the Paris Exposition Universelle in 1900 (figures 2.11–2.13). With the alpine reds of its carpet and its meadow-green wallpaper, this room—despite its Jugendstil tendrils—conveyed a sense of old-German *Gemüt*, to which Riemerschmid's plain wooden *Musician's Chair* added the necessary dash of *Derbheit*. In the art lover's room, Riemerschmid reversed Seidl's proportions, exploding touches of color into fields and whittling broad expanses of wood down into a single, graceful reincarnation of a rustic prototype. Riemerschmid's transposition of Hirth's full-bodied green, blue, and red for his interiors around 1900 resonated especially with Hermann Muthesius. In contrast to examples of French Art Nouveau also on display at the 1900 exposition, with their tremulous shell-pinks and dusty golds, Riemerschmid's colors were, according to Muthesius, "well thought-out, cozy, strong but never brash . . . everything is unobtrusive, middleclass, and even-tempered; but you still get *kräftige Hausmannskost*"—a hearty, home-cooked meal.[38]

These nourishing colors fortified the decor of Carl Thieme's *Speisezimmer*, the live-in family dining room—a modernized, upscale *Wohn- und Eßstube*—that Riemerschmid designed and installed at the Thiemes' Munich villa in 1902–1903. After entering the house, one reached the *Speisezimmer* by passing first through the more formal salon and then through a small reception area that connected the two larger rooms (figure 4.7, foreground). Like the late medieval *Stube*, the Thiemes' *Speisezimmer* was not only situated at a protective remove from the street door, but also functioned as a multipurpose living room, designed to accommodate work and play in addition to family dining. In conceiving this *Speisezimmer*,

FIGURE 4.7

Richard Riemerschmid, *Speisezimmer (living-dining room) in the Thieme House*, Munich, 1903, Architekturmuseum der TUM. © 2021 Artists Rights Society (ARS), New York / VG Bild-Kunst, Bonn.

Riemerschmid had reenvisioned the old-fashioned *Wohnstube* for the twentieth century while maintaining its hallmarks of comfort—plentiful light, warmth, and *wood*—throughout the process of transformation.

The *Speisezimmer*'s southern exposure meant that, like the old-German *Wohnstube*, it claimed the brightest natural light of any room on the villa's ground floor. But Riemerschmid improved on nature's illumination by installing an artful arrangement of electric fixtures: two intersecting rings of small light bulbs were mounted directly into the ceiling and sheathed in glass petals, so that the bulb itself, extending daringly beyond the petals, formed the center of each burning blossom. These luminous lilies stemmed from a colorfully painted medallion stenciled with interlacing circlets of leafy vines. Positioned directly beneath the ceiling decoration, a large carpet, already brilliant in hearty alpine reds, blues, greens, and golds, was set ablaze by the sparkling lights (figure 4.8). This avant-garde textile was practically an abstract painting in its own right: within a geometric frame patterned in blue and green stylized vines punctuated by diamond-shaped red buds, a central pool of volcanic red, orange, and yellow bubbles burst against the border's cooler vegetation. For each hue he employed, Riemerschmid provided both its warm and its cool tone, pairing these to approximate the effects of natural light.

Riemerschmid's homage to Nature was supported not only by Hirth's vision of a Renaissance "color-world" borrowing its paints from nature's palette, but also by the color theories of Bavarian physicist Wilhelm von Bezold, also active in Munich during the 1870s. Bezold championed complementary colors as he found them in his natural surroundings, explaining that red "forms a good pair with either of the colors green or blue, which dominate in nature."[39] According to Bezold, the combination of red, blue, and green, when applied to interior décor, exerted a "magic influence . . . which a landscape covered with fresh green, under a cloudless sky, exercises upon every human being."[40] In 1901, critic Karl Scheffler too acknowledged this natural color conjunction as working a kind of universal magic upon human beings: "It is all one needs," he writes, "to become happy enough to dance."[41]

Scheffler identified a room's *Bekleidung* (cladding)—specifically, its wallpaper and carpets—as the generator of that interior's "mood." The carpet was permitted to be "energetically colored" as it was never beheld separately from the totality of the room but was instead experienced constantly, "always colorfully present to the eye."[42] Riemerschmid's energetic red, blue, and green carpet approached nature's full complement. The sheer size and central position of the Thieme carpet meant that, just as Scheffler suggested, its optical force could not be taken in at a glance;

FIGURE 4.8

Richard Riemerschmid, *Hand-knotted Carpet
for Speisezimmer in the Thieme House*,
Munich, 1903. Münchner Stadtmuseum,
Sammlung Angewandte Kunst. © 2021
Artists Rights Society (ARS), New York / VG
Bild-Kunst, Bonn.

instead, it impressed its "dance-happy" mood on the family as their feet pressed into its fibers. This was the affective capacity of modern *Kunstgewerbe*—the new art that no longer demanded the undivided optical attention of a viewer, but instead infiltrated the occupant's mood, instilling its *Gemüt*, over time, within her very being.

Illuminated by the electric ceiling fixtures, the *Speisezimmer* carpet was not simply a material bearer of color, but a reflector and emitter of light, joining the two brass-clad columns that supported the room's basket-handle arch entrance, the glinting brass hardware of the furniture, and the *Heizkörperverkleidung* (heater cladding). These glimmering brass plates strung together with glass beads covered the steam-heating unit stationed opposite the south-facing windows, against the *Speisezimmer*'s north wall. Riemerschmid's design for the heater housing united the old-German *Stube*'s dual amenities of light and warmth in a single, practical yet artistic solution. Standing in for the *Stube*'s tile stove, the raised, reflective surfaces of the *Heizkörperverkleidung*'s linked brass plates both assumed and enhanced the aesthetic function of the old tile stove's shiny, lead-glazed tiles. As warm air passed through the brass curtain, the suspended plates swayed and clinked together, alerting the ear to the welcome emission of heat while simultaneously dispersing and activating light to cheer the heart and amuse the eye. The associations of warmth and camaraderie, which over several centuries had reflected from the motionless surface of the tile stove, were now brought to life in the shifting, shimmering plates of Riemerschmid's modern heating unit as a direct result of its utilitarian function. The late medieval *Stube* had solved the problem of the dirty, smoky open fireplace by containing and concealing altogether the kinetic element of fire; Riemerschmid's twentieth-century solution, still more hygienic, resurrected the flicker and crackle of the living flame.

Although the modern steam heater had displaced the traditional tile stove, tiles were still present in Riemerschmid's *Speisezimmer*. Above built-in wooden benches, violet-glazed stoneware tiles circled the room at eye level before yielding to the smooth, unornamented upper wall. The built-in wooden seating was a formally reductive version of the convention begun in the late-medieval *Stube* and quoted in the *Seidlzimmer*; the simple whitewashed wall too had been a feature of the alpine *Stube*, an element that Seidl had admired and employed repeatedly in his own interiors; and finally, the ceramic tiles, though stripped from their former comrade, the stove, and deployed instead as a modern, hygienic, and modestly ornamental wallcovering, formed at one of its corners a *wall fountain*—the hand-washing basin familiar both from the late medieval *Stube* and again from its 1870s reincarnations.[43]

These congenial exchanges of color and light were the results of Riemerschmid's *Materialgerechtigkeit*: he had bestowed artistic and utilitarian justice in equal measure on dyed wool fibers, brass plates, and glazed stoneware tiles in the Thiemes' *Speisezimmer*. These attentions were more than enough to satisfy the needs of *Gemüt*. But *Derbheit*, too, demanded its due in this cozy, modern *Wohnstube*; and its demands were furnished by wood.

Muthesius commended Riemerschmid in 1904 for being the first designer of his generation to "allow the sheer loveliness of the wood grain to be seen once more, and even accentuated in his furniture."[44] Riemerschmid's imposing mahogany sideboard, stationed on the *Speisezimmer*'s east wall, materialized Muthesius's assertion (figure 4.9). The massive sideboard acted both as an extension and a culmination of the wooden benches that lined the *Speisezimmer*'s walls. Each cabinet door framed a unique set of intarsia panels, whose puzzle-like construction, meticulously executed by the Munich carpentry firm of Kohlbecker & Sohn, exuded the characteristic "loveliness" of Riemerschmid's wood grain. The sideboard was undoubtedly *derb*: in addition to its simplified, rough-hammered hardware, its overall aesthetic impact was produced solely and inherently by the character of wood, with its natural grain, figures, and flaws. But the warm red glow of the mahogany and its intricate inlays, whose swirling, hypnotic configurations were crafted with masterful skill and precise calculation, refined and redefined "rough" Munich *Derbheit*, inflecting it with the "imagination and feeling" hitherto reserved for *Gemüt*. Riemerschmid had once again inverted the old-German formula, so that *Derbheit* now served as *Gemüt*'s accent, and what one might call Riemerschmid's *Prinzip des Bundten*—"principle of the colorful"—now presided where Hirth's *Prinzip des Braunen* ("principle of brown") had once held sway.

Hirth had argued that it was an interior's materials that defined its social character: "massive constructions of timber," for example, exuded a powerful realism that precluded all pretentiousness.[45] Amid the plush red upholstery and golden appliqués of the Thiemes' salon, Riemerschmid's stocky wooden wardrobe stood out like a hard fact (figure 2.21). Compared with the mahogany sideboard's elaborately figured cupboards, the magnolia wardrobe's simple, flat doors were shockingly *derb* and powerfully "real"—or, in the language of the new *Kunstgewerbe*, *sachlich*. Within the sober expanses of its plain wooden doors, the wardrobe's peering, opalescent "eyes" reflected the soul of the salon—its *Gemüt*—back upon its occupants. In conjunction with its tough, defiant stance, these mother-of-pearl fragments instilled imagination and feeling directly *within* this model of *Derbheit*, synthesizing

FIGURE 4.9

Richard Riemerschmid, *Sideboard for Speisezimmer in the Thieme House*, Munich, 1903. Münchner Stadtmuseum, Sammlung Angewandte Kunst. © 2021 Artists Rights Society (ARS), New York / VG Bild-Kunst, Bonn.

Munich's old-German dialectic in a single piece of modern furniture. While the wardrobe's *Derbheit*—its staunch material presence—made it hearty, it was this infusion of *Gemüt* that elevated heartiness to heart and *soul*.

THE *GEIST* IN THE MACHINE

At the same time that he was working on the Thiemes' Speisezimmer and salon, Riemerschmid was becoming one of the most important designers for the Dresdner Werkstätten für Handwerkskunst, the Dresden furniture and housewares firm run by his colleague and soon-to-be brother-in-law, Karl Schmidt.[46] The Dresdner Werkstätten (renamed Deutsche Werkstätten in 1907) employed progressive artist-designers, including Riemerschmid's Munich colleague Peter Behrens, the Austrian Joseph Maria Olbrich, Charles Rennie Mackintosh from Scotland, and the English Mackay Hugh Baillie Scott, in an attempt to offer the public an artistic alternative to the historicist furniture then available on the market. Schmidt cultivated the use of machines in the production of "artistic handwork," dedicating his Dresden Workshops to the creation of "furniture which is so arranged that each domestic furnishing best serves its purpose"—*Zweckmäßigkeit*—and to the *Sachlichkeit* that "expresses this purpose in its form."[47]

Schmidt's connection of the practical, utilitarian aspects of *Sachlichkeit* with a vision of German production that incorporated both the tangible processes of design and fabrication, as well as the more ephemeral sensibility of "German-ness," positioned his Dresdner Werkstätten to stand as an example of successful modern manufacture at the Third German Applied Arts Exhibition in the summer of 1906. The Workshops displayed twenty-six showrooms (seventeen outfitted by Riemerschmid) in their own separate exhibition hall. Occupying the focal point of popular and critical attention at the 1906 Dresden Exhibition, Schmidt's Dresdner Werkstätten—and Riemerschmid in particular—acted as the catalyst of this pivotal point in the history of design.

The exhibition's impact on the fate of modern design began with its selection process. Unlike previous applied arts exhibitions in Germany, during which various well-established organizations and manufacturing firms simply purchased exhibition space to show products of their own choosing, the 1906 exhibition's organizational committee—dominated by progressive local architects, artists, and designers—chose individual objects based on aesthetic and utilitarian merit rather than the reputation or legacy of the firms that produced them. The immediate result was an exhibition that showcased not just modern aesthetics, but the latest means of production. The more lasting effect, however, was the escalation of existing tensions between traditional craftspeople and conventional manufacturers on one side, and modern designers and progressive firms on the other. The term *Kunstgewerbe* and its component parts—"art" and "industry"—accrued new connotations at odds with the values associated with the traditional crafts. The exhibition's emphasis on the significance of art in the development of modern German industry and the artist's capacity to determine its destiny alienated practitioners of traditional handcraft, to whom the term *artist* seemed both pretentious and superfluous: Was the craftsman not already an artist, designer, and maker himself?

A new, explicit and specialized notion of art, or *Kunst*, as a status or quality that only an artist could bestow, became the exhibition's leitmotif, reappearing in each of its three sections: *Kunst* (Art), *Kunsthandwerk* (Artistic Handcraft), and *Kunstindustrie* (Art-Industry). The category of *Kunst* included not only *bildende Kunst*, or "fine art," but also *Raumkunst*: "spatial art," or the art of the interior, embracing in theory all aspects of dwelling and daily life. The category titled *Kunsthandwerk* was ostensibly devoted to traditional handcraft; however, the addition of the prefix *Kunst* to the familiar concept of *Handwerk* implied that these displays comprised not simply German vernacular craft that had stood the test of time, but specific examples of craft that had been deemed most "artistic" by the selection committee. *Kunsthandwerk* was, in a sense, the pendant concept to the final category, *Kunstindustrie*, the former signifying those objects made by hand, and the latter absorbing those manufactured with the help of machines. The inclusive yet ambiguous *Kunstgewerbe* had been fractured into two fraternal terms, related by opposition rather than affinity. The polarity of *Kunsthandwerk* and *Kunstindustrie* at Dresden in 1906 mirrored the practical and ideological conflicts erupting within the *Kunstgewerbebewegung* itself.

And yet, though the *Kunsthandwerk* and *Kunstindustrie* sections at Dresden in 1906 implied the existence of sharp demarcations between the two categories, in practice the two production philosophies frequently overlapped. According to Dresden-based critic Erich Haenel, the central theme of the Dresden exhibition was not the segregation of artistic handcraft and artistic industrial production, but the nature of their relationship.[48] Somewhat ironically, at the same time that the Dresdner Werkstätten dominated the displays of *Kunstindustrie* at the Dresden exhibition, *Handwerkskunst* (literally, "handwork art") was part of their name.

Although hand-working methods were practiced at the Dresden Workshops, hand-craft was never pursued or exalted simply for its own sake; rather, emphasis was placed on efficiency and quality in the production of practical, durable furniture and housewares for customers of varying income levels, by employing the most appropriate means available to execute each specific task.[49] In his privileging of this flexible, "democratic" approach to production over an insistence on handcraft alone, Schmidt corroborated the view Muthesius had expressed in his 1902 article "Kunst und Maschine" ("Art and Machine"): "Today wherever handwork is promoted as the ideal, one has to reckon with artificial economic conditions. Immediately that remarkable cultural image pops up, which William Morris and the English artist-socialists disseminated, that begins as an 'art by the people and for the people,' but ends in products so expensive that only the richest can afford them."[50]

Another vocal critic of exclusive adherence to handcraft in modern applied arts production was liberal politician and art enthusiast Friedrich Naumann, whose ideas and policies exerted a significant influence on Schmidt and his vision for the Dresden Workshops. Like Muthesius, Naumann believed that utilitarian objects of a high aesthetic caliber were the key to revitalizing German society and culture—and that these could only be made available to the general German public if machine technology were employed in their production. However, Naumann rejected the notion that machines should be used in the manufacture of objects that could be produced more efficiently by hand or, conversely, that machines should be used to make objects appear handcrafted. Machines should not replace crafting hands but must develop instead forms suited to their own mechanized means of mass production. It was the designer's task, then, to "spiritualize" the machine through new aesthetic forms capable of expressing its "soul."[51] Nauman's seminal essay on this topic, "Art in the Age of the Machine," from 1904, explored the significance of industrial production and machine technology for Germany's artistic culture. Naumann called for a new German style, based on the aesthetics and capacities of machines, to transform Germany's applied arts production and so to realize the spirit of the modern age.[52] By 1905, in technical collaboration with Schmidt's Workshops, Riemerschmid had developed his serially producible furniture, as Naumann expressed it, "from the spirit of the machine."[53] And in 1906, this machine furniture became the main attraction of the Workshops' extensive displays of *Kunstindustrie* at the first exhibition of modern design in Germany.

In "Art and Industry," his essay for the exhibition's official catalog, Naumann proposed that "the highest art is simply the most pleasing combination of mechanized production processes."[54] Riemerschmid's machine furniture was the first program of industrial furniture in Germany; it was intended to demonstrate the potential of the machine in the fabrication of high-quality, artistic furniture. And it became the mascot of the modern *Kunstindustrie* displayed at Dresden in 1906. Its standardized parts were produced in a serial process fueled by the most modern power tools, including an electric-powered band saw for cutting profiles and an electric-powered surface planer to achieve a consistently uniform thickness in all components of a particular piece of furniture. Although band saws and planers had been in use in larger furniture manufactories since the 1870s, the application of electric power was new in the early twentieth century. New too was the notion that a relatively small-scale manufacturer could use such advanced machinery in the production of "art furniture."

In the Dresdner Werkstätten's separate *Kunstindustrie* exhibition building, visitors encountered fourteen displays of interiors featuring the machine furniture arranged in domestic ensembles, as well as a fully functioning workshop, where they witnessed the new electric-powered woodworking machines in action as the component parts were fabricated, assembled, and painted in rapid succession. Disassembly procedures—important both to industrial commerce and to increasingly itinerant modern lifestyles—were also demonstrated: a sturdily built cupboard could be dismantled and packed for shipping in five minutes. However, the machine furniture also reflected the interdependent relationship of *Kunstindustrie* and *Kunsthandwerk* that defined the state of the applied arts at Dresden: while it relied upon mechanical processes for cutting and profiling, each chair, table, cupboard, and bookcase had to be assembled and finished by hand.

Naumann pointed out that while small housewares—cutlery, for example—had been mass-produced for decades, visitors to Dresden in 1906 were "experiencing the industrialization of artistic carpentry" for the first time as they toured the displays of Riemerschmid's machine furniture.[55] The machine furniture realized Naumann's desire, articulated in his 1904 essay "Art in the Age of the Machine," to witness the development of mechanized production through the artistic guidance of a designer who truly understood the "spirit of the machine" and its potential for modern art. The machine furniture, then, had a twofold significance. Culturally, it represented the successful harnessing of the machine in the advancement of the New German Art; but its inherent reproducibility also had social implications: the democratization of modern art—the dissemination of "good taste" to all levels of society.

Like the standardized component construction that facilitated the machine furniture's reproducibility, accessibility to all types of households—from the factory worker to the businessman—was built into its design. Riemerschmid designed three different lines of machine furniture to accommodate a range of income levels. The cheapest line, *Collection I*, included a living-dining room, bedroom, and kitchen priced at a total of 570 marks (figure 4.1). These three basic suites were made from spruce stained in Riemerschmid's "alpine" colors: red or blue for the living-dining room, green for the bedroom set, and red for the kitchen. The vernacular sensibility of these traditionally "peasant" colors was reinforced by iron hardware on the bedroom and kitchen furniture, as well as rustic-looking, leafy, wreath-shaped ornaments stenciled over selected cupboard panels. Brass hardware distinguished the living-dining room as a space where one might also receive visitors—just as the *Stube* would have been several centuries before. While the colorfully stained wood and iron fittings seemed to equate the modern lower-income household with peasant interiors of bygone days, standardized manufacturing techniques meant that all surfaces were smoother and more regular—more practical for work and more hygienic to maintain—than they would have been in an alpine cottage. *Collection II* included the same basic kitchen furniture with a few added pieces; in this more expensive configuration intended for middle-class consumers, however, the cheerful red stain was replaced by a more sophisticated gray lacquer finish. To this was added a living-dining room in mahogany with bronze fittings and a bedroom in larch with iron fittings (figure 4.10); the entire set was priced at 1,200 marks. The third and most expensive collection (for 2,600 marks) offered more specialized rooms characteristic of an upper-middle-class household, such as a reception room, a gentleman's study (figure 4.11), and a young girl's bedroom set; this *Collection III* was executed primarily in smoked oak with iron hardware and mahogany with bronze.[56]

Riemerschmid's machine furniture seemed to combine the familiar *Derbheit* of the Bavarian peasant vernacular—a rough-and-ready charm—with the modern *Derbheit*, or spare, no-nonsense practicality and relentless reproducibility of the machine. Naumann applauded these qualities as they enabled the designer to disseminate well-made furniture to the consuming public while at the same time giving consumers a lesson in taste—educating them about the *Geist*, or spirit, of the machine that defined the age in which they were living. Naumann was aware, however, that to convey this spirit, "machine furniture" had to express *Stimmung* and *Gemüt*—feeling and imagination: it had to possess what he called a "soul" and

a "personality," the characteristic qualities that distinguished "machine art" from the morass of machine-made products.[57] To keep his machine furniture affordable, Riemerschmid had had to limit both the materials and methods used in its production: *Stimmung* and *Gemüt* were instilled through aesthetic subtleties, artistic details such as the colors of paints, stains, and lacquers; the stenciled ornaments applied sparingly here and there; the warmth and sheen of brass and bronze or the dull, cool resistance of iron in all its workaday integrity. But before all of these, Riemerschmid enlisted the crisp frugality of pine, the mellow gravity of oak, and the dark exoticism of mahogany—the poetics of wood.

FIGURE 4.10

Richard Riemerschmid, *Machine Furniture: Bedroom from Collection II* (larch pine with iron fittings), Dresden 1906, in *Das Deutsche Kunstgewerbe 1906*, 163.

A FOREST IN THE LIVING ROOM

The more costly the machine furniture, the *woodier* its wood. While sets for working families were stained in red, green, and blue, those designed for consumers with deeper pockets renounced both colorful surface treatments and applied ornaments in favor of the decorative effects of the wood itself. Within the standardized parameters of the machine furniture's construction, middle-class and upper-middle-class dwellers could enjoy ornament that was entirely unique: the particular character of the grained surface on a cupboard door, for instance, with all of its natural idiosyncrasies and imperfections, personalized what would otherwise have been

FIGURE 4.11

Richard Riemerschmid, *Machine Furniture: Gentleman's Study from Collection III* (smoked oak with iron fittings), Dresden 1906, in *Das Deutsche Kunstgewerbe 1906*, 161.

an impersonal piece of furniture, by uncovering the personality of the individual piece of wood.

In an article that appeared right before the opening of 1906 Dresden exhibition, Nuremberg art historian Paul Rée set himself the task of discovering "what Richard Riemerschmid means for the artistic life of our times."[58] One of Riemerschmid's great strengths as a designer, Rée asserted, was his ability to determine the specific value of every material for which he designed and to see its own peculiarities in their best light. "It is as if," Rée wrote, "he saw through to the materials' innermost essence and designed exactly how they themselves would, were they able to develop artistic forms for themselves."[59] For Rée, this uncanny ability to penetrate to the essence of a specific material and determine its nature—to, in the language of *Sachlichkeit*, get down to *die Sache*—was the primary way in which Riemerschmid both reflected and defined the artistic life of the modern age. Erich Haenel, discussing the machine furniture in a review of the Dresden exhibition, claimed that Riemerschmid had wedded the aesthetics of his designs so inextricably to their users' mechanical and psychological needs—the needs of the *soul*—that "we instinctively accept his work as if it were a necessity of our artistic culture."[60] Haenel continued by citing Friedrich Naumann, who, "when he wants to describe Riemerschmid, starts with wood and Riemerschmid's uncommon capacity to recognize its soul."[61]

Naumann wrote in his Dresden catalog essay that whereas once Germany had known great "poets of words," now, in the twentieth century, it could claim "poets of wood."[62] German culture had exchanged the Goethes of its Romantic age for "Holz-Goethes," like Schmidt and Riemerschmid. But the role of the wood poet in Naumann's assessment of modern *Kunstindustrie* was not purely romantic. A poet without a printer and publisher, Naumann argued, was an unhappy poet. "There is a barbarity in the notion of printing Goethe's poems," Naumann admitted, "but Goethe himself wanted them to be printed."[63] Using the Romantic poet and his poems as metaphors, Naumann explores the tension between the human desire to experience unique, individual works of art and the necessity for the work of art—whether poem or chair—to be reproduced and disseminated if its influence is to be felt by society as a whole. Reproduction, Naumann insisted, was the keynote of industrial art, and industrial art was the new art of modern Germany.[64]

As if to symbolize the paradox of the machine furniture—objects whose designs were infinitely reproducible, but whose naturally serendipitous materials made each one unique—the cozily arranged installations of furniture at Dresden in 1906 were graced by color lithographs of famous masterworks. Leonardo's *Mona*

Lisa hung to the right of a large cupboard in the living room of *Collection I*; Raphael's *Sistine Madonna* stood guard over the bed in *Collection II*; and Holbein's 1523 *Portrait of Erasmus* sobered the gentleman's study in *Collection III*. Chromolithography—a technology only slightly older than those involved in the production of Riemerschmid's machine furniture—could, like the Dresdner Werkstätten's woodworking machines, offer the inimitable soul of the work of art to every household in Germany.

The lithographic reproduction that hung in Riemerschmid's second gentleman's study displayed at Dresden in 1906—Carl Thieme's *Herrenzimmer*—was the likeness of Erasmus's contemporary, Albrecht Dürer. The humanist Erasmus might well have approved of the machine furniture study, designed and fabricated for the German "everyman," but Dürer, the self-possessed and self-imaged artist, looked out on a specially commissioned, consciously artistic interior designed specifically and exclusively for one individual: the *Herr* or lord of the fashionable villa in Munich's Georgenstraße. A later commentary on the Dresden installation in the *German Carpenter's Journal* confirmed its status as the unique creation of an artist to articulate the individual tastes and accomplishments of a cultivated client: "The *Herrenzimmer* bespeaks not simply an owner rich in earthly goods, but a harmoniously ordered, determined personality. The exquisitely coffered, gracefully decorated and sensitively illuminated ceiling, the felicitous architecture of the walls, crowned with a wonderfully cut, enclosed frieze, speak—like the cupboard, desk, and chairs—the language of noble unanimity and egality."[65]

Riemerschmid's *Herrenzimmer* for Herr Thieme was viewed at Dresden in an entirely different light from its machine furniture counterpart. While Carl Thieme's *Herrenzimmer* lacked the universality and accessibility of machine art, it expressed the one-of-a-kind character or warm personality that Georg Hirth had associated with the "German Room of the Renaissance" in the 1880s. And, as if in support of Hirth's view, Riemerschmid's room made direct allusions to that golden age of Germanic art and culture that Hirth had advocated as a model for modern living. Riemerschmid's sturdy-looking, slanting-backed wooden chairs and large, slab-like wooden work desk, all supported by surprisingly elaborate turned legs, recall what Beate Menke refers to in her study of the Thieme interiors as "late Gothic" precedents.[66] Embracing not only the furnishings but the room's interior architecture within the scope of its design, encompassing the aesthetic sensibilities of artist and client, and referring to the Renaissance as the touchstone of German artistic culture, Riemerschmid's *Herrenzimmer* design was not an example of *Kunstindustrie*, as were his machine furniture suites, but instead of *Raumkunst*: the room itself was a work of art.

"The felicitous architecture of the walls" of Thieme's study, noted in the *German Carpenter's Journal*, suggests a new understanding of interior design as a form of art in which architecture, applied art, and even fine art could finally be united. Haenel's essay on the concept of *Raumkunst* in the Dresden catalog describes this new art form as a rapprochement of applied art and architecture, in which "*Kunstgewerbe* has become the art of interior design, it has become the technique of the comfortable room, it has become *Raumkunst*."[67] *Raumkunst* was the mirror of the inhabitant's peculiar nature, his thoughts and moods. The rooms in which he "worked and ate, made music and slept" should not be a "haphazard system of ceiling and walls, windows and doors, filled up with furniture and rugs, pictures and light fixtures; they should be an *organism* . . . they should retain the character of an individual artistic creation."[68] Haenel's description veers dangerously close to Adolf Loos's infamous depiction of the poor little rich man's all too "complete" interior: the museum-like dwelling that in Loos's polemic is not in the least livable, but is in fact deadening. In actuality, however, *Raumkunst* eschewed the cold, curated interior of Loos's cautionary tale, revitalizing instead Hirth's vision of a German Renaissance of everyday art (*Alltagskunst*)—in which the natural materials that constituted each room glowed like jewels, and art was embedded in daily life. As in the Renaissance, so too in the age of the machine "the modern man . . . will not have his art framed on the wall or packed up in nice clean files and conserved within drawers; instead, he will feel his art as the invigorating breath that breathes through his house and all of its housewares: art as room-art [*die Kunst als Raumkunst*]."[69] Once more in the twentieth century, *Raumkunst* and *Alltagskunst* went hand in hand: the Italian's gods could keep their palaces; Germans would live every day in houses—comfortably—like men.

For Muthesius, all of Riemerschmid's Thieme interiors represented simple German *Volkskunst*.[70] But Carl Thieme's 1905–1906 *Herrenzimmer* was arguably simpler and more overtly German than any of Riemerschmid's previous rooms for the Thieme family. In contrast to the salon and family living-dining room with their colorfully painted accents, rich velvets, and intricately stained inlays, Riemerschmid restricted himself in the study to three primary materials: brass, elephant leather, and wood. The *Herrenzimmer* was far woodier than either of the previous rooms: its built-in cabinetry and bookshelves grew out of floor-to-ceiling paneling in larch pine; the large wooden Renaissance-style desk abutted one wooden wall, while a broad, heavy wooden cupboard stood against the adjacent wall—where Dürer's portrait hung. The *Herrenzimmer* revived Hirth's image of the wood-loving, forest-dwelling German: it was here, as Naumann observed, that the German forest seemed to have "moved into the German living room."[71] Hirth's principle of brown was hard at work in this man's room, where color was even scantier than it had been in Seidl's *Wohnstube* three decades earlier, and the naked pinewood harmonized with the natural leather upholstery. The subdued expanses of leather and wood were interrupted only by accents of brass: standing in for Seidl's cheerful tile stove was once again Riemerschmid's signature steam-heating unit (figure 4.12), this time clad in a curtain of diamond-shaped plates. Toward the top of each wooden wall panel was fixed a small, shining brass square with a protruding hook from which the room's framed lithographs were suspended by long wires. These brass hooks functioned paradoxically: while inherently ornamental, as tools they enabled the display of further ornaments (figure 4.12). And as if to counter the room's otherwise earthy, woody tones, the entire space was crowned with a coffered brass ceiling illuminated by evenly spaced electric fixtures.

Had Riemerschmid chosen to coffer the *Herrenzimmer*'s ceiling in wood instead, the room's Renaissance-style back stools—nestled into its cozy built-in eating corner with wooden benches, where a wooden table covered in a white embroidered cloth awaited the visitor—would have harked effortlessly back to Seidl's 1870s *altdeutsche Renaissance Wohnstube*. But where Seidl's room had featured the alpine convention of the white-washed wall, Riemerschmid's study seemed to delve further into history for its point of reference: the grainy wood walls of Carl Thieme's room evoked the fully wood-lined, incubating "box" of the fourteenth-century *Stube*. Dürer's meticulous rendering of the pine ceiling panels in his 1514 etching of St. Jerome's study bears an uncanny resemblance to the pine wall panels in the 1906 photograph of Riemerschmid's modern study. Riemerschmid's broad work desk, too, seems to derive its form from the desk at which the industrious saint is bent over his wooden lectern. Both Dürer and Riemerschmid appear to have reveled in the tangible *Derbheit*, the characteristic roughness, of wood as the material of the German interior.

The lively, evocative texture of Riemerschmid's revived *altdeutsche* Renaissance room was due not simply to its plain pine, but to the way in which that pine was worked. While the back stools were not produced in standardized components as in the fabrication of the machine chair, the presence of the modern machine was still felt throughout the construction of Carl Thieme's *Herrenzimmer*. An

FIGURE 4.12

Richard Riemerschmid, *Herrenzimmer showing brass-curtained steam-heating unit* (left), square brass picture hooks, and brass-clad ceiling, Dresden 1906, in *Das Deutsche Kunstgewerbe 1906*, 159.

electric-powered surface planer ensured the flat planes and neat corners of the back stools' seats and backs, while the stylized multiple-ball turnings on the legs were crafted with the aid of an electric-powered lathe.[72] The study's robust, brawny cupboard, with its four prominent bosses protruding unabashedly from its double-paneled doors, modeled an eye-catching effect of modern machine-assisted carpentry, for which Riemerschmid received significant attention in the press surrounding the 1906 exhibition (figure 4.13). The cupboard's pine surfaces—along with the room's other furniture and wood-paneled walls—were described in contemporary literature as having been "brushed," so that the wood's soft, smooth surface was scoured away and the denser, deeply textured woodgrain beneath stood out in raw relief. Although the result was similar to that of sandblasting or etching, the visual impact of this new brushed wood was antique: it looked like "a weathered signpost."[73]

The *Leipziger Illustrierte Zeitung* (*Leipzig Illustrated Newspaper*) noted how this modern technique exposed the expressive soul of the wood, drawing from it "all of the charms and idiosyncrasies that Nature has given it and exploiting them to artistic effect. It coaxes decoration out of the material itself, while at the same time laying bare its internal structure."[74] Here decoration was no longer a process of applying, but instead of stripping away; a second description of the grainy surface relief, in the applied arts journal *Kunst und Handwerk*, pronounced it "entirely fused with its structural substrate." While the brass-clad ceiling acted as a superficial layer or "dress," the exposed woodgrain was the wood's "bare skin."[75]

Riemerschmid's twentieth-century revival of the nineteenth-century's Renaissance revival room had elicited an unmistakably modernist response: that beauty resulted not from "dressing up," but revealed itself instead in the process of undressing, in the stark material presence of the wood, itself. The wood's bare skin was self-referential: it pointed to the real thing, the Kantian *Ding an sich*—the cupboard's thingliness. For Muthesius, the characteristically textured surface of Riemerschmid's cupboard doors amounted to its "physiognomy": this downright *derb* surface communicated the cupboard's "defiant" personality.[76] The way it looked was the way it felt. And the way it felt—both as object and *subject*—was the way it was. The tactile roughness of Riemerschmid's walls and furniture—their palpable *Derbheit*, simple and rustic, like a weather-beaten wooden sign—enacted the forthrightness, the artlessness, of *Sachlichkeit*.

But the *German Carpenter's Journal* checks any temptation to view Riemerschmid's room as naive, "undesigned," or literally "artless." The multiple allusions

FIGURE 4.13

Richard Riemerschmid, *Cupboard for the Herrenzimmer at the Thieme House*, 1906. Münchner Stadtmuseum, Sammlung Angewandte Kunst. © 2021 Artists Rights Society (ARS), New York / VG Bild-Kunst, Bonn.

to *Derbheit* are tempered here by a description of nothing less than *Gemüt*: "One has become used to thinking of Riemerschmid as a modern, middleclass architect, whose work has no place in the Crown of Art, where the wondrous dreams of the 'Thousand and One Nights' live; but in this study he delivers sufficient proof that his art transcends sheer material beauty and technique. Despite all fitness for purpose, comfort, and coziness, the room's ultimate effect is one of richness and ease. The suggestively hung likenesses of Richard Wagner and Dürer confirm above all that we find ourselves here in an Arcadia of music, painting, and science."[77] While fitness for purpose (*Zweckmäßigkeit*), comfort, and coziness all testify in one way or another to the informal, down-to-earth familiarity of *Derbheit*, the room's ultimate effect transcends this: it reaches the high cultural mark of *Gemüt*. Stepping into Riemerschmid's study was, for someone like Muthesius, to enter a new age, in which art had finally become, as he had predicted, a "common necessity." It must indeed have felt like entering Arcadia.

IN THE FORM OF A THING

At home in Munich, in the autumn of 1906, after the fanfare of the Dresden exhibition had subsided, the *Herrenzimmer*'s bare wood panels, where *no* pictures hang, make Dresden's lithographs seem even more suggestive (figures 4.2 and 4.14). But why were images of Dürer and Wagner chosen to hang in the exhibition context, and what, precisely, do they suggest? The *German Carpenter's Journal* interprets the selection of these portraits of German cultural icons as linking Riemerschmid's woody study to a more expansive national artistic culture, typically represented by literature, music, and fine art of the past. Rée invokes these "old masters" regularly as he strives to situate Riemerschmid's work within the German artistic canon. Like the German artists of past centuries, Rée believed, Riemerschmid always sought to express with great sensitivity the spirit and texture of life as it was lived in his own time. "Here," Rée wrote, "the artistic mother tongue has been rediscovered."[78] Dürer's *Self-Portrait* of 1500—a painting that, throughout its history, has been taken to mark the dawn of a new age—might have hung in Riemerschmid's exhibited room as a symbol of cultural rebirth, ripe for appropriation by twentieth-century German designers who wanted to renew and reform the world of their forefathers. Rée recalled the sentiments of nineteenth-century architect Gottfried Semper (in many senses the founder of Germany's modern *Kunstgewerbe*), who believed that

FIGURE 4.14

Richard Riemerschmid, *Herrenzimmer installed at the Thieme House*, Munich, autumn 1906. Architekturmuseum der TUM. © 2021 Artists Rights Society (ARS), New York / VG Bild-Kunst, Bonn.

the state of applied art could only improve when designers could once more hear the *Urmelodien*—the ancient melodies—of art sounding in their ears. According to Rée, these ur-melodies "sounded in Riemerschmid's works, as if ringing out from ancient times."[79] Engaging with Riemerschmid's art, Rée believed, "one is reminded of Dürer in multiple ways."[80] And so Dürer peered from Riemerschmid's wood-paneled wall as if overseeing the reconstruction of his world. But within the context of this spiritual and material renovation project, Dürer's likeness carried an even more pointed meaning for Riemerschmid's study, for its contents—and for the foundational modernist concept of *Sachlichkeit*.

In 1906, at this crucial stage in the development of German applied art—the moment in which *Kunstindustrie* or art-industry was emerging as the most radical, but also most accessible and livable, expression of modern art—*Sachlichkeit* connoted not merely an approach to modern form but also a particular perception and expression of the modern self. *Sachlichkeit* was that which not simply defined the self but externalized and materialized it—made it visible, tangible. In its capacity to turn things inside out, then, *Sachlichkeit* was perhaps not so new: Has this not always been the project, more or less, of all true self-portraiture?

The breathtaking naturalism and painstaking detail of Dürer's *Self-Portrait* have, ever since its creation, made it the object of compulsive fascination. Even today, time is somehow suspended as visitors pause to contemplate it in Munich's Alte Pinakothek. In Dürer's time, it was reported that the painter's dog was once found licking the portrait's surface, having mistaken his master's likeness for the master himself. Remarkable to Renaissance and to modern eyes alike was the way that each strand of hair on the artist's head, as well as each blade of fur on the border of his coat, seemed to possess real, individual, material life. Art historian Joseph Koerner has referred to this magnetic quality in Dürer's painting as the "magical presence or quiddity of the painted world."[81] Koerner has explored the significance of hair and fur in the 1500 *Self-Portrait*, drawing special attention to Dürer's sensuous fingering of his furry lapel. For Koerner, Dürer's touching of the voluptuous substance is a twofold gesture: the touch is at once a reminder of the painting's dog-deceiving illusionism—an "index of painterly craft"—and a reference to the painter's own physical, material presence—the body as the self.[82]

Dürer points to what is (in his painter's mirror) directly before him: *das Ding an sich*, the thing in itself—or, in this case, *him*self. In his *Self-Portrait* of 1500, "Dürer is absorbed not in what he sees but in what he touches," Koerner writes. "Touching the fur signals the sitter's interiority; it draws him inward toward his body as into his 'self.'"[83] But Dürer's fingers touch and point at the same time. Anatomically speaking, Dürer points at his heart, the physical engine of his material self—the center of his bodily being. Like Riemerschmid's cupboard, whose smooth outer mantle was peeled back to uncover the wood's rough skin, Dürer's gesture of self-reference is disarmingly *derb*, matter-of-fact—*sachlich*. To the cupboard's declaration, "I am nothing but wood," the man responds, "I am nothing but flesh." In the year 1500, however, as Koerner has shown, the heart was understood as more than a functional organ or a lump of flesh: it was the material housing of the spirit, or soul. By virtue of the mirror, which erected for the painter a real, physical barrier but which is dematerialized—invisible—for the viewer, matter and spirit are collapsed on the hard wood panel that constitutes the painting's surface. In his act of self-imaging, Dürer points simultaneously to what is before and what lies within. His gesture, equating surface with substance, is one of *Sachlichkeit*. The old-German dialectic, at play in Riemerschmid's modern furniture, mimicked Dürer's motions, pointing now before, to the woody heart of *Derbheit*, and now within, to the ineffable soul of *Gemüt*. But Riemerschmid's modernist synthesis removes the mirror, the barrier of likeness: the thing—body and soul—exists in itself.

In his 1904 essay "Art in the Age of the Machine," Friedrich Naumann describes the "endless *Sachlichkeit*" of modern, mechanized industrial life as a process of "depersonalization" that "leaves in the dark background of the soul a room that does not want to be illuminated with electric light, that will not be regulated, the room of lost passions and primal emotions."[84] Naumann argues that what most Germans truly desire is not this *Sachlichkeit*, not what he too calls the *Ding an sich*, but instead the seductive "appearance" or charming "ambience"—the *Stimmung*. But Naumann then proceeds to complicate the term *Stimmung*: "Depth and superficiality coexist in *Stimmung*. *Stimmung* is in part the first impression gained from a fleeting glance . . . and in part a harking back to the most elemental sensations of happiness, pain—the movements of the soul."[85] Though *Stimmung* purports to be all atmosphere and caprice, its visible, tactile surface qualities—like flamboyant blossoms organically one with the colorless, subterranean roots that nourish them—actually tap the depths of true emotion and feeling. What begins in Naumann's text as a feud between a rigid *Sachlichkeit* and a riotous *Stimmung* ends in their reconciliation and fraternal relation. Like *Sachlichkeit*, *Stimmung* is a reflexive principle: but while *Stimmung* works from the outside in, *Sachlichkeit* works "from the inside out." This book has offered many words to mark the German preoccupation with what lies "inside": *Gemüt* (imagination or feeling), *Seele* (soul), and *Geist* (spirit or mind) are but a few. In 1907, Riemerschmid stated, as if echoing his friend Naumann, that the forms of modern objects must come "from the spirit [*Geist*] of the machine."[86] But it was this same spirit—of the modern machine—that had already enabled Riemerschmid to reveal the soul of the most natural, elemental, ur-material: wood.

Naumann's contribution to the Dresdner Werkstätten's displays at the 1906 exhibition was a small brochure included in the firm's sales catalog and titled "Der Geist im Hausgestühl" ("The Spirit in Domestic Furnishings"). It was here that Naumann wrote what might in retrospect be understood as the keynote not only of the exhibition's new *Kunstindustrie* and *Raumkunst*, but of this formative passage in the development of modern design—and, as such, of Germany's entrance into what Muthesius had defined as a *New Age of Art*. In Riemerschmid's "Arcadian" *Herrenzimmer*, with Dürer's likeness as its emblem, new-old furnishings "animated by the spirit of the machine" could "rebuild the world of Albrecht Dürer from the inside out—not in the sense of a 'Renaissance' of leftover, antediluvian notions, nor as an artificial rejuvenation of ossified social constructs, but as a rebirth of living naturalness."[87]

For Dürer, the natural world had been not simply that which he touched, but that which touched him: nature felt and internalized gave life to his art. In comparing Riemerschmid to the "old master," Rée writes that, as was the case with Dürer, it was the "nature of the things themselves" that give life to Riemerschmid's art.[88] Koerner acknowledges that, in his own time, "Dürer was conscious of his role as inventor of a new notion of art in Germany, one founded upon the authentic and irreducible presence of the artist in his works."[89] Riemerschmid's new notion of German art arose not from his own artistic persona, however, but from *Sachlichkeit*: the authentic and irreducible presence of the *thing*. His practical, modern artworks were not self-portraits of the artist who designed them but living portraits of the *things themselves*. It was Dürer's keen perception of this thingliness of things, documented in his momentous likenesses of the world around him, that resonated in Riemerschmid's modern *Alltagskunst*. In *The German Room of the Renaissance*, George Hirth cited Dürer's own reflections on this essential process of revelation and renewal capable of rebuilding the world: "Through this, the secret treasure of the heart will be revealed: through the work of art—the new creature, which one creates in his heart, in the form of a thing."[90]

5

FILLING EMPTY HANDS

The little baby tankards offer themselves in an orderly fashion to the loving embrace of
the empty hand, while the large jug seems in his already half-tipping motion, to be just
waiting for the moment when he will be next called upon to perform his accommodating
service with drink.
—Hermann Muthesius[1]

When Dresden's Third German Applied Arts Exhibition closed its doors on October
31, 1906, the New Age of Art that Hermann Muthesius had foreseen at the dawn of
the twentieth century seemed already well underway. As Muthesius had predicted,
the art on view at Dresden was not the cold, exclusive art of the museum, but an
intimate, inclusive art approaching the status of "common necessity" for modern
cultural life. In fact, modern life seemed, to Muthesius and to many of his architect
and designer contemporaries, the only legitimate basis for the development of a
new art. The notion of *artistic culture* that Muthesius and his cohort promoted was
actually, as architectural historian John Maciuika has argued, "a euphemism for
a program extending well beyond the realm of aesthetics."[2] In Maciuika's analysis, the Dresden exhibition, much more than a mere showcase of the new *Kunstgewerbe* (art-industry), articulated a persuasive didactic program focused on three
specific aspects of modern life that the exhibition's organizers identified as key to
the prosperity of their "harmonious" New Age of Art: modern production methods;
the relationship between artist-designers and producers; and the question of who
could claim ownership rights to the designs for the new products. All three prongs

of Dresden's program disturbed the traditional craftspeople and manufacturers united in the Trade Association for the Economic Interests of Applied Art (Fachverband für die wirtschaftlichen Interessen des Kunstgewerbes). But it was above all the increasing prominence of the modern artist-designer and the increasingly powerful role that this interloper seemed to play—not simply in changing the look of familiar products, but in determining the way they were made, as well as their competitive force on the commercial market—that alienated and infuriated members of the Fachverband.

Dresden's *Exhibition Newspaper* celebrated the fact that Richard Riemerschmid's "technically as well as artistically thoroughly exemplary" machine furniture was "produced up to ninety percent by machine and therefore comparatively affordable, so that even those of lesser means can afford to buy these items."[3] This combination of circumstances was the threat most feared by the Fachverband: a renowned artist (no nameless artisan) had designed a remarkably versatile line of furniture specifically for reproduction through modern machine technology; this furniture was recognized by the design intelligentsia not just as artistic, but as technically excellent as well; and—the most galling point of all—because Riemerschmid's furniture was almost entirely machined in one way or another, just about anyone could buy it. And just about anyone might well choose to buy it instead of the more "traditional" furniture that had, almost overnight, become both more expensive and less fashionable than its artist-designed counterpart. Finally, adding insult to injury, what appeared to the Fachverband as a deadly compact between the modern artist-designer and modern mechanized production was advertised in the machine furniture's very name.

THE SIGNIFICANCE OF *KUNSTGEWERBE*

In January 1907, Kaiser Wilhelm II approved new copyright laws that elevated the artist (including the designer) to the status of producer, with legally defensible rights to the designs he or she produced.[4] That very same month, Muthesius took a step that, together with the new copyright laws and the recent Dresden exhibition, represented both a consolidation of the modern Art-Industry Movement's progressive position and a categorical rejection of all the Fachverband stood for. On his new appointment as first chair of Berlin's Trade Academy (Handelhochschule), Muthesius gave an opening speech for his lecture series on modern art-industry in which he denounced the outdated nineteenth-century practices of traditional craftspeople and manufacturers: holding these primarily responsible for Germany's poor reputation as a producer of "tasteless" goods, he proclaimed that "the future belongs to those producers who subscribe to the new movement."[5] This inaugural speech defined modern art-industry's significance for modern Germany in three senses: artistic, cultural, and economic.

"Every visitor to the Dresden exhibition," Muthesius asserted, "must first have been struck by the fact that all the work on show, from a small piece of embroidery to a fully decorated and furnished room, spoke a distinctive artistic language." And what was more important for Muthesius—and more injurious to the Fachverband—the artistic language heard at the 1906 exhibition had "nothing in common with that of the old applied art, which was in its heyday in the 1880s and 1890s."[6] Muthesius felt that while the artistic significance of the *Kunstgewerbe* had been much discussed during the first years of the twentieth century, its cultural significance was only beginning to be charted, and its economic significance was the province of the future.[7] However distant the economic fruition of art-industry might seem in 1907, Muthesius's speech described a relation in which the *Kunstgewerbe*'s artistic and cultural capacities would ultimately benefit the national economy by fueling the development of a modern class of goods that would be highly competitive, both with the old-fashioned products they sought to replace and on the international market. Even in 1907, Muthesius claimed, it was already becoming clear that it was "by no means an act of commercial suicide to give one's allegiance to the modern movement."[8] The Dresden exhibition, with its celebration of modern, mechanized production methods, shone as the beacon of an art-industrial future where manufacture was efficient and its results affordable to all. And Dresden's didactic program of art for daily life (*Alltagskunst*) had already more than implied the significance of well-designed, efficiently produced furniture for the cultural education, or *Bildung* of the German *Volk*.

Muthesius made clear that *cultural education*, as he called it, must be the focus not only of the Art-Industry Movement but of its objects as well:

The art-industry has before it an educative [*erzieherische*] task of eminent significance. And in this it has already stepped beyond the boundaries generally assigned to it in its popular conception; it is becoming more than art-industry: it is becoming a means of cultural education [*kulturelles Erziehungsmittel*]. Art-industry's goal is to instruct today's social classes and lead them back to dignity, veracity, and middleclass simplicity. If it succeeds in this, it will penetrate to the depths of our cultural life and achieve the most far-reaching conse-quences. It won't just transform the German apartment and house, it will directly affect the character of our generation, because instruction in the decent, appropriate [*anständigen*] design of the rooms in which we live can in essence only be the education of character.[9]

This project of *Erziehung*—the German term for education that included the moral implications of proper upbringing, guidance, and even "good breeding"—Muthesius assigned not to his professional colleagues in the progressive Art-Industry Movement but to the much humbler products of art-industry: the *things themselves*. It was up to these inanimate objects to impress themselves on their users, to mold the character of a generation, and, without words, to instruct modern occupants in the "decent" (*anständigen*) design of their rooms. Everyday things like egg cups and mustard pots were to become the cultivators—the *teachers*—of modern German society (figure 5.1).

Muthesius's use of the word *anständig* to describe the modern interiors that the new art-industry objects were designed to inspire is simultaneously opaque and re-vealing. *Anständig*, which may be translated rather innocuously as "appropriate" or "suitable," or more pointedly as "proper," "modest," or even "decent," gives no tan-gible description of the modern interior or modern art-industry. To learn that the new industrial art will instruct dwellers in the appropriate or decent arrangement of their rooms is to learn nothing concrete about how those rooms were supposed to look. However, Muthesius's word choice is enmeshed with the rhetoric of *Sach-lichkeit*, articulated as early as the 1890s. *Anständigkeit*'s appropriateness and suit-ability recall the conditions of "realistic architecture" laid out by Richard Streiter in 1896, elaborated and illustrated soon after by Alfred Lichtwark in his discussion of the appropriateness of vernacular architecture to its regional milieu, and of the suitability of simple, functional furniture to the "practical purpose" of domestic life.[10] Muthesius himself had explored *Sachlichkeit*'s notion of suitability or "fit" in his comparison of the modern dwelling to a well-made suit, while Adolf Loos had stitched this suit into a symbol for *Sachlichkeit*'s weightier, *anständiger* values of mod-esty, propriety, and decency. The progressive modern man was *modestly* clothed, lived in a *decent* apartment, and owned *proper* things. His entire experience, from the design of his material possessions to that of his character, was rationalized by *Sachlichkeit*.

The apprehension and resentment that the Dresden exhibition had sparked among the Fachverband's members ignited into open rage after Muthesius's

FIGURE 5.1

Richard Riemerschmid, *Mustard Pot &
Egg Cup* (fine-grained stoneware), 1902.
Münchner Stadtmuseum, Sammlung
Angewandte Kunst. © 2021 Artists Rights
Society (ARS), New York / VG Bild-Kunst, Bonn.

inflammatory statements in his January 1907 lecture. This controversy, publicized as the "Muthesius Case," became a focus for heated debates over modern versus traditional methods of production, ultimately galvanizing the more progressive art-industry proponents into their own camp. The notion of an organization of those who might gain through the development of the modern art-industry—artist-designers, architects, industrialists, retailers—had already been germinating at the Dresden exhibition in 1906. Architect Fritz Schumacher, the exhibition's chief organizer, noted a "principle of brotherly association between artists and firms" that seemed to warrant the formation of an organization where this fraternal attitude could be fostered; through the channels of such an organization, Friedrich Naumann's political agenda of industrial and commercial expansion might also be advanced.[11] Naumann's notion of *Qualitätsarbeit*, or "quality work," had made a strong impression on the Dresdner Werkstätten's Karl Schmidt, who had at his disposal the tools to put Naumann's social and economic concerns into visual and material practice. Together, Naumann and Schmidt desired to nurture the *Kunstgewerbe*'s progressive gains at Dresden through the founding of a national organization.[12]

And it was Schmidt who gave this organization its simple, straightforward yet comprehensive name: Deutscher Werkbund (German Work Alliance). During the Werkbund's first meeting, held in Munich on October 5–6, 1907, Schmidt argued that the term *Kunstgewerbe* had exhausted its usefulness for modern artists and industrialists alike because it could no longer encompass the modern culture of trade and industry in the artistic, economic, and social dimensions that Muthesius had outlined.[13] While Schmidt himself played a prominent role in the formalities of the Werkbund's founding, his Dresden Workshops (Dresdner Werkstätten)—which had, just a few months earlier, merged with its Munich competitor, the Workshops for Home Furnishing (Werkstätten für Wohnungs-Einrichtung), to become the German Workshops (Deutsche Werkstätten)—played an integral and practical one.

The new Werkbund chose the Deutsche Werkstätten ("DeWe") in Dresden as the location for its headquarters, but Schmidt's enterprise had already been serving as a model for the Art-Industry Movement ever since its vast displays at the 1906 exhibition. Muthesius cited the DeWe, "which in eight years have evolved from modest beginnings into a concern that employs cabinetmakers by the hundreds and measures its turnover in millions," as proof that allegiance to the new art-industry would not result in "commercial suicide."[14] The DeWe represented not simply the union of northern and southern competitors, but, much like the German Werkbund, a consolidation of progressive art-industrial interests at a national level: in the Deutscher Werkstätten, the new Deutscher Werkbund found an established example of the success that its modern principles might yield.

But while the connections between the Werkstätten and the Werkbund were strong, both ideologically and practically, a second branch of German art-industry offered the Werkbund a production model that was perhaps less obvious but ultimately more illuminating of the Werkbund's vision for a relationship among materials, workmanship, and design in modern German manufacture. This was the historic German stoneware industry, whose determination to modernize its designs for the new century prompted it to employ progressive German artists—chief among them, Richard Riemerschmid. Riemerschmid's collaboration with German stoneware manufacturers exemplified the partnership between artist-designer and established German industry upon which the Werkbund was founded. The objects generated through this partnership were the kind of *Kunstgewerbe* that could mold "the character of a generation." This chapter looks at Riemerschmid's things in action, following them from fabrication to circulation, and showing how and why the Werkbund deployed his stonewares as agents of its cultural agenda. Drawing together multiple strands of his singular modernism, it explores the ways in which the past—nineteenth-century historicism, the regional vernacular, and the historical construct of *Germanness*—could inform the design of not only an early twentieth-century present, but its future as well. And it demonstrates how *Sachlichkeit*'s satellite concepts—*Zweckmäßigkeit* (fitness for purpose) *Materialgerechtigkeit* (justice to materials), and especially *Qualität* (quality)—coalesced in Riemerschmid's thingly things to enhance their cultural currency.

Qualität was concretized in Riemerschmid's vessels made of stoneware clay, both a natural and a national resource in Werkbund terms. In "The Significance of *Kunstgewerbe*," Muthesius relates an object's quality to three primary factors: the nature of the materials from which that object is made, the appropriateness of the workmanship with which it is formed, and the sensitivity of the modern artist-designer to both of these factors when formulating his design (for machine production). For Muthesius, the quality relation of materials and workmanship was a *sachlich* one: the material of a quality product must demonstrate its "inner truthfulness" in visible form, and this tangible honesty could only be revealed as a result of the proper process of fabrication. "For sound workmanship," Muthesius believed, "is none other than the outward and visible sign of an inward truth."[15]

In 1908, the Werkbund's first president, Munich architect and professor Theodor Fischer (who ten years before had designed the *Kleinkunst* room at Munich's 1897

Glaspalast exhibition, where Riemerschmid and his artist-designer colleagues had brought Jugendstil to public attention), strove to explicate the Werkbund's special usage of *Qualität*. "Quality means in our language: 'anständig,'" Fischer declared.[16] For both Muthesius and Fischer, *Qualität* meant more than materials and workmanship. The quality object was not simply well made, it was appropriate, suitable, proper, and decent. *Qualität* became, on the lips of Werkbund members, a marker of morality.[17] The history of Riemerschmid's intervention in the German stoneware industry is the history of *Qualität*: it traces the development of *quality* from an ordinary, everyday word to the theoretical foundation of the prewar Werkbund.

Qualität in design resulted from an approach or attitude of *Sachlichkeit*. Muthesius argued that *Sachlichkeit*'s "iron principles of design according to purpose, material and construction" were what guaranteed a quality object.[18] These iron principles admitted no "simulations and substitutes"; in 1907, Muthesius declared, with the force of *Sachlichkeit*'s logic: "No simulation of any kind: let every object appear to be what it is!"[19] But as Muthesius also knew, letting an object "appear to be what it is" was not just a matter of iron principles. His affectionate and memorable description of Riemerschmid's 1903 beer service for the stoneware manufacturer Reinhold Merkelbach, with its "little baby tankards" and "large jug in his already half-tipping motion," proves that *Sachlichkeit*'s relation of appearance and essence was, in Riemerschmid's case, far more complex than a simple equation of purpose, material, and construction (figures 2.19, 5.2, and 5.7).

The "little baby tankards" escaped Muthesius's iron principles to perform Streiter's original *Sachlichkeit* of character, qualities, and feeling.[20] Without words, Riemerschmid's things spoke to Muthesius: their utility was inseparable from their personality—their *playfulness*. And yet, for Muthesius and Werkbund reformers like him, these playful personas were not vaudevillians; they were earnest actors in a serious plot. What was it, then, that these apparently clownish beer mugs actually offered to empty German hands? These tipsy little things sober up in the context of a larger, nationalist cause gathering steam between the Werkbund's founding in 1907 and its first major exhibition in 1914 from May through mid-August—when it was cut short by the outbreak of World War I. During a time when an imperialist Germany was not only striving to modernize and standardize at home, but also struggling to maintain control of its colonies in Africa and Asia, Riemerschmid's cheerful beer mugs became model servants, placing solid, reassuringly German values into the "empty hands" of the young nation's "cultural aristocracy": the educated middle class.

FIGURE 5.2

Richard Riemerschmid, *Tankard for 1903 Beer Service* (Reinhold Merkelbach). Münchner Stadtmuseum, Sammlung Angewandte Kunst. © 2021 Artists Rights Society (ARS), New York / VG Bild-Kunst, Bonn.

At the turn of the twentieth century, the German stoneware industry found itself in aesthetic and economic crisis. The Kannenbäckerland, or "Jug-Baking Country"— the small region of western Germany to the east of the Rhine, between the Rivers Sieg and Lahn, and situated in the southwestern portion of the Westerwald (western forest) mountain range—had seen better days. Kannenbäckerland had earned its nickname for more than five centuries of utilitarian pottery production—nearly six hundred years of cobalt-stained, salt-glazed tankards, jugs, and punch bowls known as Westerwald stoneware. Three primary production centers at Höhr, Grenzau, and Grenzhausen grew up around the lower Westerwald mountains, which contained the largest and richest deposits of stoneware clay constituents in northwest Europe. This natural resource fueled the development of the Westerwald industry from its fourteenth-century production for local markets to its international renown in the sixteenth and seventeenth centuries.[21]

The material character of Westerwald clay—fine-grained and plastic, yet durable and sanitary owing to its high firing temperature—suited it not only to a variety of utilitarian, domestic forms from preserving jars to chamber pots, but also to the elaborately embellished drinking vessels that became fashionable during the sixteenth century and won the Westerwald potters recognition as fine craftsmen (figure 5.3).[22] Rhineland beer mugs and kitchen crockery, traded across Europe and Britain and exported as far as North America, Africa, and Asia, came to be identified with reliability and authenticity: the word *Westerwald* bespoke German quality.[23]

By the eighteenth century, Westerwald stoneware had secured a reputation for usefulness; but by the nineteenth century this reputation was all it had left. The eighteenth century saw Westerwald stoneware already assuming a narrower market niche as primarily functional pottery, appropriate to the utilitarian needs that imported fineware, such as tin-glazed earthenware, failed to meet. But the discovery of white kaolin clay near Dresden in the early eighteenth century and the rapid development of European porcelain that followed foretold the total eclipse of Westerwald stoneware as a decorative ceramic.[24] During the nineteenth century, as porcelain became increasingly affordable to the middle class for everyday use, stoneware began to seem crude. The Westerwald firms rallied to the nationalist historicism of the Gründerzeit, but their intricate copies of German Renaissance vessels, though technologically progressive, attracted only fleeting consumer

FIGURE 5.3

Baluster Jug (stoneware), Westerwald, 1600–
1625. The Metropolitan Museum of Art, New
York. Robert A. Ellison Jr. Collection, Gift of
Robert A. Ellison Jr., 2014.

interest.[25] By 1900, flea markets were flooded with blue-and-gray beer mugs whose only remaining value resided in the pewter of their lids.[26]

At the 1900 Paris Exposition Universelle, the juxtaposition of "dusty" Westerwald stoneware with the dazzling spectrum of glazes and innovative, Asian-inspired forms of French "art pottery" proved humiliating, not only for the Rhineland firms, but for the new German nation. In desperation, and with Prussian government support, the Westerwald turned to progressive German artists for a solution to what applied arts professor Ernst Zimmermann called an "artistic emergency."[27] Zimmermann argued in 1900 that the industry's modern problems could not be solved simply by reclothing Westerwald vessels in historicist forms, nor could one superficially tart up the somber stonewares by sheathing them in flashy colored enamels. But if the emergency could not be remedied by novelty and fashion, then how could Westerwald stonewares be made to appeal to modern German consumers, yet retain their dignity as time-honored products of Germany's cultural heritage? According to Muthesius's 1907 speech, "the impulse to break free of fancy dress and face up to the circumstances of our own time" had been "the prime motivating power of the new movement in *Kunstgewerbe*."[28] But what lay beneath that "fancy dress" was the question with which the Westerwald preoccupied itself.

Sachlichkeit, in its mission to reveal the character of the thing, offered a means of rejuvenation both untainted by the novelties of fashion and also *bodenständig*: rooted in the German soil.[29] The appearance and texture of regional, vernacular materials—like the cobalt-stained, salt-glazed skin of Westerwald stoneware—announced *Sachlichkeit*'s presence. To be *sachlich*, an object had to shed its fancy dress and reveal its inner self. Zimmermann's reform strategy for the Westerwald, stemming from a dual appreciation for its material product and its cultural heritage, was pure *Sachlichkeit*. He believed that modern artistic and technological reforms must engage not merely with visible surface but with practical and cultural substance, with "the actual, current circumstances in the ceramics industry, which are the direct result of its history and *Bodenbeschaffenheit* [fundamental character]."[30] Zimmermann's opposition of the term *Bodenbeschaffenheit* (literally, "ground character") with words like *novelty* and *fashion* set the tone for the Westerwald's twentieth-century modernization, grounded in the character of the clay itself. At *Sachlichkeit*'s expressive heart lay a hard kernel of materiality that would be excavated, celebrated, and eventually proselytized by the Werkbund as *Qualität*.

Between the Westerwald's embarrassment at Paris in 1900 and the 1907 founding of the Werkbund, the indigenous Rhineland industry underwent rigorous technical and aesthetic modernization. The collaboration among manufacturers, technicians, and artists necessary to achieve its reincarnation would stand as a model for the Werkbund's symbiotic vision for art and industry. The product of this union was envisioned as a useful, affordable *Alltagskunst*. And this new everyday art should establish a modern German style rooted so deeply in German culture that it could weather the whims of fashion, and integrated so completely into contemporary everyday life that it would be experienced as the natural, material expression of an indigenous people, or *Volk*. Westerwald stoneware clay was the German soil itself; and high-fired Westerwald stoneware pottery was that soil petrified and perpetuated.

"No matter where the whims of fashion lead," Zimmermann wrote in 1903, "the beer mug will always stick with stoneware."[31] In discussing the influence of the vernacular in German design reform, historian Maiken Umbach has proposed that "on a conceptual level, the notion of the 'vernacular' bound together the two decisive components of this reform project: the tradition of craftsmanship and a sense of geographical 'rootedness' that countered the threatening alienation between people and the material culture of modernity."[32] Riemerschmid's salt-glazed beer mugs eased drinkers into modern life by giving them something familiar and concrete—rock solid—to hold on to. The history of Westerwald stoneware as indigenous resource, geographically specific material, vernacular craft process, and utilitarian tradition adapted by modern designers for cosmopolitan life in the twentieth century reveals the paradox inherent in shaping a modern German identity. For although the stoneware industry strove toward technological innovation and mass production, it did so in order to recover the Westerwald's lost glory. The Westerwald aspired to what Susan Stewart has called a "future-past": a utopian state in which the idealized image of a bygone era is resuscitated.[33] But by infusing their modern, reproducible designs with signs of regional handcraft, designers for Westerwald firms not only ensured the survival of craft in the machine age but also constructed material evidence of Germany's ambivalent engagement with modernity. The vernacular idyll—an idealized vision of a timeless, preindustrial Arcadia distinct and exempt from the recent, historical past of the—was central to the conception of modern German design. Westerwald stoneware's embodiment of this vernacular past helped it to define a modern sense of German quality.

But the first significant interaction between modern art and the stoneware industry resulted from the Westerwald's collaboration with a foreigner. In 1901, the Westerwald District Council appealed to Belgian Henry van de Velde to bring his renowned Art Nouveau design sensibility to Westerwald products. Although van de Velde had little prior experience with stoneware, his designs for other media were already well known in Germany and greatly admired among its progressive design reform circles. Indeed, it was just the year before, in August 1900, that van de Velde (and Riemerschmid) had been instrumental in revitalizing Krefeld's struggling silk and dressmaking industries in collaboration with Friedrich Deneken, director of Krefeld's Kaiser Wilhelm Museum. In addition to his celebrated avant-garde interiors, van de Velde's participation in a public campaign to rejuvenate the native industry of a German manufacturing center suffering at the hands of the French fashion industry had aligned him with the nationalist cause of German design reform, making him a highly desirable candidate to update the outdated Westerwald wares.

Van de Velde's new designs inspired the hope of progress in Kannenbäckerland, presenting the possibility of a fresh approach to its age-old industry and earning him the historical title of "catalyst" of the modern Westerwald. He received most acclaim for his attempts at expanding the conventional Westerwald glaze palette by using colorful, high-fired, Asian-inspired glazes on decorative vases (figure 5.4).[34] At Krefeld, van de Velde's goal had been the artistic elevation of the modern woman's dress as an alternative to Paris fashion. Van de Velde's strategy proved more appropriate to Krefeld silks than to Westerwald stoneware, however: while his dresses had offered German women an escape from fashion, his pots seemed to rely too heavily on current aesthetic trends to be altogether free of fashion. Despite the new life he injected into tired German stoneware through the cachet of his colorful, modern vases, van de Velde's preoccupation with formal concerns blinded him to the Westerwald's two core values: craft and utility. Zimmermann wrote in 1903 that van de Velde's stonewares owed too much to the "international" (i.e., French and Asian) influence of Art Nouveau—but that the designs of Munich artist Richard Riemerschmid demonstrated true *Materialschätzung*, or affectionate appreciation for the material.[35]

In 1900, after the success of Riemerschmid's *Room of an Art Lover* at the Paris World's Fair, the Westerwald firm of Reinhold Merkelbach approached him to design

FIGURE 5.4

Henry van de Velde, *Stoneware Vase
manufactured by Reihold Hanke*, 1902.
Mallams Oxford. © 2021 Artists Rights
Society (ARS), New York / c/o Pictoright
Amsterdam.

modern beer vessels, inviting him to visit the manufactory in order to experiment directly with the clay and work with the firm's technicians.[36] Riemerschmid's close collaboration with Reinhold Merkelbach resulted in a redefinition of craftsmanship for the machine age and the adaptation of the Westerwald's utilitarian vernacular for the modern middle-class consumer. His designs constituted a new conception of stoneware that seemed refreshingly modern compared with nineteenth-century historicist wares, yet restrained and functional in contrast to van de Velde's undulating vases. Period reviews praised Riemerschmid for expressing the "right feeling" for the tough, dense clay body in simple, sturdy forms. One critic argued that Riemerschmid's stonewares were more successful than his designs in any other material, while another claimed that through his keen understanding of the material itself, Riemerschmid followed "in the footsteps of the old potters."[37]

But Riemerschmid's appreciation for the material went beyond the stoneware clay to embrace the history of its technology—its craft. His rationalized sphere-and-cylinder construction of a 1902 jug (and its own "little babies"), decorated in a blue-and-gray lozenge pattern, was designed for serial production and also for domestic use (figure 5.5). Its broad surfaces and simplified forms were visually modern, as well as being easy to use and clean. These aspects of Riemerschmid's design contrast starkly with the more complex, ornamented form of a seventeenth-century Westerwald baluster jug (figure 5.3); however, Riemerschmid's dripping geometry shares more with the seventeenth-century decoration than cobalt pigment. The old baluster jug's complicated decorative scheme was achieved by hand through a combination of techniques, including the application of a molded frieze, as well as the stamping, rouletting, and incising of the clay surface. During the incising process, known in the Westerwald as the *scratch technique*, a sharp tool was used to outline ornaments in the unfired, leather-hard clay, after which cobalt oxide was applied within the voided areas. But Riemerschmid's incised lozenges, while they allude to the Westerwald's decorative traditions and convey the sense of time-honored craftsmanship, were not "hand-crafted" in the conventional sense. Though carved into the body of a model jug initially, the "scratched" lozenges became reliefs when this original jug was cast to form a hollow mold, within which jug after identical jug could then be thrown. Rather than being painstakingly incised one by one, the lozenges were thus imprinted all at once into the jug's surface as the technician pressed the clay against the mold; the cobalt stain was applied later within the impressions. This serial production process enabled Merkelbach to manufacture hundreds of identical vessels—each one ostensibly unique. Zimmermann immediately

hailed Riemerschmid's modernized scratch technique as a "great leap forward" in its adaptation to "modern mechanized production."[38] By perpetuating the illusion of one-of-a-kind, hand-decorated pottery, while at the same time facilitating a production process in which form and ornament were created simultaneously in one infinitely repeatable step, Riemerschmid's design not only advanced Westerwald technology but, more significantly, bridged the gap between vernacular craft and the modern demand for affordable and hygienic products. His modern stonewares fetishized Westerwald craft within their rationalized, reproducible forms, repackaging regional tradition for a new national market.

Riemerschmid used his modern scratch technique to integrate the generous body of a bulbous brown jug with its invitingly rounded handle in a single, powerful

FIGURE 5.5

Richard Riemerschmid, *Jug and Tankards*
(design drawing, left; vessels manufactured
by Reinhold Merkelbach, right),
stoneware with cobalt decoration, 1902.
Architekturmuseum der TUM; Quittenbaum.
© 2021 Artists Rights Society (ARS), New
York / VG Bild-Kunst, Bonn.

spiral incision (figure 5.6). This vessel, designed in 1902, performed a second, symbolic integration of traditional craft and modern technology when it was fabricated in 1910 with a speckled brown surface. While van de Velde had explored arty, "foreign," colored glazes, Riemerschmid became involved in the revival of iron-brown surface treatments based on the archaeological study of sixteenth-century stonewares excavated during the 1890s near the ancient Rhineland city of Cologne. Although the Cologne stoneware tradition was historically and geographically distinct from that of the Westerwald, Reinhold Merkelbach capitalized on its nationalist resonance as a unique product of the German Renaissance in appropriating and reviving *kölnisch* stonewares. Like Riemerschmid's Renaissance-inflected *Herrenzimmer* (gentleman's study) at Dresden in 1906, his Cologne stonewares adapted history for modern use.

Shortly after 1905, in attempts to replicate the surface treatments of the pieces excavated at Cologne, technicians at Reinhold Merkelbach rediscovered the technique of applying a layer of iron-bearing slip beneath the salt glaze: if exposed to oxygen during firing, the iron particles oxidized and speckles developed in the brown slip. The suggestion of antique patina that the speckles conveyed was achieved, however, through a distinctly modernist approach to surface decoration that relied solely on the inherent properties and processes of materials rather than intentionally applied ornament.[39] But while the "brushed" wood surfaces of Riemerschmid's 1906 study furniture required a modern machine-powered process to produce an intentionally aged effect, the modern "patina" of Merkelbach's speckled stonewares came naturally—during the chemical process of oxidation.

In addition to this *braun geflammt* or "oxidized brown" effect, a second rediscovered technique—*kölnisch braun*, or "Cologne brown"—featured cobalt relief ornaments that turned a shiny black when fired under a layer of iron-brown slip. These warm, inviting shades of brown ale and Bavarian *Schwarzbier* lent Riemerschmid's 1903 beer jug a new degree of "appropriateness" in the fulfillment of its task (figure 5.7). In a process similar to his modern scratch, Riemerschmid's relief ornaments were again fabricated simultaneously with his vessels. This time, in order to mimic the meticulously handcrafted reliefs on vessels excavated at Cologne, Westerwald technicians pressed cobalt-colored clay into depressed areas of molds before throwing their pots within them so that the cobalt clay adhered to the pot as it was being thrown. After the pots were dipped in brown slip and then fired, these "applied" ornaments emerged in glossy black. A review of Riemerschmid's *kölnisch braun* vessels noted reassuringly that "although the decorations,

FIGURE 5.6

Richard Riemerschmid, *Jug Designed for Reinhold Merkelbach* (model no. 1729, 1902), executed in gray stoneware with *braun geflammt* (oxidized brown) surface treatment, 1910. Philadelphia Museum of Art: Purchased with the Haney Foundation Fund, the Bloomfield Moore Fund, and the Edgar Viguers Seeler Fund, 1987, 1987-10-1. © Artists Rights Society (ARS), New York / VG Bild-Kunst, Bonn.

FIGURE 5.7

Richard Riemerschmid, *Jug from* Beer
Service *designed for Reinhold Merkelbach*
(jug model no. 1758 S) in 1903, executed in
gray stoneware with *kölnisch braun* surface
treatment, 1910. Quittenbaum. © 2021
Artists Rights Society (ARS), New York / VG
Bild-Kunst, Bonn.

which are comparatively sparse and employed in startling ways, have sprung from a strictly modern design, they still nestle against the body of the vessel as the old reliefs did."[40]

Critics hailed the fabrication of these new "antique" browns as a technological advance; here, however, technology was understood not simply as a progressive force, but rather as a means for reclaiming the lost pinnacle of Westerwald production—and German achievement. Both Reinhold Merkelbach's appropriation of Cologne's historic, regional tradition and the positive critical reception of the *kölnisch* Renaissance stoneware's adaptation for the modern Westerwald industry signal the expressly modern attitude toward the vernacular adopted by a recently unified Germany that was seeking national cultural currency in the regional riches of its past. While Cologne and the Westerwald had evolved separate stoneware traditions, to early twentieth-century eyes, both were time-honored, authentic, and indisputably German. In the firm's bid for the status of Germany's preeminent modern stoneware producer, Reinhold Merkelbach amalgamated regional traditions into a consolidated, modern *German* vernacular—the geographical equivalent, perhaps, of the chronological pastiche known as the old-German Renaissance.

This hybrid German vernacular was interpreted as not only newer but also better than its historical counterparts. The new *kölnisch* browns, according to contemporary glaze chemists, were even richer and more vibrant than their sixteenth-century prototypes.[41] These brown slipwares, which both referred to and improved upon the long-forgotten pottery of Cologne with the tools, techniques, and materials of the Westerwald, became synonymous with Riemerschmid's modern designs for Reinhold Merkelbach between 1905 and 1915.[42] Their enactment of a nostalgia-driven progress exemplifies the Westerwald's complex yet cautious approach to modernism. That Riemerschmid's "great step forward" was taken "in the footsteps of the old potters" aligns his accomplishment for the Westerwald with Jeffrey Herf's description of Germany's paradoxical "reactionary modernism"—in which the development of technology was aggressively promoted and celebrated for its "magical" ability to recreate a faded era in a new-and-improved Technicolor.[43] This "future-past" modernism, improving the present in order to reclaim a distant idealized past, made the Westerwald industry a valuable asset to the Werkbund in 1907: its products were practical, tangible examples of how a modern German culture of the everyday—an *Alltagskultur*—might look.

Austrian critic, architectural theorist, and Werkbund member Joseph August Lux warned in 1908 that the concept of *Qualität* in the production of modern applied art involved much more than aesthetics; it encompassed social, economic, and "life" issues that were literally "out of the artist's hands": "If the artist is only the designer, then he only has control of the drawing, and is able only to impress forms upon industrial products. [But] if the artist is also the craftsman [*Handwerker*] and therefore the fabricator, then he has in his very hands that quality [*Qualität*] that is the result of the most affectionate, personal work, guided by an intimate knowledge of and devotion to the material—a quality that testifies to the joy of the creator's soul, to the spirit of his work, and is at the same time an essential feature of artwork itself. This is the quality that the word *Qualität* invokes when it is spoken."[44] Although Riemerschmid was neither *Handwerker* (craftsman) nor *Techniker* (technician), his hands-on, inventive collaboration with Reinhold Merkelbach demonstrated that "intimate knowledge of and devotion to the material" that Lux understood as both the recipe for and the key ingredients of *Qualität*. In their synthesis of tradition and progress, Riemerschmid's new designs adapted not only aesthetics but also materials and technology for contemporary use. His modern vernacular positioned the Westerwald to serve as a prime example for the Werkbund in its campaign to revitalize German culture through the development of modern, "quality" products.

Qualität took on special significance in Werkbund discourse between the organization's 1907 founding and its first major exhibition at Cologne in 1914. Although it would seem simply to imply something well made, the Werkbund used *Qualität* in a more exacting sense, to mark specific products that met its technical and aesthetic standards. Recent cultural scholars have wrestled, as did Werkbund members themselves, with the Werkbund's appropriation of *Qualität*, noting a tendency toward abstract, ambiguous jargon. The Werkbund's first president, Theodor Fischer, while he equated the concept of quality with *Anständigkeit* (honesty, propriety, and decency), stressed in his keynote speech at the Werkbund's first annual meeting in 1908 that the word *Qualität* was not to be determined by a particular definition. "Just as we would not all agree on the same concept of beauty," Fischer remarked, "so it's very necessary to allow the concept of quality to change according to the individual and the particular branch of industry."[45] At the Werkbund's seventh annual meeting six years later, however, designer and Werkbund member August Endell protested that "the unfortunate word quality in the Werkbund program" had led to "dire misunderstandings. For 'quality' means in the end nothing more than to make something well, and that is simply self-evident."[46] Like Endell, the notoriously opinionated Adolf Loos, though not a Werkbund member himself, was also wary of *Qualität*. To Loos, the Werkbund's emphasis on the artist-designer as the designated originator of the quality product was misguided. Like Muthesius, Loos argued that the quality (and beauty) of everyday objects stemmed from their fulfillment of function, as well as the appropriate use of modern technology in their fabrication; however, unlike Muthesius, Loos believed that this kind of quality evolved naturally through proper attention to function and workmanship in all kinds of production, not by way of the omnipotent hand of a specially appointed artist-designer.[47]

But the opinions of dissenters did not prevent modern Westerwald stoneware from being understood by Werkbund members generally as a quintessential quality product. *Qualität* was founded on the modernist vernacular idyll. To Muthesius, simple vernacular forms, evolved in response to utilitarian needs, were perfectly suited for adaptation to a practical modern lifestyle. In his 1907 address, which functioned in part as a review of products on show at Dresden in 1906, Muthesius praised Riemerschmid's modern stonewares, whose forms and functions were derived from vernacular prototypes that had stood the test of time by transcending the influence of fashion.[48] Muthesius's notion of an unpretentious, ahistorical, "styleless" German material culture that had evolved naturally from a primeval vernacular for contemporary use was central to the concept of *Qualität*: a measurement of inherent worth that outweighed both historical style and commercial value. And yet, in contrast to Loos's undesigned vernacular, Muthesius's styleless vernacular depended on the guiding force of the artist-designer: the vernacular was the raw material—the natural, national resource—that required intervention and cultivation from the proper source—namely, Werkbund-sanctioned artists. Modern products earned the title of *quality products* in part by being made of German materials and produced in honest, efficient, modern ways, but it was their design by an artist who believed in the importance of the "proper" materials and processes that sealed their quality status in Werkbund eyes.

Art-industrial products labeled as *Qualität* demonstrated the successful evolution of preindustrial regional craft for modern national industry, since *Qualität* began with the material itself. Ernst Berdel, chief glaze chemist at the Westerwald's government-funded Royal Ceramics Technical College in Höhr (established by the Prussian government in 1876 to spur the modernization of the Westerwald industry), equated stoneware with authentic German culture because it "grew out of the ground, which contained the most delectable clay deposits."[49] Muthesius targeted the inappropriate use of materials as the primary cause for "cheap and nasty" products; where indigenous natural resources, such as stoneware, were concerned, the misuse of materials actually squandered the national wealth. The remedy, Muthesius concluded, was for the designer to study the precise character of the material, which would, in turn, dictate the most suitable forms and best methods of construction. His Werkbund colleague, Stuttgart museum director Gustav Pazaurek, characterized Westerwald stoneware as a "beautiful, hard, manly material" that required appropriate handling. While firms that resorted to applying low-fired, colored enamels to their stoneware beer mugs as cheap marketing gimmicks were accused of emasculating stoneware, Riemerschmid and the designers who followed his example were applauded for restoring stoneware to its primal virility.[50]

Qualität claimed the focus of the Werkbund's first annual meeting at Munich in 1908. In his address to the association on this occasion, Muthesius proposed quality work as a remedy for Germany's relative shortage of indigenous raw materials—only *Qualität* would allow the nation to compete in the world market. Muthesius went on to describe the Werkbund as an "organization of experts that seeks to enlighten, teach, and educate the greater public about the concept of quality. [It] seeks through its activities to have an effect like yeast among the entire *Volk*."[51] *Qualität*'s leavening effect, however, was to be achieved most directly not through the Werkbund's activities, but through the exploits of quality things, themselves.

At the same meeting, the role of the hand in the production of "quality work" (*Qualitätsarbeit*) was a key theme of President Theodor Fischer's address, "The Ennoblement of the Trades in Collaboration with Art, Industry, and Handwork." The Werkbund vision of quality workmanship dictated the collaboration of modern art, industrial technology, and traditional craft. Although the Werkbund was a diverse body of individuals whose views were frequently in conflict with one another, its fundamentally progressive formal and technological agenda, developed in opposition to the products and practices of the traditional trades, appeared to favor machine production. For Muthesius and his supporters, mechanized production was indeed key, not only to the development of modern forms, but to creating a modern *Alltagskultur* by equipping the middle class with *Qualität* through the mass production of reliable, artistic, and affordable products. But as the title of Fischer's speech suggests, while the Werkbund rejected neither the concept nor the practice of handcraft in 1908, both were being rethought. And the age-old ceramics industry was the template for this redefinition of craft in the context of modern production. "Today in this technological age," Fischer states, "one remembers reluctantly—or not at all—that machines have been around for a good long time; that, for example, the potter's wheel is also a machine. . . . There is thus no rigid boundary between tools and machines. A person can create quality work [*Qualitätsarbeit*] with the tool or with the machine, as soon as he has come to terms with it as a tool."[52]

While the first concern of the Werkbund's 1908 conference was to demonstrate and establish that *Qualitätsarbeit* could be produced in collaboration with machines, banishing handwork from the lexicon of production was not part of the agenda. In the Westerwald model, new methods of manufacture only supported and celebrated the stoneware industry's legendary hand-driven achievements, while at the same time emphasizing the fact that potters' hands *had* employed machines from the industry's very inception. In 1912, Berdel decreed that the modern forms and decorations generated by serialized, mechanized processes were so "harmonious and organically unified" that he could confidently compare them to the best sixteenth- and seventeenth-century examples. But it was the increase in production resulting from new techniques that made these examples of quality work available for everyday use.[53]

The artist-designer played the central role in the Werkbund's restructuring of the relationship between traditional craft and mechanized industry because, as is evident in the example of the new scratch technique that Riemerschmid had developed for Reinhold Merkelbach while designing modern beer mugs in 1902, it was the artist whose design determined the negotiations between hand and machine. The collaboration of progressive designers and technicians at Westerwald firms had effectively replaced both the excessive embellishments of historicism and the undesirable idiosyncrasies of handcraft with standardized, sanitized pottery that spoke at once of heritage and hygiene. A new kind of Westerwald craftsmanship strengthened the modern industry's symbolic connection to its vernacular heritage. Through an evolution of the technology already inherent in its craft, the Westerwald had, by 1910, begun to reclaim its lost title of *Qualität*.

MODEL SERVANTS

Qualität referred not just to materials as such, but to materials in action—that is, to process. And the formal implications of *Sachlichkeit*, the ways in which an object's form expressed its character, were inseparable from the object's function: from the purpose of the thing. In his 1908 account of the state of modern design in Germany, Lux wrote that Riemerschmid's objects "act as if they really were individual beings, characters who have their own moods and follow their own rules . . . All the housewares are given expressive faces, inspiring droll, gnome-like thoughts."[54] Lux's Werkbund colleague Paul Rée concurred with this assessment, noting the curious way Riemerschmid's things seemed to "affect us like beings who, while they are intended to serve us, do so gladly and willingly, with faces that testify to their inner cheerfulness and freedom." Rée concluded that "die Sache"—the task at hand or, in this case, the *purpose*—was everything to Riemerschmid.[55]

Form, function, purpose, and service: these components of *sachlich* design point to a definition of utility modeled on the perceived virtues of human servitude. Both Lux and Rée were writing at a time when domestic servants were still *de rigueur* for most wealthy middle-class households, but when the role and necessity of the servant were at the same time beginning to be questioned. While it would not be until the mid-1920s that Austrian architect Grete Schütte-Lihotsky's scientifically designed, amenity-stocked "Frankfurt kitchen" was to position the middle-class housewife as the "domestic engineer" capable of *manning* the household solo, without a maid and cook, even in the first decade of the twentieth century, material objects and appliances were beginning to suggest themselves as replacements for servants in the bourgeois home. These new "cheerful and free" domestics were model servants who performed their tasks "gladly and willingly"—in contrast, perhaps, to their more complex and troublesome human counterparts. Even Riemerschmid's humble egg cup and mustard pot, each poised on three stubby feet, seem to be bustling happily toward the user. Domestics are no longer needed; the things themselves are already on their way!

But in Rée's touting of the new inanimate servant as a model for the more conventional animate one, can we hear a note of discomfort—even guilt? Why was it appealing—or important—for one's everyday things to be cheerful, free, happy, and willing? In addition to shifts in social roles and class status in early twentieth-century Germany, this rather new nation's recently achieved status as an imperial power—with colonies in present-day Burundi, Rwanda, Tanzania, Namibia, Cameroon, Gabon, Congo, Central African Republic, Chad, Nigeria, Togo, Ghana, and New Guinea, as well as numerous Micronesian islands—meant that power relations among people of different socioeconomic classes and ethnicities throughout the German Empire were a topic of interest, controversy, and anxiety.[56] What was the proper (*anständig*) position of the educated middle-class German in relation to the colonized person in Africa or Asia? Was it not implicit in the arguments made by middle-class arbiters of German culture like Rée, Lux, and Muthesius—through their naturalizing rhetoric of home and *Heimat*—that both the ideal servant and the ideal colonial subject should serve the master-colonizer with an attitude of cheerfulness and "freedom"? Perhaps, then, just as Riemerschmid's chairs did not simply accommodate their sitters but actively instructed them on how to sit, so modern German housewares could teach not only how to serve, but how to master.

The inculcating power of Riemerschmid's stonewares extended beyond interpersonal (or interthingly) dynamics to inner values. For Rée, the rough, gritty texture of Riemerschmid's salt-glazed stoneware tankards expressed a "manly honesty," conveying a distinct sense of *Biergemütlichkeit*—"beer-coziness"—to all who drank from them. But Rée's formulation of cheerful servitude seems almost restrained in contrast to Muthesius's earlier description of the "little baby tankards" in Riemerschmid's 1903 beer service for Reinhold Merkelbach, which "offer themselves . . . to the loving embrace of the empty hand," along with the large jug that is "just waiting for the moment when he will next be called upon to perform his accommodating service with drink." While one might imagine that Muthesius, soon to become an aggressive proponent of *Typisierung*, or standardization in design, would eschew the notion of biomorphic playfulness, he seems unable to contain himself before Riemerschmid's beer mugs. As serendipitous as the exuberant responses of these earnest Werkbund members might seem, however, they were not coincidental. An animated quality object, whose *sachlich* form both showcased the essential nature of its materials and enabled it to act out its purpose within the middle-class German home, was the ideal candidate for advancing the Werkbund's grassroots agenda.

Muthesius identified in the Bavarian artist's designs "art in that special, Germanic sense," a craftsmanship and character that were "rooted in the soil [*bodenwüchsig*] . . . the art of daily life."[57] Riemerschmid's stonewares evoked a folk past, realizing a common ideal of rustic German life through their animation of everyday utilitarian functions. But his beer service not only recalled preindustrial traditions of making and use, it was also eminently usable in modern life. The conviviality associated with centuries of durable Westerwald stoneware could now be reenacted with updated versions of time-honored vessels. This performative aspect of the new stoneware allowed middle-class Germans to participate in a modern culture indexically connected to a common, idealized past through the material of the clay itself. And it was the clay, in turn, that determined the economic force of *Qualität* as indigenous product, national resource, and cultural symbol. Modern stoneware's potential to combine culture with commerce in a recognizably German product tantalized Werkbund reformers like Muthesius and Osthaus, who enlisted the modernized Westerwald in their campaign for *Qualität*.

Stoneware's attraction for the Werkbund was due in large part to its reification of the specifically German cultural ideology of *Kultur*. Like stoneware, *Kultur* implied an indigenous, inherent Germanness predating and resisting the inhibiting structures of foreign civilization, or *Zivilisation*. While *Zivilisation* signified the encroachment of foreign fashions, *Kultur* stood increasingly for that which was felt to be innately and enduringly German. Characterized by intellectual freedom, *Kultur* was reflected and protected by the *Bildungsbürgertum*—the educated or "cultured" middle class.[58] Muthesius described the new German applied art as a "means of cultural education"—or *Bildung*—in his 1907 address: he identified it as an agent of *Kultur*.[59] Werkbund reformers capitalized on the middle-class connotations of *Kultur* in the concept of *Lebenskunst*, or "life art," an aestheticization of the everyday and its objects.[60] The fetishizing of everyday life as the heart of all German culture endowed utilitarian objects like Riemerschmid's stonewares with a moral "fitness for purpose" beyond their practical one—as bearers of "Germanness."

In *Moderne Kultur*, a two-volume edited guide to modern domesticity published in 1907, art critic and Werkbund member Karl Scheffler discussed the idea of *Alltagskunst* through an exploration of connections between German art and German life.[61] In articles on subjects from kitchen crockery to religion, Scheffler, along with other prominent intellectuals and artists, attempted to synthesize cultural pedagogy into a modern bourgeois ideology. *Moderne Kultur* dubbed the *Bildungsbürgertum* the modern stewards of *Kultur*. By educating the middle class about modern *Qualitätsware* (quality wares), *Moderne Kultur* encouraged discerning consumers to enact practical reforms from the inside out: beginning in the domestic interior, but overflowing inevitably (it was hoped) into public life. Through their purchases, householders could infuse modernity with Germanness: the acquisition of household items was to be understood not merely as an expression of personal taste, but as an act of cultural allegiance.

Moderne Kultur implied in its title an evolution of German culture for modern life: the preindustrial, spiritual force of *Kultur* was to ground the destabilizing aspects of modernity, including industrial capitalism. If a modern German culture were to be disseminated through consumer goods, the problematic ambivalence of the *Bildungsbürgertum* toward modern consumerism—or capitalist fashion—had to be counteracted through the stamp of *Kultur* on modern products. The vernacular motif (a marker of handcraft imprinted on the industrially produced beer mug, for instance) representing the values of usefulness, simplicity, authenticity, and permanence was the emblem necessary to redeem consumer capitalism and so harmonize the turbulence of modern life. Friedrich Naumann, writing the Werkbund's first propaganda pamphlet in 1908, attributed this redemptive power to the underlying principle of *Qualität*, which would not only produce better quality German housewares, but also "raise the value of labor, improve the worker's status, increase joy in work, and thus reverse the trend to proletarianization hitherto associated with the advance of capitalism."[62]

In its section on ceramics, *Moderne Kultur* applauded the Westerwald's revival of "long-forgotten" techniques and their adaptation to modern products. Like Muthesius, Scheffler championed the work of Riemerschmid, who, he claimed, combated the forces of *Unkultur* (unculture) with his stoneware vessels for Reinhold Merkelbach.[63] Riemerschmid embraced modernity, and with Merkelbach he exploited the potential of technology; but he remained clad in the armor of *Kultur* throughout by allowing stoneware's preindustrial heritage to guide his designs. As early as 1901, Scheffler had discussed the concept of the *Kulturprodukt*—a man-made product (distinct from a "gift of Nature") whose design had been culturally engineered to inculcate the values of *Kultur* in the modern German *Volk*.[64] By 1910, modern Westerwald stoneware had become a *Kulturprodukt*: a product whose market value was (or should be) secondary to—and determined by—its cultural value, or *Qualität*.

THE EVANGELIZING OBJECT

Stil and *Mode*, or style and fashion, functioned, as Frederic Schwartz has pointed out, as opposing discursive terms analogous to *Kultur* and *Zivilisation* in the Werkbund's approach to product design and marketing. In Heinrich Pudor's 1910 article "Practical Suggestions for the Achievement of *Qualitätsware*," the sociologist and dress reform advocate exemplified this *Stil/Mode* polarity with an emphatic statement: "Fashion is the transient, Style is the enduring."[65] Viewed in the light of economist Werner Sombart's chapter "Economy and Fashion" in his seminal *Modern Capitalism* of 1902, fashion signified not only changing tastes in dress, but also the experience of social and cultural life as a unique product of the modern economy—including the design of utilitarian objects. In his 1908 *Art-Industry and*

Culture (*Kunstgewerbe und Kultur*) Sombart criticized the Werkbund's project of *Bildung*—cultural education through industrial art objects—believing that modern art-industry illustrated the negative economic effects of modern technology harnessed by capitalism.[66] The fast-paced, ever-changing fashion that Sombart personified as capitalism's "favorite child" was, however, a serious concern to Werkbund members.[67] It was fractious fashion's chaotic shifting of "styles"—all too familiar to Werkbund members from the nineteenth-century's parade of historicist idioms and from the more recent absorption of Jugendstil into the stylistic lexicon of industrial mass production—that the Werkbund sought to arrest (or at least circumvent), through the establishment of a unifying modern German style based on vernacular prototypes, yet practical for modern life and immune to fashion's fancies.

In "The Problem of Style," an article that appeared in the April 1908 issue of *Dekorative Kunst*, sociologist Georg Simmel concluded that "style is the aesthetic attempt to solve the great problem of life."[68] Simmel noted that while modern people seemed to have an endless roster of styles from which to choose in outfitting their homes, in antiquity as well as periods during the Middle Ages, a single, unified style provided a "general foundation for life." "Where only one style is conceivable," Simmel proposed, "every individual expression grows organically from it; it has no need to search for its roots; the general and the personal go together without conflict in a work."[69] Werkbund members believed that a modern yet enduring German style could purge the modern economy of its addiction to fashion.

The crusade to cleanse industrial capitalism with *Kultur* was expressed in the title of the Werkbund's 1912 yearbook, *The Spiritualization of German Work*. The yearbooks, produced as the organization's public face, were to function as educational yet practical handbooks for industrialists and retailers; as such, they exemplified the integration of Werkbund theory and practice.[70] In conjunction with didactic articles that included Muthesius's landmark assessment of Werkbund achievement, "Where Do We Stand?" in which he proclaimed that German quality products must begin to exert an influence on the foreign market, the 1912 yearbook published lavish photographs of industrially produced quality wares endorsed by the Werkbund, including several pages of modernized Westerwald stonewares.[71]

The most drastic measure in the Werkbund's campaign to spiritualize the German economy in the name of *Qualität* was the *Deutsches Warenbuch*, or *German Warebook*, a catalog published jointly in 1915 by the Werkbund, the Dürerbund (a cultural reform organization and forerunner of the Werkbund), and four retail merchants' associations.[72] Although the *Warenbuch* appeared only after the outbreak of the First World War, it was planned already in 1913 as a catalog of *Wertarbeit* (work of value): exemplary mass-produced goods for household use. The *Warenbuch* was designed to "exert a significant influence on culture in general" since, as the introduction pointed out, "good products advance a people not only economically, but also morally and artistically."[73] As proof of their worth (*Wert*) or quality (*Qualität*), the products selected for the catalog by the Dürerbund-Werkbund Association (but manufactured by various companies) were each stamped individually with a *Wertmarke*, or mark of value. This symbol was printed boldly in the catalog's accompanying text so as to be easily recognized by consumers when choosing actual products.

Deutsches Warenbuch readers were thoroughly schooled in the principles of both technology and taste. The introductory text included a two-page definition of *quality work*, a lamentation on cheap products, a warning against the deceptions of fashion, and a brief education in the principles of mass-produced wares, concluding with the assurance that quality products could indeed be fabricated through modern industrial means. This closing argument had been advanced as early as the Dresden exhibition of 1906 and reiterated by Muthesius, Fischer, and numerous other Werkbund members leading up to the *Warenbuch*'s publication in 1915. Generous sections were devoted to the proper employment of materials and decoration. Finally, each medium was treated individually: its material nature, the techniques of its fabrication, the appropriate strategy for its design, and the practical application of these designs in the home were all systematically addressed.[74] The section on modern ceramics limited stoneware to sturdy, established, utilitarian forms, prohibiting it from imitating other materials, such as wood or metal. The *Warenbuch* implicitly refuted van de Velde's earlier proposal of a more colorful glaze palette for stoneware by insisting that its "natural" and "proper" colors were the traditional blue and gray, or the revived *kölnisch* browns. But even these restrained glaze colors should not be applied so thickly as to obscure the familiar orange-rind texture of the stoneware clay body beneath.[75]

The *Warenbuch*'s numerous photographs provide invaluable information about Werkbund-sanctioned *Qualität* (figure 5.8). Without a word, Riemerschmid's robust, *sachlich* beer mugs put into practice the principles outlined in the *Warenbuch* text. Here *Sachlichkeit* offered an antidote to what the Werkbund labeled the seductions and delusions of fashion, as Riemerschmid's mugs bared their essence to the viewer: the way they looked was the way they *were*. What one saw was perhaps more profoundly what one got than had ever been the case in industrial capitalism's brief history: at a glance, the educated middle-class consumer could understand not

K 300   K 301   K 302   K 303   K 304
Steinzeugkrüge

K 305   K 306   K 307   K 308   K 309
Krug   Becher   Becher   Krug   Kanne

only the functional purpose of these mugs, but the materials from which they were made and the tradition to which they referred. *Sachlichkeit* articulated a symbolic yet direct link from visual form to the network of theoretical and material "qualities" embedded in *Qualität*.

While some period critics indicted the *Deutsches Warenbuch* as an insidious form of advertising by the ostensibly not-for-profit Werkbund, its defenders maintained that its *sachlich* approach and presentation acted precisely to reclaim capitalism for *Kultur* by stripping the commodity of its guises. Many saw the Dürerbund-Werkbund

FIGURE 5.8

Stoneware tankards (including designs by Richard Riemerschmid) published by the Dürerbund-Werkbund Genossenschaft in the *Deutsches Warenbuch*, 1915, 101. The Metropolitan Museum of Art, The Thomas J. Watson Library Copy Photograph.

Wertmarke as nothing more than the Werkbund's "brand"—but the underlying purpose of the *Wertmarke* was to redeem the brand from fashion or, as Schwartz has argued, to "separate the brand from capital" and restore it to a sign of inherent worth by denoting the actual value of an object rather than its superficial "look." In the pursuit of this goal, the *Warenbuch* traced a second relationship between *Qualität* and *Sachlichkeit* through the visual presentation of its *Wertarbeit*. Schwartz has discussed the *Warenbuch*'s "deadpan" black-and-white photographs of products arranged in orderly rows as a means of transcending capitalist fashion by presenting true quality goods as standardized "types"—objects that had emerged from a process of design evolution as modern examples of established utilitarian predecessors.[76] Printed below the *Warenbuch* photographs was neither the designer's name nor any descriptive caption, but simply the object's type—"mug" or "jug," for instance—followed by a model number. Rather than dazzling consumers with choice, the *Warenbuch* presented them with tasteful, prechosen types: survivors of the Werkbund's "natural selection" by way of *Qualität*.

Just as the capitalist brand implied the capricious tyranny of Fashion, so the "type" heralded the arrival of the definitive modern German *Style*. With the *Warenbuch*'s publication in 1915, the Westerwald's heritage of regional craft had been incorporated into what the Werkbund promoted as a national language of symbolic form, in which the value of a pot could be read on its salt-glazed surface. The modern-scratch spiral on Riemerschmid's industrially cast *Warenbuch* mug number 303 traced not simply the technical steps from model to mass-product, but an evolution of decoration from vernacular craft to modern *Sachlichkeit*, marking, as it did so, the material connection between original and replica, in which the hand of the potter became the ghost in the machine.

In the discussion following Theodor Fischer's 1908 address to the Werkbund on the collaboration of art, industry, and handwork, Richard Riemerschmid was the first to speak. In a response that was characteristically plain spoken and straightforward in its style and heartfelt in tone, Riemerschmid expressed the need to move beyond the Werkbund's fastidious (and evidently already overburdened) collection of rhetorical terms, such as *art*, *industry*, and *handwork*—not to mention *Sachlichkeit* and *Qualität*—to arrive at the solid, material truth that he believed to be their essence: "Now I would like to express one final wish: that we abandon words as soon as possible and move on to deeds; even with the most beautiful and best words we will never accomplish much. This [Werkbund discourse] seems to me very similar to parents who try to bring up their children with instruction and good advice—through words—rather than by examples and actions: they won't get very far that way. Working and making alone will lead us to our goal."[77] This father of the modern Westerwald, whose own working and making had, ironically perhaps, generated a veritable material culture of words in the German prewar discourse on design, now pled for silence, a silence in which his things—like the mug that would soon announce itself wordlessly to the readers of the *Deutsches Warenbuch*—could speak for themselves.

On the eve of war, at the Werkbund's landmark exhibition in Cologne during the summer of 1914, Ernst Berdel, the Westerwald's chemist and chronicler, made a proclamation about his new-old German industry. He seized the rampant, intoxicating energy of the moment—a "beautiful, hard, manly" energy as yet untainted by the violence to come—as a chance to link, once and for all, the past achievements and future promise of the Werkbund with the resurrection of stoneware, through the triumph of *Qualität*: "The industry of Kannenbäckerland will, as it has already done so frequently in the undulating passage of its history, find and fight for justice with its own strength. It carries the future within itself!"[78] But it was neither the Werkbund nor even stoneware itself that had secured the Westerwald's survival: it was the designer of extraordinary things who had engineered vernacular modernism's "loving embrace" by delivering the gritty texture of the German past into the hands of the modern German *Volk*.

6

CELLS AND SOULS

I entreat you . . . to think that life is not empty nor made for nothing, and that the parts of it fit one into the other in some way; and that the world goes on, beautiful and strange and dreadful and worshipful.
—William Morris[1]

This book has placed Riemerschmid's *Kunstgewerbe*—his extra-ordinary objects or "living things"—at the core of his creative practice. Instead of considering these things as secondary to, or a by-product of, his larger-scale, architectural achievements, it has proposed his graphic design, interior ornament, clothing, furniture, and household objects as intimately expressive of a creative sensibility derived from a profound fascination with and affection for the human body. His modern objects were and are constitutive of an everyday, lived modernity that looks and feels strikingly different from its more familiar depictions in the history of modern design. But this culminating chapter goes deeper by examining Riemerschmid's approach to pattern-making as a schema of his design *thinking*. Riemerschmid was, both at the opening of his career in the 1890s and at its close in the 1950s, a *Grafiker*: a graphic artist whose training and disposition as a draftsman and painter persisted throughout his design work.[2] It is surprising, then, that Riemerschmid's patterns have received little attention in accounts of his career, and next to no critical interpretation. In this final chapter, I propose that if Riemerschmid's things form the bones of his practice, then his graphic patterns constitute its marrow.

Riemerschmid's patterns—realized in, on, and through fabrics, wallpapers, and carpets, but many of them simply drawings—are visual ideas: nonverbal thoughts externalized on drafting paper. A single form is a single idea, while a pattern is the intercourse of many: a discourse of forms. Over the course of his long life, Riemerschmid drew thousands of patterns, generating more than one hundred alone in the few years before his death. Their gregarious forms swarm across and spill over the edges of myriad leaves and slips of paper from 1898 to 1957, delineating the arc of his career. The thought-images materialized in Riemerschmid's patterns connect his two primary preoccupations: a compulsion for optical play across media, and a compact with the organic as model and muse in the designing of modern life.

While this book has addressed the most innovative and influential period of Riemerschmid's object design—the two decades flanking 1900—its final chapter reaches beyond this formative period. It explores how and suggests why, at the same time that Riemerschmid's professional responsibilities increased and his designs became ever simpler and absent of ornamental qualities, his two-dimensional pattern designs became increasingly imaginative and complex. Riemerschmid's reorientation toward a more reductive design aesthetic during and after the First World War coincides with dramatic shifts in fashion and taste toward a sleeker, sparer aesthetic—commonly associated with interwar *Sachlichkeit* and exemplified in designs from the Bauhaus, in Neues Bauen architecture, and in International Style Modernism generally.

From the late 1910s to the early 1930s, Riemerschmid took on many demanding roles and was occupied with numerous and extensive projects. He continued to work closely with his brother-in-law Karl Schmidt's Deutsche Werkstätten, for which he had planned and helped to execute the garden city of Hellerau outside of Dresden between 1907 and 1912—home to the factory, its workers, and their director.[3] From 1913 to 1924, he directed the Münchner Gewerbeschule (Munich School of Industrial Art) and subsequently the Kölner Werkschulen (the Cologne design school he modernized at the request of Mayor Konrad Adenauer) from 1926 to 1931. Riemerschmid also chaired the Deutscher Werkbund (which he had cofounded in 1907) from 1921 to 1926. And during the early 1930s, he contended with the impact of the rise of fascism and anti-Semitism in Germany. Taking all of these commitments and concerns into account, the notion that Riemerschmid would seek to streamline his design practice at both the micro level of the individual object and the macro level of the category or type of object he designed is understandable. Simply put, as time went on, he had bigger (and in some senses, better) uses for his time.

In the context of his fewer and steadily simplified designs for objects, then, his intricate, decidedly decorative, yet optically challenging patterns appear to present an anomaly, a curiosity—a *puzzle*. Certain pieces of Riemerschmid's pattern-puzzle appear at various times and in varied ways to interlock with the established tenets of modern design. But, as anyone who has attempted to complete a jigsaw puzzle knows, pieces that initially appear to fit may ultimately fail to do so. The following pages examine both these "fits" and, more revealingly, their *counterfits*. For it is the failure of Riemerschmid's patterns to conform, both to his greater oeuvre and to the history of modernism, that sets them—and their creator—apart.

A KIND OF SOUL

In one of the earliest histories of Jugendstil, published in the 1930s, Riemerschmid's close friend, Hamburg painter and art critic Friedrich Ahlers-Hestermann, describes how Riemerschmid's fundamental views on aesthetics had been formed several decades earlier—by Nature itself. Ahlers-Hestermann recounts a conversation of Riemerschmid's with architect Gabriel von Seidl in which Riemerschmid recalled lying in a summer meadow, while still a young painter, with his "head full of the future." But it was the immediate present that, at that very moment, attracted his attention. Right there before his eyes, lush green plants, on whose leaves insects crawled with tiny, precise movements, revealed to him the answer to the question of form. "Forms? Here they are—down to the very structure: every sprouting blade, each projection of twig and leaf, the wing casings of the insects—everything!"[4]

For Riemerschmid, the love of materials was one with the love of nature: Nature placed its riches—wood, minerals, clay—into the artist's hands. It was Nature, then, who truly conceived and formed the artist. Years later, at the Werkbund's first annual conference in 1908, Riemerschmid made an impassioned argument for the love and understanding of materials as the primary indicator of artistic genius. He proposed that gifted proponents of craft and design, including carpenters and even factory owners, might merit the title of *artist* more than their counterparts in the fine arts did. The gift of artistry, Riemerschmid believed, could never be given by the academy, but was bestowed directly by Nature upon her beloved. Those who could immerse themselves in the contemplation of a flower, or of flowing, glittering water just as easily as they could lose themselves in devotion while reading Goethe, approached this intuitively creative state of the natural artist. *Stimmung* (imaginative feeling or affect), Riemerschmid averred, while it distinguished the greatest examples of art, could so easily be found in the commonest manifestations of nature.[5]

But Riemerschmid's homage to nature in 1908 was neither a sweeping generalization, nor a purely metaphorical flourish. Rather, it references a specific set of discourses stemming from early nineteenth-century philosophy and science, which had been rediscovered and reinterpreted at the turn of the twentieth century. To complete his modern definition of *artist*, Riemerschmid compares the process of working with craft materials directly to the growth process of plants: "If I am correctly instructed, botanists have recently been talking a great deal about the souls of plants, and they are constantly accumulating more evidence that, in a certain sense, one can really attribute to the plant a kind of soul. He in whose hands the dead material comes to life, so that it too acquires a kind of soul, and then, as if of its own accord searches for its own most genuine form, reacts to stimuli, grows and becomes—he is an artist!"[6] By 1908, Riemerschmid had been commended many times for understanding the "souls" of his materials. Following politician Friedrich Naumann's 1906 remark that Riemerschmid possessed the "uncommon capacity" to recognize the soul of wood, the Munich art historian and critic (and Riemerschmid's close friend) Walter Riezler noted in 1908 that every material was at the same time "happy and *sachlich*" in Riemershmid's hands.[7] However, Riemerschmid's own explicit relation in 1908 of "plant souls" to the souls of materials makes two important revelations: first, that Riemerschmid was aware of contemporary debates in botanical science and understood them in analogy to modern artistic practice; and second, that the shared characteristic, in Riemerschmid's thinking, between the plant soul and the "kind of soul" he ascribes to the material that "comes to life . . . searches . . . reacts . . . grows and becomes" was animation—*motion*.

Identifying animation as the indicator of the soul's presence and sentience was, however, neither original to Riemerschmid nor new to metaphysics. Aristotle had claimed, in his 350 BCE "De Anima (On the Soul)," that the soul was defined not simply as a thing's vital essence or "essential whatness," but that an inanimate object could not properly be considered to possess a soul because it would have to have "*in itself* the power of setting itself in movement and arresting itself."[8] If the soul (*anima*) is what animates, then animation—*voluntary* motion—is what denotes the presence of a soul. Ecological humanities scholar Janet Janzen explores the revival of interest, around 1900, in nineteenth-century vitalism and nature philosophy in "a world that has suddenly become animated—through the increasing popularity of moving pictures and through inventions that were increasingly present in daily life: the streetcar, the automobile and even electricity."[9] Janzen notes that Aristotle considered the plant's soul to be of the lowest possible order—only "nutritive," while animals possessed souls that were both "nutritive and perceptive," and human souls were nutritive, perceptive, *and* "rational." But Aristotle's pupil Theophrastus, "the father of botany," allowed (as Riemerschmid does) that plants were sentient beings capable of responding voluntarily to their environment.[10]

The philosophical tradition of *vitalism*—a collection of beliefs sharing the common contention that life processes cannot be explained solely through *mechanism*, the material composition and physical/chemical performances of living bodies, but that some other animating principle, force, or power resides in and enlivens all living things—has been active since the time of Aristotle, through the seventeenth-century philosophy of Spinoza, and continues today. However, historian of art and culture Oliver Botar has discussed the *neovitalism* or *critical vitalism* emerging at the turn of the twentieth century as distinct from its predecessors and successors.[11] As Frederick Burwick and Paul Douglass note in their anthology on neovitalism, the shift that truly enabled a new, more "sophisticated" approach to vitalism around 1900 was the transition, during the nineteenth century, from a matter-based physics to an energy-based physics: whereas old, "naive" vitalism had posited a substance or fluid as the energizing force of being, critical vitalism located life's vital force in process and dynamic impulse—rather than a specialized or "magical" kind of matter.[12]

Neovitalism's focus on impulse, energy, and *movement* grew up and intertwined with *nature philosophy*: that peculiarly German branch of early nineteenth-century thought germinated in the soil of German Idealism and Romanticism, which historian of the philosophy of science Michael Heidelberger has described as proposing "an organic-dynamic worldview as opposed to the atomistic-mechanistic outlook of modern science."[13] A third vine in the neovitalist interlace was the neo-Romantic *Lebensphilosophie* or "life philosophy," which, epitomized by the work of Friedrich Nietzsche, took its cue from contemporary developments in biology, prioritizing the dynamic processes of living and deemphasizing human dominance in the natural world—exploring instead the connectedness of all life. At the core of *Lebensphilosophie* was the impassioned insistence on an exuberant *expression* of life, an opposition to anything that inhibited or opposed the life force, and a near deification of youth as the life's quintessence.[14] In the 1890s, Jugendstil artists drank long draughts from the spring of *Lebensphilosophie*; and its counterpart, neovitalism, has been understood as the accepted ideology of the *Lebensreform*

(Life Reform) movement, of which Riemerschmid was an influential proponent.[15] Indeed, Riemerschmid's reference in his 1908 speech to the ensouled material that "grows and becomes" signals his grounding in *Lebensphilosophie*, which defined itself around the biological activity of growth and the more mystical, metaphysical process of *becoming*.

Read in the turn-of-the-century context of neovitalism, *Lebensphilosophie*, and neo-Romanticism, Riemerschmid's analogy of imaginative absorption—whether in a flower, a flowing stream, or Goethe's writings—takes on heightened significance. Nature philosophy stood at the heart of Goethe's endeavors as thinker, poet, fiction writer—and scientist. Where botanical science, founded on the eighteenth-century taxonomic system of Linnaeus, sought to understand plants objectively from the outside, Goethe and other German nature philosophers desired to understand them more empathically, "from within."[16] In the tradition of Theophrastus, Goethe saw plants as constantly in motion, undergoing incessant change (metamorphosis), and acting always as part of a larger system or group; it was impossible for Goethe to view any plant as a static object or isolated individual.[17]

While distinct from its contemporary counterpart in natural science, nature philosophy was yet in many ways engaged with it. The drawings of biologist and popularizer of Darwinism in Germany, Ernst Haeckel, for instance, though dependent on scientific technology for the sources of their imagery, demonstrate a dynamism and organic interwovenness that would appear sympathetic to Goethe's vision of an animated nature (figures 6.6 and 6.9). Haeckel articulated his biologically defined worldview in 1863 as *monism*, a term drawn from earlier metaphysical usage to indicate a system based upon a single ultimate principle or kind of being. Haeckel's monism, however, refers not to metaphysics but to the physical, empirical world of natural science; for Haeckel, monism was "that unifying conception of nature as a whole."[18]

And yet, while Haeckel brought the belief in a unified creation down from heaven to earth, he simultaneously rejected any narrowly mechanistic or reductively materialist doctrine, arguing that matter—organic and inorganic—was not dead but alive, animated by what he called *Seele*, or soul. In fact, as Alfred Kelly has shown in his work on the dissemination of Darwinism in Germany, Haeckel understood himself as heir to the tradition of Spinoza and Goethe: he believed that these thinkers "saw nature as a single universal substance that was both matter and spirit—a universe of animated matter."[19] The nature of this substance (or soul) became the question around which Haeckel's scientific inquiries turned, as his theories veered more and more toward the mystical and the nineteenth century drew to its close. His publication in 1899 of *Die Welträtsel* (*The World-Riddle*), which examined this very question, marked his steady drift, since the beginning of his career at midcentury, toward the metaphysical. Botar has argued that Haeckel's "synthesis of hard science and metaphysics" made his project especially appealing to "those artists who sought such a position themselves," and his concurrent publication of the hugely popular and highly aestheticized volumes of *Art Forms in Nature* (between 1898 and 1904) suggests that a similar synthesis of the empirical and the artistic had also been accomplished by the turn of the century.[20]

But even before Haeckel's espousal of the term *Seele* in his vitalist theory of monism, psychophysicist Gustav Theodor Fechner had begun to argue specifically for the existence of souls in plants, publishing two books on this topic: *Nanna—or On the Soul Life of Plants* (1848) and *Zend-Avesta—or On the Things of Heaven and the Afterlife: From the Standpoint of Meditating on Nature* (1851), in which he broadened his soul theory to include the stars and the universe more expansively, claiming most provocatively of all that the entire material, *animated* world was "God's body."[21] In *Nanna*, Fechner principally pushes back against skepticism toward plant animation, arguing that neither brain nor nervous system was a prerequisite for the experience—or apprehension—of an inner life. Fechner reasoned that, just as the same note could be produced by pressing a key on the piano or a key on the organ (even though the piano produced its sound via a string, while the organ produced its sound by means of a pipe), so *animation*—the marker of the soul's habitation in a body—did not require a particular organ for its production.[22]

At the time of its original publication in the mid-nineteenth century, Fechner's work on the souls of plants was widely ridiculed and dismissed as unscientific. However, more than fifty years later, in 1908—the same year that Riemerschmid compared craft materials to the souls of plants—Fechner's *Nanna* was reissued with an introduction by the science fiction writer Kurd Lasswitz, who argued that while "the educated public shook their heads over [*Nanna*]" in 1848, in 1908 "it is being read constantly in new editions . . . for the times have changed."[23] Indeed, aesthetic discourse around 1900, increasingly preoccupied with questions of perception—including psychologist Theodor Lipps's theory of *Einfühlung* (empathy) and the subjective *Wirkung* (effect) of aesthetic objects upon the perceiver—provided a uniquely hospitable climate for the notion that plants might have an inner life or soul, and that this soul might communicate with other souls through physical movement. These New Aesthetics, then, laid fertile ground for the new critical vitalism to "grow and become" within the thinking and practice of twentieth-century German designers, steeped as they had been in the *Lebensphilosophie* of Jugendstil. The quasi-mystical approach to natural science that at this time shared ground with neovitalism, *Lebensphilosophie*, and monism came to be called the New Biology.

The New Biologists' preoccupation with animation as the primary indicator of the presence of life defined their *biocentrism*: the cluster of neo-Romantic and neovitalist discourses so vociferous at the turn of the twentieth century.[24] And biocentrism's revolution around motion adds a dimension to the New Aesthetics of perception and empathy that both complicates and explicates the work of its practitioners. In 1905, just three years prior to Lasswitz's reprinting of Fechner's *Nanna*, the Austro-Hungarian biologist and science fiction writer Raoul Heinrich Francé, a devotee of Haeckel's and a self-avowed biocentrist, published *Das Sinnesleben der Pflanzen* (*The Sensory Life of Plants*), a staunchly anti-Linnaean text in which Francé argues both for the animated, sentient life of plants, and for humans' dynamic *experience* of them—or, in the empathic sense, *with* them—in their own natural environment.[25] According to Francé:

The plant moves its whole body as freely, easily and gracefully as the deftest animal—just much more slowly. The roots burrow searchingly into the soil, the buds and shoots complete measured cycles, the leaves and blossoms nod and shiver in response to change, the tendrils circle searchingly and reach out with their ghostly arms into their surroundings—but the superficial person passes by and takes the plant for rigid and lifeless, because he doesn't take the time to tarry for an hour by her side. But the plant has time, that's why she doesn't hurry; for the giants of Flora's Realm live through the centuries while beholding at their feet countless human generations ripening and decaying.[26]

Francé's tone is somewhere between science and magic: he describes with precision and wonder the growth and development of plants, while at the same time imbuing them with personalities—of fairies, giants, and ghosts. In 1908, Lasswitz would write that Fechner's contribution to the discourse of science was to determine "how much truth hid behind the fairy tale" of sentient, soulful plants.[27] This fairytale rhetoric, deeply rooted in the previous century's romantic and ethnographic fascination with folklore, reverberates through descriptions of Riemerschmid's designs. Muthesius's delight in 1904 at the enchanted stoneware tankards that "offer themselves" to the drinker's hand is followed in 1908 by Joseph August Lux's more prosaic yet no less fanciful account of Riemerschmid's things as "individual beings, characters who have their own moods and follow their own rules" and inspire "droll, gnome-like thoughts." Around 1908, then, the language of the fairy tale draws together plants and objects as things that possess the capacity for voluntary motion, even if we are too hasty—or too "superficial"—to tarry with them till they do. In plants, it was slow, yet scientifically observable movement that communicated the presence of a soul; in objects, it was animation—imagined through design. Fechner's theory was, in essence, a cosmic *Sachlichkeit*: beholding the moving, *living* thing was seeing its soul.

A natural world constantly in motion was, by its animated nature, asymmetrical—*irregular*. Francé condemned Linnaeus for having "murdered" nature by arresting that very dynamism that Riemerschmid understood as the primary object of artistic absorption—and devotion: wherever Linnaeus went, Francé imagines, "the laughing brook died, the glory of the flowers withered, the grace and joy of our meadows was transformed into withered corpses, which this 'true botanist' collected into folios of his herbarium, and whose crushed and discolored bodies he described in a thousand minute Latin terms."[28] Analogous to this desiccating botany was a tradition of botanical drawing known to date to at least as early as 50 CE that stopped active nature in its tracks, frequently displaying it in a rigid and symmetrical aspect best suited to close scientific scrutiny.

This "freezing" of plant life in botanical drawing is intimately entwined with the development of vegetal ornament in modern Europe. In the mid-nineteenth century, British design reformers—including Owen Jones and his pupil Christopher Dresser, a German-trained botanist and, later, an innovative designer—employed the ideal static, formal symmetry of plants not simply in the design of decorative motifs, but especially in Dresser's case, as a model for the structural design of objects as well (figure 6.1). Although Dresser recognized growth, change, and even sickness and deformity as unavoidable in actual, living nature, he adhered to an ideal or perfected template of nature in the development and propagation of his design theories.[29] In the first decades of the twentieth century, a good deal of modern design still followed Dresser's example, regularizing nature's anomalies and smoothing over its defects.

Riemerschmid's patterns check modernism's regularizing impulse, however: while they obey symmetry at the level of the repeat, they tend to flout its regulations within the repeat's structural matrix. The wild tangle of vines of a 1902 textile pattern bearing what appear now as leaves, now as heart-shaped blossoms, and now as blushing fruit (figure 6.2), seems a visualization of Goethe's iconic statement, "All is

FIGURE 6.1

Christopher Dresser, *Floral Pattern*, 1883 (based on an earlier design). Graphite, ink, gouache. The Metropolitan Museum of Art, New York. Purchase, Lila Acheson Wallace Gift, 1992.

FIGURE 6.2

Richard Riemerschmid, *Textile Pattern Drawing* (F4A), 1902. Architekturmuseum der TUM. © 2021 Artists Rights Society (ARS), New York / VG Bild-Kunst, Bonn.

Leaf!" by which the nature philosopher strove to express his wonder at each part of the plant in continuous metamorphic motion: either transforming out of or transforming into the leaf. Riemerschmid's early patterns present a means of depicting in a static image, spread over the surface of everyday fabrics, this wondrous, ever-changing motion of plants. While the delicate vines and pods of an elegant jacquard silk woven at Krefeld in 1902 might have acted as a model for Francé's searching tendrils reaching out with their "ghostly arms" (figure 6.3), a rustic printed cotton with a motif of irregular heart-shaped leaves in navy blue, punctuated at what appear to be random intervals by clusters of scarlet berries—four, three, two, and now and then a small, lone, bright fruit—was put into production at Schmidt's Dresdner Werkstätten in 1905 and featured in Paul Rée's 1906 review of Riemerschmid's designs in *Dekorative Kunst* as an example of a modern German fabric that was simple, practical, and fanciful at all once (figure 6.4).[30]

An upholstery fabric bearing a vine motif with leaves made up of soft, rounded diamond-shapes in the bright, complementary colors familiar from Riemerschmid's paintings and graphic designs of the 1890s demonstrates at the same time his devotion to nature's forgiving geometry and what art historian Ruth Grönwoldt has called a "new direction in décor," promoted by the Dresdner Werkstätten (figure 6.5). The small motif of this machine-made textile was unpretentious, unimposing,

FIGURE 6.3

Richard Riemerschmid, *Jacquard-woven Silk*, Krefeld, 1902. Architekturmuseum der TUM. © 2021 Artists Rights Society (ARS), New York / VG Bild-Kunst, Bonn.

FIGURE 6.4

Richard Riemerschmid, *Printed Cotton F20* (design, left; fabric manufactured by Dresdner Werkstätten, right), 1905. Architekturmuseum der TUM. © 2021 Artists Rights Society (ARS), New York / VG Bild-Kunst, Bonn.

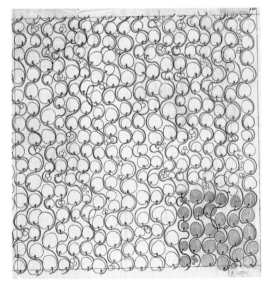

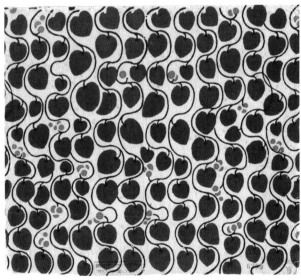

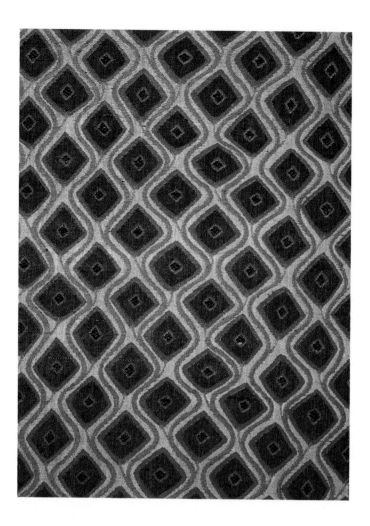

FIGURE 6.5

Richard Riemerschmid, *Cotton/Acetate Upholstery Fabric* for the Dresdner Werkstätten, 1905. Münchner Stadtmuseum, Sammlung Mode/Textilien/Kostümbibliothek. © 2021 Artists Rights Society (ARS), New York / VG Bild-Kunst, Bonn.

versatile—appropriate for use in a variety of contexts by a broad swath of modern middle-class consumers. And yet, as Grönwoldt notes, the pattern spreads out across the fabric with "great assurance" and "empathy" (*Einfühlung*), softening any harshness that such a strong, geometric motif in contrasting colors might risk.[31] While the geometric forms of the leaves appear at first glance to repeat themselves, a careful examination reveals thirty different leaf shapes within a single repeat.[32] Modern and pragmatic in its simplicity, geometry, and versatility, the 1905 upholstery textile yet evoked a familiar natural world populated with patterned irregularities—like the turning leaves of an autumn tree: all similar in principle but each unique in reality, and each gradually changing hue at its own, particular pace, maintaining its individuality while perpetuating the reassuring pattern perceived as "tree." We know Nature's organized anomalies best through our lifelong experience of the body—our own, and those of others—which we understand to be symmetrical in theory, but know as rather motley in the flesh. Riemerschmid, born with one brown and one blue eye, may have known especially well that organic life is, all at once, structured and regulated, unruly and unraveling. Even the very cells of life are alike in structure while unique in form.

Riemerschmid's pattern-making process, in which irregular forms crept and bloomed across tightly gridded graph paper like vines over a trellis, enacted the dependence of asymmetry on symmetry—the *permission* that rationalism gives to irrationality. His patterns require structure if only for the purpose of wriggling free of it—to prove their living thingliness. As if redrawing the grid beneath nature's own patterns, over the course of the eighteenth and nineteenth centuries natural science had—with the aid of the microscope—revealed structures far deeper than those apparent to the naked eye; microscopy had seemed almost magically to *produce* structure and order where none had previously been presumed to exist. Breathtaking examples of these microscopic architectures can be found in Haeckel's studies of the radiolarian, a sea-dwelling protozoan of about 0.1 mm to 0.2 mm in size, which secretes an elaborate glassy exoskeleton (typically made of silica) to protect its single cell. Haeckel's intricate drawings of multiple radiolarian species—each housed by a different form—not only revealed Nature's previously unimagined capacities as the tiniest, most meticulous of architects, but also exposed a nakedly clear relationship between the animating essence (in this case, not the soul but the *cell*) and its outer housing, or form (figure 6.6) The shimmering energy of Haeckel's turn-of-the-century radiolaria is also projected by the wiggling pulsations of the radial bursts that propel themselves across a sea of bubbling protoplasm in one of

Cyrtoidea. — Flaschenstrahlinge.

Riemerschmid's very first wallpaper patterns for Munich's Vereinigte Werkstätten from 1899 (figure 6.7).

Understood through our closest lens—the unaided human eye—the pattern created by Riemerschmid's 1905 furnishing textile is a stylized vine; but interpreted through the eye of the microscope, it may also be read as a system comprising more fundamental though far more minute natural structures: not the leaves but the *cells* of the vine, made up, in the simplest terms, of cell wall, vacuole, and nucleus (figure 6.8). Magnifying our view to consider Riemerschmid's patterns as visions "under the microscope," we might also begin to connect the neovitalist belief in the souls of plants with the natural scientist's technological revelation and empirical study of the cells of plants. The conflation of the definition of *cell* as the smallest functional unit capable of life and the vitalistic definition of *soul* as animating essence had, by the time of Riemerschmid's patterns, been explored implicitly in the New Biology—and more specifically in Haeckel's "world-riddle" of that mysterious "substance" that was at once matter and spirit, cell and soul. Haeckel's drawings depict this balance between science and religion nonverbally, intuitively—artistically: what appears initially in *Art Forms in Nature*'s plate 34 as a symmetrically arranged collection of green-and-red geometrical patterns turns out to be highly magnified groups of *Melethallia* green algae, their cell structure and life-impulse expressed all at once in the optical dazzle of green fields and red dots (figure 6.9).

The word *cell* was first used in reference to Nature's micropatterns (entirely invisible to humans until the invention of the microscope at the very end of the sixteenth century) by British nature philosopher Robert Hooke in his 1665 *Micrographia, or Some Physiological Descriptions of Minute Bodies Made by Magnifying Glasses with Observations and Inquiries Thereupon*. Hooke chose the Latin *cella*—storeroom or chamber—to indicate the smallest individual, repeated unit that made up the magnified structure of a piece of cork wood. The connotation of the cell as the chamber where something is stored, or *someone* is kept, separate and distinct from others, is significant both in its communication of division—implying the existence of a wall

FIGURE 6.6

Ernst Haeckel, Pl. 31 (Cyrtoidea) in *Kunstformen der Natur*, 1899–1904, Library of Congress, Prints and Photographs Division, Washington, DC.

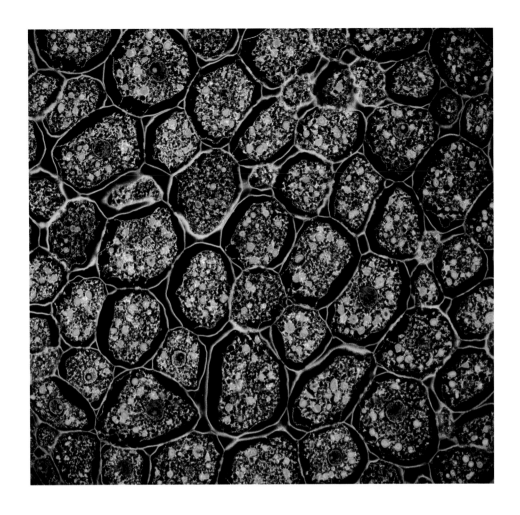

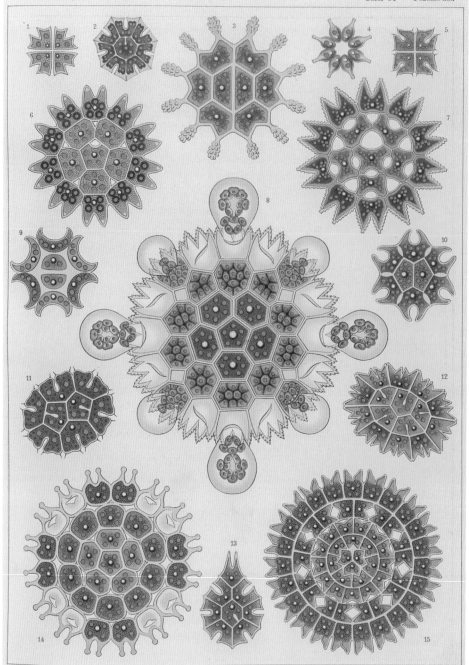

Melethallia. — Gesellige Algetten.

or barrier—and of repetition: this little unit can be reproduced over and over, and though it need not be an exact replica of the cell before or next to it, it will be theoretically and structurally homologous. In the case of Riemerschmid's patterns, the cell is the smallest unit of distinct visual information—the blueprint of his design philosophy, his approach to mass-reproducible modernity, and his understanding of *life*. Riemerschmid's pattern cell is infinitely repeatable, applicable, and adaptable: capable of spreading itself across surfaces "of its own accord" and "with great assurance"—filling up empty space with "empathy."

FAUX BOIS TROMPE L'OEIL

Harnessing microscopic imagery for design was a turn-of-the-century phenomenon. In 1900, one of Haeckel's tiny radiolaria served as the model for the so-called *Porte Binet*—the monumental entrance that French architect René Binet designed for the Paris World's Fair. But a subtler understanding of nature's previously invisible designs not merely as discrete objects but more comprehensively, more cosmically, as all-encompassing, constantly regenerating, and potentially infinite *patterns* came from a far humbler source: the model book. Increasingly popular during the nineteenth century, model books gathered together a variety of printed and photographic "raw material"—images taken from nature and architecture, among other sources—for artists and designers to use as inspiration. But in 1902, Martin Gerlach, an established Viennese publisher of model books who had also trained as a designer, released the first model book to contain microscopic photography: *Formenwelt aus dem Naturreiche* (A World of Forms from Nature's Realm).[33] Gerlach's photographer Hugo Hinterberger promoted microscopic images as a new and unique resource capable of inspiring the artist's creativity without predetermining his scope or limiting his imagination to forms familiar to the naked eye.[34] *Formenwelt* marked its distinction from didactic biological texts by privileging aesthetic

FIGURE 6.9

Ernst Haeckel, Pl. 34 (Melethalia) in *Kunstformen der Natur*, 1899–1904. Library of Congress, Prints and Photographs Division, Washington, DC.

drama over more rationalist taxonomic criteria. In plate 5, close-up, conventional photographs of wood grain, bark, and petrified wood fossils have been juxtaposed with magnified images of the same objects to form a montage of reticulated lines and amoeba-like blotches, while the lozenge-like, attenuated cells of garden snails butt up against the lacy patterns of tree cells in plate 20 (figure 6.10).[35]

In 1902 and 1903, as German designers began to avail themselves of Gerlach's new *World of Forms*, Riemerschmid was modernizing the interiors of the Thieme House in Munich. Looking through the lens of the microscope at the large, red-and-green wool carpet in the Thieme's dining room—previously encountered in chapter 4 (figure 4.8)—we exchange our bird's-eye view of an alpine meadow for an exploded image of Haeckel's concentrically arranged algae. Or perhaps we find the delicate lace of Nature's invisible realm, the intricate matrix of Riemerschmid's most beloved material: wood. Examined through the modern technology of natural science, Riemerschmid's carpet brought the German forest into the German living room in a manner both radical and explicit: not, as his furniture did, by mimicking the grain of its outward surface, but by suggesting its interior structure in cross-section. The large, concentric rings of the Thieme carpet, though they recall the annual rings familiar from the trunks of those awesome "giants of Flora's Realm," (attended, perhaps, by creeping mosses and red-capped mushrooms), are better understood as a cross-section of that giant's miniature appendage—the slender stem connecting delicate leaves to skeletal branches (figure 6.11).

Beheld as a magnified wood stem, the carpet's rings of mottled red "bubbles" translate to xylem: the tubular cells that convey water from the tree's roots upward. Each year, a new ring of xylem forms so that the number of rings—expanding ever outward in the same arrangement as Riemerschmid's carpet design—indicates the tree's age. The stem's outer ring, analogous here to the carpet's denser blue-and-green pattern framing the red center, is made up of a closer-knit tissue of phloem cells, those which transport food from the leaves to the other parts of the tree. Separating the xylem from the phloem is the cambium, the tissue where new xylem and phloem cells are generated and which finds its stylized counterpart here in the thick, dark, geometric border of alternating blue and green bars between the carpet's two distinct sections. Even viewed as a purely abstract pattern, the carpet's design is energetic: hot reds pulse against cool greens and blues, while the linear, striped pattern of the frame strikes out from the round, full, throbbing circles of the interior, each pattern suggesting both different types of motion and rates of speed.

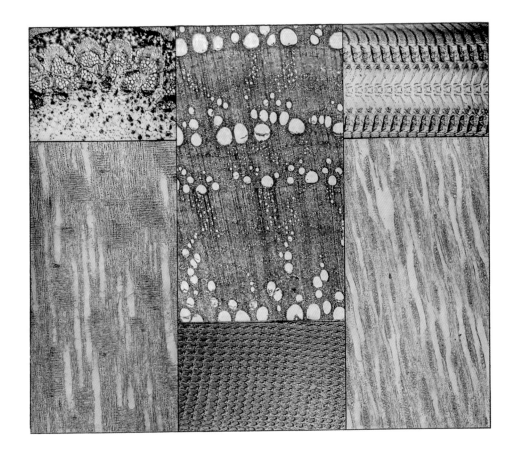

FIGURE 6.10

Martin Gerlach, *Formenwelt aus dem
Naturreiche* (A World of Forms from Nature's
Realm) (Vienna: Martin Gerlach & Co., 1902–
1904), plate 20: "1 Cross-section of plant
tissue. – 2 Radial section of a hardwood. – 3
Cross-section of a hardwood. – 4 Lingual
plate of a land snail. – 5 Lingual plate of an
aquatic snail. – 6 Tangential section of a
hardwood."

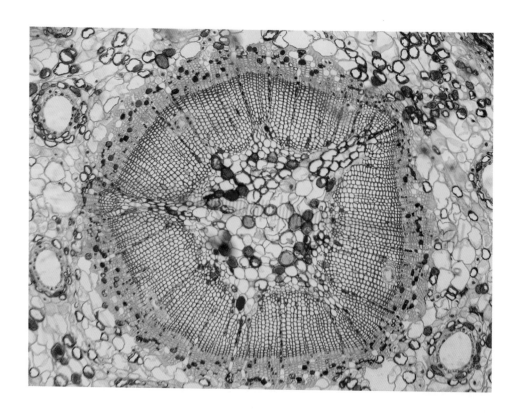

FIGURE 6.11

*Microscopic shot: stem of first-year
Pinus taiwanensis, cross section* by
石川 Shihchuan. https://www.flickr.com
/photos/40891106@N08/4569896543
(CC BY-SA 2.0).

Considered as bursting bubbles and creeping vines, the pattern adopts nature's dynamics. But apprehended at the cellular level, with the abstracted xylem and phloem not just busy in their own delivery of nourishment to the organism of the tree, but being themselves manufactured in the cambium tissue, the pattern does more than approximate motion: it actually illustrates the essential *activity* of botanical life. The carpet becomes, in short, a sort of picture or diagram in which the "material [wood] comes to life . . . acquires a kind of soul . . . searches for its own most genuine form, reacts to stimuli, grows and becomes."

But wood's natural, visible patterning is equally a manifestation of its inherent growth and becoming. Wood grain is an index of wood's essential nature as a living substance that continues to fluctuate and, as Riemerschmid described it, "react to stimuli" in all phases of its materiality: even after the tree's death, its "soul" lives on in the form of furniture. And Riemerschmid's critical renown for perceiving and expressing the soul of wood stemmed from his uncanny ability to design furniture so as to reveal its inherent "charms."[36] Riemerschmid's furniture for the gentleman's study displayed at the 1906 Third German Applied Arts Exhibition in Dresden revealed the ornamental properties of the wood by blasting its surface so that its grain was not just visible but tangible: standing out in shallow relief as pattern became fused with texture, surface and substance were *one* (figure 4.13). This approach to surface decoration rejected applied ornament while at the same time quite literally "hunting back" the artwork or aesthetic object to its "medium."[37] This "truth to materials," originating in the Arts and Crafts principles of William Morris in the 1860s and extending for at least a century through Minimalist painting, sculpture, and design of the 1960s, was central to Riemerschmid's designs for objects in the two decades flanking 1900. But during the years of the First World War, his patterns begin bending the "truth" of medium specificity.

Many of Riemerschmid's designs for objects and furniture around the turn of the twentieth century are those of a painter feeling his way from the graphic to the plastic. Design drawings for ceramics and furniture of this period exhibit the cross-hatching, gestural mark-making, and illusionistic chiaroscuro already characteristic of his bold pencil sketches and pen-and-ink drawings of the 1890s. Indeed, in stark contradistinction to the sand-blasted bas-relief of Riemerschmid's 1906 Dresden cupboard, an inlaid tabletop from 1905 reads like a meticulously rendered pencil drawing, the various grained veneers arranged to create the form of a cross, from which a diamond formed by the precisely placed, striated wood surfaces radiates outward (figure 2.16). Far from emphasizing the tactility of the wood as a warm, living, pliant material offering its natural self for carving or blasting, the 1905 table presents the user with a flat, patterned surface—almost like a built-in tablecloth—that denies depth and resists illusion.

Startling in contrast, then, are a group of wallpaper patterns designed more than a decade later in 1917. Playing with an enduring convention in wallpaper design, these patterns create the illusion of textured wood grain or wood paneling on flat, pasted paper. *Faux bois* (the fashionable French term for this "fake wood" surface treatment) was lambasted throughout its history, first by nineteenth-century British design reformers including Owen Jones and William Morris, and then more ironically in the modernist artworks of Pablo Picasso and Georges Braque, beginning in 1912 with their "synthetic" Cubist paintings: composite images collaged together from newspaper clippings, advertisements, sheets of music, drawings, and illusionistic wallpapers—including *faux bois* (figure 6.12). *Faux bois* wallpaper still thrives today, ranging in tone and meaning from the perennial ersatz kitsch to the luxurious (and ironic) postkitsch chic.

In the first of his two volumes on art pedagogy, published in the same year as his wood patterns were executed, Riemerschmid contested the academic, strictly mimetic rendering of nature as a teaching method for young artists. And yet he went on to assert that "nature is the source from which all art emanates, all form is taken from here, so that it is no more indispensable for the artist to emulate what Nature has already performed than it is to make his eye see and his hand skilled."[38] Riemerschmid's belief in nature as the source of all artistic form, coupled with his rejection of any slavish copying of the natural world, sheds light on the ways in which his three sequential patterns from 1917 engage with the *faux bois* tradition, as well as the significance of their deviation from its naturalism (figure 6.13).

Riemerschmid's designs consist of bold, black-and-white lines articulated in closely concentric pointed oval or double-ogival forms that interlock with one another to form an impenetrably dense field of pattern. Close looking reveals that here too, curious anomalies persist within the overall regular, palpably rhythmic pattern. Yet these quirks are not numerous or random enough to suggest any attempt at naturalism: the verisimilitude necessary for *faux bois* to function as an ersatz material has been avoided. On the contrary, Riemerschmid's wood patterns are highly aestheticized, alluding perhaps to *book matching*, a veneering technique in which pieces of wood veneer are mirrored, obverse to reverse, so that the grain in the two abutting pieces resembles the two pages of an open book. And yet this is no ironically luxe revision of a cheap stand-in; neither is it Picasso's semiotic

FIGURE 6.12

Pablo Picasso, *Guitar and Wine Glass*, 1912. Collage and charcoal on board, 18⅞ × 14¾ in. (47.9 × 37.5 cm). Bequest of Marion Koogler McNay. © McNay Art Museum / Art Resource, NY. © 2021 Estate of Pablo Picasso / Artists Rights Society (ARS), New York

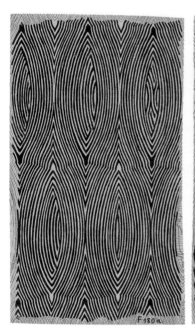 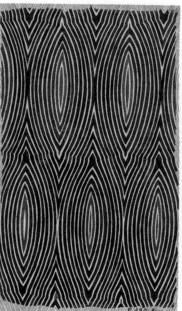 

vision in which fake wood (already a surrogate) might stand in for any object in a cubist collage, depending simply on the shape into which the obliging *faux bois* is cut, and its placement within the composition. But if Riemerschmid plays neither Picasso's semiotic game nor the half-admiring, half-mocking game in which "art" colonizes "kitsch," then what sort of game is he playing in his weirdly woody wallpapers of 1917?

These patterns are puzzles. And their solution lies in a particular kind of *looking*—in fact, their solution *is* looking. The regular repetition of the ogival contour in each pattern in Riemerschmid's F180 series generates a sense of continuous expansion and contraction, an optical vibration that conveys two direct, intuitive

FIGURE 6.13

Richard Riemerschmid, *Patterns F180a, F180b, F180c*, 1917. Architekturmuseum der TUM. © 2021 Artists Rights Society (ARS), New York / VG Bild-Kunst, Bonn.

messages to the eye—and brain. First, these patterns, while they *remind* one of woodgrain, are immediately recognizable as something special, distinct from the disinterested fruits of nature: they are artist-made puzzles deliberately calculated by a human mind and calibrated by a human hand to produce an effect on the viewer—to create *Wirkung*. Second, true to the empathic nature of *Wirkung*, blurring the boundaries between subject (viewer) and object (pattern), these patterns demand perceptual participation; it is impossible to look at them without being drawn in. And once immersed, it becomes difficult to reason through or trace out the pattern cognitively: while the pattern's idiosyncrasies—the varying, apparently shifting forms that inhabit the centers or apertures of each ogive—pretend to offer penetration to the eye and resolution to the mind, both are caught and held on the humming surface. Then the gaze softens, focus becomes diffuse, and perception melts into sensation.

It might be more accurate to say that perception is arrested not on but *in* the pattern's surface. Although the intellect understands the pattern as flat, just as dye stains fabric, so the eye sinks into, merges with, and actually perpetuates the oscillation of form. It is almost as if the collapse of surface into substance enacted by the sandblasted skins of Riemerschmid's furniture at Dresden in 1906 was transposed through these patterns into a purely optical experience: a haptic vision in which physical contact is manufactured by the nervous system and internal to the body. And this sensation of optical touch—an empathic looking—is accentuated by the patterns' simultaneous likeness to and divergence from natural wood. While they evoke the familiar sensation of stroking a wood surface, thereby triggering an internal simulation of touch, they work at the same time to defamiliarize—making strange that well-known sensation by activating form in ways that destabilize the sense of a flat, strokeable plane. Rather than encountering wood simply as an external object, the subject (viewer) is compelled by the pattern's optical trickery to "do" or to "be" wood: to enter into it, travel through it, *feel with it*.

Riemerschmid's game of *faux bois trompe l'oeil*, then, blended optical play with tactile diversion. And like a true puzzle, it compelled the viewer to activate it; in fact, it required the viewer's participation for its own actualization. The empathic aesthetics of Riemerschmid's wood-games resonates with Theodor Lipps's descriptions of *Einfühlung*, summarized by Lipps's better-known student, art historian Wilhelm Worringer, in his seminal *Abstraktion und Einfühlung* (*Abstraction and Empathy*) of 1908. "Aesthetic enjoyment is objectified self-enjoyment," Worringer recites, "to enjoy aesthetically means to enjoy myself in a sensuous object diverse from myself, to empathise myself into it." Worringer continues, quoting Lipps's 1903 *Aesthetics: The Psychology of Beauty and Art* directly: "What I empathise myself into is life. And life is energy, inner working, striving and accomplishing. In a word, life is activity. But activity is that in which I experience an expenditure of energy. By its nature, this activity is an activity of the will. It is endeavour or volition in motion."[39]

Lipps expands his theory of aesthetic perception as a fundamentally empathic experience, to characterize it as active, energetic, and dynamic. Life—like a game or puzzle—is inherently *in progress*. When the game is no longer in play, when the puzzle is solved, neither can lay claim to its original name—just as the cessation of life is not a mere modification thereof, but takes a new name: death. Lipps identified voluntary, directed motion—a visible striving toward something—as the hallmark of aesthetic empathy. His focus on animation echoes in the New Biology's contemporaneous insistence on organic life as constantly in motion and in the neovitalists' biocentric worldview in which a plant was not only capable of sensation and motion but also exerted its will and communicated through movement. Riemerschmid transferred this preoccupation with movement in 1908 to the artist's material, which "of its own accord searches for its own most genuine form, reacts to stimuli, grows and becomes." This activity of the will—in plants, materials, and patterns—was the externalization of the living soul.

Riemerschmid, so lauded for his capacity to perceive wood's soul, seems in these grained, graphic labyrinths to be actively searching for that very thing. In a material sense, these patterns are less than wood—*not wood at all*. But in a metaphysical sense, they "emulate what nature has already performed" by simulating and activating wood's essence: more ideal, more eternal, and more *alive* than any wooden object could ever be. The Munich neovitalist philosopher, psychologist, and contemporary of Riemerschmid's, Ludwig Klages, understood images as "the souls of things."[40] In creating these images, Riemerschmid moves both onward and *in*ward from wood's multiple (sur)faces, displayed across his array of household objects, to conceive and enact its collective soul. His 1917 wallpaper designs are—like plant cells—living blueprints, coursing with energy and endowed by their creator with the agency to pull us into their surfaces and set us in motion along the passages of their intricate circuitry, sweeping us away in the swirls and eddies of rings and grain. In the currents of the soul-image, acting and signifying—*being* and *meaning*—are one and the same. *Sachlichkeit*'s structure of surface and substance collapses completely: everything is surface—the surface *is* the thing. And yet in this very flatness, an infinite space opens up. In the perceptual play of Riemerschmid's patterns, *Sachlichkeit* is no longer compressed within the material strata of surface and substance but expands into the illimitable realm of image and idea. This is the space of the soul.

VERTIGINOUS *WIRKUNG*

In *Abstraction and Empathy*, Worringer discusses Lipps's belief in two modes of aesthetic empathy: positive and negative. Simply put, *positive empathy* is an experience of pleasure generated by a sense of harmony between the perceptive "activity" that the aesthetic object requires and the perceiver's inherent desire to "act" or perceive in the required fashion. Lipps constructs this relation in his typically animated, personified style: "If I can give myself over to the activity demanded of me without inward opposition, I have a feeling of liberty."[41] After quoting this passage from Lipps's 1903 *Aesthetics*, Worringer concludes that "apperceptive activity becomes aesthetic enjoyment in the case of positive empathy, in the case of the unison of my natural tendencies to self-activation with the activity demanded of me by the sensuous object."[42] *Negative empathy*, on the contrary, is marked by conflict between the subject's natural inclination toward *self-activation* (what the subject wants to do or feel) and the sort of activation (activity) that the aesthetic compels. This conflict or disharmony generates frustration and displeasure. Lipps notes, too, that these two empathic modes are the origins of the terms *beautiful* and *ugly*: the pleasure experienced in positive empathy with a sensuous object we understand as beauty; the friction or conflict we experience in negative empathy we call ugliness.[43]

Worringer's treatise turns on the contemporary assumption among Lipps and his Munich circle that *positive empathy* was experienced during the viewer's absorption into representational or narrative works of art, while abstract art was lacking in the capacity to foster empathy and was therefore culturally inferior to naturalism. But Worringer, taking his cue from Austrian art historian Alois Riegl's 1893 *Stilfragen: Grundlegungen zur eine Geschichte der Ornamentik* (*Problems of Style: Foundations for a History of Ornament*), argues for abstraction as a human psychological need for self-actualization, self-expression independent from nature. "Just as the desire for empathy as the basis for aesthetic experience finds satisfaction in organic beauty," Worringer continues, "so the desire for abstraction finds its beauty in the life-renouncing inorganic, in the crystalline, in a word, in all abstract regularity and necessity."[44] Again building on Riegl's discussion of the *Kunstwollen*—artistic volition or "the will to art"—Worringer imagines a "will to abstraction," in which geometric abstraction, detached from the outer world of nature and belonging instead to the inner world of the psyche or soul, provided its creator with a sense of spiritual satisfaction or repose as "the only absolute form that could be conceived and attained by man."[45]

Reading Riemerschmid's patterns as illustrations of Worringer's theories would be at best a conjectural venture. However, taking into account Worringer's relationship to Lipps in Munich, as well as his pervasive influence on the trajectory and interpretation of modernist aesthetics from the time of *Abstraction and Empathy*'s publication in 1907 onward, we might well consider the development of Riemerschmid's patterns—from their naturalistic origins around 1900 to their stylized naturalism during the years of the First World War to the geometric abstraction of the Third Reich—in relation to a "will to abstraction."[46] Worringer employs the monist rhetoric of biocentrism to argue for abstraction as the organic connection between natural (or vegetal) and artificial (or geometric) ornamentation. "Both styles," he persists, "linear as well as vegetal ornament . . . represent at bottom an abstraction, and their diversity is, in this sense, really only one of degree; just as, in the eyes of a monist, organic regularity . . . differs only in degree from that of the inorganic-crystalline."[47] Riemerschmid's patterns from the early to mid-1930s, and especially a series from 1934, the year following the accession to power of the National Socialist German Workers' Party (NSDAP), exchange the natural forms of plants for a convulsive linear abstraction—an optical assault that churns the flat surface and grips the perceiver with *negative empathy*.

Toward the end of World War I and in its aftermath, Riemerschmid's designs for furniture and household objects undergo a marked shift in aesthetic. Forms become simpler and more straightforward, in many cases more conventional: the playfulness and animation of the prewar designs is swallowed up in sobriety, and ornament survives only in the naturally aesthetic qualities of materials. During the same period, by contrast, Riemerschmid's patterns become gradually denser and more complex, growing into intricate puzzles that interlock to create the illusion of three-dimensional form. Over the course of 1917, the year of his *faux bois trompe l'oeil*, the patterns tend increasingly toward total abstraction, finally relying entirely for their *Wirkung* on the interaction of geometric forms. And quite unlike his placid, undemanding furniture of the same vintage, these graphic works become more and more active—resisting the confinement of a single visual register, refusing to lie still. It is as if the life force or soul had been drained from the furniture and poured into the patterns, where Riemerschmid's prewar penchant for animation meets his new predilection for abstraction, spawning restless, agitated images that seem to rattle the bars of their page (figure 6.14).

If we consider Riemerschmid's abstract patterns as a kind of animated geometry—a living puzzle—both historical and personal events of this period become essential "pieces." Before looking more closely at the patterns of 1934, then, we must lay out some of these key chronological pieces. Riemerschmid's transition toward abstract patterning in 1917 took place between his return in 1916 from voluntary military service as a training officer of the First Bavarian Field Artillery Regiment in Munich (figure 6.15) to resume his directorship of the Münchner Kunstgewerbeschule (Munich School of Industrial Art), and the loss of his eldest son, Helmut, killed in action in France in July 1918.[48] (Maria Wüllenkemper notes the profound effect of the son's death upon his father by recounting that Riemerschmid, who delighted in playing his viola, never touched the instrument again from this time forward.) Riemerschmid continued at the Kunstgewerbeschule (which he had directed since 1913) until 1924, concurrently taking an active and influential role in the proceedings of the Werkbund. Offering his 1905 machine furniture as a tangible argument, Riemerschmid assumed a decisive position in the Werkbund's *Typisierung* or "standardization" debates, siding with Hermann Muthesius to support the concept of the *type* in design and its significance for streamlining furniture production and providing quality products for a broadening clientele.[49] Riemerschmid was named chair of the Werkbund in 1921, an office he held until 1926.

Between 1926 and 1931, Riemerschmid led the Kölner Werkschulen, whose new, straightforward, pragmatic name—Cologne "Work Schools"—reflected the project assigned to Riemerschmid by Cologne's major, Konrad Adenauer (later the first chancellor of the Federal Republic of Germany from 1949 to 1963), to reorganize and update the city's erstwhile Kunstgewerbe und Handwerkschulen (Schools of Art-Industry and Handcraft) in order to align them more closely with the modern, practical, hands-on approaches to design pedagogy promulgated through the Werkbund. In 1931, however, as one of the myriad consequences of the 1929 market crash and worldwide economic crisis, Riemerschmid's contract as director of the Werkschulen was not renewed, and at age sixty-three he returned with his wife, Ida, to their hometown of Munich. The termination of Riemerschmid's position in Cologne was for him the first in a series of blows to his aspirations for the reform of design and its pedagogy. The period that followed was one of disillusionment and defeat, as Riemerschmid witnessed much of what he had worked for throughout

FIGURE 6.14

Richard Riemerschmid, *Pattern F172*, 1917.
Architekturmuseum der TUM. © 2021 Artists
Rights Society (ARS), New York / VG Bild-
Kunst, Bonn.

FIGURE 6.15

Officer Richard Riemerschmid on a Horse, Field-Artillery Regiment 1 Prince-Regent Luitpold, April 4, 1914. Münchner Stadtsarchiv.

his career as a *Lebensreformer* (a utopist who had come of age in the 1890s) defamed and destroyed in the inexorable process of the *Gleichschaltung* or "Nazification" of, among numerous cultural institutions, the German Werkbund—the organization that Riemerschmid not only led from 1921 to 1926 but also had cofounded in 1907.

The Werkbund, too, had not been immune to the economic hardships that ended Riemerschmid's tenure in Cologne. And at the time of his return to Munich in 1931, its financial struggles were compounded by political attacks from both right and left. While committed socialists and communists condemned the Werkbund as politically effete and oblivious to the material needs of the masses, Nazi ideologue Alfred Rosenberg's Kampfbund für deutsche Kultur (Combat League for German Culture) assailed the Werkbund as a malignant example of the "Marxist-Jewish" cultural degeneration endemic (for the Nazis) to the politically liberal Weimar Republic (1919–1933). As historians Paul Betts and Alan Steinweis have shown, however, the stereotype of Nazi aesthetics as a unilateral "blood and soil" vernacular is inaccurate. In fact, it was the Nazis' simultaneous (and shrewd) embrace of what Betts has referred to as a "softened Bauhaus modernism"—akin to Riemerschmid's sleeker, yet more stolid furnishings of the late 1920s and 1930s—that led many Werkbund members to believe that the party might yet be sympathetic to its aims.[50] And the Kampfbund, for its part, attracted to the Werkbund as a potential talisman of Nazi "progressivism," proposed a merger of the two organizations early in 1933. Although the Werkbund initially rebuffed this overture, both financial and political security were becoming every day more imperative to its survival. Ultimately, the Werkbund's abject position—exploited not just by the Nazi Kampfbund but also, internally, by the conservative contingent of its membership—delivered it into fascist hands. On June 10, 1933, the Werkbund's thirty-member executive council voted almost unanimously to join with the Kampfbund, instating architect Carl Cristoph Lörcher, president of the Bund Deutscher Architekten (BDA, or Association of German Architects) and Nazi Party member, as the Werkbund's new leader.

The June 10 Kampfbund merger was immediately followed by the circulation among non–Nazi Party members of a compulsory questionnaire requesting details of occupational and personal background, and, as a result of this, the expulsion from the Werkbund of all Marxists and Jews. The *Führerprinzip* (the Nazi-devised "Leader Principle," which granted absolute legal authority to Adolf Hitler and, by extension, to his appointed leader of every German cultural organization) then began to be implemented throughout the Werkbund and its regional affiliates. During the next few months, this would prove devastating for Riemerschmid, who was at that time leader of the Münchner Bund (the Werkbund's Munich branch), as well as a much-respected, long-standing, and influential member of the national Werkbund, though not a member of the Nazi Party. Riemerschmid's correspondence with the Werkbund from this period is painful to read as it documents the steady tightening of the Kampfbund's vise around the once democratic and, on the whole (up to this point), progressive organization.

Shortly before the June *Gleichschaltung*, Riemerschmid had received a letter from the Werkbund's secretary, Otto Baur, filling him in on the plans for the merger and mentioning the Werkbund's dealings with Rosenberg and the new Nazi Minister of Propaganda, Joseph Goebbels. Baur asked that Riemerschmid keep the central Werkbund in Berlin abreast of the goings-on in Munich.[51] As the weeks and months pass, however, this congenial reciprocity vanishes from Riemerschmid's correspondence with the Werkbund. Lörcher begins pressuring Riemerschmid to bring conservative Munich architect Karl Johann Fischer (a BDA and NSDAP member) onto the executive board of the Münchner Bund, and then—most gallingly for Riemerschmid—to cede his own position as Münchner Bund leader to Fischer and to install him as its authoritarian *Führer*. Riemerschmid, in addition to recognizing the fact that Johann Fischer's assumption of Münchner Bund leadership would mean his own deposition therefrom, felt strongly that Fischer was neither creatively suited to nor particularly interested in—and, most importantly, not equipped to lead—the Münchner Bund. Fischer was not an *artist*, in Riemerschmid's sense of the word, as expressed in his 1908 speech to the Werkbund. But it was the Nazi-controlled Werkbund's ambiguity and hypocrisy—its fundamental lack of *Sachlichkeit*—in handling "the matter at hand" that seems to have rankled and disillusioned Riemerschmid most. In a letter to Lörcher on July 17, he writes bitterly:

You know that I would very much like to continue to participate in the work of the Werkbund, but I can only bestow my energies and my trust in the service of the Werkbund's comprehensive tasks if its affairs are clear to me, and if I know that trust will be returned for trust. If you do not find in me "a capable character, proven by his achievements" [here Riemerschmid quotes a description of J. Fischer in a previous letter from Lörcher], and if you believe that this description fits Herr Fischer better, then it is right to make that clear right now and to give the Munich leadership over to Herr Fischer.[52]

On September 22, 1933, Riemerschmid received a letter on behalf of Lörcher by his Werkbund and party colleague Winfried Wendland, officially severing the Werkbund's ties to the Münchner Bund, "releasing" it from its role as the Werkbund's regional affiliate in Bavaria. A new Bavarian regional Werkbund office, the Landesgruppe Bayern, would now be headed by Johann Fischer, and any members of the Münchner Bund "who value their membership in the Werkbund" were to apply to him.[53]

As Werkbund historian Joan Campbell has asserted, Lörcher's attacks on the highly respected Riemerschmid, at the time in his sixty-fifth year, alienated many Werkbund members who might otherwise have accepted its new order.[54] A few days after Riemerschmid's receipt of Wendland's and Lörcher's letter, Riemerschmid wrote to his friend, the designer Fritz Ehmcke in Widdersberg, Upper Bavaria, pleading with him to retain his membership in the Münchner Bund, even if he resigned from the Werkbund itself. Riemerschmid writes on September 26, "I don't want to have anything to do with the Werkund, with the leadership as it is now."[55] The following day, less than a week after the Münchner Bund's connection with the Werkbund had been dissolved by Lörcher, Riemerschmid composed the final version of a statement on the Münchner Bund's behalf, insisting on its value as an independent organization and naming himself and his close friend, Theodor Fischer, among those who would perpetuate it without the Werkbund's participation—or blessing. Riemerschmid's final text (prior drafts had been heavily edited with the help of Fischer, who no doubt recognized the political and personal danger to Riemerschmid of issuing such a public statement) stressed the necessity for artistic freedom, opposing this fundamental right of the artist to political affiliation:

He who truly bears the title of artist and whose appearance is rare, lives by the requirements of his inner being in a world that turns away from fleeting realities of the moment . . . He is, on the whole, a quintessentially apolitical person. Many of these true artists have stayed far away from the great national movement, not out of opposition, but because they were on different paths . . . Accordingly, it is understandable that precisely those whose artistic input would have been most valuable have been absent from the Kampfbund, both in its inception and its development . . . Earnest, true art conveys a meaningful image of a *Volk* to posterity, but not always in its own time.[56]

In his closing line, Riemerschmid declared that the Münchner Bund would not be guided by any particular program or set of rules (doubtless referring to the

Werkbund's recent fate at the hands of Nazi bureaucracy) but instead by the principle of *Qualität*. Riemerschmid's equation of *Qualität* with artistic freedom in 1933 represents an ironic reversal of August Endell's fears in 1914 for the potential of this vague term to become a kind of programmatic Werkbund jargon and to cause "dire misunderstandings." Whereas indeterminacy had seemed a liability to Endell in the Werkbund's 1914 context, in the socially draconian Third Reich, *Qualität* offered creative sanctuary in its very failure to specify, to limit, to categorize. It was, perhaps, Riemerschmid's last grasp at the artistic utopia that had been gradually but steadily slipping through his fingers since the turn of the century.

For the next half year, the Münchner Bund maintained its independence by, according to Campbell, "playing off the Prussian authorities against the Bavarian," and select members continued to meet privately at Theodor Fischer's Munich villa.[57] But in the new year, rather than allow itself to be absorbed into the conservative Munich Kunstgewerbeverein (Arts and Crafts Association), the Münchner Bund agreed to disband. In contrast to his painstaking letters to Lörcher and the Kampfbund-Werkbund of the year prior, a terse yet poignant entry from Riemerschmid's diary on February 6, 1934, reads: "Membership meeting. Dissolution and then to wrap things up, a pint at the Bayerischer Hof. In the evening Beethoven."[58] The Werkbund itself did not survive much longer. Over the course of that year, it became increasingly reactionary and unrecognizable to the majority of its pre-*Gleichschaltung* members; it was dissolved by 1935, to be reinstated only well after World War II was over, in 1950.[59]

The series of sharp, jagged patterns that appeared almost exactly a year after the Werkbund's disastrous merger with the Kampfbund in June 1933, and in the direct aftermath of the Münchner Bund's disbanding in early 1934, are striking in their diametric formal opposition to the undulating curves and sinuous tendrils of Riemerschmid's prewar patterns. While Riemerschmid persists in deploying irregularities within a regularly calculated matrix or repeated motif, the *Wirkung* (effect) that this strategy generates in his 1934 patterns is far removed from the gently pulsating organic biocentrism of his earlier vines, blossoms, pods, tree rings, stems, and cells. The layered cruciforms of a pencil-and-ink pattern dated May 26, 1934, interrupted, as it were, by abrupt bars of black and white flung at the pattern in all manner of malformed geometries, creates a frantic visual rhythm—or perhaps the intentional negation thereof: while the pattern's matrix provides the time signature, the invisible pattern-player seems *out of time*, jolting and jarring the "listener" as he willfully misses the beat (figure 6.16).

FIGURE 6.16

Richard Riemerschmid, *Pattern FLM 331*, 26
May, 1934. Architekturmuseum der TUM.
© 2021 Artists Rights Society (ARS), New
York / VG Bild-Kunst, Bonn.

A similar pattern executed less than a fortnight later, on June 6, 1934, again deliberately destabilizes, as each attenuated, uneven, off-kilter cross radiates cruciform waves that crash against each other with the pent-up force of dissonance (figure 6.17). The *Sturm-und-Drang* of both patterns is marvelously and terrifyingly orchestrated: where regular repetition begat optical illusion in Riemerschmid's woody patterns of 1917, here it is the very distortions in the cross-forms, with their inscrutable interlocks, unfathomable overlays, insistent disruptions, and frustrated frictions, that produce a simultaneous sensation of penetration and impenetrability, attraction and repulsion—a precarious, vertiginous push-and-pull that at once worries the surface, unnerves the eye, and unsettles the stomach. Riemerschmid's cross-patterns are nothing short of a performance of Lipps's and Worringer's theoretical *negative empathy*, in which the perceiver is compelled to "feel with" the image, yet recoils from what she feels.

But the form that Riemerschmid disturbs to create these fractured lines is no Catholic crucifix, nor it is a generically geometric figure: it is the *eizernes Kreuz*, or Prussian Iron Cross, first used as a Prussian military decoration toward the end of the Napoleonic Wars in 1813, next in the Franco-Prussian War of 1870–1871, and then in the Wilhelmine Empire (1871–1918) and First World War (1914–1918), when a "W" for Wilhelm II of Prussia was placed at its center and it began to be recognized as a symbol of honor not just for the Kingdom of Prussia, but for the entire (now unified) German Empire (figure 6.18). For Riemerschmid—born on the cusp of Germany's 1871 unification, coming of age at the height of Wilhelmine nationalism, serving as a training officer in World War I, and consigning his firstborn son to a premature death on foreign soil in 1918 for the glory of the Fatherland—the Iron Cross may well have vibrated by 1934 with an ambivalence and anxiety to equal the agitation of his optical-visceral snarls. Right at the heart of what masquerades as a system of "pure" geometric forms, this symbolic saboteur explodes Worringer's "primitive," ideal repose in abstraction with mutually amplifying bursts of visual and emotional conflict: attraction and repulsion, attachment and rejection—love and betrayal.

Riemerschmid's design work dwindled alarmingly from 1934 onward, and during the war years (1939–1945) he was involved in few private projects and took on no public commissions.[60] And so his renewed investment at this time in graphic work may represent less of a voluntary return than a forced retreat. But in addition to the severely narrowed sphere of engagement under the Nazi regime that would naturally have turned his creative spirit inward, the significance of Riemerschmid's

FIGURE 6.17

Richard Riemerschmid, *Pattern FLM 334*, 6
June, 1934. Architekturmuseum der TUM.
© 2021 Artists Rights Society (ARS), New
York / VG Bild-Kunst, Bonn.

FIGURE 6.18

WWI Prussian Iron Cross, 1914.
Germanisches Nationalmuseum, Nuremberg.
Photo: M. Runge.

1934 Iron Cross patterns as private rather than public, personal rather than professional, is underscored by the fact that on May 19, 1933—less than a month before the Werkbund's *Gleichschaltung*—the Nazi government had officially prohibited symbols of German history and the German state from being used in any way that might damage their dignity.

Riemerschmid's anxiously ambiguous Iron Crosses would have appeared not simply inexplicable but heretical to Nazi propagandists, and their public circulation would have constituted a professional liability, as well as a personal danger to their artist. Their actual function, then, may have been as a mechanism for the externalization of thought and feeling—a graphic grappling with events and emotions—for a man who wrote little and spoke less about what he thought and felt: a riveting, repetitive, physical process through which he might come to grips both with what had passed and what was passing, and experience it as a living thing outside of, yet still intimately connected to, himself. Here, the repetition inherent in the process of pattern-making traces the psychological compulsion to repeat, first explored in 1914 by Sigmund Freud in "Remembering, Repeating and Working-Through," and then in greater depth in his 1920 "Beyond the Pleasure Principle."[61] Freud identifies and analyzes the compulsion to repeat a past traumatic situation or event as an attempt to master (in the present) that which had been beyond one's control to master at the time of its occurrence. The irony, however, is that by the simple virtue of its "pastness," the event is now forever beyond one's reach—hence, monumentally unmasterable. Riemerschmid's feverish Iron Cross patterns (and the even more unsettling patterns that followed) seem to perform all at once (and over and over) the cycle of trauma, struggle for control, and its inevitable loss that compels the nervous hand to trace and rehearse the ruminations of an anxious mind.

As public evidence of the Nazi campaign against the "misuse" of German symbols, one of the Werkbund's first charges in its new service to the NSDAP in the summer of 1933 was its Away with National Kitsch! exhibition in Cologne.[62] The primary target of this exhibition was the commercialization and trivialization of the *Hakenkreuz*, the forked cross—or swastika. An ancient Eastern symbol of auspiciousness, the swastika (from the Sanskrit *svastika*, meaning "good fortune" or "well-being," and still employed today in sacred contexts within Buddhism, Hinduism, Jainism, and Odinism) had drawn attention during the nineteenth century in connection with ethnographic study and archaeological findings—specifically, those of German archaeologist Heinrich Schliemann in his excavations at Troy. After World War I, several far-right nationalist movements in Germany adopted the symbol, ostensibly to represent an imagined connection between its mystical Eastern origins and the "true" German *Volk* as being of Aryan descent. The Nazi Party formally adopted the forked cross as its symbol in 1920.

Long before its appropriation as a Nazi symbol, a European fascination had developed around the swastika's aesthetic qualities, and Hitler seized on its powerful potential to create *Wirkung* by selecting it as the central motif in the design of NSDAP propaganda. As early as 1925, in his notorious *Mein Kampf*, Hitler discusses the care he took to integrate the ancient symbol, with attention to order and correctness in composition and proportion, into his design for the flag of his envisaged empire. The Nazi banner's palette—black, white, and red—referenced the colors of the Second (Wilhelmine) Reich's flag while eschewing the Weimar Republic's black, red, and gold, thereby creating a symbolic visual lineage for the Third Reich that elided the "degenerate" episode of Weimar liberalism. But perhaps most significant in terms of design was the choice to orient the forked cross, carefully staged within its white circle set against a red ground, not as if "kneeling," shin flush with the ground, but instead on the "point" of one "fork," so that it appears perpetually in motion—*spinning*. The Nazis' infamous pageantry capitalized on the dynamism of their new emblem, sometimes actually enacting it, as was the case with a parade of the Hitler Youth carefully choreographed into the form of a gargantuan, revolving swastika at a rally on August 27, 1933 (figure 6.19). Two days later, on August 29, while still deep in the throes of his excruciating and humiliating negotiations with Lörcher and the new Nazified Werkbund regarding the leadership of the Münchner Bund, Riemerschmid drew a sparse, tentative-looking pattern based on the form of the swastika (figure 6.20).

But it was not until almost a year later, directly on the heels of his Iron Crosses, in July and August 1934, that Riemerschmid would return to this most freighted symbol. Both his crosses and his swastikas belong to a disarming contingent of patterns developed, over the summer of 1934, from purely abstract—yet profoundly unsettling—systems of forms. In a pen-and-ink pattern dated July 3, 1934, squared-off spirals jostle one another, upsetting any possibility of military order (figure 6.21). While each one curls up differently into a rectilinear snail shell, each is yet connected to its neighbors by an uneven, searching line that tempts the eye to trace it, but almost immediately foils the attempt. The pattern's complex striations recall Riemerschmid's romance with wood grain. Ultimately, though, the angular geometry of these lines separates them from plant life; and their lack of uniformity—now thickening, now attenuating—divorces them from any mechanical connections,

creating instead a kind of alternative organicism: neither animal nor vegetal. The boxy whirlpools feel off balance, as if any one of them might at any moment break free of its centripetal force and come unsprung. But together they create a mesmeric optical experience: an intense vibration of uneven black and white lines that suddenly "flips," doing away momentarily with the spiraling squares and presenting in their place a puzzle of floating diamonds, constructed alternately from horizontal and vertical lines, so that one set of diamonds retreats while the other advances, appearing to hover above the surface of the page. The overall effect of these fidgety forms and the illusions they create is a nervous disturbance, a profound lack of ease.

FIGURE 6.19

Hitler Youth parade in the form of a swastika to honor the Unknown Soldier. August 27, 1933. *Facing History and Ourselves.* https://www.facinghistory.org/resource-library/image/hitler-youth-swastika-formation.

FIGURE 6.20

Richard Riemerschmid, *Pattern FLM 358*, 29
August, 1933. Architekturmuseum der TUM.
© 2021 Artists Rights Society (ARS), New
York / VG Bild-Kunst, Bonn.

A month later, another pattern mimics not just the spiraling motion but the iconic form of the NASDP's tightly controlled symbol itself (figure 6.22). Dated August 1, 1934, F 418 makes the most recognizable use of the jealously guarded *Hakenkreuz*. Nine boxy spirals of squared black lines are connected to and set in motion—*driven*, in fact—by a black swastika that appears to rotate, like a turbine, at the center of each. And each of these nine swastikas is poised at a different angle, apparently captured by the artist at a distinct point in its rotation, which in turn generates (as a turbine would) the particular direction and shape of its whorl. The spirals, too, are connected to one another in Riemerschmid's characteristically intricate interlace (how much has passed since the Paris *Art Lover's Room* in 1900!), into which the viewer is compelled to enter, but the way out of which she will never find. But these interlocking gyrations, while they suggest a synchronized, orderly motion like that of the Hitler Youth pageants, effect quite the opposite *Wirkung*. These are skewed and skewing "downward spirals," whose perpetual yet uneven rotations threaten—like the traumatic events that propelled them—to spiral out of control.

In *Abstraction and Empathy*, Worringer cites Lipps's view that "geometrically uniform [*regelmäßig*] figures are an object of pleasure because the apprehension of them, as a whole, is natural to the soul, or because it is, to a particularly great extent, in conformity with a propensity in the nature or essence of the soul."[63] The state-sanctioned designs of the *Eisernes Kreuz* and the *Hakenkreuz*, regardless of the personal and cultural associations that arose in response to them and clung to them in conjunction with their political meanings, conformed, in their abstract designs, to the soul-pleasing, law-abiding order of geometric regularity. In the purely aesthetic, nondiscursive terms of Worringer's discourse, these symbols generate *positive empathy*. Conversely, then, it is through Riemerschmid's graphic acts of irregulation and *dysregulation*—generating, in turn, immediate, intuitive *negative empathy*—that he subverts the symbols of the Third Reich.

FIGURE 6.21

Richard Riemerschmid, *Pattern FLM 344*, 3 July, 1934. Architekturmuseum der TUM. © 2021 Artists Rights Society (ARS), New York / VG Bild-Kunst, Bonn.

FIGURE 6.22

Richard Riemerschmid, *Pattern F 418*, 1
August 1934. Architekturmuseum der TUM.
© 2021 Artists Rights Society (ARS), New
York / VG Bild-Kunst, Bonn.

Had they become public, Riemerschmid's Iron Cross patterns would certainly have signaled to the Nazis cultural "degeneracy" and warranted censure of his already frail design practice. But his swastika patterns from the summer of 1934 were positively treasonous. (In a mere three years' time, the Nazis' infamous Degenerate Art Exhibition of 1937 would open in Munich, drawing over a million visitors in its first six weeks.[64]) The 1934 pattern series were of necessity, then, deeply private exercises, contemplations, meditations—but of what nature? The answer to this final puzzle may be found again in the puzzle itself: in its skewing, distorting, and *warping* of the most prized and protected symbol of Third Reich—a motif which, ironically, lent itself easily to abstraction, distortion, and dissonance by those who abhorred its implications.

Riemerschmid was not alone in his subversion of the swastika. However, unlike the overtly political messages artfully embedded in Dada artist John Heartfield's bitingly satirical photomontages for Berlin's communist *Arbeiter Illustrierte Zeitung*, like his "Blood and Iron" of 1934 (figure 6.23), it was not the discursive "message" of Riemerschmid's patterns but their perceptual effect that registered and communicated their subversive *Wirkung*.[65] As the perceiver participates in the pattern, she activates it, experiencing *with its designer* the discomfort, disorientation, and confusion that propelled its design. This *negative empathy*, while uncomfortable, immerses the viewer directly in the current of Riemerschmid's critique. His own absorption in the process of abstraction allowed him to think through *feeling*—to simultaneously undergo sensation and wrestle with cognition in the complex interweaving of forms that adulterated the "purity" of geometric abstraction with powerfully symbolic iconography. These were the by-products (if not benefits) of a compulsion to repeat, executed not in life, but on paper.

On September 1, 1939, the same day that German troops invaded Poland, Hitler reinstated the use of the Iron Cross, removing the Prussian "W" of World War I and officially converting it to a national, German symbol of honor by placing at its very center—like the centrifuge of one of Riemerschmid's August 1, 1934, spirals—the poised, turbine-like swastika of the 1920 banner described in *Mein Kampf* (figure 6.24). Eight days later, on September 9, 1939 (less than a week after France and Britain declared war on Germany), medic Gerhardt "Gert" Riemerschmid, the artist's second son and the baby of the family, was killed in action in Leczyca, Poland (figure 6.25). The letter that notified his father and mother of their son's death would bear the emblem of the newly minted Iron Cross with its forked cross for a heart.

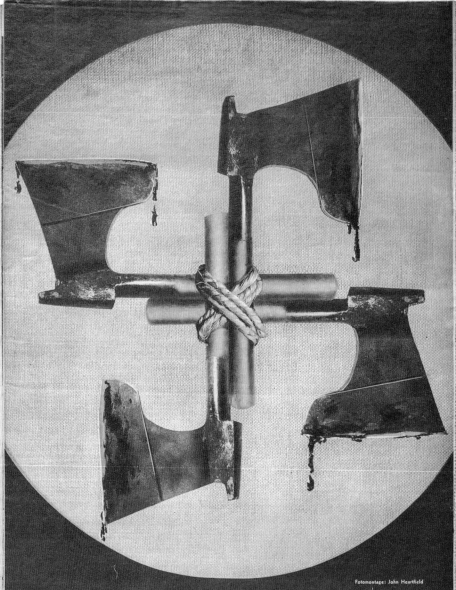

Fotomontage: John Heartfield

Der alte Wahlspruch im „neuen" Reich:

BLUT UND EISEN

FIGURE 6.23

John Heartfield, *Blut und Eisen*, 1934. Reproduced
in *A-I-Z: die Arbeiter-illustrierte Zeitung aller Länder*.
Getty Research Institute, Los Angeles (87-S194).
© The Heartfield Community of Heirs / Artists
Rights Society (ARS), New York, 2021.

FIGURE 6.24

Third Reich Iron Cross, 1939. Germanisches
Nationalmuseum, Nuremberg. Scan: C. Merz.

FIGURE 6.25

"Gerhardt in green field uniform, Christmas 1915" (written by Ida Riemerschmid on the back of the photograph). Germanisches Nationalmuseum, Deutsches Kunstarchiv und Historisches Archiv, Nuremberg.

"A LIVING THING
WITH HOPE IN IT"

A large stoneware punch bowl accompanied by a set of matching cups that Riemer-schmid designed for Reinhold Merkelbach in 1902 (figure 7.1) embodies the extraordinary thingliness of his designs in a manner unparalleled and to a degree unsurpassed by the other thingly things that inhabit this, his book. The generous globe, bearing down on its three stubby feet (apparently with weight enough to splay them), speaks fecundity in its very form. And its little rounded cups—which ask to be lifted by their handles and cradled in the palm of the hand—seem to have spawned from the bowl's pregnant roundness like seeds from a pod, or young from a womb. The decorative pattern, too, whether vines that creep or bubbles that rise, is ebullient—generating, celebrating, and overflowing with life—its small, starry spangles like the heady effervescence of sweet, sparkling wine. In its relation of container and contents, image and being, this family of things plays out its *Sachlichkeit* for all not simply to behold, but actively to partake of. The congeniality binding these things to one another, and in turn bringing their users together in convivial contact, expands and extends their *Sachlichkeit* beyond pedestrian functionalism and even beyond the *Sachlichkeit* of character, qualities, and feeling evoked and explored in this book. As Adolf Behne would express it years later in 1926, here "each *Sache* is a nodal point" in a thingly *society*—a social matrix of people and things. The *Sache* is the thing that both links and communicates, "a crossing point," as Behne has it, "of relations between human being and human being."[1]

    These relations—vectors of sociability traced from each thing to its neighboring thing—form the patterns of life. Half a century later, a pen-and-ink pattern dated

FIGURE 7.1

Richard Riemerschmid, *Punchbowl Set*
(stoneware), manufactured by Reinhold
Merkelbach, 1902. Münchner Stadtmuseum,
Sammlung Angewandte Kunst. © 2021
Artists Rights Society (ARS), New York / VG
Bild-Kunst, Bonn.

October 1, 1956, loosely drawn over a grid of faintest pencil, retraces the steps in Riemerschmid's lifelong process of patterning, which, as we have seen, functioned as a kind of matrix for his grander project as a designer (figure 7.2). The turbulent, striated whorls rippling out in 1956 recall the funneling motifs of the 1930s; the concentric striations suggest both the wooden furniture and wood grained patterns of the 1910s; and the scattered confetti of small blue squares, floating on the surface of the whirlpools, brings to mind the irregular "cells" of Riemerschmid's early, organic motifs on both punch bowls and printed cottons. A single, tiny red square at the page's right-hand edge is by now a familiar peccadillo—perhaps a stain from one of the bright red berries scattered here and there among the blue-leafed vines of his 1905 printed cotton (figure 6.4). Looking closer, we see that the hand that held the pen was shaking: faltering strokes stop and start, as if control was lost—then caught and, momentarily, held again. Riemerschmid drew this pattern when he was eighty-eight, just six months before his death on April 13, 1957.

Throughout Riemerschmid's life and across the media for which he designed, patterning served as a kind of graphic gardening: a planting of marks, or sowing of seeds, that would grow out from the order of their inception into a wild and wondrous tangle. His intertwining patterns, though they are sparser and simpler—more *sachlich* in form and construction—than those of Arts and Crafts progenitor William Morris, share with Morris's patterns a complex symbiosis of visual elements that inhabits a no-man's-land between the natural and artificial. In language that could also be used to describe Riemerschmid's later patterns, Morris scholar Caroline Arscott describes Morris's 1876 *Honeysuckle* pattern (figure 7.3):

The pattern units repeat. The underlying structures do register in the viewer's mind even if they are hard to grasp as we observe the detail. We are able to appreciate the rhythmic disposition of forms in two dimensions. The naturalistic observation does not for a moment make the viewer think that a real scene is being depicted; we know that things do not grow quite like this in any garden or hedgerow. And yet there is a response in the viewer to the subject of these co-dependent living elements, a familiarity when taken close up to the pulsing weave. Morris's designs use the ornamental interlock, interlace, plaiting and pattern repeat to suggest a unity of living substance which references the human body, and which can be understood to reference the community.[2]

Design historian Nikolaus Pevsner identified Morris in 1936 as the "first pioneer" of what he termed the "Modern Movement."[3] The trajectory of this book

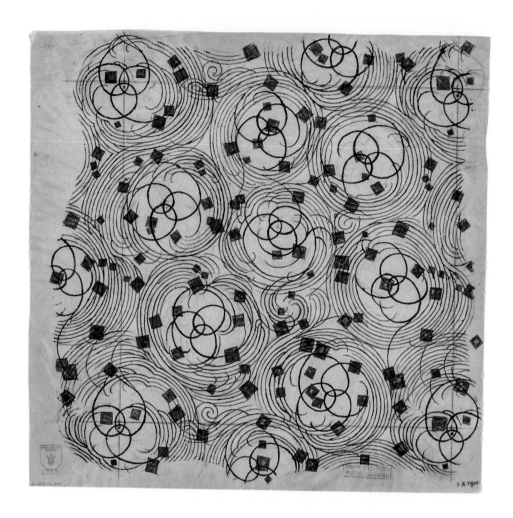

FIGURE 7.2

Richard Riemerschmid, *Pattern*, 1 October,
1956. Architekturmuseum der TUM. © 2021
Artists Rights Society (ARS), New York / VG
Bild-Kunst, Bonn.

FIGURE 7.3

William Morris, *Honeysuckle* (printed cotton),
1876. The Metropolitan Museum of Art, New
York, Theodore M. Davis Collection, Bequest
of Theodore M. Davis, 1915.

has diverged sharply and intentionally from the lineage that Pevsner traced from Morris to Walter Gropius in 1936. And yet, recognizing similarities between Morris and Riemerschmid—both believers in design as the most effective means of social reform; both instinctual pattern-makers, like nest-building birds or web-weaving spiders; and both disciples of Nature—helps to complete the puzzle of Riemerschmid's designs as this book draws to its close. Morris's tightly knit, dynamic *Honeysuckle* pattern, inspired by, indebted to, strongly suggestive of plant growth—and yet ultimately divorced from it by the regular, cognitive calculations and repetitions accessible only to the human mind, eye, and hand—unfurls a template for the richly entangled modernism that Riemerschmid pursued throughout his life: first overtly in the organic, animated lines, vines, and limbs of his designed objects around 1900, and later on covertly, taking his organic imagination "underground" into modernism's unconscious.

On Riemerschmid's seventieth birthday in 1938, liberal politician Theodor Heuß (first president of the Federal Republic of Germany after World War II) named Riemerschmid a "constructive-thinking Son of Nature."[4] These five words count for much more than their sum in understanding Riemerschmid's work and its meaning for modernism. Arscott's relation of Morris's dynamic patterning to his thinking—his connection, in her estimation, between the symbiosis of plants, the interrelated, living systems of the body, and the interdependence of members in a community—resonates with Riemerschmid's own project and his approach to it, as expressed through his patterns. The perpetual motion of Riemerschmid's patterns, while it stems from the biocentric, neovitalist understanding of a soul-motion in plants, is the same current that electrifies the embraces of the embattled bodies in his early figure studies and overflows into his now hospitable, now haunting household things. But before, beneath, and beyond these externalized modes of movement, the motion of patterning is the motion of *thought*: it is the externalization, on paper, of mental prowling, pacing, and retracing of steps.

By the time of his 1956 pattern, Riemerschmid had seen dashed to pieces by the atomic force of historical events his professional aspirations for an honest, practical, yet aesthetically gratifying system of design based on collaboration between artist and materials. His utopian dreams for interdependent community life centered on the life-giving principles of *Lebensphilosophie* were simultaneously shattered. According to Maria Wüllenkemper, Riemerschmid's defacto biographer, it was through his bitter personal experience of the Nazis' despotism and the crisis of his Münchner Bund that he was, for the first time, forced to face defeat: his faith in the inviolability of art and the artist could not survive the Third Reich.[5] By 1950, Riemerschmid had lost three of his four children: his two sons to the two wars and, soon after, his younger daughter Gertrud—a doctor who died in Africa in 1946 (figures 7.4 and 7.5). Only Ilse Riemerschmid would survive her parents.

Perhaps the motion that churned Riemerschmid's patterned surfaces, then, was not just nervous repetition but compulsive *puzzling*—repeated, ruminative, and increasingly faltering attempts to put the pieces together again: to prove that, as Morris wrote to a suffering friend in the *Honeysuckle* year of 1876, "life is not empty nor made for nothing, and that the parts of it fit one into the other in some way; and that the world goes on, beautiful and strange and dreadful and worshipful."[6] Arscott interprets Morris's empathic attempt to give comfort as an expression of his core belief in "the principles of pattern as the one thing that takes the individual beyond despair."[7] For Riemerschmid, the act of patterning gathered unruly, unsettling, and perhaps even unbearable parts together, weaving them into an interdependent, intelligible order—a new creature, separate from the natural world yet, like Nature itself, an eternally self-perpetuating whole.

In the closing lines of his 1881 lecture before the Working Men's College at Queen's Square in Bloomsbury, entitled "Some Hints on Pattern-Designing," Morris identifies the stakes of his project—both the immediate project of patterning, and the grander one of designing for modern life:

I have had to talk to you tonight about popular art, the foundation on which all art stands. I could not go through the dreary task of speaking to you of a phantom of bygone times, of a thing with no life in it; I must speak of *a living thing with hope in it*, or hold my peace; and most deeply am I convinced that popular art [or design] cannot live if labour is to be forever the thrall of muddle, dishonesty, and disunion. Cheerfully I admit that I see signs about us of a coming time of order, goodwill, and union, and it is that which has given me the courage to say to you these few last words, and to hint to you what in my poor judgment we each and all of us who have the cause at heart may do to further the cause.[8]

Morris's speech bristles with implications: above all, it maps his passion for the practice of design onto his passion for social justice. At the same time, it registers the nature of Morris's modernism, the quality of thought that marked him, in Pevsner's eyes, as its original pioneer: his recognition of "popular art"—or contemporary utilitarian design—as "the foundation on which all art stands." This was Morris's bequest to Riemerschmid and the German design reformers launching

FIGURE 7.4

Ida Riemerschmid with her four children
(from left to right): Helmut, Ilse, Gerhardt,
and Gertrud (standing behind), Pasing
bei München, April 1915. Germanisches
Nationalmuseum, Deutsches Kunstarchiv
und Historisches Archiv, Nuremberg.

FIGURE 7.5

Ida, Richard, and Gerhardt Riemerschmid
in Munich, ca. 1930. Germanisches
Nationalmuseum, Deutsches Kunstarchiv
und Historisches Archiv, Nuremberg.

their careers just at the time of Morris's death in 1896. It was the reason that in 1898 Munich's United Workshops drew their name from the craft workshops in Morris's utopian, socialist novel *News from Nowhere* of 1890; and it was also the reason that, after the turn of the twentieth century, Hermann Muthesius, along with other German design reformers discussed in this book, began to refer to modern German design as "the New German Art."

But it is Morris's allusion to popular art or modern design as a "living thing" that brings him nearest to Riemerschmid. And this insistence on design as *alive* explains too why, when his publicly proclaimed "truth to materials" doctrine would seem to have dictated his eschewal of all illusionism on the flat surface, his flat patterns continue to generate what Arscott calls a "pulsing weave." "As we take in the surface pattern *and* complexification in depth," she writes, "we feel the force of the analogy between floral or vegetal design and the organic substance of the human body."[9] It is Morris's "complexification in depth" that Pevsner overlooks (or ignores), and it is this oversight (or ignorance) that allows him to a draw a confident, straight, modernist line from Morris to Gropius, a line that pauses only momentarily at Riemerschmid before it hastily overtakes him. But what if "truth to materials" had been read not in Morris's *words* but in his wordless images of thought—as the perception and experience of "surface pattern *and* complexification in depth"? And what if *Sachlichkeit* had been determined not by a jumble of theoretical discourses, but by modern design's "living things" themselves? It could then be understood—or better, *felt*—in the presence of these things not as soulless "objectivity," but as the intimate, inseparable unity of body and soul.

The noblest patterns, Morris determined, "are those where one thing grows visibly and necessarily from another."[10] Riemerschmid's patterns will neither lie flat nor sit still because they are—and will always be—*growing*. As Morris writes, "the parts of [them] fit one into the other in some way," but this way is dynamic, ever shifting and changing—growing and becoming—thanks to the embodied, empathic relation between the pattern's *Wirkung* and the participant's perception. Riemerschmid's patterns, though far from the cool "objective" *Sachlichkeit* of the *type* and the Bauhaus, enact warm-blooded *thingliness* in a definitive, wordless way that ultimately puts to silence this book's many attempts to define it. At and *as* the heart of his design thinking, Riemerschmid's patterns—like multiplying cells or clambering vines—override and overrun any insipid, simplistic "truth" to the flat surface, to create something that is neither image nor object, but a new *thing in itself*.

A pattern from May 1917, whose grainy, book-matched ogives assign it a place in Riemerschmid's *faux bois* series, sets itself apart through a strange act of *becoming*: from the core of each ogive peeps a small white flower (figure 7.6). Silhouetted against the cavity of densely packed horizontal lines from which it emerges, and in contrast to the curving, vertical lines of the closely striated frame that surrounds it, each one of the twenty different flower forms in a single repeat is arrestingly simple: a flat, white blossom clipped just below the sepal, defined only by the slender line that articulates its contours. As Arscott writes of Morris's *Honeysuckle*, "we know that things do not grow quite like this in any garden or hedgerow," and yet they did grow *just like this* in Riemerschmid's mind—or in his heart. This pattern is neither picture of nor *part of* something else: it is an original thought, an autonomous thing.

Morris's biographer, E. P. Thompson, explores the image of the heart in Morris's epic saga, *The Earthly Paradise*—completed in 1868, the year of Riemerschmid's birth. In verses concerning the "Man Who Never Laughed," an individual alienated from the world around him, Morris relates how "all the folk he saw were strange to him," and concludes that "Like empty shadows by his eyes they passed, / The world was narrowed to his heart at last."[11] For Thompson, the vision of the world "narrowed" to "the solitary individual's heart" prefigures Morris's steady disillusionment as his efforts toward the reforms necessary for his envisioned socialist revolution began to seem ever more unattainable in the evening of his life.[12] We have seen how Riemerschmid's world had narrowed, as the result of events far more cataclysmic than those Morris had experienced half a century earlier, until both his professional and personal life must have seemed, as they did to the mirthless man in *The Earthly Paradise*, like "four walls, hung with pain and dreams."[13] But in her analysis of Morris's patterns, Arscott proposes that "as the world closes in to the four walls of the heart, the heart expands to the space of a dwelling."[14]

This solitary, yet self-sustaining and *animating* chamber of the heart is that same "space of the soul," the monastic cell of thinking-and-feeling that opens up on the site of Riemerschmid's physically flat patterns—like a white flower rising from wood's dark heart. It is the place where that primary, primal, and illimitable *Sachlichkeit* that binds image and idea is germinated—the seed of all of the many living things that are the objects of Riemerschmid's modernism, and the subjects of this book. These are not, as Riemerschmid wrote in 1933, mere outward, fleeting realities, but the fundamental requirements of the "inner being." They are, as Albrecht Dürer defined the true artwork, "the secret treasure of the heart . . . the

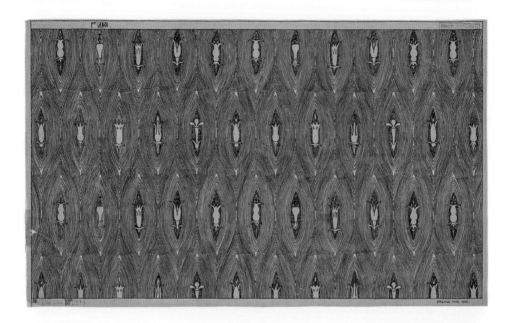

FIGURE 7.6

Richard Riemerschmid, *Pattern F180*, May
1917. Architekturmuseum der TUM. © 2021
Artists Rights Society (ARS), New York / VG
Bild-Kunst, Bonn.

FIGURE 7.7

Ida and Richard Riemerschmid
Reading, Munich, 1950. Germanisches
Nationalmuseum, Deutsches Kunstarchiv
und Historisches Archiv, Nuremberg.

new creature, which one creates in his heart, in the form of a thing." This "one" is rare; it is Riemerschmid's ideal creator: "he in whose hands the dead material comes to life, so that it too acquires a kind of soul, and then, as if of its own accord searches for its own most genuine form, reacts to stimuli, grows and becomes—he is an artist!"[15] And it is Riemerschmid's "earnest, true art" that places in the hands of posterity objects more practical, more palpable, more *real*—feeling forms filled with meanings for a modern *Volk*—than any image could ever be. The spark of attraction, struck first between dead material and living artist's hand, is rekindled in each new embrace of useful thing and needy user. Fueled by this shared desire, inanimate object bursts into living thing.

But perhaps the heart of Richard Riemerschmid was not, in the end, quite a solitary chamber. Perhaps, just as the white flowers bloomed from the hearts of his wood patterns, something yet unblighted budded from his own, like the irrepressible daffodils—the first signs of spring—placed in a slender vase on the table at which an elderly Richard and Ida sit alone together, quietly reading (figure 7.7). Perhaps, like the blossoms in the tree rings, *this* was the true engine of the patterns of Riemerschmid's life. Ida survived Richard by only six years, joining him in Munich's Gräfeling Cemetery in 1963. A note in her hand to the mayor of Munich, dated April 13, 1957, reads: "Thank you for your kind words on the passing of my husband, but you will understand and allow me, today, to be brief."[16]

ACKNOWLEDGMENTS

This book has been a long time coming. Consequently, there are more people I would like to thank for making its publication possible than there is room in its final pages. And so, I will save these last words for those whose support has meant the most to me—and to Riemerschmid—and to whom, I believe, his book will mean most. At this long-awaited moment of completion, I feel indebted above all to my research assistant at Bard Graduate Center (BGC), Elizabeth Koehn, for her tireless, diligent, efficient, thoughtful, and cheerful support throughout all aspects of preparing the manuscript for publication. It is not the slightest exaggeration to say that I could not have done this without her.

This project really began at Bard Graduate Center during my master's study there in the early 2000s, when my advisor, Amy Ogata (upon whose good counsel I still rely), introduced me to Art Nouveau—with which I have since formed a long-term relationship. It seems fitting, then, that I should be writing this now from the desk in my office at BGC. I wish to thank Bard Graduate Center's director, Susan Weber, and dean, Peter Miller, for their support of my work and of this project in particular. Teaching at BGC, my intellectual life is continually enriched by my esteemed colleagues; I am especially grateful for the guidance, support, and encouragement of Catherine Whalen and Michele Majer. I am thankful every day for my BGC MA and PhD students, who think with me about things, and who keep me on my toes. Bard Graduate Center's commitment to the study of the history of design and material culture is truly unique; this book could not have sprung from any other soil.

I am grateful to those farther along the path: to Edward S. Cooke, Jr., for supervising this project in its infancy; to Robin Schuldenfrei for recognizing its contribution to the field; to Timothy Barringer for reassuring me of its value while I sought its proper home; to Christopher Long for his critiques, counsel, and above all for the milk of human kindness; and to Elizabeth Otto for tirelessly reading drafts, selflessly cheering me on, and introducing me to Victoria Hindley at MIT Press. I thank Victoria for believing in this project. Her experience, guidance, and wisdom have made this the book it wanted to be.

Research for this book was made possible through the institutional support of Yale University, the Beinecke Rare Book and Manuscript Library, the Berlin Program for Advanced German and European Studies, the Central European History Society, and the Wolfsonian. Its production was supported by a grant from the Graham Foundation for Advanced Studies in the Fine Arts. Embedded in its pages is the expertise of many generous individuals in Germany. First, I would like to thank Maria Wüllenkemper, whose excellent monograph, *Richard Riemerschmid (1868–1957): "Nicht die Kunst schafft den Stil, das Leben schafft ihn"* (2009), both supported my own study and freed me to write the book I aspired to write. I am likewise indebted to Winfried Nerdinger, whose 1982 exhibition catalog, *Richard Riemerschmid vom Jugendstil zum Werkbund: Werke und Dokumente*, was an important resource throughout my research. I thank Professor Nerdinger, too, for welcoming me at the Technische Universität München in 2008 and taking the time to share his thoughts with me. I am most grateful for a morning spent with Helmut Bauer in the storage facility of the Münchner Stadtmuseum in the summer of 2014, during which Dr. Bauer not only shared his insights, but also prompted me to pursue key avenues of inquiry by confirming some of my deepest intuitions about Riemerschmid's design thinking.

Munich became for me a second home over the course of this project. I owe hearty thanks to Antonia Voit and Elisabeth Stürmer at the Münchner Stadtmuseum; to Karin Althaus at the archives of the Städtische Galerie im Lenbachhaus; to Josef Straßer at the Neue Sammlung of the Pinakothek der Moderne; and to Michaela Rammert-Götz at the archives of the Vereinigte Werkstätten. Most of all, I extend my warmest gratitude and endless admiration to archivist Anja Schmidt at the TUM's Architekturmuseum, whose great kindness, unfailing accuracy, and indefatigable good cheer have contributed immeasurably to this book.

The wonderful staff at the Germanisches Nationalmuseum's Deutsches Kunstarchiv in Nuremberg have supported the development of this project since its inception in 2007 and have been especially helpful in its culminating weeks; I would like to thank in particular Susanna Brogi and Laura Metz for their generosity in providing beautiful photographs of Riemerschmid and his family. I retain special fondness for the staff of Krefeld's Deutsches Textilmuseum, where I spent an illuminating few days in 2008; I am especially thankful to Isa Fleischmann-Heck for her hospitality and expertise.

It is simply not possible to thank my family adequately for their gifts and sacrifices over the arc of this project. My heart is with Bjorn and Brynja—the rosy apples of my eye—for their curiosity, their affection, and their joy. I dedicate this book to my parents, Sally and Jon, who taught me to think, to write, and to *discern*. They ever go with me.

In their spirit, I acknowledge, finally, the long life and devoted work of Ida Riemerschmid (1873–1863): professional, mother, comrade, and lover. I am convinced—as I study these pages for the last time before sending them into the world—that if not for her, none of this could have been.

NOTES

INTRODUCTION

1. Hermann Obrist, "Der Zukunft unserer Architektur," *Dekorative Kunst* 4, no. 9 (June 1901): 334.

2. Thomas Mann, "Gladius Dei," in *Tristan. Sechs Novellen* (Berlin: S. Fischer Verlag, 1903), 1. Born in the north German port city of Lübeck, Mann (1875–1955) lived in Munich from 1891 to 1933.

3. See Kathryn Bloom Hiesinger, *Art Nouveau in Munich: Masters of Jugendstil* (Munich: Prestel-Verlag, 1988); Klaus-Jürgen Sembach, *Art Nouveau. Utopia: Reconciling the Irreconcilable* (Cologne: Taschen, 2002); Maria Makela, *The Munich Secession: Art and Artists in Turn-of-the-Century Munich* (Princeton, NJ: Princeton University Press, 1990); and Nikolaus Pevsner, *Pioneers of the Modern Movement from William Morris to Walter Gropius* (New York: Museum of Modern Art, 1936).

4. For discussions of *Typisierung*, see Joan Campbell, *The German Werkbund: The Politics of Reform in the Applied Arts* (Princeton, NJ: Princeton University Press, 1978); and Frederic J. Schwartz, *The Werkbund: Design Theory & Mass Culture before the First World War* (New Haven, CT: Yale University Press, 1996).

5. See Frederic J. Schwartz, "Marcel Breuer Club Chair," in *The Bauhaus 1919–1933: Workshops for Modernity*, ed. Harry Bergdoll and Leah Dickerman (New York: Museum of Modern Art, 2009), 228.

6. Schwartz, "Marcel Breuer Club Chair," 230.

7. Schwartz, 228.

8. See, for example, Kathleen James-Chakraborty, ed., *Bauhaus Culture: From Weimar to the Cold War* (Minneapolis: University of Minnesota Press, 2006); Barry Bergdoll and Leah Dickerman, eds., *The Bauhaus 1919–1933: Workshops for Modernity* (New York: Museum of Modern Art, 2009); Jeffrey Saletnik and Robin Schuldenfrei, eds., *Bauhaus Construct: Fashioning Identity, Discourse and Modernism* (London: Routledge, 2009); T'ai Smith, *Bauhaus Weaving Theory: From Feminine Craft to Mode of Design* (Minneapolis: University of Minnesota Press, 2014); Robin Schuldenfrei, *Luxury and Modernism: Architecture and the Object in Germany, 1900–1930* (Princeton, NJ: Princeton University Press, 2018); and Elizabeth Otto, *Haunted Bauhaus: Occult Spirituality, Gender Fluidity, Queer Identities, and Radical Politics* (Cambridge, MA: MIT Press, 2019).

9. Valuable discussions of Riemerschmid's objects and furniture are included in Maria Wüllenkemper, *Richard Riemerschmid (1868–1957): "Nicht die Kunst schafft den Stil, das Leben schafft ihn"* (Regensburg: Schnell & Steiner, 2009), as well as Winfried Nerdinger, *Richard Riemerschmid vom Jugendstil zum Werkbund. Werke und Dokumente* (Munich: Prestel Verlag,

1982). Other sources include Sonja Günther, *Interieurs um 1900. Bernhard Pankok, Bruno Paul und Richard Riemerschmid also Mitarbeiter der Vereinigte Werkstätten für Kunst im Handwerk* (Munich: Wilhelm Fink, 1971); Beate Menke, *Die Riemerschmid-Innenausstattung des Hauses Thieme Georgenstraße 7* (Munich: Tuduv Verlag, 1990); and Hans Wichmann, *Deutsche Werkstätten und WK-Verband 1898–1990: Aufbruch zum neuen Wohnen* (Munich: Prestel, 1992).

10. Conversation with Winfried Nerdinger at the Technische Universität München, May 2, 2008.

11. Riemerschmid, *Diskussion von der Verhandlung des Deutschen Werkbundes zu München am 11. und 12. Juli 1908* (Leipzig: R. Voigtländer Verlag, 1908), 35. Courtesy of the Werkbund-Archiv, Berlin.

12. Pevsner, *Pioneers of Modern Design* (New Haven, CT: Yale University Press, 2005), 22. Originally published in 1936 as *Pioneers of the Movement from William Morris to Walter Gropius* by the Museum of Modern Art.

13. Heidegger delivered this lecture at the Bayerischen Akademie der Schönen Künste at the end of World War II and published it subsequently in his 1954 *Vorträge und Aufsätze*. I employ Albert Hofstadter's translation of the text: Heidegger, "The Thing," in *Poetry, Language, Thought* (New York: Perennial Library, 1975), 163–180.

14. Heidegger, 166.

15. Heidegger, 166.

16. Heidegger, 172.

17. Bill Brown, "Thing Theory," *Critical Inquiry* (Autumn 2001), 5.

18. Diana Coole and Samantha Frost, eds., *New Materialisms: Ontology, Agency, and Politics* (Durham, NC: Duke University Press, 2010).

19. Jane Bennett, *Vibrant Matter: A Political Ecology of Things* (Durham, NC: Duke University Press, 2010).

20. Coole and Frost, *New Materialisms*, 4.

21. Gustav Hartlaub, "Zum Geleit," in *Ausstellung "Neue Sachlichkeit": Deutsche Malerei seit dem Expressionismus* (Mannheim: Städtische Kunsthalle, 1925). Translated in *The Weimar Republic Sourcebook*, ed. Anton Kaes, Martin Jay, and Edward Dimendberg (Berkeley: University of California Press, 1995), 492.

22. Otto Dix, "Der Objekt ist Primare," *Berliner Nachtausgabe*, December 3, 1927; translated as "The Object is Primary," in *Art in Theory 1900–2000: An Anthology of Changing Ideas*, ed. Charles Harrison and Paul Wood (Malden, MA: Blackwell Publishing, 2003), 408.

23. Max Beckmann, "Creative Credo," in *Tribune der Zeit und Kunst. Eine Schriften-Sammlung, Schöpferische Konfession*, ed. Kasimir Edschmid (Berlin: Erich Reiß Verlag, 1920), 13:61–67. Translated in *Weimar Republic Sourcebook*, 487–489.

24. See Roh, *Nach-Expressionismus, Magischer Realismus: Probleme der neuesten europäischen Malerei* (Leipzig: Klinkhardt und Biermann, 1925), and also Misch Orend, "Der magische Realismus," *Klingsohr: Siebenbürgische Zeitschrift* 5 (January 1928): 25–27.

25. The phrase "form follows function" is commonly associated with the Bauhaus, but the original phrase, "form ever follows function," has been attributed to American architect Louis Sullivan during the early years of the twentieth century. However, this basic functionalist

concept reaches even further back, to the architectural theory of American sculptor Horatio Greenhough (1805–1852).

26. See Richard Pommer and Christian F. Otto, *Weissenhof 1927 and the Modern Movement in Architecture* (Chicago: University of Chicago Press, 1991); and Barbara Miller Lane, *Architecture and Politics in Germany 1918–45* (Cambridge, MA: Harvard University Press, 1985).

27. Rosemarie Haag Bletter cites and translates this passage from Behne's *Neues Wohnen—Neues Bauen* (1927) in her excellent introduction to Adolf Behne, *The Modern Functional Building*, trans. Michael Robinson (Santa Monica, CA: Getty Research Institute for the History of Art and the Humanities, 1996), 53n128.

28. Dudenredaktion, *Duden. Das Stilwörterbuch* (Mannheim: Dudenverlag, 2017), 2:649–650.

29. Heidegger, "The Thing," 172.

30. Mallgrave's translation of Wagner in "From Realism to *Sachlichkeit*: The Polemics of Architectural Modernity in the 1890s," in *Otto Wagner: Reflections on the Raiment of Modernity*, ed. Mallgrave (Santa Monica, CA: Getty Center for the History of Art and the Humanities, 1993), 283.

31. Mallgrave, "From Realism to *Sachlichkeit*," 287.

32. Mallgrave, 289.

33. See Mallgrave.

34. See Mark Jarzombek, "The Discourses of Bourgeois Utopia, 1904–1908, and the Founding of the German Werkbund," in *Imagining Modern German Culture*, ed. Françoise Forster-Hahn (Washington, DC: National Gallery of Art, 1996), 127–145.

35. Aristotle, "De Anima (On the Soul)," in *The Basic Works of Aristotle*, ed. Richard McKeon, trans. J. A. Smith (New York: Modern Library, 2001), 555.

36. Aristotle, "De Anima," 556.

37. Aristotle, 556.

38. Aristotle, 556.

39. George Eliot, *Silas Marner: The Weaver of Raveloe* (New York: Modern Library, 2001), 25–26. Originally published in 1861.

40. Aristotle, "De Anima," 555.

41. See Debora Silverman, *Art Nouveau in Fin-de-Siècle France: Politics, Psychology, and Style* (Berkeley: University of California Press, 1989), 79–106.

42. See Hilke Peckmann, "Ausdruck und Innerlichkeit. Der Körper als Träger seelischer Stimmung," in *Die Lebensreform: Entwürfe zur Neugestaltung von Leben und Kunst um 1900*, ed. Kai Buchholz (Darmstadt: Verlag Häusser, 2001), 2:217–219.

43. See Klaus Wolbert's essay, "Körper zwischen animalischer Leiblichkeit und ästhetisierender Verklärung der Physis," in *Die Lebensreform*, 2:153–154.

44. See Haeckel's *Die Radiolarien* (1862) and *Kunstformen der Natur* (1899–1904). For secondary literature on Haeckel, see Kurt Bayertz, "Biology and Beauty: Science and Aesthetics in Fin-de-Siècle Germany," in *Fin de Siècle and Its Legacy*, ed. Mikuláš Teich and Roy Porter (Cambridge: Cambridge University Press, 1990), 279–295; Olaf Breidbach, *Visions of Nature: The Art and Science of Ernst Haeckel* (Munich: Prestel Verlag, 2006); and Robert J. Richards,

The Tragic Sense of Life: Ernst Haeckel and the Struggle over Evolutionary Thought (Chicago: University of Chicago Press, 2008).

45. C., "Das Neue Schauspielhaus in München," *Dekorative Kunst* 4, no. 9 (June 1901): 367.

46. Hermann Muthesius, "Die Kunst Richard Riemerschmids," *Dekorative Kunst* 7, no. 7 (April 1904): 273.

47. See Endell's letter to Kurt Breysig of October 15, 1897, excerpted and discussed in Tilmann Buddensieg, "The Early Years of August Endell: Letters to Kurt Breysig from Munich," *Art Journal* 43, no. 1 (Spring 1983): 46.

48. For further biographical information on Riemerschmid and his family, see Wüllenkemper, *Richard Riemerschmid*, 13–17.

49. See Alex Ross, *Wagnerism: Art and Politics in the Shadow of Music* (New York: Farrar, Straus and Giroux, 2020).

50. See Martin Ellis, Timothy Barringer, and Victoria Osborne, *Victorian Radicals: From the Pre-Raphaelites to the Arts & Crafts Movement* (Munich: Prestel, 2018).

51. See Amy Ogata, *Art Nouveau and the Social Vision of Modern Living: Belgian Artists in a European Context* (Cambridge: Cambridge University Press, 2001).

52. For more on Endell's design philosophy, see Zeynep Çelik Alexander, "Affecting: Endell's Mathematics of Living Feeling," in *Kinaesthetic Knowing: Aesthetic, Espistemology, Modern Design* (Chicago: University of Chicago Press, 2017), 97–130.

53. See Buddensieg's translation of Endell's undated letter from the spring of 1896 in "Early Years of August Endell," 45–46.

54. On *German holism*, see Anne Harrington, *Reenchanted Science: Holism in German Culture from Wilhelm II to Hitler* (Princeton, NJ: Princeton University Press, 1996). See also Stacy Hand, "Embodied Abstraction: Biomorphic Fantasy and Empathy Aesthetics in the Work of Hermann Obrist, August Endell, and their Followers" (PhD diss., University of Chicago, 2008), 9–10.

55. Buddensieg, "Early Years of August Endell," 42.

56. Endell, "Formenschönheit und dekorative Kunst," originally published in *Dekorative Kunst* 1 (1897–98): 75–77 and *Dekorative Kunst* 2 (1898): 119–125; excerpted and translated as "The Beauty of Form and Decorative Art," in *Architecture and Design 1890–1939*, ed. Tim and Charlotte Benton (London: Open University Press, 1975), 21.

57. See Çelik Alexander, *Kinaesthetic Knowing*, 104.

58. See Buddensieg, "Early Years of August Endell," 46.

59. See Buddensieg's excerpt from an 1897 letter from Endell to his cousin Breysig, "Early Years of August Endell," 44.

60. Maria Makela, "Munich's Design for Living," *Art in America*, February 1989, 146.

61. See Obrist, "Der Zukunft unserer Architektur," 348.

62. Obrist, 334.

63. Obrist, 329.

64. Obrist, 330.

65. Obrist, 332.

66. Obrist, 334–335.

67. Obrist, 336.

68. For a thorough discussion of Riemerschmid's house in Pasing bei München, see Wüllenkemper, *Richard Riemerschmid*, 44–58. The Münchner Schauspielhaus interiors are discussed at length in chapter 3 of the current work.

69. Obrist, "Der Zukunft unserer Architektur," 348.

70. Translations are my own unless otherwise noted. With the exception of proper nouns, I have chosen to italicize German words (with the exception of proper nouns) throughout this text to emphasize not only their special meanings, but also their aural texture and cadence.

71. Klaus-Peter Arnold, *Vom Sofakissen zum Städtebau: Die Geschichte der Deutschen Werkstätten und der Gartenstadt Hellerau* (Dresden: Verlag der Kunst, 1993).

72. See Hans Belting's discussion of Nietzsche on German identity in *The Germans and Their Art: A Troublesome Relationship*, trans. Scott Kleager (New Haven and London: Yale University Press, 1998), 31–32.

73. Bill Brown, ed., *Things* (Chicago: University of Chicago Press, 2004), 4–5.

74. Riemerschmid, *Diskussion von der Verhandlung des Deutschen Werkbundes*, 36–37.

CHAPTER 1

1. Friedrich Nietzsche, "On the Despisers of the Body," 1883 in *Thus Spoke Zarathustra: A Book for Everyone and Nobody*, trans. Graham Parkes (Oxford: Oxford World's Classics, 2005), 142.

2. Bill Brown, "Thing Theory," in *Things*, ed. Bill Brown (Chicago: University of Chicago Press, 2004), 1–30.

3. Winfried Nerdinger, ed., *Richard Riemerschmid vom Jugendstil zum Werkbund. Werke und Dokumente* (Munich: Prestel Verlag, 1982), 16–17.

4. Walter Benjamin, "On the Mimetic Faculty," in *Walter Benjamin: Selected Writings* vol. 2, part 2, ed. Michael W. Jennings, Howard Eiland, and Gary Smith (Cambridge, MA: Bellknap Press, 1999), 720.

5. Bruno Latour, "Where are the Missing Masses? The Sociology of a Few Mundane Artifacts," in *The Object Reader*, ed. Fiona Candlin and Raiford Guins (New York: Routledge, 2009), 237.

6. George Eliot, *Silas Marner: The Weaver of Raveloe* (New York: Modern Library, 2001), 33. Originally published in 1861.

7. See Zeynep Çelik Alexander, *Kinaesthetic Knowing: Aesthetics, Epistemology, Modern Design* (Chicago: University of Chicago Press, 2017), 119–120.

8. See Oliver A. I. Botar and Isabel Wünsche, eds., *Biocentrism and Modernism* (New York: Routledge, 2017).

9. Çelik Alexander, *Kinaesthetic Knowing*, 32.

10. Hermann von Helmholtz, "The Recent Progress of the Theory of Vision," in *Popular Lectures on Scientific Subjects* (New York: D. Appleton and Company, 1885), 308–309. See also Çelik Alexander's discussion of Helmholz in *Kinaesthetic Knowing*, 27–32.

11. See Charles Le Brun, *Méthode pour apprendre à dessiner les passions: proposé dans une conférence sur l'expression générale et particulière* (Amsterdam: François van-der Plaats, 1702); and Johann Caspar Lavater, *Physiognomische Fragmente, zur Beförderung der Menschenkenntniß und Menschenliebe*, 4 vols. (Leipzig: Weidmann und Reich, 1775–1778).

12. See Çelik Alexander, *Kinaesthetic Knowing*, 109–110.

13. Claude-Nicholas Ledoux, *L'architecture considerée sous le rapport de l'art, des moeurs et de la legislation* (Paris, 1804).

14. William James, "What Is an Emotion?," *Mind* 9, no. 34 (April 1884): 189–190.

15. Duchenne de Boulogne, *Mécanisme de la physionomie humaine, ou analyse eléctro-physique de l'expression des passions* (Paris: Jules Renouard, 1862). See also Çelik Alexander, *Kinaesthetic Knowing*, 111–112.

16. See Maria Wüllenkemper, *Richard Riemerschmid (1868–1957): "Nicht die Kunst schafft den Stil, das Leben schafft ihn"* (Regensburg: Schnell & Steiner, 2009), 25–27.

17. See Hilke Peckmann, "Ausdruck und Innerlichkeit. Der Körper als Träger seelischer Stimmung," in *Die Lebensreform: Entwürfe zur Neugestaltung von Leben und Kunst um 1900*, ed. Kai Buchholz (Darmstadt: Verlag Häusser, 2001), 2:153–154.

18. For further discussion of the *Gründerzeit* climate as it relates to the decorative arts, see John Heskett, *German Design 1870–1918* (New York: Taplinger Publishing Company, 1986), 11–12.

19. See Maria Makela, *The Munich Secession: Art and Artists in Turn-of-the-Century Munich* (Princeton, NJ: Princeton University Press, 1990), 121. See also Michael Hau, *The Cult of Health and Beauty in Germany: A Social History, 1890–1930* (Chicago: University of Chicago Press, 2003), 15–16.

20. Rainer Maria Rilke, *Worpswede: Fritz Mackeusen, Otto Modersohn, Fritz Overbeck, Hans am Ende, Heinrich Vogeler* (Bielefeld/Leipzig: Velhagen and Klasing, 1903), 13; and Karl Marx and Friedrich Engels, "The Manifesto of the Communist Party," in *The Marx-Engels Reader*, second ed., ed. Robert C. Tucker (New York: W. W. Norton & Company, 1978), 476.

21. See Peckmann, "Der Mensch im Zustand ursprünglicher Natürlichkeit. Reformkonzept und Thema in der Kunst," in *Die Lebensreform*, 2:217–219.

22. Annette Wagner, "Natur als Resonanzraum der Seele," in *Die Lebensreform*, 2:165.

23. Klaus Wolbert, "Körper zwischen animalischer Leiblichkeit und ästhetisierender Verklärung der Physis," in *Die Lebensreform*, 2:339–340.

24. Fechner published his *Elemente der Psychophysik* (*Elements of Psychophysics*) in 1860. See Peckmann, "Ausdruck und Innerlichkeit," 153.

25. See Kai Buchholz, "Seele," in *Die Lebensreform*, 2:147–148. See also Richard T. Gray, *About Face: German Physiognomic Thought from Lavater to Auschwitz* (Detroit: Wayne State University Press, 2004).

26. Nietzche, *Thus Spoke Zarathustra*, 142.

27. Nietzsche quoted in Wolbert, "Körper," 340.

28. Thomas Mann in Heinz Thiersch, ed., *Wir fingen einfach an. Arbeiten und Aufsätze von Freunden und Schülern um Richard Riemerschmid zu dessen 85.Geburtstag* (Munich: Richard Pflaum Verlag, 1953), 12.

29. See Wüllenkemper, *Richard Riemerschmid*, 17–18, 47.

30. Jean Moréas, "Le Symbolisme," *Supplément littéraire du Figaro*, September 18, 1886, 150; excerpted and translated as Jean Moréas [Ioannes Papadiamantopoulos], "A Literary Manifesto—Symbolism (1886)," in *Symbolist Art Theories: A Critical Anthology*, ed. Henri Dorra (Berkeley: University of California Press, 1994), 150–152.

31. Morehead, *Nature's Experiments and the Search for Symbolist Form* (University Park: Pennsylvania State University Press, 2017), 14.

32. Gustave Kahn, "Réponse des symbolistes," *L'Evénément*, September 28, 1886.

33. Michelle Facos, *Symbolist Art in Context* (Berkeley: University of California Press, 2009), 9.

34. Debora Silverman, *Art Nouveau in Fin-de-Siècle France: Politics, Psychology, and Style* (Berkeley: University of California Press, 1989), 77.

35. Morehead, *Nature's Experiments*, 15.

36. Wüllenkemper, *Richard Riemerschmid*, 24.

37. See Makela, *Munich Secession*.

38. See Wüllenkemper, *Richard Riemerschmid*, 34.

39. Peg Weiss, *Kandinsky in Munich: The Formative Jugendstil Years* (Princeton, NJ: Princeton University Press, 1979), 81.

40. Weiss, *Kandinsky in Munich*, 81n5.

41. Rodolphe Rapetti, *Symbolism*, trans. Deke Dusinberre (Paris: Flammarion, 2005), 49.

42. Çelik Alexander, "Kinaesthetic Impulses: Aesthetic Experience, Bodily Knowledge, and Pedagogical Practices in Germany, 1871–1918" (PhD diss., Massachusetts Institute of Technology, 2007), 23.

43. Harry Francis Mallgrave, *Architecture and Embodiment: The Implications of the New Sciences and Humanities for Design* (London: Routledge, 2013).

44. Mallgrave, *Architecture and Embodiment*, 13.

45. Mallgrave, 14.

46. Robert Vischer, *Über das optische Formgefühl. Ein Beitrag zur Aesthetik* (Leipzig: Hermann Credner, 1873); translated as "On the Optical Sense of Form: A Contribution to Aesthetics" in *Empathy, Form, and Space: Problems in German Aesthetics 1873–1893*, ed. Harry Francis Mallgrave (Los Angeles: Getty Center for the History of Art the Humanities, 1994), 89–123.

47. Juliet Koss, *Modernism after Wagner* (Minneapolis: University of Minnesota Press, 2010), 67.

48. See Mallgrave and Ikonomou's discussion of Vischer's theory in *Empathy, Form, and Space*, 25.

49. Vischer, "On the Optical Sense of Form," 93–94.

1. Ernst Jentsch, "On the Psychology of the Uncanny," translated by Roy Sellars in *Angelaki* 2, no. 1 (1995), 11. Originally published as "Zur Psychologie des Unheimlichen" in 1906.

2. Heinrich Wölfflin, "Prolegomena zu einer Psychologie der Architecture," in *Kleine Schriften (1886–1933)*, ed. Joseph Gantner (Basel: Schwabe, 1946), 13–47. Originally published in 1886.

3. Wölfflin, "Prolegomena to a Psychology of Architecture," in *Empathy, Form, and Space: Problems in German Aesthetics, 1873–1893*, ed. Harry Francis Mallgrave and Eleftherios Ikonomou (Los Angeles: Getty Center for the History of Art and the Humanities, 1994), 160.

4. Zeynep Çelik Alexander, "Kinaesthetic Impulses: Aesthetic Experience, Bodily Knowledge, and Pedagogical Practices in Germany, 1871–1918" (PhD diss., Massachusetts Institute of Technology, 2007), 139.

5. Gustav Floerke, *Zehn Jahre mit Böcklin* (Munich, 1901), 14. Quoted in Rodolphe Rapetti, *Symbolism*, trans. Deke Dusinberre (Paris: Flammarion, 2005), 48.

6. Van de Velde, "Allgemeine Bemerkungen zu einer Synthese der Kunst," *Pan* 5, no. 4 (1899–1900): 261–270. Originally published in 1895 as "Aperçus en vue d'une synthèse d'art." See also E. P. Thompson, *William Morris: Romantic to Revolutionary* (London: Merlin Press, 1955).

7. Amy Ogata, *Art Nouveau and the Social Vision of Modern Living: Belgian Artists in a European Context* (Cambridge: Cambridge University Press, 2001); and "Belgium and France: Arts, Crafts, and Decorative Arts," in *The Arts & Crafts Movement in Europe and America*, ed. Wendy Kaplan (Los Angeles: Thames & Hudson, in association with the Los Angeles County Museum of Art, 2004), 218–245.

8. Zeynep Çelik Alexander, *Kinaesthetic Knowing: Aesthetics, Epistemology, Modern Design* (Chicago: University of Chicago Press, 2017), 145–146. See also Irene Gammel, *Baroness Elsa: Gender, Dada, and Everyday Modernity* (Cambridge, MA: MIT Press, 2002), 72–120.

9. Hand, "Embodied Abstraction: Biomorphic Fantasy and Empathy Aesthetics in the Work of Hermann Obrist, August Endell, and Their Followers" (PhD diss., University of Chicago, 2008), 139–140.

10. Theodor Lipps, *Raumästhetik und geometrisch-optische Täuschungen* (Leipzig: J. A. Barth, 1897), 347.

11. See Harry Francis Mallgrave, "From Realism to *Sachlichkeit*: The Polemics of Architectural Modernity in the 1890s," in *Otto Wagner: Reflections on the Raiment of Modernity*, ed. Mallgrave (Santa Monica: Getty Center for the History of Art and the Humanities, 1993), 292.

12. Streiter, "Aus München," *Pan* 2, no. 3 (1896), 249.

13. Alfred Lichtwark, *Übungen im Betrachten von Kunstwerken* (Berlin: Cassirer, 1914), 18. Originally published in 1897.

14. Lichtwark, "Der Praktische Zweck," *Dekorative Kunst* 1, no. 1 (October 1897): 24–27.

15. Streiter, "Aus München," 249. See also Stanford Anderson, "*Sachlichkeit* and Modernity, or Realist Architecture," in *Otto Wagner*, 339.

16. Streiter, "Aus München," 249.

17. Lichtwark, "Palastfenster und Flügeltür," *Pan* 2, no. 1 (1896): 58.

18. Van de Velde, "Ein Kapitel über Entwurf und Bau moderner Möbel," *Pan* 3, no. 4 (1897), 263.

19. Henry van de Velde, *Récit de ma vie: Anvers, Bruxelles, Paris, Berlin* (Paris: Flammarion, 1992–1995), 1:325.

20. Van de Velde, "Entwurf und Bau moderner Möbel," 261.

21. Jutta Thamer, "Die Eroberung der Dritten Dimension. Raum und Fläche bei Henry van de Velde," in *Henry van de Velde: Ein europäischer Künstler seiner Zeit*, ed. Klaus-Jürgen Sembach and Birgit Schulte (Cologne: Wienand Verlag, 1992), 159–160.

22. Makela, "Munich's Design for Living," *Art in America*, February 1989, 145.

23. For further discussion of the 1897 Glaspalast exhibition, see Sabine Wieber, "The German Interior at the End of the Nineteenth Century," in *Designing the Modern Interior*, ed. Penny Sparke et al. (Oxford: Berg, 2009), 53–64.

24. See "Program of the Committee of the Section for Decorative Arts of the 7th International Art Exhibition in the Königlicher Glaspalast, Munich, February 24, 1897," translated in Kathryn Bloom Hiesinger, *Art Nouveau in Munich: Masters of Jugendstil* (Munich: Prestel-Verlag, 1988), 169.

25. See Makela, "Munich's Design for Living," 145.

26. William Morris, *News from Nowhere: An Epoch of Rest* (London: Kelmscott Press, 1890).

27. See Hiesinger's introduction to *Art Nouveau in Munich*, 11–23.

28. Hiesinger, *Art Nouveau in Munich*, 12–16, 169–170.

29. Paul Schultze-Naumburg, "Die Dresden Kunstausstellung," *Dekorative Kunst* 2, no. 9 (June 1899): 91.

30. Hermann Muthesius, *Style-Architecture and Building-Art: Transformations of Architecture in the Nineteenth Century and Its Present Condition*, intro. and trans. Stanford Anderson (Santa Monica, CA: Getty Center for the History of Art and the Humanities, 1994), 86.

31. See Dolf Sternberger, *Über Jugendstil* (Frankfurt am Main: Insel Verlag, 1977), 70.

32. Walter Benjamin, "On the Mimetic Faculty," in *Walter Benjamin: Selected Writings*, ed. Michael W. Jennings, Howard Eiland, and Gary Smith, vol. 2., part 2 (Cambridge, MA: Belknap Press, 1999), 721.

33. Hand, "Embodied Abstraction," 168, 203.

34. Ludwig Klages, *The Biocentric Worldview: Selected Essays and Poems by Ludwig Klages*, ed. John B. Morgan, trans. Joseph D. Pryce (London: Arktos, 2013). Despite his important contributions to Lebensphilosophie and biocentrism, Klages's right-wing politics make him a historically problematic figure. His citation in this book does not constitute an endorsement of his political views or those of his publishers.

35. See Haeckel's *Kunstformen der Natur*; and Gustav Theodor Fechner, *Nanna, oder über das Seelenleben der Pflanzen* (Leipzig: Leopold Vos, 1848).

36. Van de Velde's theory is articulated in "Die Linie," *Die Zukunft* 10, no. 49 (September 6, 1902): 385–388.

37. Joseph August Lux, *Das neue Kunstgewerbe in Deutschland* (Leipzig: Klinkhardt & Biermann, 1908), 145.

38. Muthesius, "Die Kunst Richard Riemerschmids," *Dekorative Kunst* 7, no. 7 (April 1904): 273.

39. Rée, "Richard Riemerschmid," *Dekorative Kunst* 9, no. 7 (April 1906): 286.

40. Rée, "Richard Riemerschmid," 286.

41. Rée, 266.

42. Rée, 266.

43. Muthesius, "Der Weg und das Endziel des Kunstgewerbes," *Dekorative Kunst* 8, no. 5 (February 1905): 181–190, and *Dekorative Kunst* 8, no. 6 (March 1905): 230–238. Reprinted as "Der Weg und Ziel des Kunstgewerbes" in *Hermann Muthesius: Kunstgewerbe und Architektur* (Jena: Eugen Diedrichs, 1907).

44. Muthesius, "Die Kunst Richard Riemerschmids," 254–256.

45. Maiken Umbach, "The Deutscher Werkbund and Modern Vernaculars," in *Vernacular Modernism: Heimat, Globalization, and the Built Environment*, ed. Maiken Umbach and Bernd Hüppauf (Stanford, CA: Stanford University Press, 2005), 114–140.

46. See Umbach and Hüppauf, "Introduction: Vernacular Modernism," in *Vernacular Modernism*, 1.

47. Umbach and Hüppauf, 8.

48. Umbach and Hüppauf, 11.

49. Umbach and Hüppauf, 9.

50. Umbach and Hüppauf, 9–10.

51. Umbach and Hüppauf, 13.

52. Umbach, "Deutscher Werkbund and Modern Vernaculars," 125.

53. See Rée, "Richard Riemerschmid," 298; and Lux, *Das neue Kunstgewerbe*, 146.

54. Rée, "Richard Riemerschmid," 298.

55. Karl Jaspers, *Heimweh und Verbrechen* (Leipzig: FCW Vogel, 1909).

56. Muthesius, "Die Kunst Richard Riemerschmids," 283.

57. See, for example, Lichtwark, "Palastfenster und Flügeltür," 57–60.

58. Rée, "Richard Riemerschmid," 286. The modernization of German stoneware is the subject of chapter 5.

59. Muthesius, "Die Kunst Richard Riemerschmids," 278.

60. Rée, "Richard Riemerschmid," 266.

61. Rée, 272.

62. Jentsch, "Uncanny," 11.

63. Jentsch, 13.

64. Benjamin, "On the Mimetic Faculty," 720.

65. Jentsch, "Uncanny," 13.

66. Jaspers, *Heimweh und Verbrechen*, 12–13.

67. Jentsch, "Uncanny," 11.

68. Jentsch, 9.

69. Anthony Vidler, *The Architectural Uncanny: Essays in the Modern Unhomely* (Cambridge, MA: MIT Press, 1992), 63.

70. Vidler, *Architectural Uncanny*, 23.

71. Sigmund Freud, *The Uncanny*, translated by David McLintock in *The Uncanny* (New York: Penguin, 2003), 121–162. Although the essay was first published in 1919, Freud appears to have begun work on it in 1913. See the introduction to the original German text, "Das Unheimliche," in *Sigmund Freud. Studienausgabe Band IV. Psychologische Schriften*, ed. Alexander Mitscherlich, Angela Richards, and James Strachey (Frankfurt am Main: S. Fischer Verlag, 1970), 242.

72. Vidler, *Architectural Uncanny*, 23.

73. Freud, *Uncanny*, 150.

74. Freud, 153, 156.

75. Vidler, *Architectural Uncanny*, 25.

76. Vidler, 24.

77. Freud, *Uncanny*, 126–134.

78. Vidler, *Architectural Uncanny*, 3.

79. Vidler, 4.

80. Muthesius, "Die Kunst Richard Riemerschmids," 276.

81. Rée, "Richard Riemerschmid," 272.

82. John Bell, "Playing with the Eternal Uncanny," in *The Routledge Companion to Puppetry and Material Performance*, ed. Dassia N. Posner, Claudia Orenstein, and John Bell (New York: Routledge, 2015), 46.

83. Bell, "Eternal Uncanny," 49.

84. Bell, 46.

85. Van de Velde to Riemerschmid, December 13, 1901, Schriftlicher Nachlaß Richard Riemerschmid, Deutsches Kunstarchiv, Germanisches Nationalmuseum, Nuremberg (RR Papers, DKA).

86. Van de Velde, "Ein Kapitel über Entwurf und Bau moderner Möbel," 261.

87. Steve Tillis, *Toward an Aesthetics of the Puppet: Puppetry as Theatrical Art* (New York: Greenwood Press, 1992), 7.

88. Brown, *Things* (Chicago: University of Chicago Press, 2004), 4; emphasis in original.

CHAPTER 3

1. Robert Vischer, *Über das optische Formgefühl. Ein Beitrag zur Aesthetik* (Leipzig: Hermann Credner, 1873); translated as "On the Optical Sense of Form: A Contribution to Aesthetics," in *Empathy, Form, and Space: Problems in German Aesthetics, 1873–1893*, ed. Harry Francis Mallgrave (Los Angeles: Getty Center for the History of Art and the Humanities, 1994), 89–123.

2. The Münchner Schauspielhaus is today the Münchner Kammerspiele im Schauspielhaus. See Maria Wüllenkemper, *Richard Riemerschmid (1868–1957): "Nicht die Kunst schafft den Stil, das Leben schafft ihn"* (Regensburg: Schnell & Steiner, 2009), 74–92; Winfried Nerdinger, ed.,

Richard Riemerschmid vom Jugendstil zum Werkbund. Werke und Dokumente (Munich: Prestel Verlag, 1982), 387–388, 471; and Edda and Michael Neumann-Adrian, *Münchens Lust am Jugendstil. Häuser und Menschen um 1900* (Munich: Buchendorfer Verlag, 2005), 113.

3. Hocheder to Riemerschmid, May 5, 1901, Schriftlicher Nachlaß Richard Riemerschmid, Deutsches Kunstarchiv, Germanisches Nationalmuseum, Nuremberg (RR Papers, DKA).

4. Letter from Berlepsch-Valendas to Riemerschmid, April 20, 1901, excerpted in Nerdinger, *Richard Riemerschmid*, 471.

5. See Zeynep Çelik Alexander's discussion of Wölfflin's *Prolegomena* in "Looking: Wölfflin's Comparative Vision," in *Kinaesthetic Knowing: Aesthetics, Epistemology, Modern Design* (Chicago: University of Chicago Press, 2017), 65–66.

6. Vischer, *Über das optische Formgefühl*, 89–123.

7. See Mallgrave and Ikonomou's discussion of Vischer's theory in *Empathy, Form, and Space*, 25.

8. Juliet Koss, "On the Limits of Empathy," *Art Bulletin* 88, no. 1 (March 2006): 139–157.

9. Vischer, "On the Optical Sense of Form," 101.

10. Mark Wigley, "The Antifashion Fashion," in *White Walls, Designer Dresses: The Fashioning of Modern Architecture* (Cambridge, MA: MIT Press, 1995), 127–154.

11. See Mallgrave's translation of Schmarsow's text in *Architecture and Embodiment: The Implications of the New Sciences and Humanities for Design* (London: Routledge, 2013), 125.

12. Muthesius, "Dress and Dwelling," in *Style-Architecture and Building Art: Transformations of Architecture in the Nineteenth Century and Its Present Condition, 1902,* ed. and trans. Stanford Anderson (Los Angeles: Getty Center for the History of Art and the Humanities, 1994), 80.

13. Hermann Muthesius, "Kultur und Kunst: Betrachtungen über das deutsche Kunstgewerbe," *Deutsche Monatsschrift für das gesamte Leben der Gegenwart* 3, no. 7 (April 1904): 85.

14. Hermann Muthesius, "Die Kunst Richard Riemerschmids," *Dekorative Kunst* 7, no. 7 (April 1904): 283.

15. Muthesius, "Kultur und Kunst," 73–74.

16. Adolf Loos, "Von einem armen, reichen Manne," first published on April 26, 1900, and reprinted in *Ins Leere Gesprochen, 1897–1900* (Paris: Éditions George Crès et Cie, 1921), 159–163.

17. Loos, "The Story of the Poor Little Rich Man (1900)," in *Adolf Loos: On Architecture*, trans. Michael Mitchell (Riverside, CA: Ariadne Press, 2002), 52.

18. Koss, *Modernism after Wagner* (Minneapolis: University of Minnesota Press, 2010), 68.

19. See Mallgrave, "Introduction," in Gottfried Semper, *Style in the Technical and Tectonic Arts; or Practical Aesthetics, 1860–1863,* trans. Harry Francis Mallgrave and Michael Robinson (Los Angeles: Getty Research Institute, 2004), 51.

20. Mallgrave, "Introduction," 50.

21. See Mallgrave and Ikonomou's summary of Semper's *Bekleidung* principle in *Empathy, Form, and Space*, 33.

22. Semper, *Der Stil in den technischen und tektonischen Künsten; oder, Praktische Aesthetik: Ein Handbuch für Techniker, Künstler und Kunstfreunde* (Frankfurt am Main: Verlag für Kunst und Wissenschaft, 1860; Munich: F. Bruckmann, 1863), 1:445; translated as *Style in the Technical*

and Tectonic Arts; or Practical Aesthetics, introd. Harry Francis Mallgrave, trans. Mallgrave and Michael Robinson (Los Angeles, CA: Getty Research Institute, 2004).

23. Mallgrave, *Empathy, Form, and Space*, 33.

24. For more on dress reform in Germany, see Brigitte Stamm, *Das Reformkleid in Deutschland* (Berlin: Technische Universität Berlin, 1976).

25. Michael Hau, *The Cult of Health and Beauty in Germany: A Social History, 1890–1930* (Chicago: University of Chicago Press, 2003), 44–45; Patricia Cunningham, *Reforming Women's Fashion, 1850–1920* (Kent, OH: Kent State University Press, 2003).

26. See Radu Stern, *Against Fashion: Clothing as Art* (Cambridge, MA: MIT Press, 2004), 14–15.

27. See Hau, "Gender and Aesthetic Norms," in *Cult of Health and Beauty*, 55–100. See also Valerie Steele, *The Corset: A Cultural History* (New Haven, CT: Yale University Press, 2001).

28. Patricia Ober, *Der Frauen Neue Kleider. Das Reformkleid und die Konstruktion des modernen Frauenkörpers* (Berlin: Verlag Hans Schiler, 2005), 101.

29. Ober, *Der Frauen Neue Kleider*, 30.

30. Ober, 90.

31. Frederic J. Schwartz, *The Werkbund: Design Theory & Mass Culture Before the First World War* (New Haven, CT: Yale University Press, 1996), 28.

32. See Ober's discussion of Simmel in *Der Frauen Neue Kleider*, 90–93.

33. Werner Sombart, *Wirtschaft und Mode: Ein Beitrag zur Theorie der modernen Bedarfsgestaltung* (Wiesbaden: J. F. Bergmann, 1902), 14, 13.

34. Heinrich Pudor, "Praktische Vorschläge zur Erzielung von Qualitätswaren," *Volkswirtschaftliche Blätter* 9, nos. 15–16 (1910): 283.

35. See Norbert Elias, *The Civilizing Process: Sociogenic and Psychogenetic Investigations*, rev. ed. (Oxford: Blackwell Publishers, 2000), 5–30.

36. Deneken to Riemerschmid, April 3, 1900, RR papers, DKA.

37. See Mohrbutter, *Das Kleid der Frau* (Darmstadt: Verlags Anstalt Alexander Koch, 1904).

38. Van de Velde, "Das neue Kunst-Prinzip in der modernen Frauen-Kleidung," *Deutsche Kunst und Dekoration* 5, no. 8 (May 1902): 363–371; see Stern's translation, "A New Art Principle in Women's Clothing," in *Against Fashion*, 137–142.

39. See Stern, "Henry van de Velde and Germany," in *Against Fashion*, 11–22.

40. Letter from Deneken to Riemerschmid, April 3, 1900, RR papers, DKA.

41. Riemerschmid designed silks for the Krefeld firm of C. Lange in 1902.

42. Gerda Breuer, "Deneken und die Krefelder Textilindustrie," in *Der westdeutsche Impuls 1900–1914: Kunst und Umweltgestaltung im Industriegebiet. Von der Künstlerseide zur Industriefotographie. Das Museum zwischen Jugendstil und Werkbund* (Krefeld: Kaiser Wilhelm Museum, 1984), 89–93.

43. Friedrich Deneken, "Künstlerkleid und Eigenkleid," in *Zweiter Bericht des Stadtischen Kaiser Wilhelm Museums* (Krefeld, 1904); translated as "Artistic Dress and Personalized Dress," in Stern, *Against Fashion*, 146.

44. Deneken, "Artistic Dress and Personalized Dress," in Stern, *Against Fashion*, 143.

45. Maria Sèthe van de Velde, "Sonderausstellung Moderner Damenkostüme," *Dekorative Kunst* 4, no. 1 (October 1900): 41–47.

46. Van de Velde, *Die künstlerische Hebung der Frauentracht* (Krefeld: Kaiser Wilhelm Museum, 1900); translated as "The Artistic Improvement of Women's Clothing" in Stern, *Against Fashion.*

47. Van de Velde, "Artistic Improvement of Women's Clothing," in Stern, *Against Fashion*, 128.

48. Van de Velde, "New Art Principle," in Stern, *Against Fashion*, 141.

49. Van de Velde, "Artistic Improvement of Women's Clothing," 131.

50. Van de Velde, *Die künstlerische Hebung der Frauentracht*, 14.

51. Paul Schultze-Naumburg, *Die Kultur des Weiblichen Körpers als Grundlage der Frauenkleidung* (Leipzig: Eugen Diedrichs, 1901).

52. Van de Velde, "New Art Principle" in Stern, *Against Fashion*, 138–139.

53. Van de Velde, 141.

54. Van de Velde, 141–142.

55. Deneken to Riemerschmid, April 3, 1900, RR papers, DKA.

56. See Stefan Muthesius, "The 'altdeutsche' Zimmer, or Cosiness in Plain Pine: An 1870s Munich Contribution to the Definition of Interior Design," *Journal of Design History* 16, no. 4 (2003): 275–276.

57. M. S. van de Velde, "Einleitung," in *Album moderner nach Künstlerentwürfen ausgeführter Damenkleider. Ausgestellt auf der Grossen Allgemeinen Ausstellung für das Bekleidungswesen, Krefeld, 1900*, ed. Friedrich Wolfrum (Krefeld: J. B. Klein'schen Buchdruckerei, 1900), 2.

58. Deneken to Riemerschmid, April 8, 1900, RR papers, DKA.

59. Deneken to Riemerschmid, June 14, 1900, RR papers, DKA.

60. M. S. van de Velde, "Einleitung," 2.

61. Anna Muthesius, *Das Eigenkleid der Frau* (Krefeld: Kaiser Wilhelm Museum, 1903).

62. Deneken's letters to Riemerschmid, written on April 8 and July 12, 1900, respectively, RR papers, DKA.

63. *Programm der Sonderausstellung moderner Damenkostüme nach Künstlerentwürfen in der Krefelder Stadthalle vom 4. bis 13. August, 1900.*

64. Deneken to Riemerschmid, June 20, 1900, and July 5, 1900, RR papers, DKA.

65. Deneken to Riemerschmid, July 12, 1900, RR papers, DKA.

66. Deneken to Riemerschmid, July 30, 1900, RR papers, DKA.

67. Deneken to Riemerschmid, July 12, 1900, RR papers, DKA.

68. Deneken to Riemerschmid, July 30, 1900, RR papers, DKA.

69. See Heinrich Pudor's citation of a passage from the *Kölnische Zeitung*'s review of the Krefeld exhibition in *Die Frauenreformkleidung. Ein Beitrag zur Philosophie, Hygiene und Aesthetik des Kleides* (Leipzig: Hermann Seemann Nachfolger, 1903), 54. See also Brigitte Stamm, "Richard Riemerschmid: Unveröffentlichte Entwürfe zur Reformierung der Frauenbekleidung um 1900," *Waffen- und Kostümkunde* 20, no. 1 (1978): 51–56.

70. Deneken to Riemerschmid, July 30, 1900, RR papers, DKA.

71. Pudor's citation of the *Kölnische Zeitung*'s review in *Die Frauenreformkleidung*, 54.

72. Deneken to Riemerschmid, June 14, 1900, RR papers, DKA.

73. Ober, *Der Frauen Neue Kleider*, 85.

74. M. S. van de Velde, *Album moderner, nach Künstlerentwürfen ausgeführter Damenkleider*, 1.

75. M. S. van de Velde, "Sonderausstellung Moderner Damenkostüme," 46.

76. I am grateful to Münchner Stadtmuseum conservator Magdalena Gerg for her sharing her expertise in relation to the theater dress.

77. See Peter Jelavich, *Munich and Theatrical Modernism: Politics, Playwriting, and Performance, 1890–1914* (Cambridge, MA: Harvard University Press, 1985), 153–160.

78. Paul Busse, *Das Münchner Schauspielhaus im neuen Heim. Zur Erinnerung an die Eröffnungsvorstellung am 20.April 1901* (Munich: o. J., 1901), in Nerdinger, *Richard Riemerschmid*, 471.

79. Jelavich, *Munich and Theatrical Modernism*, 156.

80. Paul Busse, *Das Münchner Schauspielhaus*, 471.

81. Littmann, *Das Münchner Schauspielhaus: Denkschrift zur Freier der Eröffnung* (Munich: L. Werner, 1901), 2.

82. See Çelik Alexander, *Kinaesthetic Knowing*, 113–116.

83. See Klaus-Jürgen Sembach and Gottfried von Haeseler, *August Endell: Der Architekt des Photoateliers Elvira, 1871–1925* (Munich: Museum Villa Stuck, 1977), 34–42.

84. Hand, "Embodied Abstraction: Biomorphic Fantasy and Empathy Aesthetics in the Work of Hermann Obrist, August Endell, and Their Followers" (PhD diss., University of Chicago, 2008), 203–207.

85. Paul Busse, *Das Münchner Schauspielhaus*, 471.

86. Hermann Obrist, "Die Zukunft unserer Architektur," *Dekorative Kunst* 4, no. 9 (June 1901): 343.

87. Nerdinger, *Richard Riemerschmid*, 387–388.

88. Busse, *Das Münchner Schauspielhaus im neuen Heim*, 471.

89. Graham Dry, "The Development of the Bent-Wood Furniture Industry: 1869–1914," in *Bent Wood and Metal Furniture: 1850–1946*, ed. Derek Ostergard (New York: American Federation of Arts, 1987), 77.

90. Busse, *Das Münchner Schauspielhaus*, 471; Sonja Günther, *Interieurs um 1900. Bernhard Pankok, Bruno Paul und Richard Riemerschmid als Mitarbeiter der Vereinigten Werkstätten für Kunst im Handwerk* (Munich: Wilhelm Fink Verlag, 1971), 85.

91. C., "Das Neue Schauspielhaus in München," *Dekorative Kunst* 4, no. 9 (June 1901): 367.

92. C., "Das Neue Schauspielhaus in München," 367.

93. See the detailed verbal tour: C., "Das Neue Schauspielhaus in München," 369–371.

94. Karl Scheffler, "Notitzen über die Farbe," *Dekorative Kunst* 4, no. 5 (February 1901): 190.

95. C., "Das Neue Schauspielhaus in München," 370–371.

96. See Koss's brief description and analysis of the Schauspielhaus in *Modernism after Wagner*, 126–127.

97. Wilhelm von Bezold, *The Theory of Color in Its Relation to Art and Art-Industry*, trans. S. R. Koehler, introd. and notes Edward C. Pickering, authorized American ed., rev. and enlarged by author (Boston: Prang and Co., 1876), 195–196.

98. Busse, *Das Münchner Schauspielhaus*, 471.

99. See Koss, "Building Bayreuth," in *Modernism after Wagner*, especially pages 58–66.

100. Beate Menke, *Die Riemerschmid-Innenausstattung des Hauses Thieme Georgenstraße 7* (Munich: Tuduv Verlag, 1990).

101. Lux, *Das neue Kunstgewerbe in Deutschland* (Leipzig: Klinkhardt & Biermann, 1908), 145.

102. Bezold, *Theory of Color*, 174.

103. See Hal Foster, *Design and Crime (and Other Diatribes)* (London: Verso, 2002), 14–17.

CHAPTER 4

1. William Shakespeare, "Ariel's Song," from *The Tempest*, ed. Alden T. Vaughan and Virginia Mason Vaughan (London: Bloomsbury, 2011), 1.2, https://doi.org/10.5040/9781408160183.000 00045.

2. Friedrich Naumann, "Der Geist im Hausgestühl," in *Preisbuch Dresdner Hausgerät 1906* (Dresden: Dresdner Werkstätten für Handwerkskunst, 1906), 6.

3. For more on the topic of Dürer's and Johann Wolfgang von Goethe's influences on the modern designers of this period, see Freyja Hartzell, "Dürer, Goethe, and the Poetics of Richard Riemerschmid's Modern Wooden Furniture," in *Design and Heritage*, ed. Rebecca Houze and Grace Lees-Maffei (London: Routledge, 2022), 127–140.

4. Hermann Muthesius, "Die moderne Bewegung," in *Spemanns goldenes Buch der Kunst. Eine Hauskunde für Jedermann* (Berlin: Verlage von W. Spemann, 1901), 1067.

5. See Mark Jarzombek, "The 'Kunstgewerbe,' the 'Werkbund,' and the Aesthetics of Culture in the Wilhelmine Period," *Journal of the Society of Architectural Historians* 53, no. 1 (March 1994): 8.

6. See Erich Haenel, "Raumkunst," in *Das Deutsche Kunstgewerbe 1906: Die Dritte Deutsche Kunstgewerbe Ausstellung Dresden 1906* (Munich: Verlagsanstalt F. Bruckmann, 1906), 27.

7. Hermann Muthesius, *Style-Architecture and Building-Art: Transformations of Architecture in the Nineteenth Century and Its Present Condition*, introd. and trans. Stanford Anderson (Santa Monica, CA: Getty Center for the History of Art and the Humanities, 1994), 87–88.

8. Muthesius, *Style-Architecture*, 84.

9. Muthesius, 75.

10. Muthesius, 52.

11. Hermann Muthesius, "Die Kunst Richard Riemerschmids," *Dekorative Kunst* 7, no. 7 (April 1904): 283.

12. Joseph August Lux, *Das neue Kunstgewerbe in Deutschland* (Leipzig: Klinkhardt & Biermann 1908), 147.

13. Muthesius, *Style-Architecture*, 62.

14. Streiter, "Aus München," *Pan* 2, no. 3 (1896): 249. See my prior discussion of Streiter's *Sachlichkeit* in chapter 2.

15. Stefan Muthesius, *The Poetic Home: Designing the 19th-Century Domestic Interior* (New York: Thames & Hudson, 2009), 224–230; Hermann Muthesius, *Style-Architecture and Building-Art*, 62.

16. John Heskett, *German Design 1870–1918* (New York: Taplinger, 1980), 13–18. See also Ulrike Laufer and Hans Ottomeyer, eds., *Gründerzeit 1848–1871. Industrie & Lebensträume zwischen Vormärz und Kaiserreich* (Dresden: Sandstein Verlag, 2008).

17. Wilhelm Lübke, *Geschichte der deutschen Renaissance*, vol. 5 of *Geschichte der Baukunst*, ed. F. Krüger (Stuttgart: Ebner & Seubert, 1873), 967–968.

18. S. Muthesius, *Poetic Home*, 212.

19. S. Muthesius, 265–268.

20. Konrad Bedal, "Wohnen wie zu Dürer's Zeiten: Stuben und Wohnräume in süddeutschen, ins besondere fränkischen Bürgerhaus des späten Mittelalters," in G. Ulrich Grossmann and Franz Sonnenberger, eds., *Das Dürer-Haus: Neue Ergebnisse der Forschung. Dürer Forschungen*, vol. 1 (Nuremberg: Verlag des Germanischen Nationalmuseums, 2007), 28.

21. S. Muthesius, "The 'altdeutsche' Zimmer, or Cosiness in Plain Pine: An 1870s Munich Contribution to the Definition of Interior Design," *Journal of Design History* 16, no. 4 (2003): 276.

22. B. Bucher, *Die Kunst-Industrie auf der deutschen Ausstellung in München 1876* (Vienna: Verlag Oestereichisches Zentralkomité, 1876), 17. Translated and quoted in S. Muthesius, "Cosiness in Plain Pine," 276.

23. D. Duncker, *Über die Bedeutung der deutschen Ausstellung in München* (Berlin: C. Duncker, 1876), 18. Translated and quoted in S. Muthesius, "Cosiness in Plain Pine," 276.

24. Georg Hirth, *Das deutsche Zimmer der Renaissance: Anregungen zu Häuslicher Kunstpflege* (Munich: G. Hirths Verlag, 1880), 172.

25. S. Muthesius, "Cosiness in Plain Pine," 274.

26. Hirth, *Das deutsche Zimmer* (1880), 30.

27. Hirth, 23.

28. Hirth, 10.

29. Hirth, 25.

30. Hirth, 31.

31. Hirth, 15.

32. Hirth, 20.

33. Hirth, 65.

34. Hirth, 101, 63.

35. Hirth, 16–17.

36. Johann Wolfgang von Goethe, *Zur Farbenlehre* (Tübingen: C. G. Cotta, 1810); Michel-Eugène Chevreul, *De la loi du contraste simultané des couleurs et de l'assortiment des objets colorés* (Paris: Pitois-Levrault, 1839); Hermann von Helmholtz, *Über die Theorie der zusammeng-esetzten Farben* (Berlin: Gebrüder Unger, 1852); and Jakob von Falke, *Die Kunst im Hause. Geschichte und kritisch-ästhetische Studien über die Decoration und Ausstattung der Wohnung* (Vienna: Druck und Verlag von Carl Gerold's Sohn, 1871). See also John Gage, *Color and Meaning: Art, Science, and Symbolism* (Berkeley: University of California Press, 1999).

37. Muthesius, *Hermann Muthesius: Kunstgewerbe und Architektur* (Jena: Eugen Diederichs, 1907), 8.

38. Muthesius, "Die Kunst Richard Riemerschmids," 256.

39. Wilhelm von Bezold, Wilhelm von Bezold, *The Theory of Color in Its Relation to Art and Art-Industry*, trans. S. R. Koehler, introd. and notes Edward C. Pickering, authorized American ed., rev. and enlarged by author (Boston: Prang and Co., 1876), 195.

40. Bezold, *Theory of Color*, 196.

41. Karl Scheffler, "Notitzen über die Farbe," *Dekorative Kunst* 4, no. 5 (February 1901): 196.

42. Scheffler, "Notitzen über die Farbe," 194.

43. Beate Menke gives a detailed account of the Thieme interiors in *Die Riemerschmid-Innenausstattung des Hauses Thieme Georgenstraße 7* (Munich: Tuduv Verlag, 1990), 43–50.

44. Muthesius, "Die Kunst Richard Riemerschmids," 276.

45. Hirth, *Das deutsche Zimmer*, 153.

46. The two men became brothers-in-law when Schmidt married Riemerschmid's sister Frida in 1910. See Maria Wüllenkemper, *Richard Riemerschmid (1868–1957): "Nicht die Kunst schafft den Stil, das Leben schafft ihn"* (Regensburg: Schnell & Steiner, 2009), 111–112.

47. Karl Schmidt, *Grundungsprogramm der Dresdner Werkstätten* (Dresden, 1898); trans. and quoted in W. Owen Harrod, "The Deutsche Werkstätten and the Dissemination of Mainstream Modernity," *Studies in the Decorative Arts* 11, no. 2 (Spring–Summer, 2003): 22–23.

48. Erich Haenel, "Die Dritte Deutsche Kunstgewerbe-Ausstellung Dresden 1906," *Dekorative Kunst* 9, no. 10 (July 1906): 398.

49. See Schmidt quoted in Klaus-Peter Arnold, *Vom Sofakissen zum Städtebau: Die Geschichte der Deutschen Werkstätten und der Gartenstadt Hellerau* (Dresden: Verlag der Kunst, 1993), 185.

50. Muthesius, "Kunst und Maschine," *Dekorative Kunst* 5, no. 4 (January 1902): 141–142.

51. Friedrich Naumann, "Kunst und Industrie," in *Das Deutsche Kunstgewerbe 1906: Die Dritte Deutsche Kunstgewerbe Ausstellung Dresden 1906* (Munich: Verlagsanstalt F. Bruckmann, 1906), 32–35.

52. Naumann, "Die Kunst im Zeitalter der Maschine," *Kunstwart* 17 (1904), reprinted in *Friedrich Naumann: Werke*, ed. Heinz Ladendorf (Cologne: Westdeutscher Verlag, 1964), 6:186–201.

53. Naumann, "Der Geist im Hausgestühl," 6.

54. Naumann, "Kunst und Industrie," 34.

55. Naumann, 33.

56. Direktorium der Ausstellung, ed., *Das Deutsche Kunstgewerbe 1906. III. Deutsche Kunstgewerbe-Ausstellung Dresden 1906* (Munich: F. Bruckmann, 1906), 160–163.

57. Naumann, "Die Kunst im Zeitalter der Maschine," 189.

58. Rée, "Richard Riemerschmid," *Dekorative Kunst* 9, no. 7 (April 1906), 265.

59. Rée, 272.

60. Haenel, "Die Dritte Deutsche Kunstgewerbe-Ausstellung," 505.

61. Haenel, 505.

62. Naumann, "Kunst und Industrie," 34.

63. Naumann, 32.

64. Naumman, 34.

65. Anonymous, "Die Dritte Deutsche Kunstgewerbe-Ausstellung Dresden 1906," *Deutsche Tischler-Zeitung*, no. 51 (1912): 404. Cited in Beate Menke, *Die Riemerschmid-Innenausstattung des Hauses Thieme Georgenstraße 7* (Munich: Tuduv Verlag, 1990), 70n159.

66. Menke, *Die Riemerschmid-Innenausstattung des Hauses Thieme*, 69.

67. Haenel, "Raumkunst," 26–27.

68. Haenel, 24–25.

69. Haenel, 27.

70. Muthesius, "Die Kunst Richard Riemerschmids," 283.

71. See Maiken Umbach, *German Cities and Bourgeois Modernism, 1890–1924* (Oxford: Oxford University Press, 2009), 157n41.

72. See Menke, *Die Riemerschmid-Innenausstattung des Hauses Thieme*, 71.

73. Leopold Gmelin, "Die III. Deutsche Kunstgewerbe Ausstellung: Die Dresdner Werkstätten," *Kunst und Handwerk* 57, no. 3 (1906–1907): 75.

74. Cited in Menke, *Die Riemerschmid-Innenausstattung des Hauses Thieme*, 67n149.

75. Gmelin, "Die Dresdner Werkstätten," 75.

76. Muthesius, "Die Kunst Richard Riemerschmids," 276.

77. Anonymous, "Die Dritte Deutsche Kunstgewerbe-Ausstellung Dresden 1906," 404.

78. Rée, "Richard Riemerschmid," 266.

79. Rée, 281.

80. Rée, 281–286.

81. Koerner, *The Moment of Self-Portraiture in German Renaissance Art* (Chicago: University of Chicago Press, 1993), 163.

82. See Koerner, "The Hairy, Bearded Painter," in *Moment of Self-Portraiture*, 160–186.

83. Koerner, 160.

84. Naumann, "Die Kunst im Zeitalter der Maschine," 200.

85. Naumann, 199.

86. Richard Riemerschmid, "Zur Ausstellung München 1908," in *Ausstellung München 1908: Amtliche Mitteilungen der Ausstellungs-Leitung 1*, November 1907, 1–5 (1907), 1–5. Cited in Wüllenkemper, *Richard Riemerschmid*, 157n514.

87. Naumann, "Der Geist im Hausgestühl," 6.

88. Rée, "Richard Riemerschmid," 281–286.

89. Koerner, *Moment of Self-Portraiture*, 186.

90. Hirth, *Das Deutsche Zimmer*, 30.

CHAPTER 5

1. Hermann Muthesius, "Die Kunst Richard Riemerschmids," *Dekorative Kunst* 7, no. 7 (April 1904): 278.

2. John V. Maciuika, *Before the Bauhaus: Architecture, Politics and the German State, 1890–1920* (Cambridge: Cambridge University Press, 2005), 158.

3. M. Buhle, "Kunstindustrielle Maschinen und Werkstaetten," in *Dritte Deutsche Kunstgewerbeausstellung Dresden 1906, Ausstellungszeitung*, no. 7 (April 1906), as quoted in Maciuika, *Before the Bauhaus*, 144–145n26.

4. Maciuika, *Before the Bauhaus*, 161.

5. Hermann Muthesius, "Die Bedeutung des Kunstgewerbes. Eröffnungsrede zu den Vorlesungen über modernes Kunstgewerbe an der Handelhochschule in Berlin," *Dekorative Kunst* 10, no. 5 (February 1907): 190.

6. Muthesius, "Die Bedeutung des Kunstgewerbes," translated as "The Significance of Applied Art," in *The Theory of Decorative Art: An Anthology of European & American Writings, 1750–1940*, ed. Isabelle Frank (New Haven, CT: Yale University Press, 2000), 74.

7. Muthesius, "Significance of Applied Art."

8. Muthesius, 80.

9. Muthesius, "Die Bedeutung des Kunstgewerbes," 183.

10. Lichtwark, "Palastfenster und Flügeltür," *Pan* 2, no. 1 (1896): 57–60; and "Der Praktische Zweck," *Dekorative Kunst* 1, no. 1 (1897): 24–27.

11. Maciuika, *Before the Bauhaus*, 163–165.

12. Joan Campbell, *The German Werkbund: The Politics of Reform in the Applied Arts* (Princeton, NJ: Princeton University Press, 1978), 19.

13. Maciuika, *Before the Bauhaus*, 165.

14. Muthesius, "Significance of Applied Art," 80.

15. Muthesius, 77.

16. Theodor Fischer, "Die Veredlung der Gerwerblichen Arbeit im Zusammenwirken von Kunst, Industrie und Handwerk," *Verhandlung des Deutschen Werkbundes zu München am 11. Und 12. Juli 1908* (Leipzig: R. Voigtländer Verlag, 1908), 5. Courtesy of the Werkbund-Archiv, Berlin.

17. See Campbell's discussion of the Werkbund's founding in *German Werkbund*, 19–20.

18. Siegfried Gronert, "Simmel's Handle: A Historical and Theoretical Design Study," in *Design and Culture* 4, no. 1 (March 2012): 62.

19. Muthesius, "Significance of Applied Art," 77, 82.

20. See the discussion of architect Richard Streiter's 1896 definition of *Sachlichkeit* in chapter 2.

21. David Gaimster, *German Stoneware, 1200–1900: Archaeology and Cultural History* (London: British Museum Press, 1997), 251–253.

22. Ernst Jaffé, "Neue deutsche Steinzeugkunst," *Kunstindustrie und Kunstgewerbe* 1 (1913): 95.

23. Gaimster, *German Stoneware*, 124, 251.

24. Gaimster, 252.

25. Gaimster, 325.

26. Jaffé, "Neue deutsche Steinzeugkunst," 383.

27. Ernst Zimmermann, "Die künstlerische Nothlage der Westerwälder Steinzeugindustrie," *Kunst und Handwerk* 50 (1899–1900): 76–83.

28. Muthesius, "Significance of Applied Art," 76.

29. Itohan Osayimwese, *Colonialism and Modern Architecture in Germany* (Pittsburgh: University of Pittsburgh Press, 2017), 107–108. See also Kenny Cupers, "Bodenständigkeit: The Environmental Epistemology of Modernism," *Journal of Architecture* 21, no. 8: 1226–1252.

30. Zimmermann, "Die künstlerische Nothlage," 76.

31. Zimmermann, "Steinzeugkrüge von Richard Riemerschmid," *Kunst und Handwerk* 54 (1903–1904): 270.

32. Maiken Umbach, "The Deutscher Werkbund and Modern Vernaculars," in *Vernacular Modernism: Heimat, Globalization, and the Built Environment*, ed. Maiken Umbach and Bernd Hüppauf (Stanford, CA: Stanford University Press, 2005), 124.

33. Susan Stewart, *On Longing: Narratives of the Miniature, the Gigantic, the Souvenir, the Collection* (Durham, NC: Duke University Press, 1993), 14–24.

34. Gaimster, *German Stoneware*, 330–331.

35. Zimmermann, "Steinzeugkrüge von Richard Riemerschmid," 269.

36. Beate Dry-von Zezschwitz, "Vorbemerkung zu Riemerschmids Keramischen Arbeiten," in *Richard Riemerschmid: Vom Jugendstil zum Werkbund*, ed. Winfried Nerdinger (Munich: Prestel Verlag, 1982), 313.

37. Jaffé, "Neue deutsche Steinzeugkunst," 384; H. H., "Die Keramische Ausstellung im Berliner Kunstgewerbemuseum," *Keramische Monatshefte* 7, no. 10 (October 1907): 148.

38. Zimmermann, "Steinzeugkrüge von Richard Riemerschmid," 269–271.

39. Gaimster, *German Stoneware*, 326.

40. H. H., "Die Keramische Ausstellung," 148.

41. Ernst Berdel, "Die Moderne Entwickelung der Westerwälder Industrie," *Sprechsaal* 45 (1912): 83–85, 99–101.

42. Gaimster, *German Stoneware*, 326.

43. Jeffrey Herf, *Reactionary Modernism: Technology, Culture, and Politics in Weimar and the Third Reich* (Cambridge: Cambridge University Press, 1984).

44. Lux, *Das neue Kunstgewerbe in Deutschland* (Leipzig: Klinkhardt & Biermann, 1908), 246–247.

45. Fischer, "Die Veredlung der Gewerblichen Arbeit," 5.

46. Endell in *Die Werkbund-Arbeit der Zukunft und Aussprache darüber. 7.Jahres Versammlung des Deutschen Werkbundes vom 2. bis 6.Juli in Köln* (Jena: Eugen Diedrichs, 1914), 57–58.

47. Campbell, *German Werkbund*, 30.

48. Muthesius, "Die Bedeutung des Kunstgewerbes."

49. Berdel, "Die Moderne Entwickelung der Westerwälder Industrie," 83.

50. Gustav E. Pazaurek, "Neues Steinzeug von Albin Müller," *Dekorative Kunst* 14, no. 4 (January 1911): 178.

51. Muthesius's address to the 1908 meeting is translated and quoted in Maciuika, *Before the Bauhaus*, 168n96.

52. Fischer, "Die Veredlung der Gewerblichen Arbeit," 8–9.

53. Berdel, "Die Moderne Entwickelung der Westerwälder Industrie," 101.

54. Lux, *Das neue Kunstgewerbe*, 146, 147–148.

55. Paul Johannes Rée, "Richard Riemerschmid," *Dekorative Kunst* 9, no. 7 (April 1906): 266. See Rée's reference to "Biergemütlichkeit" on page 286.

56. On German colonialism and power relations, see Sebastian Conrad, *German Colonialism: A Short History*, trans. Sorcha O'Hagan (Cambridge: Cambridge University Press, 2012); Susanne Kuss, *German Colonial Wars and the Context of Military Violence* (Cambridge, MA: Harvard University Press, 2017); Nina Berman, Klaus Mühlhand, and Patrice Nganang, eds., *German Colonialism Revisited: Africa, Asia, and Oceanic Experiences* (Ann Arbor: University of Michigan Press, 2014); Michael Perraudin and Juergen Zimmerer, eds., *German Colonialism and National Identity* (New York: Routledge, 2015); and Volker Langbehn, ed., *German Colonialism, Visual Culture, and Modern Memory* (New York: Routledge, 2012).

57. Muthesius's article "Die moderne Bewegung," in *Spemanns goldenes Buch der Kunst. Eine Hauskunde für Jedermann* (Berlin: Verlag von W. Spemann, 1901), para. 1032.

58. Norbert Elias, *The Civilizing Process: Sociogenic and Psychogenetic Investigations*, rev. ed. (Oxford: Blackwell Publishers, 2000), 5–30.

59. Maciuika, *Before the Bauhaus*, 162.

60. Mark Jarzombek, "The 'Kunstgewerbe,' the 'Werkbund,' and the Aesthetics of Culture in the Wilhelmine Period," *Journal of the Society of Architectural Historians* 53, no. 1 (1994): 7–19.

61. Karl Scheffler, "Kultur und Kunst" and "Kunst und Leben," in *Moderne Kultur: Ein Handbuch der Lebensbildung und des Guten Geschmacks*, ed. Eduard Heyck and Marie Binder Diers (Stuttgart: Deutsche Verlags-Anstalt, 1907), 1:17–92; 93–112.

62. Campbell, *German Werkbund*, 17–18.

63. Karl Scheffler, "Keramik," in *Moderne Kultur*, 1:232.

64. Scheffler, "Notitzen über die Farbe," *Dekorative Kunst* 4, no. 5 (February 1901): 183–196.

65. Heinrich Pudor, "Praktische Vorschläge zur Erzielung von Qualitätswaren," *Volkswirtschaftliche Blätter* 9, no. 15–16 (1910): 283. Quoted in Frederic J. Schwartz, *The Werkbund: Design Theory & Mass Culture before the First World War* (New Haven, CT: Yale University Press, 1996), 29.

66. See Campbell's discussion of Sombart's book *Kunstgewerbe und Kultur* (written in 1906 but published in 1908), in *German Werkbund*, 30–31.

67. Werner Sombart, *Wirtschaft und Mode: Ein Beitrag zur Theorie der modernen Bedarfsgestaltung* (Wiesbaden: J. F. Bergmann, 1902), 13. See the illuminating discussion of Sombart in Schwartz, *Werkbund*, 28–29.

68. Georg Simmel, "Das Problem des Stiles," *Dekorative Kunst* 11, no. 7 (April 1908). Translated in David Frisby and Mike Featherstone, eds., *Simmel on Culture: Selected Writings* (London: Sage Publications, 1997), 217.

69. Frisby and Featherstone, *Simmel on Culture*, 216. Siegfried Gronert opposes Simmel's understanding of the concept of style as the key to the unification of modern German *Kunstgewerbe* with Muthesius's focus on the "iron principles" of *Sachlichkeit*. See Gronert, "Simmel's Handle," 62.

70. Bernd Nicolai, ed., *Die Durchgeistigung der deutschen Arbeit. Jahrbuch des deutschen Werkbunds 1912*, reprint (Berlin: Gebrüder Mann, 1999), 5.

71. Muthesius, "Wo Stehen Wir?," in *Die Durchgeistigung der deutschen Arbeit*, ed. Bernd Nicolai, 11–26.

72. Josef Popp, *Deutsches Warenbuch*, (Munich: Dürerbund-Werkbund Genossenschaft, 1915), xvii.

73. Popp, *Deutsches Warenbuch*, xvii.

74. Popp, xxi–xxxiii.

75. Popp, section on "Keramik," xxxiv.

76. Schwartz, *Werkbund*, 141–145.

77. Richard Riemerschmid, *Diskussion von der Verhandlung des Deutschen Werkbundes zu München am 11. und 12. Juli 1908* (Leipzig: R. Voigtländer Verlag, 1908), 36–37.

78. Berdel, "Die Moderne Entwickelung der Westerwälder Industrie," 101.

CHAPTER 6

1. Excerpted from a letter Morris sent to a friend in March 1876, and reprinted in J. W. Mackail, *The Life of William Morris*, vol. 1 (London: Longmans, Green, 1901), 328.

2. Dr. Helmut Bauer, Münchner Stadtmuseum, in a 2014 conversation.

3. Sources on Hellerau include Maria Wüllenkemper, *Richard Riemerschmid (1868–1957): "Nicht die Kunst schafft den Stil, das Leben schafft ihn"* (Regensburg: Schnell & Steiner, 2009); Klaus-Peter Arnold, *Vom Sofakissen zum Städtebau: Die Geschichte der Deutschen Werkstätten und der Gartenstadt Hellerau* (Dresden: Verlag der Kunst, 1993); Clemens Galonska and Frank Elstner, *Gartenstadt/Garden City of Hellerau* (Chemnitz: Palisander Verlag, 2007); and Hans Wichmann, *Deutsche Werkstätten und WK-Verband 1898–1990: Aufbruch zum neuen Wohnen* (Munich: Prestel, 1992).

4. Friedrich Ahlers-Hestermann, *Stilwende: Aufbruch der Jugend um 1900*, 2nd. rev. ed. (Berlin: Verlag Gebr. Mann, 1956), 42.

5. Riemerschmid, *Diskussion von der Verhandlung des Deutschen Werkbundes zu München am 11. und 12. Juli 1908* (Leipzig: R. Voigtländer Verlag, 1908), 34–37.

6. Riemerschmid, *Diskussion von der Verhandlung*, 34–35.

7. Erich Haenel quotes Naumann in "Die Dritte Deutsche Kunstgewerbe-Ausstellung Dresden 1906," *Dekorative Kunst* 9, no. 12 (August 1906): 505. See also Walter Riezler, "Neue Arbeiten von Richard Riemerschmid," *Deutsche Kunst und Dekoration* 9, no. 3 (1908): 170.

8. Aristotle, "De Anima (On the Soul)," in *The Basic Works of Aristotle*, ed. Richard McKeon, trans. J. A. Smith (New York: Modern Library, 2001), 556.

9. Janet Janzen, *Media, Modernity and Dynamic Plants in Early 20th Century German Culture* (Leiden: Brill Rodopi, 2016), 14–15.

10. Janzen, *Dynamic Plants*, 8–9.

11. Botar, "Defining Biocentrism," in *Biocentrism and Modernism*, ed. Oliver A. I. Botar and Isabel Wünsche (London: Routledge, 2016), 17; E. Benton, "Vitalism in Nineteenth-Century Scientific Thought: A Typology and Reassessment," *Studies in the History and Philosophy of Science* 5, no. 1 (May 1974): 18.

12. Frederick Burwick and Paul Douglass, eds., *The Crisis in Modernism: Bergson and the Vitalist Controversy* (Cambridge, MA: Cambridge University Press, 1992).

13. Michael Heidelberger, *Nature from Within: Gustav Theodor Fechner and His Psychophysical Worldview*, trans. Cynthia Klohr (Pittsburgh: University of Pittsburgh Press, 2004), 325. Originally published as *Die innere Seite der Natur: Gustav Theodor Fechners wissenschaftlich-philosophische Weltauffassung* in 1993.

14. Herbert Schnädelbach, *Philosophy in Germany 1831–1933*, trans. Eric Matthews (Cambridge: Cambridge University Press, 1984), 139.

15. Wolfgang Krabbe, *Gesellschaftsveränderung durch Lebensreform: Strukturmerkmale einer sozialreformerischen Bewegung im Deutschland der Industrialisierungsperiode* (Göttingen: Vandenhoeck & Ruprecht, 1974), 108.

16. See Janzen, *Dynamic Plants*; and Heidelberger, *Nature from Within*.

17. Johann Wolfgang von Goethe, *Der Versuch die Metamorphose der Pflanzen zu erklären* (Gotha: bey Carl Wilhelm Ettinger, 1790).

18. Ernst Haeckel, *Monism as Connecting Religion and Science: The Confession of Faith of a Man of Science* (London: Adam and Charles Black, 1894), 3.

19. Alfred Kelly, *The Descent of Darwin: The Popularization of Darwinism in Germany, 1860–1914* (Chapel Hill: University of North Carolina Press, 1981), 24.

20. Botar, "Defining Biocentrism," 21–24.

21. Heidelberger, *Nature from Within*, 119.

22. Gustav Theodor Fechner, *Nanna, oder Über das Seelenleben der Pflanzen* (Leipzig: Leopold Voss, 1848); reprinted as *Nanna: Über das Seelenleben der Pflanzen*, ed. Michael Holzinger (Berlin: Michael Holzinger, 2016), 37.

23. Kurd Lasswitz, "Introduction," in Gustav Fechner, *Nanna, oder über das Seelenleben der Pflanzen* by Gustav Fechner (Leipzig: Voss, 1908), iv, https://archive.org/details/nannaoderberdasoolassgoog/page/n11/mode/2up. See also Janzen's discussion of this passage in *Dynamic Plants*, 13.

24. Oliver A. I. Botar and Isabella Wünsche, eds., *Biocentrism and Modernism* (New York: Routledge, 2017).

25. Raoul Heinrich Francé, *Das Sinnesleben der Pflanzen* (Stuttgart: Kosmos Gesellschaft der Naturfreunde, 1905); translated as *Germs of Mind in Plants* (Chicago: C. H. Kerr & Co., 1905).

26. Francé, *Das Sinnesleben der Pflanzen*, 14.

27. See Lasswitz, "Introduction," iv.

28. Francé, *Das Sinnesleben der Pflanzen*, 13.

29. Christopher Dresser, *The Art of Decorative Design* (London: Day and Son, 1862).

30. Rée, "Richard Riemerschmid," *Dekorative Kunst* 9, no. 7 (April 1906), 303.

31. Ruth Grönwoldt, *Art Nouveau Textil-Dekor um 1900* (Vienna: MAK, 1980), 230.

32. Brigitte Tietzel, "Stoffmuster des Judgendstils," *Zeitschrift für Kunstgeschichte* 44, no. 3 (1981): 281.

33. Martin Gerlach, ed., *Formenwelt aus dem Naturreiche* (Leipzig: Gerlach & Co, 1902–1904).

34. Hugo Hinterberger, "Die Mikrographie im Dienste der Kunst," in *Jahrbuch für Photographie und Reproduktionstechnik* 16, ed. Josef Maria Eder (Halle: Wilhelm Knapp Verlag, 1902), 192.

35. For more on Gerlach, see Astrid Mahler and Elborg Forster, "A World of Forms from Nature: New Impulses for the Aesthetic of *Jugendstil*," *Visual Resources* 23, nos. 1–2: 21–37.

36. *Leipziger Illustrierte Zeitung* 1906, cited in Beate Menke, *Die Riemerschmid-Innenausstattung des Hauses Thieme Georgenstraße 7* (Munich: Tuduv Verlag, 1990), 67n149. See chapter 4.

37. Clement Greenberg, "Towards a Newer Laocoön," *Partisan Review* 7 (July–August 1940): 296–310.

38. Richard Riemerschmid, *Künstlerische Erziehugsfragen I* (Munich: Flugschriften des Münchner Bundes, 1917), 3.

39. See Lipps, *Aesthetik: Psychologie des Schönen und der Kunst* (Hamburg: Leopold Voss, 1903). Quoted in Worringer, *Abstraktion und Einfuhlung: ein Beitrag zur Stilpsychologie* (München: R. Piper & Co. Verlag, 1908), translated by Michael Bullock as *Abstraction and Empathy: A Contribution to the Psychology of Style* (New York: International Universities Press, 1953), 5. I cite the English translation here and hereafter.

40. See mention of Klages in chapter 2, as well as Stacy Hand's more extensive discussion in "Embodied Abstraction: Biomorphic Fantasy and Empathy Aesthetics in the Work of Hermann Obrist, August Endell, and Their Followers" (PhD diss., University of Chicago, 2008), 152.

41. Worringer cites this passage from Lipp's *Aesthetik* in *Abstraction and Empathy*, 6.

42. Worringer, *Abstraction and Empathy*, 7.

43. Lipps, *Aesthetik*, 247.

44. Worringer, *Abstraction and Empathy*, 4.

45. Worringer, 36.

46. In our conversation at the Münchner Stadtmuseum on May 27, 2014, Helmut Bauer mentioned Worringer's *Abstraction and Empathy* and American art historian George Kubler's

Shape of Time: Remarks on the History of Things (New Haven, CT: Yale University Press, 1962) as having special relevance for Riemerschmid's approach to design.

47. Worringer, *Abstraction and Empathy*, 60.

48. For more of Riemerschmid's biography, see Wüllenkemper, *Richard Riemerschmid*, 13–22; and for this specific reference, see pages 19–20.

49. For more on Riemerschmid's role in the *Typisierung* debates, see Wüllenkemper, *Richard Riemerschmid*, 162–168.

50. See Betts, *The Authority of Everyday Objects: A Cultural History of West German Industrial Design* (Berkeley: University of California Press, 2004), 30; and Alan Steinweis, *Art, Ideology, and Economics in Nazi Germany: The Reich Chambers of Music, Theater, and Visual Arts* (Chapel Hill: University of North Carolina Press, 1983), 16–20.

51. Letter from Otto Baur, Geschäftsführer des DWB, to Richard Riemerschmid on April 5, 1933. Werkbund-Archiv, Berlin.

52. Letter from Riemerschmid in Pasing-bei-München to Carl Cristoph Lörcher, July 17, 1933, Werkbund-Archiv, Berlin.

53. Letter from Winfried Wendland, acting leader of the DWB, on behalf of Carl Lörcher to Riemerschmid, September 22, 1933, Werkbund-Archiv, Berlin.

54. Campbell, *The German Werkbund: The Politics of Reform in the Applied Arts* (Princeton, NJ: Princeton University Press, 1978), 253.

55. Letter from Riemerschmid to Ehmcke, September 26, 1933, Werkbund-Archiv, Berlin.

56. Riemerschmid, statement on behalf of the Münchner Bund, September 27, 1933, Werkbund-Archiv, Berlin.

57. Campbell, *German Werkbund*, 253.

58. Wüllenkemper, *Richard Riemerschmid*, 231.

59. See Campbell, *German Werkbund*, 258–263.

60. See Wüllenkemper, *Richard Riemerschmid*, 247–250.

61. Sigmund Freud, "Erinnern, Wiederhohlen und Durcharbeiten," *Internationale Zeitschrift für Psychoanalyse* 2, no. 6 (1914): 485–491; and *Jenseits des Lustprinzips* (Vienna: Internationaler Psychoanalytischer Verlag, 1920).

62. See Ernst Hopmann's brief review of the exhibition, "Fort mit dem nationalen Kitsch!" in the Werkbund's journal *Die Form: Zeitschrift für gestaltende Arbeit* 8 (August 1933): 255. See also Betts's discussion of the National Kitsch exhibition in *Everyday Objects*, 31–34.

63. See Worringer's discussion of Lipps in *Abstraction and Empathy*, 65.

64. Stephanie Barron, ed., *"Degenerate Art": The Fate of the Avant-Garde in Nazi Germany* (Los Angeles: LACMA, 1991); and Olaf Peters, ed., *Degenerate Art: The Attack on Modern Art in Nazi Germany* (New York: Prestel and Neue Galerie, 2014).

65. Sabine T. Kriebler, *Revolutionary Beauty: The Radical Photomontages of John Heartfield* (Berkeley: University of California Press, 2014); and Andrés Mario Zervigón, *John Heartfield and the Agitated Image: Photography, Persuasion, and the Rise of the Avant-Garde Photomontage* (Chicago: University of Chicago Press, 2012).

1. Behne, *The Modern Functional Building*, trans. Michael Robinson, with an introduction by Rosemarie Haag Bletter (Santa Monica, CA: Getty Research Institute for the History of Art and the Humanities, 1996), 53n128. Originally published in 1926 as *Der Moderne Zweckbau* by Drei Masken Verlag.

2. Arscott, "Four Walls/Heart and Flesh," in *William Morris and Edward Burne-Jones: Interlacings* (New Haven, CT: Yale University Press, 2008), 97.

3. Pevsner, *Pioneers of the Modern Movement from William Morris to Walter Gropius* (New York: Museum of Modern Art, 1936), 24.

4. Theodor Heuß, *Frankfurter Zeitung*, June 21, 1938. Cited in Maria Wüllenkemper, *Richard Riemerschmid (1868–1957): "Nicht die Kunst schafft den Stil, das Leben schafft ihn"* (Regensburg: Schnell & Steiner, 2009), 21n85.

5. Wüllenkemper, *Richard Riemerschmid*, 244.

6. Excerpted from a letter Morris sent to a friend in March 1876, and reprinted in J. W. Mackail, *The Life of William Morris*, vol. 1 (London: Longmans, Green, 1901), 328.

7. Arscott, "Four Walls/Heart and Flesh," 103.

8. Morris, "Some Hints on Pattern-Designing: A Lecture Delivered at the Working Men's College, London, on December 10, 1881," in *The Collected Works of William Morris*, vol. 22 (Cambridge: Cambridge University Press, 2012), 205.

9. Arscott, "Four Walls," 98.

10. Morris, "Hints on Pattern-Designing," 199.

11. Thompson quotes *The Earthly Paradise* in *William Morris: Romantic to Revolutionary* (London: Merlin Press, 1955), 124.

12. Thompson, *William Morris*, 124–125.

13. See Thompson's citation of Morris in *William Morris*, 124.

14. Arscott, "Four Walls," 98.

15. Riemerschmid, *Diskussion von der Verhandlung des Deutschen Werkbundes zu München am 11. und 12. Juli 1908* (Leipzig: R. Voigtländer Verlag, 1908), 34–35.

16. Letter from Ida Riemerschmid to Oberbürgermeister Wimmer, April 13, 1957. Landeshauptstadt München Stadtarchiv.

BIBLIOGRAPHY

ARCHIVES AND COLLECTIONS

Archiv der Akademie der Künste, Berlin

Archiv der Vereinigten Werkstätten für Kunst im Handwerk, Munich

Archiv des Kaiser Wilhelm Museums, Krefeld

Deutsches Textilmuseum, Krefeld

Germanisches Nationalmuseum, Nuremberg

Hamburg Museum für Kunst und Gewerbe

Kunstgewerbemuseum Berlin

Künstlerischer Nachlaß Richard Riemerschmid (design drawings, plans, photographs), Architekturmuseum der Technischen Universität München

Künstlerischer Nachlaß Richard Riemerschmid (sketchbooks and works on paper) Sammlungsarchiv, Städtische Galerie im Lenbachhaus und Kunstbau München

Landeshauptstadt München Stadtarchiv

Münchner Stadtmuseum

Museum der Dinge: Werkbundarchiv, Berlin

Schriftlicher Nachlaß Richard Riemerschmid (papers, personal photographs), Deutsches Kunstarchiv, Germanisches Nationalmuseum, Nuremberg (RR papers, DKA)

Stadtarchiv Dresden

PRINTED SOURCES

Ahlers-Hestermann, Friedrich. *Stilwende: Aufbruch der Jugend um 1900*, second revised edition. Berlin: Verlag Gebr. Mann, 1956.

Anderson, Stanford. "*Sachlichkeit* and Modernity, or Realist Architecture." In *Otto Wagner: Reflections on the Raiment of Modernity*, edited by Harry Francis Mallgrave, 323–360. Santa Monica, CA: Getty Center for the History of Art and the Humanities, 1993.

Anonymous. "Die Dritte Deutsche Kunstgewerbe-Ausstellung Dresden 1906." *Deutsche Tischler-Zeitung*, no. 51 (1912): 404.

Aristotle. "De Anima (On the Soul)." In *The Basic Works of Aristotle*, edited by Richard McKeon and translated by J. A. Smith, 534–603. New York: Modern Library, 2001.

Arnold, Klaus-Peter. *Vom Sofakissen zum Städtebau: Die Geschichte der Deutschen Werkstätten und der Gartenstadt Hellerau*. Dresden: Verlag der Kunst, 1993.

Arscott, Caroline. "Four Walls/Heart and Flesh." In *William Morris and Edward Burne-Jones: Interlacings*, 87–103. New Haven, CT: Yale University Press, 2008.

Barron, Stephanie ed. *"Degenerate Art": The Fate of the Avant-Garde in Nazi Germany*. Los Angeles: LACMA, 1991.

Bauer, Helmut. *Setz Dich! Setzen Sie sich bitte!* Munich: Münchner Stadtmuseum and Edition Bemberg, 2000.

Bayertz, Kurt. "Biology and Beauty: Science and Aesthetics in Fin-de-Siècle Germany." In *Fin de Siècle and Its Legacy*, edited by Mikuláš Teich and Roy Porter, 279–295. Cambridge: Cambridge University Press, 1990.

Beckmann, Max. "Creative Credo." In *Tribune der Zeit und Kunst. Eine Schriften-Sammlung*, vol. 13, *Schöpferische Konfession*, edited by Kasimir Edschmid, 61–67. Berlin: Erich Reiß Verlag, 1920. Translated in *The Weimar Republic Sourcebook*, edited by Anton Kaes, Edward Dimendberg, and Martin Jay, 487–489. Berkeley: University of California Press, 1995.

Bedal, Konrad. "Wohnen wie zu Dürers Zeiten. Stuben und Wohnräume in süddeutschen, ins besondere fränkischen Bürgerhaus des späten Mittelalters." In *Das Dürer-Haus: Neue Ergebnisse der Forschung. Dürer Forschungen*, vol. 1, edited by G. Ulrich Grossmann and Franz Sonnenberger, 28–60. Nuremberg: Verlag des Germanischen Nationalmuseums, 2007.

Behne, Adolf. *The Modern Functional Building*. Translated by Michael Robinson, with an introduction by Rosemarie Haag Bletter. Santa Monica, CA: Getty Research Institute for the History of Art and the Humanities, 1996. Originally published in 1926 as *Der Moderne Zweckbau* by Drei Masken Verlag.

Bell, John. "Playing with the Eternal Uncanny." In *The Routledge Companion to Puppetry and Material Performance*, edited by Dassia N. Posner, Claudia Orenstein, and John Bell, 43–45. New York: Routledge, 2015.

Belting, Hans. *The Germans and Their Art: A Troublesome Relationship*. Translated by Scott Kleager. New Haven, CT: Yale University Press, 1998.

Benjamin, Walter. "On the Mimetic Faculty." In *Walter Benjamin: Selected Writings*, edited by Michael W. Jennings, Howard Eiland, and Gary Smith, vol. 2, part 2, 721–722. Cambridge, MA: Belknap Press, 1999.

Bennett, Jane. *Vibrant Matter: A Political Ecology of Things*. Durham, NC: Duke University Press, 2010.

Benton, E. "Vitalism in Nineteenth-Century Scientific Thought: A Typology and Reassessment." *Studies in the History and Philosophy of Science* 5, no. 1 (May 1974): 17–48.

Benton, Tim, and Charlotte Benton, eds. *Architecture and Design 1890–1939*. London: Open University Press, 1975.

Berdel, Ernst. "Die Moderne Entwickelung der Westerwälder Industrie." *Sprechsaal* 45 (1912): 83–85, 99–101.

Berdel, Ernst. "Die Tonindustrie im Westerwald." *Keramische Rundschau* 17 (August 5, 1909): 419–421.

Bergdoll, Barry, and Leah Dickerman, eds. *The Bauhaus 1919–1933: Workshops for Modernity*. New York: Museum of Modern Art, 2009.

Berman, Marshall. *All That Is Solid Melts into Air: The Experience of Modernity*. New York: Penguin, 1982.

Berman, Nina, Klaus Mühlhand, and Patrice Nganang, eds. *German Colonialism Revisited: Africa, Asia, and Oceanic Experiences*. Ann Arbor: University of Michigan Press, 2014.

Betts, Paul. *The Authority of Everyday Objects: A Cultural History of West German Industrial Design*. Berkeley: University of California Press, 2004.

Bezold, Wilhelm von. *The Theory of Color in Its Relation to Art and Art-Industry*. Translated from the German by S. R. Koehler, with an introduction and notes by Edward C. Pickering. Authorized American edition, revised and enlarged by the author. Boston: Prang, 1876.

Bialostocki, Jan. *Dürer and His Critics, 1500–1971*. Baden-Baden: Verlag Valentin Koerner, 1986.

Bletter, Rosemarie Haag. "Introduction." In Adolf Behne, *The Modern Functional Building*, 1926. Translated by Michael Robinson, with an introduction by Rosemarie Haag Bletter, 47–64. Santa Monica, CA: Getty Research Institute for the History of Art and the Humanities, 1996.

Botar, Olivier A. I. "Defining Biocentrism." In *Biocentrism and Modernism*, edited by Oliver A. I. Botar and Isabel Wünsche, 15–45. London: Routledge, 2016.

Botar, Oliver A. I., and Isabel Wünsche, eds. *Biocentrism and Modernism*. London: Routledge, 2016.

Boulogne, Duchenne de. *Mécanisme de la physionomie humaine, ou analyse eléctro-physique de l'expression des passions*. Paris: Jules Renouard, 1862. Edited and translated by R. Andrew Cuthbertson as *The Mechanism of Human Facial Expression*. Cambridge: Cambridge University Press, 1990.

Bredt, E. W. "Richard Riemerschmids Schauspielhaus." *Kunst und Handwerk* 51, no. 10 (1901): 281–289.

Breidbach, Olaf. *Visions of Nature: The Art and Science of Ernst Haeckel*. Munich: Prestel Verlag, 2006.

Breuer, Gerda. *Haus eines Kunstfreundes: Baillie Scott, Mackintosh, Bauer*. Stuttgart: Axel Menges, 2002.

Breuer, Gerda. *Der westdeutsche Impuls 1900–1914: Kunst und Umweltgestaltung im Industriegebiet. Von der Künstlerseide zur Industriefotographie. Das Museum zwischen Jugendstil und Werkbund*. Krefeld: Kaiser Wilhelm Museum, 1984.

Brown, Bill, ed. *Things*. Chicago: University of Chicago Press, 2004.

Bucher, B. *Die Kunst-Industrie auf der deutschen Ausstellung in München 1876*. Vienna: Verlag Oestereichisches Zentralkomité, 1876.

Buchholz, Kai, Rita Latocha, and Hilke Peckmann, eds. *Die Lebensreform: Entwürfe zur Neugestaltung von Leben und Kunst um 1900*. 2 vols. Darmstadt: Verlag Häusser, 2001.

Buchholz, Kai. "Seele." In *Die Lebensreform: Entwürfe zur Neugestaltung von Leben und Kunst um 1900*, edited by Kai Buchholz, Rita Latocha, and Hilke Peckmann, 2:147–148. Darmstadt: Verlag Häusser, 2001.

Buddensieg, Tilmann. "The Early Years of August Endell: Letters to Kurt Breysig from Munich." *Art Journal* 43, no. 1 (Spring 1983): 41–49.

Buhle, M. "Kunstindustrielle Maschinen und Werkstaetten." In *Dritte Deutsche Kunstgewerbeausstellung Dresden 1906, Ausstellungszeitung*, no. 7 (April 1906).

Burns, Emile, ed. *The Marxist Reader: The Most Significant and Enduring Works of Marxism*. New York: Avenue Books, 1982.

Burwick, Frederick, and Paul Douglass, eds. *The Crisis in Modernism: Bergson and the Vitalist Controversy*. Cambridge: Cambridge University Press, 1992.

Busse, Paul. *Das Münchner Schauspielhaus im neuen Heim. Zur Erinnerung an die Eröffnungsvorstellung am 20.April 1901*. Munich: o. J., 1901. In *Richard Riemerschmid vom Jugendstil zum Werkbund. Werke und Dokumente*, edited by Winfried Nerdinger, 417. Munich: Prestel Verlag, 1982.

C. "Das Neue Schauspielhaus in München." *Dekorative Kunst* 4, no. 9 (June 1901): 366–373.

Campbell, Joan. *The German Werkbund: The Politics of Reform in the Applied Arts*. Princeton, NJ: Princeton University Press, 1978.

Çelik Alexander, Zeynep. "Kinaesthetic Impulses: Aesthetic Experience, Bodily Knowledge and Pedagogical Practices in Germany, 1871–1918." PhD diss., Massachusetts Institute of Technology, 2007.

Çelik Alexander, Zeynep. *Kinaesthetic Knowing: Aesthetics, Epistemology, Modern Design*. Chicago: University of Chicago Press, 2017.

Chevreul, Michel-Eugène. *De la loi du contraste simultané des couleurs et de l'assortiment des objets colorés*. Paris: Pitois-Levrault, 1839. Translated by Charles Martel as *The Principles of Harmony and Contrast of Colours, and Their Applications to the Arts*. London: Longman, Brown, Green, and Longmans, 1854.

Coole, Diana, and Samantha Frost, eds. *New Materialisms: Ontology, Agency, and Politics*. Durham, NC: Duke University Press, 2010.

Conrad, Sebastian. *German Colonialism: A Short History*. Translated by Sorcha O'Hagan. Cambridge: Cambridge University Press, 2012.

Cunningham, Patricia. *Reforming Women's Fashion, 1850–1920*. Kent, OH: Kent State University Press, 2003.

Cupers, Kenny. "Bodenständigkeit: The Environmental Epistemology of Modernism." *Journal of Architecture* 21, no. 8: 1226–1252.

Deneken, Friedrich. "Künstlerkleid und Eigenkleid." *Zweiter Bericht des Stadtischen Kaiser Wilhelm Museums*. Krefeld, 1904. Translated as "Artistic Dress and Personalized Dress," in Radu Stern, *Against Fashion: Clothing as Art*, 143–147. Cambridge, MA: MIT Press, 2004.

Deneken, Friedrich. *Programm der Sonderausstellung moderner Damenkostüme nach Künstlerentwürfen in der Krefelder Stadthalle vom 4. bis 13. August, 1900.*

Direktorium der Ausstellung, ed. *Das Deutsche Kunstgewerbe 1906. III. Deutsche Kunstgewerbe-Ausstellung Dresden 1906*. Munich: F. Bruckmann, 1906.

Dix, Otto. "Das Objekt ist Primare." *Berliner Nachtausgabe*, December 3, 1927. Translated as "The Object Is Primary," in *Art in Theory 1900–2000: An Anthology of Changing Ideas*, edited by Charles Harrison and Paul Wood, 408. Malden, MA: Blackwell Publishing, 2003.

Dorra, Henri, ed. *Symbolist Art Theories: A Critical Anthology*. Berkeley: University of California Press, 1994.

Dresdner Werkstätten für Handwerkskunst. *Preisbuch Dresdner Hausgerät, 1906*. Dresden: Dresdner Werkstätten für Handwerkskunst, 1906.

Dresser, Christopher. *The Art of Decorative Design*. London: Day and Son, 1862.

Dudenredaktion. *Duden. Das Stilwörterbuch*, vol. 2. Mannheim: Dudenverlag, 2001.

Duncker, D. *Über die Bedeutung der deutschen Ausstellung in München*. Berlin: C. Duncker, 1876.

Dry, Graham. "The Development of the Bent-Wood Furniture Industry: 1869–1914." In *Bent Wood and Metal Furniture: 1850–1946*, edited by Derek Ostergard, 53–93. New York: American Federation of Arts, 1987.

Dry-von Zezschwitz, Beate. "Vorbemerkung zu Riemerschmids Keramischen Arbeiten." In *Richard Riemerschmid: Vom Jugendstil zum Werkbund*, edited by Winfried Nerdinger, 313–315. Munich: Prestel Verlag, 1982.

Elias, Norbert. *The Civilizing Process: Sociogenic and Psychogenetic Investigations*, revised edition. Oxford: Blackwell Publishers, 2000.

Eliot, George. *Silas Marner: The Weaver of Raveloe*. New York: Modern Library, 2001. Originally published in 1861.

Ellis, Martin, Timothy Barringer, and Victoria Osborne. *Victorian Radicals: From the Pre-Raphaelites to the Arts & Crafts Movement*. Munich: Prestel, 2018.

Endell, August. "Formenschönheit und Dekorative Kunst." *Dekorative Kunst* 1 (1897–1898): 75–77 and *Dekorative Kunst* 2 (1898): 119–125. Excerpted and translated as "The Beauty of Form and Decorative Art" in *Architecture and Design 1890–1939*, edited by Tim and Charlotte Benton, 21. London: Open University Press, 1975.

Facos, Michelle. *Symbolist Art in Context*. Berkeley: University of California Press, 2009.

Falke, Jakob von. *Die Kunst im Hause. Geschichte und kritisch-ästhetische Studien über die Decoration und Ausstattung der Wohnung*. Vienna: Druck und Verlag von Carl Gerold's Sohn, 1871.

Fechner, Gustav Theodor. *Nanna, oder über das Seelenleben der Pflanzen*. Leipzig: Leopold Vos, 1848. Reprinted as *Nanna: Über das Seelenleben der Pflanzen*, edited by Michael Holzinger. Berlin: Michael Holzinger, 2016.

Fehr, Michael, Sabine Röder, and Gerhard Storck. *Das Schöne und der Alltag: Die Anfänge modernen Designs 1900–1914. Deutsches Museum für Handel und Gewerbe*. Cologne: Wienand Verlag, 1997.

Fischer, Theodor. "Die Veredlung der Gerwerblichen Arbeit im Zusammenwirken von Kunst, Industrie und Handwerk." In *Verhandlung des Deutschen Werkbundes zu München am 11. Und 12. Juli 1908*. Leipzig: R. Voigtländer Verlag, 1908.

Floerke, Gustav. *Zehn Jahre mit Böcklin*. Munich, 1901.

Foster, Hal. *Design and Crime (and Other Diatribes)*. London: Verso, 2002.

Francé, Raoul Heinrich. *Das Sinnesleben der Pflanzen*. Stuttgart: Kosmos Gesellschaft der Naturfreunde, 1905.

Francé, Raoul Heinrich. *Germs of Mind in Plants*. Chicago: C. H. Kerr, 1905.

Frank, Isabelle, ed. *The Theory of Decorative Art: An Anthology of European & American Writings, 1750–1940*. New Haven, CT: Yale University Press, 2000.

Freud, Sigmund. "Erinnern, Wiederhohlen und Durcharbeiten." *Internationale Zeitschrift für Psychoanalyse* 2, no. 6 (1914): 485–491.

Freud, Sigmund. *Jenseits des Lustprinzips*. Vienna: Internationaler Psychoanalytischer Verlag, 1920.

Freud, Sigmund. *Sigmund Freud. Studienausgabe Band IV. Psychologische Schriften*. Edited by Alexander Mitscherlich, Angela Richards, and James Strachey. Frankfurt am Main: S. Fischer Verlag, 1970.

Freud, Sigmund. *The Uncanny*. Translated by David McLintock. New York: Penguin, 2003.

Frisby, David, and Mike Featherstone, eds. *Simmel on Culture: Selected Writings*. London: Sage Publications, 1997.

Gage, John. *Color and Meaning: Art, Science, and Symbolism*. Berkeley: University of California Press, 1999.

Gaimster, David. *German Stoneware, 1200–1900: Archaeology and Cultural History*. London: British Museum Press, 1997.

Galonska, Clemens, and Frank Elstner. *Gartenstadt/Garden City of Hellerau*. Chemnitz: Palisander Verlag, 2007.

Gammel, Irene. *Baroness Elsa: Gender, Dada, and Everyday Modernity*. Cambridge, MA: MIT Press, 2002.

Gerlach, Martin, ed. *Formenwelt aus dem Naturreiche*. Leipzig: Gerlach & Co, 1902–1904.

Gmelin, Leopold. "Die III. Deutsche Kunstgewerbe Ausstellung: Die Dresdner Werkstätten." *Kunst und Handwerk* 57, no. 3 (1906–1907): 73–77.

Goethe, Johann Wolfgang von. *Der Versuch die Metamorphose der Pflanzen zu erklären*. Gotha: bey Carl Wilhelm Ettinger, 1790.

Goethe, Johann Wolfgang von. *Zur Farbenlehre*. Tübingen: J. G. Cotta, 1810.

Graul, Richard, ed. *Die Krisis im Kunstgewerbe: Studien über die Wege und Ziele der modernen Richtung*. Leipzig: Verlag von S. Hirzel, 1901.

Gray, Richard T. *About Face: German Physiognomic Thought from Lavater to Auschwitz*. Detroit: Wayne State University Press, 2004.

Greenberg, Clement. "Towards a Newer Laocoön." *Partisan Review* 7 (July–August 1940): 296–310.

Greenhalgh, Paul, ed. *Art Nouveau 1890–1914*. New York: Harry N. Abrams, 2000.

Gronert, Siegfried. "Simmel's Handle: A Historical and Theoretical Design Study." *Design and Culture* 4, no. 1 (March 2012): 55–71.

Grönwoldt, Ruth. *Art Nouveau Textil-Dekor um 1900*. Vienna: MAK, 1980.

Grossmann, G. Ulrich, and Franz Sonnenberger, eds. *Das Dürer-Haus: Neue Ergebnisse der Forschung. Durer Forschungen*, vol. 1. Nuremberg: Verlag des Germanischen Nationalmuseums, 2007.

Günther, Sonja. *Interieurs um 1900. Bernhard Pankok, Bruno Paul und Richard Riemerschmid als Mitarbeiter der Vereinigten Werkstätten für Kunst im Handwerk*. Munich: Wilhelm Fink, 1971.

H. H. "Die Keramische Ausstellung im Berliner Kunstgewerbemuseum." *Keramische Monatshefte* 7, no. 10 (October 1907): 145–149.

Haeckel, Ernst. *Die Radiolarien (Rhizopoda Radiaria): Eine Monographie*. Berlin: G. Reimer, 1862.

Haeckel, Ernst. *Kunstformen der Natur*. Leipzig: Verlag des Bibliographischen Instituts, 1899–1904.

Haeckel, Ernst. *Monism as Connecting Religion and Science: The Confession of Faith of a Man of Science*. London: Adam and Charles Black, 1894.

Haenel, Erich. "Die Dritte Deutsche Kunstgewerbe-Ausstellung Dresden 1906." *Dekorative Kunst* 9, nos. 10 & 12 (July and August 1906): 393–511.

Haenel, Erich. "Raumkunst." In *Das Deutsche Kunstgewerbe 1906: Die Dritte Deutsche Kunstgewerbe Ausstellung Dresden 1906*, 23–28. Munich: Verlagsanstalt F. Bruckmann, 1906.

Hand, Stacy. "Embodied Abstraction: Biomorphic Fantasy and Empathy Aesthetics in the Work of Hermann Obrist, August Endell, and Their Followers." PhD diss., University of Chicago, 2008.

Harrington, Anne. *Reenchanted Science: Holism in German Culture from Wilhelm II to Hitler*. Princeton, NJ: Princeton University Press, 1996.

Harrod, W. Owen. "Bruno Paul's Typenmöbel, the German Werkbund, and Pragmatic Modernism, 1908–1918." *Studies in the Decorative Arts* 9, no. 2 (Spring–Summer 2002): 33–57.

Harrod, W. Owen. "The Deutsche Werkstätten and the Dissemination of Mainstream Modernity." *Studies in the Decorative Arts* 11, no. 2 (Spring–Summer, 2003): 21–41.

Harrod, W. Owen. "Towards a Transatlantic Style: The Vereinigte für Kunst im Handwerk and German Modernism in the United States." *Studies in the Decorative Arts* 12, no. 1 (Fall–Winter, 2004–2005): 30–54.

Hartlaub, Gustav. "Zum Geleit." In *Ausstellung "Neue Sachlichkeit": Deutsche Malerei seit dem Expressionismus*. Mannheim: Städtische Kunsthalle, 1925. Translated as "Introduction to 'New Objectivity': German Painting Since Expressionism (1925)," in *The Weimar Republic Sourcebook*, edited by Anton Kaes et al., 492. Berkeley: University of California Press, 1995.

Hartzell, Freyja. "Dürer, Goethe, and the Poetics of Richard Riemerschmid's Modern Wooden Furniture." In *Design and Heritage*, edited by Rebecca Houze and Grace Lees-Maffei, 127–140. London: Routledge, 2022.

Hartzell, Freyja. "A Ghost in the Machine Age: The Westerwald Stoneware Industry and German Design Reform." *Journal of Modern Craft* 2, no. 3 (November 2009): 251–277.

Hartzell, Freyja. "A Renovated Renaissance: Richard Riemerschmid's Modern Interiors for the Thieme House in Munich." *Interiors* 5, no. 1 (2014): 5–36.

Hau, Michael. *The Cult of Health and Beauty in Germany: A Social History, 1890–1930*. Chicago: University of Chicago Press, 2003.

Heidegger, Martin. "The Thing." In *Poetry, Language, Thought*, translated by Albert Hofstadter, 163–180. New York: Perennial Library, 1975.

Heidelberger, Michael. *Nature from Within: Gustav Theodor Fechner and His Psychophysical Worldview*. Translated by Cynthia Klohr. Pittsburgh: University of Pittsburgh Press, 2004. Originally published as *Die innere Seite der Natur: Gustav Theodor Fechners wissenschaftlich-philosophische Weltauffassung* (Frankfurt am Main: Vittorio Klostermann, 1993).

Helmholtz, Hermann von. "Die neueren Fortschritten in der Theorie des Sehens." Berlin, 1868. Translated by Philip Henry Pye-Smith as "The Recent Progress of the Theory of Vision," in *Popular Lectures on Scientific Subjects*, edited by E. Atkinson, 197–316. New York: D. Appleton, 1885.

Helmholtz, Hermann von. *Über die Theorie der zusammengesetzten Farben*. Berlin: Gebrüder Unger, 1852.

Herf, Jeffrey. *Reactionary Modernism: Technology, Culture, and Politics in Weimar and the Third Reich*. Cambridge: Cambridge University Press, 1984.

Heskett, John. *German Design 1870–1918*. New York: Taplinger, 1986.

Heuß, Theodor. "Untitled." *Frankfurter Zeitung*. June 21, 1938.

Heyck, Eduard, and Marie Binde Diers, eds. *Moderne Kultur: Ein Handbuch der Lebensbildung und des Guten Geschmacks*. Stuttgart: Deutsche Verlags-Anstalt, 1907.

Hiesinger, Kathryn Bloom. *Art Nouveau in Munich: Masters of Jugendstil*. Munich: Prestel-Verlag, 1988.

Hinterberger, Hugo. "Die Mikrographie im Dienste der Kunst." In *Jahrbuch für Photographie und Reproduktionstechnik* 16, edited by Josef Maria Eder, 192–195. Halle: Wilhelm Knapp Verlag, 1902.

Hirth, Georg. *Das deutsche Zimmer der Renaissance*: *Anregungen zu Häuslicher Kunstpflege*. Munich: G. Hirths Verlag, 1880.

Hopmann, Ernst. "Fort mit dem nationalen Kitsch! " *Die Form: Zeitschrift für gestaltende Arbeit* 8 (August 1933): 255.

Jaffé, Ernst. "Neue deutsche Steinzeugkunst." *Kunstindustrie und Kunstgewerbe* 1 (1913): 95, 383–384.

James, William. "What Is an Emotion?" *Mind* 9, no. 34 (April 1884): 118–205.

James-Chakraborty, Kathleen, ed. *Bauhaus Culture: From Weimar to the Cold War*. Minneapolis: University of Minnesota Press, 2006.

Janzen, Janet. *Media, Modernity and Dynamic Plants in Early 20th Century German Culture*. Leiden: Brill Rodopi, 2016.

Jarzombek, Mark. "The Discourses of Bourgeois Utopia, 1904–1908, and the Founding of the German Werkbund." In *Imagining Modern German Culture*, edited by Françoise Forster-Hahn, 127–145. Washington, DC: National Gallery of Art, 1996.

Jarzombek, Mark. "The 'Kunstgewerbe,' the 'Werkbund,' and the Aesthetics of Culture in the Wilhelmine Period." *Journal of the Society of Architectural Historians* 53, no. 1 (1994): 7–19.

Jaspers, Karl. *Heimweh und Verbrechen*. Leipzig: FCW Vogel, 1909.

Jelavich, Peter. *Munich and Theatrical Modernism: Politics, Playwriting, and Performance, 1890–1914*. Cambridge, MA: Harvard University Press, 1985.

Jentsch, Ernst. "On the Psychology of the Uncanny." 1906. Translated by Roy Sellars in *Angelaki* 2, no. 1 (1995): 7–16. Originally published as "Zur Psychologie des Unheimlichen," *Psychiatrisch-Neurologische Wochenschrift* 8, no. 22 (August 25, 1906): 195–198 and 8, no. 23 (1 September 1906): 203–205.

Jessen, Peter. *Deutsche Form im Kriegsjahr: Die Ausstellung Köln 1914*. Munich: F. Bruckmann, 1915.

Kahn, Gustave. "Réponse des symbolistes." *L'Evénément*, September 28, 1886.

Kaplan, Wendy, ed. *The Arts & Crafts Movement in Europe and America*. Los Angeles: Thames & Hudson, in association with Los Angeles County Museum of Art, 2004.

Kelly, Alfred. *The Descent of Darwin: The Popularization of Darwinism in Germany, 1860–1914*. Chapel Hill: University of North Carolina Press, 1981.

Klages, Ludwig. *The Biocentric Worldview: Selected Essays and Poems by Ludwig Klages*. Edited by John B. Morgan and translated by Joseph D. Pryce. London: Arktos, 2013.

Klein, Ulrich. "Zur Forschungsgeschichte des Dürer-Hauses." In *Das Dürer-Haus: Neue Ergebnisse der Forschung. Dürer Forschungen*, edited by G. Ulrich Grossmann and Franz Sonnenberger, 1:99–120. Nuremberg: Verlag des Germanischen Nationalmuseums, 2007.

Koerner, Joseph Leo. *The Moment of Self-Portraiture in German Renaissance Art*. Chicago: University of Chicago Press, 1993.

Koss, Juliet. *Modernism after Wagner*. Minneapolis: University of Minnesota Press, 2010.

Koss, Juliet. "On the Limits of Empathy." *Art Bulletin* 88, no. 1 (March 2006): 139–157.

Krabbe, Wolfgang. *Gesellschaftsveränderung durch Lebensreform: Strukturmerkmale einer sozialreformerischen Bewegung im Deutschland der Industrialisierungsperiode.* Göttingen: Vandenhoeck & Ruprecht, 1974.

Kriebler, Sabine T. *Revolutionary Beauty: The Radical Photomontages of John Heartfield.* Berkeley: University of California Press, 2014.

Kubler, George. *The Shape of Time: Remarks on the History of Things.* New Haven, CT: Yale University Press, 1962.

Kuss, Susanne. *German Colonial Wars and the Context of Military Violence.* Cambridge, MA: Harvard University Press, 2017.

Lane, Barbara Miller. *Architecture and Politics in Germany 1918–45.* Cambridge, MA: Harvard University Press, 1985.

Langbehn, Volker, ed. *German Colonialism, Visual Culture, and Modern Memory.* New York: Routledge, 2012.

Lasswitz, Kurd. "Introduction." In Gustav Fechner, *Nanna, oder über das Seelenleben der Pflanzen,* iii–ix. Leipzig: Voss, 1908. https://archive.org/details/nannaoderberdasoolassg00g/page/n11/mode/2up.

Latour, Bruno. "Where Are the Missing Masses? The Sociology of a Few Mundane Artifacts." In *The Object Reader,* edited by Fiona Candlin and Raiford Guins, 229–254. New York: Routledge, 2009.

Laufer, Ulrike, and Hans Ottomeyer, eds. *Gründerzeit 1848–1871. Industrie & Lebensträume zwischen Vormärz und Kaiserreich.* Dresden: Sandstein Verlag, 2008.

Lavater, Johann Caspar. *Physiognomische Fragmente, zur Beförderung der Menschenkenntniß und Menschenliebe.* 4 vols. Leipzig: Weidmann und Reich, 1775–1778.

Le Brun, Charles. *Méthode pour apprendre à dessiner les passions: propose dans une conférence sur l'expression générale et particulière.* Amsterdam: François van-der Plaats, 1702.

Ledoux, Claude-Nicholas. *L'architecture considerée sous le rapport de l'art, des moeurs et de la legislation.* Paris, 1804.

Lichtwark, Alfred. "Der Praktische Zweck." *Dekorative Kunst* 1, no.1 (October 1897): 24–27.

Lichtwark, Alfred. "Palastfenster und Flügeltür." *Pan* 2, no. 1 (1896): 57–60.

Lichtwark, Alfred. *Übungen im Betrachten von Kunstwerken.* Berlin: Cassirer, 1914. First published in 1897.

Lipps, Theodor. *Aesthetik: Psychologie des Schönen und der Kunst.* Hamburg: Leopold Voss, 1903.

Lipps, Theodor. *Raumästhetik und geometrisch-optische Täuschungen.* Leipzig: J. A. Barth, 1897.

Lipps, Theodor. *Zur Einfühlung.* Leipzig: W. Engelmann, 1913.

Littmann, Max. *Das Münchner Schauspielhaus: Denkschrift zur Freier der Eröffnung*. Munich: L. Werner, 1901.

Long, Christopher. "The Origins and Meanings of Ornament and Crime." In *Essays on Adolf Loos*, 53–89. Prague: Kant, 2019.

Loos, Adolf. *Adolf Loos: On Architecture*. Translated and edited by Michael Mitchell. Riverside, CA: Ariadne Press, 2002.

Loos, Adolf. *Ins Leere Gesprochen, 1897–1900*. Paris: Éditions George Crès et Cie, 1921.

Lübke, Wilhelm. *Geschichte der deutschen Renaissance*. Vol. 5 of *Geschichte der Baukunst*, edited by F. Krüger. Stuttgart: Ebner & Seubert, 1873.

Lux, Joseph August. *Das neue Kunstgewerbe in Deutschland*. Leipzig: Klinkhardt & Biermann, 1908.

Maciuika, John V. *Before the Bauhaus: Architecture, Politics, and the German State, 1890–1920*. New York: Cambridge University Press, 2005.

Mackail, J. W. *The Life of William Morris*. Vol. 1. London: Longmans, Green, 1901.

Mahler, Astrid, and Elborg Forster. "A World of Forms from Nature: New Impulses for the Aesthetic of *Jugendstil*." *Visual Resources* 23, nos. 1–2: 21–37.

Makela, Maria. "Munich's Design for Living." *Art in America*, February 1989, 144–151.

Makela, Maria. *The Munich Secession: Art and Artists in Turn-of-the-Century Munich*. Princeton, NJ: Princeton University Press, 1990.

Mallgrave, Harry Francis. *Architecture and Embodiment: The Implications of the New Sciences and Humanities for Design*. London: Routledge, 2013.

Mallgrave, Harry Francis. "From Realism to *Sachlichkeit*: The Polemics of Architectural Modernity in the 1890s." In *Otto Wagner: Reflections on the Raiment of Modernity*, edited by Harry Francis Mallgrave, 281–321. Santa Monica, CA: Getty Center for the History of Art and the Humanities, 1993.

Mallgrave, Harry Francis. "Introduction." In Gottfried Semper, *Style in the Technical and Tectonic Arts; or Practical Aesthetics*, translated by Harry Francis Mallgrave and Michael Robinson, 1–67. Los Angeles: Getty Research Institute, 2004.

Mallgrave, Harry Francis, and Eleftherios Ikonomou, eds. and trans. *Empathy, Form, and Space: Problems in German Aesthetics, 1873–1893*. With an introduction by Harry Francis Mallgrave and Eleftherios Ikonomou. Los Angeles, CA: Getty Center for the History of Art and the Humanities, 1994.

Mallgrave, Harry Francis, and Eleftherios Ikonomou. "Introduction." *Empathy, Form, and Space: Problems in German Aesthetics, 1873–1893*, edited by Harry Francis Mallgrave, 1–88. Los Angeles, CA: Getty Center for the History of Art and the Humanities, 1994.

Mann, Thomas. *Tristan: Sechs Novellen*. Berlin: S. Fischer Verlag, 1903.

Marx, Karl, and Friedrich Engels. "The Manifesto of the Communist Party." In *The Marx-Engels Reader*, second edition, edited by Robert C. Tucker, 469–500. New York: W. W. Norton & Company, 1978.

Menke, Beate. *Die Riemerschmid-Innenausstattung des Hauses Thieme Georgenstraße 7*. Munich: Tuduv Verlag, 1990.

Mitscherlich, Alexander, Angela Richards, and James Strachey, eds. *Sigmund Freud: Studienausgabe Band IV: Psychologische Schriften*. Frankfurt am Main: S. Fischer Verlag, 1970.

Mohrbutter, Alfred. *Das Kleid der Frau*. Darmstadt: Verlags Anstalt Alexander Koch, 1904.

Moréas, Jean. "Le Symbolisme." *Supplément littéraire du Figaro*, September 18, 1886, 150. Excerpted and translated as Jean Moréas [Ioannes Papadiamantopoulos], "A Literary Manifesto— Symbolism (1886)." In *Symbolist Art Theories: A Critical Anthology*, edited by Henri Dorra, 150–152. Berkeley: University of California Press, 1994.

Morehead, Allison. *Nature's Experiments and the Search for Symbolist Form*. University Park: Pennsylvania State University Press, 2017.

Morris, William. *News from Nowhere: An Epoch of Rest*. London: Kelmscott Press, 1890.

Morris, William. "Some Hints on Pattern-Designing: A Lecture Delivered at the Working Men's College, London, on December 10, 1881." In *The Collected Works of William Morris*, vol. 22, 175–205. Cambridge: Cambridge University Press, 2012.

Muthesius, Anna. *Das Eigenkleid der Frau*. Krefeld: Kaiser Wilhelm Museum, 1903.

Muthesius, Hermann. "Der Weg und das Endziel des Kunstgewerbes." *Dekorative Kunst* 8, no. 5 (February 1905): 181–190 and *Dekorative Kunst* 8, no. 6 (March 1905): 230–238. Reprinted as "Der Weg und das Ziel des Kunstgewerbes," in Hermann Muthesius, *Hermann Muthesius: Kunstgewerbe und Architektur*, 1–28. Jena: Eugen Diederichs, 1907.

Muthesius, Hermann. "Die Bedeutung des Kunstgewerbes. Eröffnungsrede zu den Vorlesungen über modernes Kunstgewerbe an der Handelhochschule in Berlin." *Dekorative Kunst* 10, no. 5 (February 1907): 177–192.

Muthesius, Hermann. "Die Kunst Richard Riemerschmids." *Dekorative Kunst* 7, no. 7 (April 1904): 249–283.

Muthesius, Hermann. "Die moderne Bewegung." In *Spemanns Goldenes Buch Der Kunst: Eine Hauskunde Für Jedermann*, 1067. Berlin: Verlag von W. Spemann, 1901.

Muthesius, Hermann, ed. *Die Werkbund-Arbeit der Zukunft und Aussprächse darüber. 7.Jahres Versammlung des Deutschen Werkbundes vom 2. bis 6.Juli in Köln*. Jena: Eugen Diedrichs, 1914.

Muthesius, Hermann. *Hermann Muthesius: Kunstgewerbe und Architektur*. Jena: Eugen Diederichs, 1907.

Muthesius, Hermann. "Kultur und Kunst: Betrachtungen über das deutsche Kunstgewerbe." *Deutsche Monatsschrift für das gesamte Leben der Gegenwart* 3, no. 7 (April 1904): 74–87.

Muthesius, Hermann. "Kunst und Maschine." *Dekorative Kunst* 5, no. 4 (January 1902): 141–147.

Muthesius, Hermann. "The Significance of Applied Art." In *The Theory of Decorative Art: An Anthology of European & American Writings, 1750–1940*, edited by Isabelle Frank, with translations by David Britt, 74–82. New Haven, CT: Yale University Press, 2000.

Muthesius, Hermann. *Stilarchitektur und Baukunst. Wandlungen der Architektur und der gewerblichen Kunst im XX.Jahrhundert und ihr heutiger Standpunkt*. Mülheim-Ruhr: K. Schimmelpfeng, 1902.

Muthesius, Hermann. *Style-Architecture and Building-Art: Transformations of Architecture in the Nineteenth Century and Its Present Condition*. Introduction and translation by Stanford Anderson. Santa Monica, CA: Getty Center for the History of Art and the Humanities, 1994.

Muthesius, Hermann. "Wo Stehen Wir?" In *Die Durchgeistigung der deutschen Arbeit: Jahrbuch des deutschen Werkbunds 1912*, edited by Bernd Nicolai, 11–26. Berlin: Gebrüder Mann, 1999. Originally published in 1912.

Muthesius, Stefan. "The 'altdeutsche' Zimmer, or Cosiness in Plain Pine: An 1870s Munich Contribution to the Definition of Interior Design." *Journal of Design History* 16, no. 4 (2003): 269–290.

Muthesius, Stefan. *The Poetic Home: Designing the 19th-Century Domestic Interior*. New York: Thames & Hudson, 2009.

Naumann, Friedrich. "Der Geist im Hausgestühl." In *Preisbuch Dresdner Hausgerät, 1906*. Dresden: Dresdner Werkstätten für Handwerkskunst, 1906.

Naumann, Friedrich. "Die Kunst im Zeitalter der Maschine." In *Friedrich Naumann: Werke*, edited by Heinz Ladendorf, vol. 6, 186–201. Cologne: Westdeutscher Verlag, 1964. Originally published in *Kunstwart* 17 (1904).

Naumann, Friedrich. "Kunst und Industrie." In *Das Deutsche Kunstgewerbe 1906: Die Dritte Deutsche Kunstgewerbe Ausstellung Dresden 1906*, 32–35. Munich: Verlagsanstalt F. Bruckmann, 1906.

Nerdinger, Winfried, ed. *100 Jahre Deutscher Werkbund 1907/2007*. Munich: Prestel Verlag, 2007.

Nerdinger, Winfried, ed. *Richard Riemerschmid vom Jugendstil zum Werkbund. Werke und Dokumente*. Munich: Prestel Verlag, 1982.

Neumann-Adrian, Edda, and Michael Neumann-Adrian. *Münchens Lust am Jugendstil: Häuser und Menschen um 1900*. Munich: Buchendorfer Verlag, 2005.

Nicolai, Bernd, ed. *Die Durchgeistigung der deutschen Arbeit. Jahrbuch des deutschen Werkbunds 1912*. Berlin: Gebrüder Mann, 1999. Originally published in 1912.

Nietzsche, Friederich. *Thus Spoke Zarathustra: A Book for Everyone and Nobody*. Translated by Graham Parkes. Oxford: Oxford World's Classics, 2005. Originally published in 1883.

Ober, Patricia. *Der Frauen Neue Kleider. Das Reformkleid und die Konstruktion des modernen Frauenkörpers*. Berlin: Verlag Hans Schiler, 2005.

Obrist, Hermann. "Der Zukunft unserer Architektur." *Dekorative Kunst* 4, no. 9 (June 1901): 329–349.

Ogata, Amy F. *Art Nouveau and the Social Vision of Modern Living: Belgian Artists in a European Context*. Cambridge: Cambridge University Press, 2001.

Ogata, Amy F. "Belgium and France: Arts, Crafts, and Decorative Arts." In *The Arts & Crafts Movement in Europe and America*, edited by Wendy Kaplan, 218–245. Los Angeles: Thames & Hudson, in association with the Los Angeles County Museum of Art, 2004.

Orend, Misch. "Der magische Realismus." *Klingsohr: Siebenbürgische Zeitschrift* 5 (January 1928): 25–27.

Osayimwese, Itohan. *Colonialism and Modern Architecture in Germany*. Pittsburgh: University of Pittsburgh Press, 2017.

Ostergard, Derek, ed. *Bent Wood and Metal Furniture: 1850–1946*. New York: American Federation of Arts, 1987.

Osthaus, Karl Ernst. *van de Velde: Leben und Schaffen des Künstlers*. Hagen: Volkwang Verlag, 1920.

Otto, Elizabeth. *Haunted Bauhaus: Occult Spirituality, Gender Fluidity, Queer Identities, and Radical Politics*. Cambridge, MA: MIT Press, 2019.

Ottomeyer, Hans. *Jugendstil Möbel: Katalog der Möbelsammlung des Münchner Stadtmuseums*. With contributions by Michaela Rammert-Götz. Munich: Prestel Verlag, 1988.

Ottomeyer, Hans, and Margot Brandlhuber, eds. *Wege in Die Moderne: Jugendstil in München 1896 bis 1914*. Leipzig: Klinkhardt & Biermann, 1997.

Ottomeyer, Hans, and Alfred Ziffer, eds. *Möbel des Neoklassizismus und der Neuen Sachlichkeit: Katalog der Möbelsammlung des Münchner Stadtmuseums*. Munich: Prestel Verlag, 1993.

Pazaurek, Gustav E. "Neues Steinzeug von Albin Müller." *Dekorative Kunst* 14, no. 4 (January 1911): 176–183.

Pecht, Friedrich. *Aus dem Münchner Glaspalast*. Stuttgart: Cotta, 1876.

Peckmann, Hilke. "Ausdruck und Innerlichkeit. Der Körper als Träger seelischer Stimmung." In *Die Lebensreform: Entwürfe zur Neugestaltung von Leben und Kunst um 1900*, edited by Kai Buchholz, 2:153–154. Darmstadt: Verlag Häusser, 2001.

Peckmann, Hilke. "Der Mensch im Zustand ursprünglicher Natürlichkeit. Reformkonzept und Thema in der Kunst." In *Die Lebensreform: Entwürfe zur Neugestaltung von Leben und Kunst um 1900*, edited by Kai Buchholz, 2:217–219. Darmstadt: Verlag Häusser, 2001.

Perraudin, Michael, and Juergen Zimmerer, eds. *German Colonialism and National Identity*. New York: Routledge, 2015.

Peters, Olaf, ed. *Degenerate Art: The Attack on Modern Art in Nazi Germany*. New York: Prestel and Neue Galerie, 2014.

Pevsner, Nikolaus. *Pioneers of Modern Design*. New Haven, CT: Yale University Press, 2005.

Pevsner, Nikolaus. *Pioneers of the Modern Movement from William Morris to Walter Gropius*. New York: Museum of Modern Art, 1936.

Plöger, Ulrich, and Jürgen Schimanski. *Die Neue Ära, 1900–1930: Westerwälder Steinzeug, Jugendstil und Werkbund*. Düsseldorf: Contur-Verlag, 1987.

Pommer, Richard, and Christian F. Otto. *Weissenhof 1927 and the Modern Movement in Architecture*. Chicago: University of Chicago Press, 1991.

Pudor, Heinrich. *Die Frauenreformkleidung: Ein Beitrag zur Philosophie, Hygiene und Aesthetik des Kleides*. Leipzig: Hermann Seemann Nachfolger, 1903.

Pudor, Heinrich. "Praktische Vorschläge zur Erzielung von Qualitätswaren." *Volkswirtschaftliche Blätter* 9, nos. 15–16 (1910): 280–283.

Popp, Josef. *Deutsches Warenbuch*. Munich: Dürerbund-Werkbund Genossenschaft, 1915.

Rammert-Götz, Michaela. *Richard Riemerschmid, Möbel und Innenräume 1895–1900*. Munich: Tuduv Verlag, 1987.

Rapetti, Rodolphe. *Symbolism*. Translated by Deke Dusinberre. Paris: Flammarion, 2005.

Rée, Paul Johannes. "Richard Riemerschmid." *Dekorative Kunst* 9, no. 7 (April 1906): 265–303.

Richards, Robert J. *The Tragic Sense of Life: Ernst Haeckel and the Struggle over Evolutionary Thought*. Chicago: University of Chicago Press, 2008.

Riemerschmid, Richard. *Diskussion von der Verhandlung des Deutschen Werkbundes zu München am 11. und 12. Juli 1908*. Leipzig: R. Voigtländer Verlag, 1908.

Riemerschmid, Richard. *Künstlerische Erziehugsfragen I*. Munich: Flugschriften des Münchner Bundes, 1917.

Riemerschmid, Richard. *Künstlerische Erziehugsfragen II*. Munich: Flugschriften des Münchner Bundes, 1919.

Riemerschmid, Richard. "Zur Ausstellung München 1908." In *Ausstellung München 1908: Amtliche Mitteilungen der Ausstellungs-Leitung 1*, November 1907, 1–5.

Riezler, Walter. "Neue Arbeiten von Richard Riemerschmid." *Deutsche Kunst und Dekoration* 9, no. 3 (1908): 164–214.

Rilke, Rainer Maria. *Worpswede: Fritz Mackeusen, Otto Modersohn, Fritz Overbeck, Hans am Ende, Heinrich Vogeler*. Bielefeld/Leipzig: Velhagen and Klasing, 1903.

Roh, Franz. *Nach-Expressionismus, Magischer Realismus: Probleme der neusten europäischen Malerei*. Leipzig: Klinkhardt und Biermann, 1925.

Ross, Alex. *Wagnerism: Art and Politics in the Shadow of Music*. New York: Farrar, Straus and Giroux, 2020.

Saletnik, Jeffrey, and Robin Schuldenfrei, eds. *Bauhaus Construct: Fashioning Identity, Discourse and Modernism*. London: Routledge, 2009.

Schnädelbach, Herbert. *Philosophy in Germany 1831–1933*. Translated by Eric Matthews. Cambridge: Cambridge University Press, 1984.

Scheffler, Karl. "Kultur und Kunst." In *Moderne Kultur: Ein Handbuch der Lebensbildung und des Guten Geschmacks*, edited by Eduard Heyck and Marie Binde Diers, 1:17–92. Stuttgart: Deutsche Verlags-Anstalt, 1907.

Scheffler, Karl. "Kunst und Leben." In Heyck and Diers, *Moderne Kultur*, 1:93–112.

Scheffler, Karl. "Keramik." In Heyck and Diers, *Moderne Kultur*, 1:232.

Scheffler, Karl. "Notizen über die Farbe." *Dekorative Kunst* 4, no. 5 (February 1901): 183–196.

Schmidt, Karl. *Grundungsprogramm der Dresdner Werkstätten*. Dresden, 1898.

Schuldenfrei, Robin. *Luxury and Modernism: Architecture and the Object in Germany, 1900–1930*. Princeton, NJ: Princeton University Press, 2018.

Schultze-Naumburg, Paul. "Die Dresden Kunstausstellung." *Dekorative Kunst* 2, no. 9 (June 1899): 89–92.

Schultze-Naumburg, Paul. *Die Kultur des Weiblichen Körpers als Grundlage der Frauenkleidung*. Leipzig: Eugen Diedrichs, 1901.

Schwartz, Frederic J. "Marcel Breuer Club Chair." In *The Bauhaus 1919–1933: Workshops for Modernity*, edited by Barry Bergdoll and Leah Dickerman, 228–231. New York: Museum of Modern Art, 2009.

Schwartz, Frederic J. *The Werkbund: Design Theory & Mass Culture before the First World War*. New Haven, CT: Yale University Press, 1996.

Sembach, Klaus-Jürgen. *Art Nouveau. Utopia: Reconciling the Irreconcilable*. Cologne: Taschen, 2002.

Sembach, Klaus-Jürgen, and Gottfried von Haeseler. *August Endell: Der Architekt des Photoateliers Elvira, 1871–1925*. Munich: Museum Villa Stuck, 1977.

Sembach, Klaus-Jürgen and Birgit Schulte, eds. *Henry van de Velde. Ein europäischer Künstler seiner Zeit*. Cologne: Wienand Verlag, 1992.

Semper, Gottfried. *Der Stil in den technischen und tektonischen Künsten; oder, Praktische Aesthetik: Ein Handbuch für Techniker, Künstler und Kunstfreunde*. 2 vols. Frankfurt am Main: Verlag für Kunst und Wissenschaft, 1860; Munich: F. Bruckmann, 1863. Translated by Harry Francis Mallgrave and Michael Robinson as *Style in the Technical and Tectonic Arts; or Practical Aesthetics*. Los Angeles, CA: Getty Research Institute, 2004.

Shakespeare, William. *The Tempest*. Edited by Alden T. Vaughan and Virginia Mason Vaughan. London: Bloomsbury, 2011.

Silverman, Debora. *Art Nouveau in Fin-de-Siècle France: Politics, Psychology, and Style*. Berkeley: University of California Press, 1989.

Simmel, Georg. "Das Problem des Stiles." *Dekorative Kunst* 11, no. 7 (April 1908): 307–316.

Smith, T'ai. *Bauhaus Weaving Theory: From Feminine Craft to Mode of Design*. Minneapolis: University of Minnesota Press, 2014.

Sombart, Werner. *Wirtschaft und Mode: Ein Beitrag zur Theorie der modernen Bedarfsgestaltung*. Wiesbaden: J. F. Bergmann, 1902.

Stamm, Brigitte. *Das Reformkleid in Deutschland*. Berlin: Technische Universität Berlin, 1976.

Stamm, Brigitte. "Richard Riemerschmid: Unveröffentlichte Entwürfe zur Reformierung der Frauenbekleidung um 1900." *Waffen- und Kostümkunde* 20, no. 1 (1978): 51–56.

Steele, Valerie. *The Corset: A Cultural History*. New Haven, CT: Yale University Press, 2001.

Steinweis, Alan. *Art, Ideology, and Economics in Nazi Germany: The Reich Chambers of Music, Theater, and Visual Arts*. Chapel Hill: University of North Carolina Press, 1983.

Stern, Radu. *Against Fashion: Clothing as Art*. Cambridge, MA: MIT Press, 2004.

Sternberger, Dolf. *Über Jugendstil*. Frankfurt am Main: Insel Verlag, 1977.

Stewart, Susan. *On Longing: Narratives of the Miniature, the Gigantic, the Souvenir, the Collection*. Durham, NC: Duke University Press, 1993.

Streiter, Richard. "Aus München." *Pan* 2, no. 3 (1896): 248–252.

Thamer, Jutta. "Die Eroberung der Dritten Dimension. Raum und Fläche bei Henry van de Velde." In *Henry van de Velde: Ein europäischer Künstler seiner Zeit*, edited by Klaus-Jürgen Sembach and Birgit Schulte, 132–147. Cologne: Wienand Verlag, 1992.

Thiersch, Friedrich, ed. *Wir fingen einfach an: Arbeiten und Aufsätze von Freunden und Schülern um Richard Riemerschmid zu dessen 85.Geburtstag*. Munich: Richard Pflaum Verlag, 1953.

Thompson, E. P. *William Morris: Romantic to Revolutionary*. London: Merlin Press, 1955.

Tietzel, Brigitte. "Stoffmuster des Judgendstils." *Zeitschrift für Kunstgeschichte* 44, no. 3 (1981): 258–283.

Tillis, Steve. *Toward an Aesthetics of the Puppet: Puppetry as Theatrical Art*. New York: Greenwood Press, 1992.

Umbach, Maiken. "The Deutscher Werkbund and Modern Vernaculars." In *Vernacular Modernism: Heimat, Globalization, and the Built Environment*, edited by Maiken Umbach and Bernd Hüppauf, 114–140. Stanford, CA: Stanford University Press, 2005.

Umbach, Maiken. *German Cities and Bourgeois Modernism, 1890–1924*. Oxford: Oxford University Press, 2009.

Umbach, Maiken, and Bernd Hüppauf, eds. *Vernacular Modernism: Heimat, Globalization, and the Built Environment*. Stanford, CA: Stanford University Press, 2005.

Umbach, Maiken, and Bernd Hüppauf. "Introduction: Vernacular Modernism." In *Vernacular Modernism: Heimat, Globalization, and the Built Environment*, edited by Maiken Umbach and Bernd Hüppauf, 1–23. Stanford, CA: Stanford University Press, 2005.

van de Velde, Henry. "Allgemeine Bemerkungen zu einer Synthese der Kunst." *Pan* 5, no. 4 (1899–1900): 261–270.

van de Velde, Henry. "Das neue Kunst-Prinzip in der modernen Frauen-Kleidung." *Deutsche Kunst und Dekoration* vol. 5, no. 8 (May 1902): 363–371. Translated as "A New Art Principle in Women's Clothing," in Radu Stern, *Against Fashion: Clothing as Art*, 137–142. Cambridge, MA: MIT Press, 2004.

van de Velde, Henry. *Die künstlerische Hebung der Frauentracht*. Krefeld: Kaiser Wilhelm Museum, 1900. Translated as "The Artistic Improvement of Women's Clothing," in Radu Stern, *Against Fashion: Clothing as Art*, 125–136. Cambridge, MA: MIT Press, 2004.

van de Velde, Henry. "Die Linie." *Die Zukunft* 10, no. 49 (September 6, 1902): 385–388.

van de Velde, Henry. "Ein Kapitel über Entwurf und Bau moderner Möbel." *Pan* 3, no. 4 (1897): 260–264.

van de Velde, Henry. *Récit de ma vie: Anvers, Bruxelles, Paris, Berlin*. 2 vols. Paris: Flammarion, 1992–1995.

van de Velde, Maria Sèthe. "Einleitung." In *Album Moderner, Nach Künstlerentwürfen Ausgeführter Damenkleider. Ausgestellt auf der Grossen Allgemeinen Ausstellung für das Bekleidungswesen, Krefeld, 1900*, edited by Friedrich Wolfrum. Krefeld: J. B. Klein'schen Buchdruckerei, 1900.

van de Velde, Maria Sèthe. "Sonderausstellung Moderner Damenkostüme." *Dekorative Kunst* 4, no. 1 (October 1900): 41–47.

Vidler, Anthony. *The Architectural Uncanny: Essays in the Modern Unhomely*. Cambridge, MA: MIT Press, 1992.

Vidler, Anthony. *The Writing on the Walls: Architectural Theory in the Late Enlightenment*. Princeton, NJ: Princeton University Press, 1987.

Vischer, Robert. *Über das optische Formgefühl. Ein Beitrag zur Aesthetik*. Leipzig: Hermann Credner, 1873. Translated as "On the Optical Sense of Form: A Contribution to Aesthetics," in *Empathy, Form and Space: Problems in German Aesthetics, 1873–93*, edited by Harry Francis Mallgrave and Eleftherios Ikonomou, 89–123. Santa Monica, CA: Getty Center for the History of Art and the Humanities, 1994.

Wagner, Anette. "Natur als Resonanzraum der Seele." In *Die Lebensreform: Entwürfe zur Neugestaltung von Leben und Kunst um 1900*, edited by Kai Buchholz, Rita Latocha, and Hilke Peckmann, 2:165–184. Darmstadt: Verlag Häusser, 2001.

Weiss, Peg. *Kandinsky in Munich: The Formative Jugendstil Years*. Princeton, NJ: Princeton University Press, 1979.

Weißler, Sabine. *Design in Deutschland, 1933–1945: Ästhetik und Organisation des Deutschen Werkbundes im Dritten Reich*. Giesen: Anabas Verlag, 1990.

Wichmann, Hans. *Deutsche Werkstätten und WK-Verband 1898–1990: Aufbruch zum neuen Wohnen*. Munich: Prestel, 1992.

Wieber, Sabine. "The German Interior at the End of the Nineteenth Century." In *Designing the Modern Interior*, edited by Penny Sparke, Anne Massey, Trevor Keeble, and Brenda Martin, 53–64. Oxford: Berg, 2009.

Wigley, Mark. *White Walls, Designer Dresses: The Fashioning of Modern Architecture*. Cambridge, MA: MIT Press, 1995.

Wolbert, Klaus. "Körper zwischen animalischer Leiblichkeit und ästhetisierender Verklärung der Physis." In *Die Lebensreform: Entwürfe zur Neugestaltung von Leben und Kunst um 1900*, edited by Kai Buchholz, Rita Latocha, and Hilke Peckmann, 2:339–340. Darmstadt: Verlag Häusser, 2001.

Wölfflin, Heinrich. "Prolegomena zu einer Psychologie der Architecture." In *Kleine Schriften (1886–1933)*, edited by Joseph Gantner, 13–47. Basel: Schwabe, 1946. Originally published in 1886.

Wölfflin, Heinrich. "Prolegomena to a Psychology of Architecture." In *Empathy, Form, and Space: Problems in German Aesthetics, 1873–1893*, edited by Harry Francis Mallgrave and Eleftherios Ikonomou, 149–192. Los Angeles: Getty Center for the History of Art and the Humanities, 1994.

Wolfrum, Friedrich, ed. *Album Moderner, Nach Künstlerentwürfen Ausgeführter Damenkleider. Ausgestellt auf der Grossen Allgemeinen Ausstellung für das Bekleidungswesen, Krefeld, 1900*. Krefeld: J. B. Klein'schen Buchdruckerei, 1900.

Worringer, Wilhelm. *Abstraktion und Einfühlung: Ein Beitrag zur Stilpsychologie*. Munich: Piper, 1908. Translated by Michael Bullock as *Abstraction and Empathy: A Contribution to the Psychology of Style*. New York: International Universities Press, 1953.

Wüllenkemper, Maria. *Richard Riemerschmid (1868–1957): "Nicht die Kunst schafft den Stil, das Leben schafft ihn."* Regensburg: Schnell & Steiner, 2009.

Zasche, H. "System Van der Velde." *Weimarer Witzblatt*, March 30, 1901.

Zervigón, Andrés Mario. *John Heartfield and the Agitated Image: Photography, Persuasion, and the Rise of the Avant-Garde Photomontage*. Chicago: University of Chicago Press, 2012.

Zimmermann, Ernst. "Die künstlerische Nothlage der Westerwälder Steinzeugindustrie." *Kunst und Handwerk* 50 (1899–1900): 76–83.

Zimmermann, Ernst. "Steinzeugkrüge von Richard Riemerschmid." *Kunst und Handwerk* 54 (1903–1904): 269–271.

INDEX